DRUGS AND CRIME

Evaluating Public Policy Initiatives

Edited by
Doris Layton MacKenzie
Craig D. Uchida

SAGE Publications
International Educational and Professional Publisher
Thousand Oaks   London   New Delhi

The editors gratefully acknowledge James A. Inciardi, David N. Nurco, and Barbara Owen for their comments on earlier versions of this manuscript.

For information address:

SAGE Publications, Inc.
2455 Teller Road
Thousand Oaks, California 91320

SAGE Publications Ltd.
6 Bonhill Street
London EC2A 4PU
United Kingdom

SAGE Publications India Pvt. Ltd.
M-32 Market
Greater Kailash I
New Delhi 110 048 India

Printed in the United States of America

Library of Congress Cataloging-in-Publication Data

MacKenzie, Doris L.
    Drugs and crime: evaluating public policy initiatives / Doris
Layton MacKenzie, Craig D. Uchida.
        p.   cm.
    Includes bibliographical references and index.
    ISBN 0-8039-4456-X (cloth).—ISBN 0-8039-4457-8 (pbk.)
    1. Narcotics and crime—United States.   2. Narcotics, Control of—
United States—Evaluation.   3. Drug traffic—United States.
4. Criminal justice, Administration of—United States.   I. Uchida,
Craig D.   II. Title.
HV5825.M23   1994   93-36738
364.2'4—dc20   CIP

94 95 96 97 98 10 9 8 7 6 5 4 3 2 1

Sage Production Editor: Judith L. Hunter

Contents

PART I

Background Issues

1. Drug Control and System Improvement: Evaluating the Success of Public Policies

DORIS LAYTON MacKENZIE

This nation has been faced with an epidemic of illicit drug use and trafficking. As a result, the justice system struggles to confront the problems related to drug trafficking and use, such as increased criminal activity, drug use by children and adolescents, employment in the illegal drug distribution system by inner-city youths, prison overcrowding and the backlog of court cases, and serious illness such as AIDS. *Drugs and Crime* is a comprehensive examination of policy-relevant research. The effectiveness of programs designed to improve the functioning of the criminal justice system, in its response to the problems associated with drugs, are examined. The book is designed to be relevant to policymakers, scholars, practitioners, and students—those who must make decisions and those who will do the future research on public policies in the critical areas of drug control and system improvement.

The surge in the number of drug-involved offenders has presented enormous problems for the criminal justice system (Lurigio & Davis, 1992; Tonry & Wilson, 1990; Weisheit, 1990; Wish, 1992). Drug control and criminal justice system improvement projects have been implemented to address these problems. In his chapter, Albert Reiss discusses what has been learned about evaluation research in criminal justice and how this knowledge can be applied to research examining drug control initiatives.

Evaluations of some initiatives are just now being completed. This volume describes many of these initiatives and critically assesses current evaluation efforts. Each chapter focuses on a major policy initiative; the problem area, policies designed to address the problem, research examining the effectiveness of the policies, and policy implications of the research are discussed. The authors discuss what we know and also what we need to know. Some policies have been in effect for a sufficient amount of time to allow conclusions to be drawn from available data; others are still in the proposal stage, and in these cases, chapter authors critically examine potential policies and methods of studying the effectiveness of these policies.

Recent data from the National Institute of Justice Drug Use Forecasting (DUF) program reveals phenomenally high rates of illegal drug use in the arrested populations studied. Although we do not understand the relationship between drug use and crime in all its complexity, we do know there is a strong correlation between them, and this implies the need for interventions. We know that rates of use of three types of drugs or drug combinations are associated with increases in criminal activity. These three types of drug use are: (a) narcotic (principally heroin) addiction, (b) cocaine abuse, and (c) frequent multiple drugs (see Chaiken & Chaiken, 1982, 1990; Inciardi, 1986; Inciardi & Pottieger, 1991; Nurco, Hanlon, Kinlock, & Duszynski, 1988, 1989; for reviews of the literature). Yet we have no real knowledge of how many offenders who need and desire treatment are turned away because there are not enough programs available. Yih-Ing Hser, Douglas Longshore, and Douglas Anglin examine this issue by using the known numbers to estimate treatment needs, and they compare these results with the number of treatment program slots currently available in Los Angeles County. In addition, they make a number of recommendations regarding effective interventions that could be used for drug-involved offenders in the criminal justice system.

The public has long associated drug dealing with street gangs. Malcolm Klein and Cheryl Maxson explore the relationship between gangs and crack dealing. They find that defining the characteristics of gangs and how they are involved with drugs is much more complex than traditionally thought. In this chapter they review what is known about the connection between gangs and crack, and they examine how suitable street gangs would be as crack distribution networks. If we are to initiate successful intervention strategies, it must be with full knowledge of the distinctive characteristics of various types of gangs—their development, structure, members, and activities.

The proportion of local, state, and federal resources devoted to policing is astronomical, and this is driven in large part by the drug problem. When it became obvious that the arresting "Mr. Big" strategy was not going to solve the problem of drugs, attention turned to strategies for disrupting local drug dealing in city drug markets. David Weisburd and Lorraine Green, along with Frank Gajewski and Charles Bellucci of the Jersey City Police Department, discuss the difficulty of defining and studying street-level drug markets. They examine the characteristics of drug markets and how Jersey City developed a systematic information system that allowed the police to define and examine localized drug activities. They find a diversity in the markets that suggests the importance of developing a wide range of strategies if drug markets are to be successfully eliminated.

One of the problems that arises is how the police can most effectively interact with the larger neighborhoods within which drug trafficking occurs. Drug markets exist within communities, and many individuals in these communities are not involved in the illegal marketing. The police must deal with both the law-abiding citizens and the offenders. Debates about how the police can most effectively deal with these groups has led to two models of policing—the professional and the more contemporary community-oriented approach. Craig Uchida and Brian Forst review the development of these two policing models and report on the results of an evaluation of community policing and its effect on drug trafficking in Oakland, California, and Birmingham, Alabama.

Robert Worden, Timothy Bynum, and James Frank discuss the research examining whether abrupt increases in police activity that dramatically increase the threat of apprehension are effective in deterring drug activity. Although the theoretical rationale for the effectiveness of crackdowns has been developed, there is as yet little empirical evidence supporting the theories.

Michele Sviridoff and Sally Hillsman's chapter fills this gap by providing an evaluation of New York City's Tactical Narcotics Teams (TNT). The TNTs were designed to be relatively short-term but intensive narcotics enforcement, focusing on crack cocaine markets in the urban neighborhoods where crack is prevalent. They use a multi-method approach to examine the effects of the targeted crackdown on the market and the community.

Perhaps the most difficult problem facing police in urban environments is how to provide effective police response to the problems of drugs in public housing. As pointed out in the chapter by Wesley Skogan and Sampson Annan, crime rates in public housing are frequently higher than in other locations of the city. Special Narcotics Enforcement in Public Housing Units (NEPHUs) has been developed with the objective of reducing crime, fear of crime, and the availability of narcotics. The authors describe the development and implementation of NEPHUs in

Denver, Colorado, and New Orleans, Louisiana. Interactions with other agencies, corruption, and discontinued funding were just some of the problems that arose in the course of the evaluation.

Although less visible than the police, prosecutors play a vital role in reducing illegal drug activity and ensuring that the system fairly and efficiently adjudicates drug cases. Joan Jacoby and Heike Gramckow examine major reforms in traditional case management. Such reforms require close coordination among offices and agencies. The authors examine the police and prosecutor relationship and structures or organizations for increasing the communication and coordination between them. In the past decade Congress has passed powerful legislation, such as the RICO Act and the CCE and forfeiture statutes, with the goal of removing profits from drug trafficking and incapacitating distributors. Jacoby and Gramckow review the impact of this legislation and discuss some of the difficulties that arise in the implementation and transfer of programs from one jurisdiction to another.

In the second half of the book we turn to understanding, sanctioning, and treating drug offenders. Effectively and efficiently intervening to reduce the rate of drug use requires that the drug offender be matched to the appropriate drug treatment. All offenders do not need, nor can we afford to give them, the most intensive and intrusive treatment. In his chapter John Hepburn describes the difficulties associated with classifying drug offenders so that decisions can be made regarding the appropriate level of treatment.

The criminal justice system has searched for effective ways to reduce the rate of drug use and eliminate the criminal activities of those convicted of crimes. During the "nothing works" and "get tough" eras of the late 1970s and early 1980s, there was less emphasis on treatment and an increased emphasis on the use of prisons to incapacitate and deter. Jeffrey Fagan examines whether there is research evidence that official sanctions for drug use deter drug crimes. Using data from New York City, he examines punishment certainty and severity, and the effects on recidivism of policies and procedures that rely heavily on imprisonment as a sanction.

As prisons became filled to capacity, and the economy prohibited increased prison construction, decision makers searched for new ways of managing prisoners. At the same time the growth in the number of drug offenders, and the empirical evidence that drug treatment is effective in reducing drug use, led to increased interest in combining sanctions with treatment. The chapters by Doris MacKenzie and by Susan Turner, Joan Petersilia, and Elizabeth Deschenes examine two of the intermediate sanctions that combine programming with sanctions. Shock incarceration, or boot camp prisons, as these programs are frequently called, involve a short term of imprisonment in a military atmosphere. Although the programs appear to have begun with a "get tough" emphasis, they are increasingly being used to provide intensive programming. MacKenzie examines the programs and how drug treatment is or is not incorporated into the daily schedule of activities. An intermediate sanction used in almost all jurisdictions is Intensive Supervision Probation/Parole (ISP). The technology of urine testing is frequently combined with ISP, particularly for drug offenders. Turner, Petersilia, and Deschenes examine the implementation, system response, and impact of urine testing in sites in five states.

Although there is some evidence that drug use is declining, use and sales by juveniles in the inner city does not show such decline. Elizabeth Deschenes and Peter W. Greenwood review what is known about juvenile drug use, the overlap between delinquency and drug use, and the effectiveness of treatment approaches to reducing drug use and criminal activity.

The final chapter in this volume reviews what has been learned about drug use and the criminal justice system in the past 25 years, since the task force report on "Narcotics and Drug Abuse" was completed by the President's Commission. Four themes we see arising from these chapters are changes in policing strategies, an increased emphasis on treatment, the need for system-level planning, and the importance of research—trends we might expect to see in future criminal justice planning and evaluation.

References

Chaiken, J. M., & Chaiken, M. R. (1982). *Varieties of criminal behavior.* Santa Monica, CA: RAND.

Chaiken, J. M., & Chaiken, M. R. (1990). Drugs and predatory crime. In M. Tonry & J. Q. Wilson (Eds.), *Drugs and crime: Vol. 13. Crime and justice* (pp. 203-240). Chicago: University of Chicago Press.

Inciardi, J. A. (1986). Hooker, whore, junkie, thief; dealer, doper, cocaine freak. In J. A. Inciardi (Ed.), *The war on drugs: Heroin, cocaine, and public policy* (pp. 156-173). Palo Alto, CA: Mayfield.

Inciardi, J. A., & Pottieger, A. E. (1991). Kids, crack, and crime. *Journal of Drug Issues, 21,* 257-270.

Lurigio, A. J., & Davis, R. C. (1992). Drugs and crime: An introduction. *Crime and Delinquency, 38*(4), 419-421.

Nurco, D. N., Hanlon, T. E., Kinlock, T. W., & Duszynski, K. R. (1988). Differential criminal patterns of narcotic addicts over an addiction career. *Criminology, 26,* 407-423.

Nurco, D. N., Hanlon, T. E., Kinlock, T. W., & Duszynski, K. R. (1989). The consistency of types of criminal behavior over preaddiction, addiction, and nonaddiction status periods. *Comprehensive Psychiatry, 30,* 391-402.

Tonry, M., & Wilson, J. Q. (Eds.). (1990). *Drugs and crime: Vol. 13. Crime and justice.* Chicago: University of Chicago Press.

Weisheit, R. (1990). *Drugs, crime and the criminal justice system* (ACJS/Anderson Monograph Series). Cincinnati, OH: Anderson.

Wish, E. D. (1992). Drug abuse: Linking policy and research. *The annals of the American academy of political and social science* (Vol. 521). Newbury Park, CA: Sage.

2. Doing Evaluations in Policy Research: Implications for Drug Control Initiatives

ALBERT J. REISS, JR.

Policymakers, practitioners, and researchers search for ways to prevent and control the production, distribution, marketing, and use of drugs and their consequences and to deal [not to pun] with the prevention, intervention, adjudication, and treatment problems generated by the drug problem. In this chapter, I address briefly what we have learned in recent years about evaluation research in criminal justice and what lessons we can draw from that history for future research in evaluating drug control initiatives. These lessons will appear as a few admonitions, or warnings, that I hope will stimulate thinking about the role of evaluation in policy research. And I offer these several admonitions in the sense of counseling against fault or oversight.

The Need for and Use of Evaluation Research

All of us in this country who are concerned about problems of crime control and criminal justice have turned increasingly to evaluation research as a guide to whether we are effectively implementing our policies and whether particular programs are producing their intended results. Each branch of our government relies upon and supports evaluation research.

AUTHOR'S NOTE: A version of this chapter was presented initially as the keynote address to the Second Annual Conference on Evaluating Drug Control Initiatives, sponsored by The National Institute of Justice and the Bureau of Justice Assistance, July 8, 1991, Washington, D.C.

Congress relies quite heavily upon evaluation research, particularly upon the reports of the Program Evaluation and Methodology Division of the Government Accounting Office. In recent years that division has developed a criminal justice evaluation program, which has evaluated such criminal justice practices as prison overcrowding and programs in drug education.

It is not necessary to detail the many ways in which the Executive and Legislative branches of our government have come to rely upon evaluation research as a means of deciding how to judge the merit of particular programs, nor indeed how and why the Congress increasingly mandates evaluation research in adopting legislation and requests such information in oversight and other hearings before committees. At times, members of Congress report being overwhelmed by the conflicting results of individual studies, as in the case of drug treatment programs for offenders. Then we hear them clamoring for an evaluation of the evaluations—what we in the methodology trade refer to as a meta-analysis. Clearly, the studies funded by the National Institute of Justice, the Bureau of Justice Statistics, and the Bureau of Justice Assistance and their predecessor agencies have a major role in developing programmatic support for evaluation research. Indeed, the National Institute of Justice has recently established a Program Evaluation and Methodology Division to meet the many demands for program evaluation.

Anyone who is a court watcher is aware of the many ways that appellate justices refer to evaluation research. Justices become acquainted with evaluation studies through citations in appellate briefs. Their staffs include these briefs in drafts of majority and dissenting opinions, and the justices more and more refer to such research in majority and dissenting opinions—confining them usually, alas, to brief citation. Additionally, it could be pointed out that the Administrative Office of the U.S. Courts and the Administrative Conference—both under Mr. Chief Justice—and the U.S. Sentencing Commission do evaluation research.

Somewhere, each executive branch makes use of evaluation research on some facet of drug control in American society. What we evaluation researchers have to say, therefore, is not without consequence, but whether it is consequential is another matter. Let me turn now both to ask and to give some answers to a series of questions about evaluation research.

WHAT IS EVALUATION RESEARCH AND HOW DO WE EVALUATE?

At the risk of bringing coals to Newcastle, I begin by telling you what I mean by *evaluating* and *evaluation* and the more special term *evaluation research*.

A simple dictionary definition of *evaluate* is "to examine and judge concerning the worth, quality, significance, amount, degree, or condition of" anything of interest. If one then defines *examine* for our purposes, it is "to test by an appropriate method." To *judge* is to "form an authoritative opinion" about a matter or "to determine or pronounce after inquiry and deliberation." What should be remembered is that to evaluate is to examine *and* judge. The first admonition then is to remind that *evaluation is a matter of both examination or testing and judging.* Evaluating drug control initiatives appears to require at least two distinct, albeit related, performances; the one, research or testing, preceding the other, forming a judgment about the value of not only the test but also the results of testing.

Unfortunately, the two procedures ordinarily are separated altogether. The research person usually eschews making judgments, except insofar as he or she is convinced, improperly, that the judgment follows from the results of the test. Those who judge often dismiss the results of a test by questioning the methods of inquiry or by alleging testing bias when the results do not support their expectations or "what everyone knows is the truth of the matter." It is important to remember that neither those who test nor those who judge are unbiased in judging the outcomes of tests, and that the safeguards against biased judgments by one are not those of the other.

What must be questioned, though, is the presumption that judgment follows testing. Anyone responsible for devising a test that is part of an evaluation must be skeptical of that separation. To evaluate appropriately and effectively means that those who do the test must be as fully apprised as possible of how the test and its results are to be judged, and those interested in its results must make clear how they will judge them. This is essential for several reasons.

The first reason is that no test will be satisfactory to those interested in taking action, based on the results, unless the design takes into account the explicit criteria by which the results will be judged. This means that those who seek to draw policy or practice implications from a particular research investigation must make clear to the investigator what are their criteria; and the investigators, in turn, must build criteria into the design. If, for example, those responsible for program implementation want to know whether a given drug treatment is cost-effective, then their criteria of cost-effectiveness must be designed into the study. If a particular drug treatment, for example, has a very high cost, would it be possible to implement it for the intended population? Or, if a particular police practice requires more personnel than the department can allocate, is it worth testing, for example, a police program to wrest control of drug-deteriorated neighborhoods from drug traffickers and hold them against retaking if it will require considerable personnel for some as yet undetermined period of time? Can the department afford to allocate those resources to those neighborhoods while accomplishing its other tasks and preventing displacement of trafficking?

The second reason the basis for judgment must precede the test is to ensure that those who will judge the results will have to stipulate explicit criteria for their judgment. This probably cannot be done very well by simply stating how one might use the results and passing them on to those doing the test evaluation. Rather, some form of limited partnership is required, where those who design the investigation and those who will use the results work together during the design stage to make explicit those criteria. One likely result of this partnership is that the criteria for judgment will be clarified during this process of specification for the design.

The second admonition follows then from the first. Evaluation is not only a matter of testing and judging, but testing and judging are so inextricably interwoven that *evaluating is preferably a joint endeavor of those who test and those who judge.* They are the warp and woof of the same web. This does not necessarily mean that the joint endeavor should be resolved by having the same person or organization responsible for both. It is preferable that they are not, given the high risk that to have a stake in a matter is not to be unbiased as to its outcome.

The third reason for emphasizing the importance of judgment is that it is a mistake for persons who do the research to conclude that they alone can draw the policy implications from their research. That they can draw some implications seems obvious enough, but as Joan Petersilia (1990) rightly contends, facts do not speak for themselves. Moreover, the policy relevance cannot become clear until one tries to take into account the alternatives considered by policymakers. What we can do to help this process is design the research to permit a choice among alternatives.

There is, therefore, a third reminder here, and that is *evaluation research has its greatest utility when it permits policymakers to choose among alternatives.* In this connection, I want to emphasize that studies that evaluate a single drug treatment, for example, whether in an experimental or some other design, are of considerably less value than those that evaluate two or more treatments. A control group ordinarily cannot be considered a treatment, as I shall shortly note. Similarly, a drug evaluation study that compares different dosage levels of a treatment—not in the simple sense of amount of a drug ingested, but in any of a number of ways in which the intensity of the treatment can vary—will be a more desirable design because it will shed light on making choices. Evaluation studies must be designed so they are relevant to making choices about implementation of a policy, or choosing among two or more policies.

This fourth warning might be stated in another way: *Evaluation studies are most relevant to policymakers and practitioners when they are cast in the framework of decision models.* In the spirit of this advice, it must be emphasized that evaluation studies often can be of greater value for making choices if one of the alternatives evaluated is that which is currently being done. That is not a simple matter for evaluation, however, because often what is being done currently are practices that include a large number of elements, each of which deservedly should be evaluated separately. Although it is possible to compare some alternative with multiple practices or treatments, it is usually futile to attempt to do so because it is nigh on to impossible to specify what constitutes the practice. If one seeks to test current practice as one of the "treatments," then a first step will be to clarify what is included in the current standard of treatment. That may be in itself a most critical benefit of an evaluation study. Two examples may illustrate the point. If one is testing police interventions in controlling drug markets that use a variety of means—for example, buy and bust, knock and talk, warrant searches, and street stops—then one should determine what constitutes each treatment and what constitutes their mix. Similarly, for a drug treatment program, one needs to assess how selection is exercised and what the elements of the treatment are, as practiced.

What Shall We Evaluate, and When Is Evaluation Necessary and Useful?

Often it is noted that there are many program and practice innovations in any year in the United States. Most likely, we do not know how many different programs there are that, in one way or another, are implementing some drug control intervention. Consider, for example, that every police department in the United States has some drug enforcement practices. Moreover, many of these policies and practices are often changed, albeit usually in small ways. In addition, drug policies and programs are implemented in the criminal justice and correctional systems through prosecution, plea bargaining, sentencing, and sanctioning practices, as well as by therapeutic treatment. And, we might add, there are literally thousands of schools in the United States with programs in preventing drug abuse. One hesitates to hazard even an estimate of how many current programs there are in drug control, or how many of those innovate in one way or another in any given year. Suffice it to say that the number is large, and that it makes little sense to think of evaluating all, or even most of them.

The problem is how to find innovations where an evaluation seems to hold forth promise of gains over current practice. There may not be a wholly satisfactory answer to that search, but it does seem that we need to expend some resources on just that question: How shall we determine which innovations are worthy of evaluation, and which of them offer conditions for doing a satisfactory evaluation? In pursuing that question, means of detecting prospects for evaluation should be compared with our current alternatives for doing so, by means of such things as program solicitations and applications for evaluation awards.

It seems that the real problem is to locate innovations that both purport to show results and offer some evidence that an evaluation might aid in deciding whether they are worthy of dissemination, or at least whether additional investment will be able to determine their utility. This places a burden on those, who develop and implement programs on treatment evaluation, to provide at least minimal information that convinces others there is an effect. My fifth admonition then is that *an important starting point for evaluation is assembling evidence that a practice or current innovation produces a desired or expected effect*—or might be expected to do so with proposed changes. I am not suggesting that the evidence result from a planned evaluation—only that some evidence of an effect be offered, something that can be examined and understood by those who might conduct an evaluation.

That is only a starting point, however. We should bear in mind that most innovations, changes in practice, or proposed changes in practice either merit or require careful evaluation. Most will, upon scrutiny, have little merit, either because they are so similar to those already evaluated that there is little gain from the repetition, especially because they showed little of significance, or because the evidence of an effect is so flawed as to leave one unconvinced of the worthwhileness of proceeding further.

There may be a few instances in which there is a pronounced effect and hence little reason to demonstrate the effectiveness. A controversial example is of not only whether to evaluate but also how to evaluate the effect that furnishing clean needles or bleach to drug users and condoms to sexual partners will have on the transmission of AIDS. There is no need to evaluate whether these measures have an effect on the transmission of virus, because that is quickly established. But that is only a beginning. In such cases, we may want evaluations to answer other questions. For example, in the AIDS example, we may want to know how we can improve the adoption of such practices. In other cases where an effect has been demonstrated, for example, methadone treatment, the problem has always been to find ways to ensure compliance with methadone maintenance. To put this general point more succinctly, evaluation research is unnecessary to demonstrate an effect when effects are patently obvious, by even the most simple criteria of test and judgment.

The more difficult problem faced in all evaluation research is how to cope with unrealistic expectations from those who sponsor or who will judge the research. All too commonly, there is the unrealistic expectation that a given intervention or innovation will show, upon evaluation, to have a substantial effect—that it will be the preliminary means of practice that we have been seeking for dissemination. Paralleling this expectation is one that we should abandon any further evaluation if there are no statistically significant effects, or when significant effects appear to promise little gain. Both of these beliefs stand in the way of developing a continuing sound evaluation program akin to those we find in the physical, mental, and public health programs.

There are several lessons from policy research, and particularly from the more rigorous policy experiments, that urge the evaluation research community to press forward in both these cases, rather than abandon the effort. For indeed, the sixth caveat is that *for any experiment or evaluation the most likely result—to repeat, the most likely result—is a failure to produce an effect. The second most likely result is that a statistically significant effect is likely to be quite small. Those are starting, not end points of evaluations.* What is required is that we look to our failures to tell us the next steps to take in solving the problem. Progress will be slow and usually is measured in terms of decades rather than years. There is a parallel seventh admonition here for practitioners and policymakers: *Short-term investments in single projects with a half-life of a year or two are unlikely to make much of a gain in problem solving.* It cannot be overemphasized that this is so, whether we are trying to find a cure for a particular disease, such as AIDS, or to produce a more effective drug treatment program. The auxiliary point, which must be kept in mind, is that any solution to drug control also requires a great deal of social engineering and social change, which are not easily attained. If one can be permitted another pun, we must not blind ourselves to the quick fix.

More commonly, then, if there are effects, they will be small. Such findings should be greeted with enthusiasm, because they usually signal significant leads to how the next gains are to be made. They point in directions to work. Moreover, even small gains should not be lightly dismissed when one is dealing with a macroscopic system, such as crime in society. Even a 1% or 2% gain from a drug treatment could account for a substantial reduction in crime, for example. Perhaps most important to keep in mind is that nothing works with everything; the problem is to find out what works for whom under what conditions.

Evaluation Research Requires Investment in Partnerships

The importance of close collaboration between those who are the policymakers, and the organizational consumers of evaluation research, and those who undertake the research was discussed above. Both have important roles in designing research because each will judge its merit upon completion.

There is an equally important feature of a partnership between the practitioners, who are expected to carry out an intervention, and the investigators. The success of the intervention depends ultimately upon their cooperation in carrying out the intervention being evaluated, and in subsequently institutionalizing its implementation. Not only do practitioners have an enormous capacity to resist innovation and sabotage it during the evaluation, but also many innovations will require practitioners to give up old ways for new ones. There is no better way of doing so than by taking them as partners in the test of the innovation. Indeed, an important principle may be that evaluation research should usually involve a partnership between the research team and the organization that is the site of the test. Most successful interventions require the cooperation of site administrators and practitioners with the research team.

The next warning reminder here is that *evaluation research requires joint participation and decision making between practitioners and evaluation researchers if it is to be institutionalized when it produces significant results. And those who fund evaluation research should broker partnerships between the research community and the organizational and practitioner communities.* Indeed, the promise of a successful partnership should be a condition of funding evaluation research. The National Institute of Justice has had considerable success in brokering such partnerships in evaluating police practices in domestic violence, and currently in police practices to control street drug marketing.

If it is to succeed in the long run, evaluation research requires another kind of investment—one that pays off through partnership. It is impossible for us to anticipate when we will want to do an evaluation, and often we will want some evaluation *after* a change has been made. This is particularly the case when we are not in a position to do elaborate measurement before the change is made. Then we must depend on data from other sources, especially existing databases, a few of which are developed and maintained by federal and state governments. The National Crime Victim Survey and the more recent adoption of state-based incident reporting for Uniform Crime Reporting (UCR) are examples. For the most part, though, we must depend on the databases of other organizations, often local ones. If that is so, then if our evaluations are to be sound, we must attend to what is collected by those organizations and their quality. This can be done most effectively if we are willing to commit our time and resources to the improvement of such databases. Working with local police departments, with local hospitals and their emergency medical services and trauma centers, with local treatment programs that are privately as well as publicly sponsored, we can help them develop databases that will have utility for many different future evaluations.

Perhaps no investment in the improvement of a database for criminal justice research will have greater payoff in evaluation than the development and implementation of incident-based UCR. We are still a fair distance from developing an efficient national and local case-tracking system for criminal justice, but if and when we reach that goal, there will be substantial gains for evaluation research. The final reminder is that *wise investment in appropriate databases is essential to a sound evaluation research program in criminal justice.*

In conclusion, my hope is that my emphasis on the long-term, on partnerships, and on expectation of negative results as the likely outcome of an evaluation program does not sound pessimistic. Difficult problems take many trials, and we must be prepared to learn from failures about what to try next, rather than conclude that we should quit if it does not produce what is expected or promised. Permit me a few final puns. We must not blind ourselves to the quick fix by seeking a quick succession of highs. A slower, steady course of planned evaluations based on failures as well as successes is our destiny.

Reference

Petersilia, J. (1990). Policy relevance and the future of criminology. *Criminology, 29*, 1-15.

3. Prevalence of Drug Use Among Criminal Offender Populations: Implications for Control, Treatment, and Policy

YIH-ING HSER

DOUGLAS LONGSHORE

M. DOUGLAS ANGLIN

Estimating the number of drug users involved in the criminal justice system (CJS) and determining the needs for treatment among them are critical precursors to policy decisions. Using local arrest data and drug-use rates among arrestees, a methodology was developed to provide estimates of the number of drug users in several categories of arrestees. In 1989 Los Angeles County (adult population 6,537,000) was estimated to have 145,395 arrestees who used cocaine; 39,633 who used heroin; 193,883 who used some illicit drug; and 67,839 who used some drug by injection. (These estimates are not mutually exclusive.) Estimates of drug use in the overall criminal population, whether arrested or not during the year, indicate 371,730 cocaine users; 109,172 heroin users; 504,738 users of some illicit drug; and 190,505 users of some drug by injection. About 40% of arrestees who showed by urinalysis recent use of at least one illicit drug reported need for drug treatment. By contrast, only 5,356 cocaine users and 14,044 injection drug users were admitted to treatment in Los Angeles in 1989. Relative to their counterparts, drug-using arrestees who are Anglo, female, and

AUTHORS' NOTE: This study was supported in part by NIJ Grants 90-IJ-CX-0044 and 90-IJ-CX-0014. Drs. Hser and Anglin are also supported by Research Scientist Development Awards (DA00139 and DA00146, respectively) from NIDA. Special thanks are due to the Bureau of Criminal Statistics and Special Services, California Department of Justice, for providing the arrest data necessary for the analysis. Dr. Jan Chaiken reviewed an earlier version of this chapter and provided valuable comments, which the authors deeply appreciate. The authors also thank staff at the UCLA Drug Abuse Research Center for data analysis and manuscript preparation. Correspondence should be sent to Yih-Ing Hser, Ph.D., UCLA Drug Abuse Research Center, 1100 Glendon Avenue, Suite 763, Los Angeles, CA 90024-3511.

older reported a greater need for treatment. Strategies for meeting offender treatment needs are suggested.

Introduction

The relationship between drugs and crime has been studied extensively, and findings accumulated over 50 years have consistently shown high crime rates among drug abusers and high drug-use rates among offenders (e.g., Tonry & Wilson, 1990). In this context, historical and current policy toward illicit drug use in the United States assigns a primary responsibility for controlling drug use and its behavioral consequences to the criminal justice system (CJS). The widespread increase in the use of drugs during the 1970s and 1980s provoked additional policy implementation by the CJS and generated unprecedented rates of arrest, incarceration, and legal supervision. The impact on police, prosecution, the courts, probation, and corrections has been overwhelming in terms of workload, stretched resources, and limited options to intervene with drug-using offenders. Corrections departments have been especially affected by new admissions and by high violation rates among probationers and parolees, events that have led to overcrowding in penal facilities.

Empirical data suggest that drug use is both a direct and an indirect cause of crime. In the underground economy, drug use drives dealing and property crimes directly, and many acts of violent crime occur indirectly as a result of transaction disputes or marketing conflicts (De la Rosa, Lambert, & Gropper, 1990). Drug dealing, in particular, not only inherently involves violence, but may also lure others into criminal behavior in anticipation of large profits (Chaiken & Chaiken, 1982; Goldstein, 1985; Johnson, Goldstein, Preble, Schmeidler, Lipton, Spunt, & Miller, 1985).

Drug-dependent offenders are specifically responsible for an extraordinary proportion of crime (Chaiken, 1986; Gropper, 1985; Inciardi, 1979; Johnson et al., 1985). Studies of substance abusing offenders, especially those who use heroin and cocaine, show that they have extremely high crime rates (Ball, Rosen, Flueck, & Nurco, 1981; Ball, Shaffer, & Nurco, 1983; Chaiken & Chaiken, 1983; Collins, Hubbard, & Rachal, 1985; Johnson et al., 1985; McGlothlin, Anglin, & Wilson, 1977). Furthermore, as the severity of drug use increases, the frequency and severity of criminal behavior also rises dramatically (Chaiken & Chaiken, 1982; Chaiken, 1986; Collins et al., 1985; Speckart & Anglin,

1986a, 1986b). Moreover, criminal offenders who are regular users of hard drugs (e.g., heroin or cocaine) or of multiple drugs are typically at high risk of recidivism after release from prison (Chaiken & Chaiken, 1982; Innes, 1986, 1988; Wexler, Lipton, & Johnson, 1988).

The Drug Use Forecasting (DUF) studies (Wish, 1988), by conducting quarterly surveys in more than 20 sites in the United States, provide perhaps the most comprehensive and compelling findings nationally of the level of drug use in arrestees; importantly, urine testing rather than self-report is used as an objective measure of drug use. The general conclusions drawn from DUF data are: (a) high prevalence rates of drug use are observed among arrestees, as determined by positive urine results; (b) considerable regional variation exists in drug use patterns; and (c) relative to their drug use, drug-using arrestees report low rates of drug treatment experience.

The evidence of high drug-use rates among arrestees—together with surveys reporting similar high pre-arrest drug use among inmates (Innes, 1988)—underscores the urgent need for effective intervention for criminal offenders with a drug use problem. However, the appropriate resource allocation for drug abuse interventions within criminal populations will continue to be relatively ad hoc until adequate population-based estimates of the degree of drug use in these populations and their treatment needs become available. Regional variation in drug use patterns suggests that policymakers need to obtain local estimates as a basis for appropriate local planning, rather than relying solely on aggregate national estimates. A model using local data to develop estimates of drug use in CJS populations is developed here.

This chapter is organized in three sections. First, combining the relatively comprehensive DUF information for Los Angeles County with local criminal justice statistics, we estimate the numbers of drug users in arrestee and criminal populations for the county. Second, we provide estimates of treatment needs, mostly derived from drug-using arrestees' self-reports. Third, we recommend a number of policy strategies for effective intervention with drug users in criminal justice populations.

Estimating Drug Use in Arrestee and Criminal Populations: Los Angeles County

Official arrest data, which show the number of arrests in a given year, provide one measure, albeit imprecise, of the size of the "criminal population" (Tillman, 1987; Visher & Roth, 1986). In 1989, for example, there were more than 1.8 million felony and misdemeanor adult arrests reported in California (Criminal Justice Profile, 1989). These arrest data, however, do not indicate how many different individuals were arrested during that year; some individuals may have been arrested more than once. Moreover, because official arrest records merely correspond to specific arrest events, they do not indicate the number of times that any single member of the population was arrested within a given year. In other words, the arrest data upon which law enforcement authorities, researchers, and the public generally rely to understand the extent of crime do not directly provide information on the prevalence of arrest, that is, how many people are arrested at least once in a given time period; and the rate of arrest, that is, how often any single individual is arrested (Tillman, 1987).

Furthermore, arrests cannot be used as a single, direct measure reflecting the size of criminal populations. The failure of victims to report crimes, the failure of the police to apprehend a suspect for a reported crime, and the multiple charges often specified at arrest prevent a simple interpretation of arrest data. Because the probability of an arrest is predicated not only on the commission of a crime but also on other factors, such as the likelihood of reporting, police policy, and so on, the criminal justice system captures only a segment of the criminal population in any given time period (Blumstein, Sagasi, & Wolfgang, 1973; Greene & Stollmack, 1981). Being able to estimate the size of the total, including the "hidden," criminal population is important for policy planning and for designing more effective interventions (Hser, Anglin, Wickens, Brecht, & Homer, 1991).

Conversely, a person being arrested may be innocent of the crime suspected, and not all arrestees are habitual criminals in the sense of maintaining a lifestyle of persistent criminal activity. However, official arrest data (unless collected for the same individual over a relatively long period) do not allow an easy distinction between habitual criminals and occasional offenders.

Prevalence estimation of the number of drug users among criminal populations requires conversion of arrest events to number of arrestees, estimation of the number of criminals (including those not arrested during a specified year), and mapping of appropriate drug use rates onto these estimated populations. Finally, levels of use at an intensity to warrant treatment must be estimated to determine the proportion of arrestees needing treatment intervention. For application purposes, we use the California Bureau of Criminal Statistics (BCS) data, which are comprehensive in coverage of arrest records, and Drug Use Forecasting

(DUF) data, which contain drug use rates,[1] drug treatment history, and reported treatment need among local arrestees. Our application uses data for 1989, the most recent year for which relevant information is available.

Our procedures for estimating the size of the arrestee population of a given year involve matching arrest records within that year using unique identifiers. This record matching provides both estimates of total arrestees and the distribution of frequency of arrest. A truncated Poisson model is applied to the arrest distribution to obtain estimates of criminals, including those not apprehended for arrest during 1989 (Hser et al., 1991). For estimating the number of drug users among these arrestee and criminal populations, we apply a simple population projection method (Hser et al., 1991), which maps drug use rates observed in DUF to the estimates of the respective populations. The applications illustrated here consider differences in gender, ethnicity,[2] and types of offenses[3] so as to increase the precision of estimates. One important note is that because our data contain no information on juvenile arrests, all our analyses deal only with adult (18 years of age or older) criminal and drug-using populations. Figure 3.1 summarizes data sources and estimation procedures that have been employed in this application.

METHODOLOGICAL ISSUES

The method described provides estimates rather than precise measures of prevalence of drug use among offender populations. Several inherent limitations of the methodology must be considered. First, converting arrest records (an event-based measure) to obtain the number of arrestees (a person-based measure) requires successful matching of records. We matched arrest records for 1989 by unambiguous personal identifiers within gender and ethnic groups.

A second set of potential biases is derived from the assumption that the observed arrest distributions follow a Poisson distribution. Because the application of the Poisson model requires the fitting of the distribution, we applied the model separately for each gender and ethnic group and empirically tested this assumption for each subgroup. The fitting for the Other ethnic group was unacceptable, and therefore the estimation model was not applied to this group. Instead, the number of unobserved arrestees in this Other group was estimated by assuming that the ratio of unobserved to observed arrestees in the Other ethnic group was in proportion to that derived for the other three groups combined (Anglo, Hispanic, and African-American).

Drug Use Prevalence Among CJS Populations

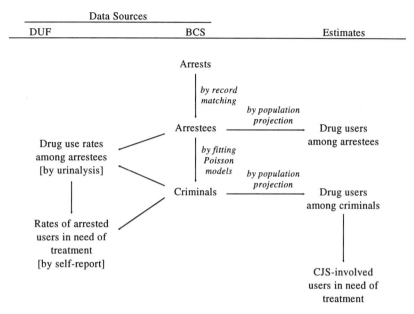

Figure 3.1. Data Sources and Estimation Procedures: Los Angeles County

A third methodological and conceptual issue is that data on arrests were analyzed in the context of an interest in estimating criminals, that is, all persons committing crimes, regardless of whether arrested. As we described earlier, many factors other than the commission of a crime influence the probability of arrest. Although we have not been entirely able to avoid the potential biases, we estimate the number of criminals separately for each gender and ethnic group, assuming that homogeneity within these subgroups will reduce the biasing effects of uncontrolled factors.

Finally, the representativeness of the DUF samples and, therefore, the adequacy of mapping DUF-derived drug use rates to the total arrestee and criminal populations may be questionable. DUF is not a probability sample. Some offenses are purposefully oversampled (e.g., felony property crimes), others are purposefully undersampled (e.g., drug possession and sales), and some offenses are excluded (e.g., traffic violations, vagrancy, warrants, and alcohol use). Therefore, as we have done, it is necessary to consider offense type, as well as gender and ethnicity, in using DUF drug use rates to project to the total arrestee population.

Furthermore, in line with our earlier discussion of the underlying meaning of an arrest, many of the arrests in the BCS data are for offenses such as traffic violations or vagrancy, those least likely to be covered by DUF. However, most citizens and policymakers are more concerned with the more serious offenses, which are better covered by DUF (see Note 3). Therefore, in estimating the criminal population, we use the term *lawbreakers* for estimates based on all offenses in the BCS data, and the term *criminals* for estimates based on offenses covered by DUF. This latter category is more likely to represent individuals involved in more serious crimes.

ESTIMATION RESULTS

Our application results are estimates of the number of arrestees and lawbreakers or criminals and the number of drug users within these populations. These results are summarized in Table 3.1. (Detailed information showing the steps of estimating the number of drug users in various categories is given in Appendix A. Briefly, for each type of drug, the population projection, or synthetic estimation, method was applied to map DUF use rates to BCS arrestees, taking into consideration offense type, gender, and ethnicity.) The total number of arrests in Los Angeles County in 1989 (525,503) yields an estimate of 436,509 arrestees, with a mean number of 1.2 arrests per arrestee. This figure is well within other annual estimates (U.S. Senate, Committee on the Judiciary, 1990; Wish, 1990). The estimated number of lawbreakers is 1,409,577, and that of DUF-identified criminals is 684,024. Based on the 1990 census for Los Angeles County, California (California State Census Data Center, 1991), these estimates indicate an arrest rate of about 8,000 arrests per 100,000 adult population. Among the Los Angeles County adult population of 6.53 million, 6.6% had been arrested at least once in 1989, 22% are estimated to be lawbreakers, and 10% are estimated to be more serious criminals.

Estimates of drug use among arrestees show that 145,395 used cocaine, 39,632 used heroin, 193,883 used some illicit drug, and 67,839 used some drug by injection. The corresponding numbers among the estimated criminal population were 371,730 cocaine users, 109,172 heroin users, 504,738 users of some illicit drug, and 190,505 users by injection. DUF data also show that among the arrestees with a positive urine test, 76% reported a history of drug dependence, and 67.8% reported having a current drug dependence problem. Based on the estimates of those who

Table 3.1 Estimates of Drug-Using Arrestees/Criminals in Los Angeles, 1989 (Based on DUF and BCS Data, 1989)

	Male				Female				Total
	Anglo	African-American	Hispanic	Other	Anglo	African-American	Hispanic	Other	
All Offense Categories									
Total Number of Arrests	113,653	112,605	207,978	15,610	27,149	25,890	19,602	3,016	525,503
Total Number of Estimated Arrestees	98,670	87,399	169,640	14,797	23,816	22,076	17,190	2,921	436,509
Total Number of Estimated Lawbreakers	392,251	212,386	492,419	45,636	101,296	78,994	72,947	13,648	1,409,577
Estimated *Lambda* (Rate of Arrest per Lawbreaker)	0.29	0.53	0.42	0.11	0.27	0.33	0.27	0.07	
DUF-Offense Categories									
Total Number of Arrests	61,842	89,851	120,031	7,320	18,231	22,580	15,452	2,218	337,525
Total Number of Estimated Arrestees	51,059	67,318	89,001	7,044	15,324	18,942	13,390	2,139	264,217
Total Number of Estimated Criminals	156,048	147,732	190,126	16,776	50,989	62,311	52,600	7,442	684,024
Estimated *Lambda* (Rate of Arrest per Criminal)	0.40	0.61	0.63	0.08	0.36	0.36	0.29	0.07	

continued

Table 3.1 Continued

| | Male | | | Female | | | |
	Anglo	African-American	Hispanic/Other	Anglo	African-American	Hispanic/Other	Total
Drug Users (Among DUF-Offense Categories)							
Cocaine Rate	0.34	0.76	0.46	0.58	0.79	0.54	
Among Arrestees:	17,512	51,136	44,487	8,935	14,955	8,370	145,395
Among Criminals:	53,056	112,276	95,175	29,574	49,226	32,423	371,730
Heroin Rate	0.15	0.08	0.16	0.22	0.09	0.40	
Among Arrestees:	7,499	5,667	15,148	3,363	1,687	6,268	39,632
Among Criminals:	23,407	11,819	33,104	11,218	5,608	24,017	109,172
Any Illicit Drug Rate	0.71	0.87	0.61	0.82	0.85	0.74	
Among Arrestees:	36,382	58,486	59,004	12,546	16,042	11,423	193,883
Among Criminals:	110,794	128,527	126,210	41,811	52,964	44,431	504,738
Any IVDU Rate	0.35	0.17	0.20	0.42	0.24	0.55	
Among Arrestees:	17,924	11,676	18,844	6,388	4,560	8,447	67,839
Among Criminals:	54,617	25,114	41,380	21,415	14,955	33,023	190,505

used some (at least one) illicit drug, it is estimated that at least 131,453 arrestees and 342,212 serious criminals in Los Angeles County were in need of treatment in 1989 for their drug dependence problems. According to the California Drug Abuse Data System (CAL-DADS, 1990), however, there were only 14,044 drug-injecting users and 5,356 cocaine users admitted to treatment in Los Angeles County in 1989. The huge disparity between the estimated numbers of drug users in CJS populations needing treatment and the number of all drug users in treatment leads to a discussion of treatment need and utilization, which occurs in the next section.

The estimation results reported above are high, which is consistent with other findings that are based on DUF (Wish, 1990), and we do not know of any other independent and equivalent estimates or sources that allow an appropriate comparison. Factors discussed in the methodological issues section may have influences on the resulting estimates, and the assumptions need to be carefully validated.

The analysis also sheds light on differences in arrest rates among subgroups. Although the mean numbers of arrests in each subgroup arrestees differ slightly, the *lambdas*[4] estimated from the truncated Poisson model vary more widely. *Lambda* of the truncated Poisson model is the mean number of arrests per offender, including those not arrested. In general, females have a lower arrest rate than males. African-Americans and Hispanics have a higher arrest rate than Anglos. More serious criminals (those included by DUF) have a higher arrest rate than lawbreakers generally. Male African-Americans and Hispanics are overrepresented in arrest statistics, which appears to result largely from the greater prevalence of arrest and the higher arrest rates within ethnic minority populations. The relative magnitudes of the estimates among subgroups seem to confirm those found in other relevant studies (Tillman, 1987; Wish, 1987).

Treatment Needs

PREVALENCE OF TREATMENT NEED

Continuing our application of methods for estimating drug use, treatment need, and treatment utilization, this section uses survey and urinalysis data collected in the Los Angeles DUF to estimate, for the year 1989, the number of criminals who needed drug treatment. The prevalence estimation procedure used here parallels the procedure used above to estimate the size of criminal populations. This section also examines variation in probable treatment need by ethnicity and gender in a multi-variate context to determine relative differences between subgroups.

In accord with the analysis strategy reported in Gerstein and Harwood (1990), "probable need for treatment" is assumed if (a) the arrestee's urinalysis was positive for any illicit drug; and (b) the arrestee reported at least one of the following: dependence on any illicit drug, current enrollment in drug abuse treatment, or current need for treatment.

It is important to note that although the first criterion is objective (not based on self-report), probable need as defined by Gerstein and Harwood (1990) cannot be established without some self-reported indication of need as well. One self-reported measure, current enrollment in treatment, is at least probably factual. The other two are perceptual. The possible bias introduced by self-reported criteria is discussed below.

Under the Gerstein and Harwood (1990) criteria, probable need is indicated for 38.7% of Los Angeles County arrestees interviewed in DUF during 1989. If it can be assumed that treatment needs are similar among non-arrested drug-using criminals, our estimation procedure indicates that 274,247 drug-using criminals probably needed drug abuse treatment in 1989. In contrast, there were only 38,602 public treatment admissions in Los Angeles County during this year (CAL-DADS, 1989). Comparisons between the treatment admission information and estimated numbers of CJS-involved drug users needing treatment show the tremendous shortage of treatment capacity to meet the probable need.

DEMOGRAPHIC DIFFERENCES
IN PROBABLE TREATMENT NEED

In considering the expansion of local treatment capacity to serve this unmet need for treatment, possible ethnic and gender differences should be examined. If, for example, unmet need is higher among women than among men, addition of new treatment slots may not efficiently serve the unmet need unless services available through those new slots are geared to address women's concerns (e.g., prenatal care and child care). Similarly, if unmet treatment need is higher among African-Americans or Hispanics than among Anglos, it may be important to ensure that a suitable number of new slots are made available in ethnic neighborhoods, or are planned to provide treatment protocols designed for cultural congruence.

To our knowledge, no previous research has directly examined ethnic and gender patterns in treatment need in any drug-using population. An alternative source of hypotheses regarding such variability is provided by studies of demographic patterns in treatment entry. Some studies have found that African-American and Hispanic drug users are less likely than Anglo drug users to enter treatment for drug abuse (Desmond & Maddux, 1984; Little, 1981; Rounsaville & Kleber, 1985). However, the Treatment Outcome Prospective Study (TOPS) found that African-Americans and Hispanics have, on average, a greater number of treatment episodes than Anglos (Hubbard, Marsden, Rachal, Harwood, Cavanaugh, & Ginzburg, 1989). Some studies on gender patterns in drug abuse treatment entry have reported that female drug users are less likely to be in treatment (Hubbard et al., 1989; Stevens, Arbiter, & Glider, 1989).

Treatment entry studies, however, mostly reflect treatment participation or utilization patterns and are of limited value for examining demographic differences in treatment need among more general drug user populations. Another limitation of most treatment entry studies has been their reliance on bivariate analysis. Multivariate analysis needs to be considered to avoid possible confounding due to uncontrolled factors.

DUF data afford an opportunity to directly examine demographic patterns in probable treatment need in a population of drug-using arrestees. It is important to reiterate that, under the Gerstein and Harwood (1990) definition, treatment need is considered probable if the arrestee himself or herself reports needing treatment or being dependent on an illicit drug. The criterion of current enrollment in treatment was met by only 3% of Los Angeles arrestees. Thus most cases of probable need are identified on the basis of self-reported need or drug dependence.

For comparability with previous studies of treatment entry, we use logistic regression techniques to determine, first, whether any bivariate differences exist in probable treatment need by ethnicity, gender, or age. We then test these demographic variables in a multivariate analysis so that any effects of subsample composition can be taken into account.

To maximize the statistical power of the analysis, we use a data set combining all Los Angeles DUF data from October 1987 to January 1990. Cases are included in this analysis if they reported use of any illicit drug within the past 30 days, or if their urinalysis tested positive for any illicit drug. This second eligibility criterion was added to avoid any bias that might result from underreported recent use. The resulting sample includes 2,417 recent drug users, or roughly 57% of the total number of arrestees ($n = 4,212$) interviewed at Los Angeles DUF sites. The gender breakdown of the study sample is 64.7% men and 35.3% women. The ethnic breakdown is 39.6% African-American, 36.7% Hispanic, and 23.6% Anglo. (Roughly 85% of Hispanics in DUF are of Mexican descent.)

The crude (bivariate) odds ratios indicate that probable need, as defined earlier, is less prevalent among Hispanic than among Anglo drug-using arrestees (odds ratio = 0.73, p = .0005). African-Americans and Anglos are not significantly different (odds ratio = 1.08, p = .36). The gender comparison indicates that probable need is significantly more prevalent among female drug users (odds ratio = 1.36, p = .0003). Finally, with age split at the mean (27.8 years), probable need is significantly more prevalent among older arrestees (i.e., those over 28) (odds ratio = 1.23, p = .01).

In the multivariate analysis, adjusted odds ratios indicate the relationship of each predictor to treatment need after other predictors are taken into account. The significant bivariate relations were confirmed. With all three demographic predictors in the equation, probable need remains less prevalent for Hispanic drug users (odds ratio = 0.70, p = .025), more prevalent among female drug users (odds ratio = 1.30, p = .003), and higher among older drug users (odds ratio = 1.20, p = .033). The multivariate analysis also reveals a marginally significant difference between African-Americans and Anglos, with probable treatment need less prevalent among African-Americans (odds ratio = 0.84, p = .10).

These results are consistent with the findings from treatment entry studies, cited above, indicating that the need for drug abuse treatment is less prevalent among African-American and Hispanic drug users. Though its statistical significance is marginal, the finding for African-Americans illustrates the importance of examining treatment need through multivariate techniques. The possibility that treatment need might be less prevalent among African-American drug users, as indicated in this fairly simple multivariate analysis, was obscured in the bivariate analysis. (The African-American subsample includes higher proportions of women and older arrestees compared with other ethnic groups. This explains why probable need among African-Americans was obscured in the bivariate analysis.)

The finding for gender is at odds with the hypothesis, drawn from treatment entry studies, that treatment need is less prevalent among female drug users. In this sample of drug-using arrestees, probable need appears more prevalent, not less so, among women than among men. Note that these findings may be unique to Los Angeles in 1989, as the prevalence of recent drug use among arrestees (as estimated by DUF) varies across time and place. Similarly, it is possible that treatment need may vary with time and geographic location, including findings regarding differences by ethnicity and gender.

In addition, we would add two important qualifiers. First, men are probably less likely than women to perceive or report dependence/need (Longshore, Hsieh, & Anglin, 1991), and this difference could partly or entirely explain the finding that probable need is higher among women. Conversely, Hispanics and African-Americans may be less likely than Anglos to acknowledge or recognize dependence/need. Future research should examine demographic differences in the relationship between intensity of drug use and perceived dependence/need, and explore the reasons for any such differences. Furthermore, it may be advisable to conduct intensive outreach among arrestees (and others) who use illicit drugs at high levels of intensity but do not perceive a need for treatment. Our findings suggest that such users are likely to be African-American, Hispanic, or male. Second, treatment need is not synonymous with treatment demand. Arrestees for whom probable need is indicated may not actually present themselves for treatment. Costs of treatment, geographic proximity to treatment providers, and other factors could work against treatment demand, even among drugs users who perceive a need for treatment. As noted above, this is one reason why treatment entry studies are of limited value as indicators of demographic differences in probable need. Questions of access aside, treatment demand may also be influenced by the drug user's own perception of problems posed by his or her dependence on drugs, the expected outcomes of treatment, and other subjective factors.

ESTIMATION CONCLUSIONS

The preceding analyses and results have shown that drug use by lawbreakers and criminals is extensive in Los Angeles County. In 1989 about 200,000 arrestees and approximately 500,000 criminals could have tested positive for some illicit drug use. We have also seen that while treatment need is high, treatment participation is low, and current treatment capacity in the county is inadequate to meet the demand. Given these high proportions and numbers, policy strategies for intervention with drug-abusing offenders are of paramount importance, especially in light of the continuing responsibility by the criminal justice system for controlling illicit drug use and the related criminality.

Strategies for Identifying and Meeting Treatment Needs of Offenders

In this section, we discuss several policy recommendations for identifying and providing treatment to CJS-involved drug users. Consistent

7231

with findings from the epidemiological perspective presented in previous sections, several general guidelines for identifying and treating drug-using criminals are provided, based on relevant evaluation results.

Several extensive reviews of the literature (Anglin & Hser, 1990, 1991; Wexler, Lipton, & Johnson, 1988) have supported the view that interventions for drug abuse can be effective, even with the criminal populations. In these groups, however, special features may be necessary to maximize the chance of success, and certain program structures may be required to achieve the optimal benefit. The following recommendations are drawn from practitioner experience and from guidelines established by the National Institute of Justice.

1. Pre-Incarceration

To reduce crime, CJS strain, and AIDS risk, concentrate on chronic heroin, cocaine, and injection drug users. Abuse of amphetamines and PCP may merit special attention in selected localities, but the majority of arrests appear to be related to either heroin or cocaine.

All persons who are arrested should be tested for drug use, especially heroin and cocaine. Many chronic drug users have contact with the criminal justice system about once per year (Wexler, Lipton, & Johnson, 1988), usually through arrest, and this contact should be seized as an opportunity to detect and assess any drug use and to present treatment options (Toborg, Bellassai, Yezer, Carver, Clark, & Pears, 1986). Records of urinalyses should be maintained in court and corrections files, along with other pertinent information, for use in determining suitability for pretrial release or for sentencing if they are convicted.

Arrestees who test positive in urinalyses and who show other indications of substance abuse should be targeted for further assessment and required to attend orientation and preliminary intake procedures while they are in detention, as a first step toward placing them in treatment, either while incarcerated or on their return to the community (Collins et al., 1985; Toborg, Levin, Milkman, & Center, 1975). When possible, those arrested primarily for drug abuse or possession should be considered for community-based sentencing and intervention programs rather than sentenced to jail or prison.

2. Inmate Programs

Chronic drug users who are sentenced to jail or prison should be enrolled in treatment programs, on either a voluntary or a compulsory basis. Despite the widely held view among CJS personnel that rehabilitation efforts aimed at such individuals are ineffective (Carter & Klein, 1976; Lipton, Martinson, & Wilks, 1975), significant research results indicate that corrections-based treatment can have a substantial impact on the behavior of chronic drug-abusing offenders (Anglin & Hser, 1990; Anglin & McGlothlin, 1984; DeLeon, 1984; DeLeon, Andrews, Wexler, Jaffe, & Rosenthal, 1979; Gendreau & Ross, 1987; McGlothlin et al., 1977; Sells & Simpson, 1976a, 1976b, 1976c; Wexler, Lipton, & Foster, 1985).

On release to probation or parole, the period of subsequent legal supervision should be a lengthy one. Dependence on opiates and other illicit drugs is a chronically relapsing condition. Except in a minority of cases, several cycles of treatment, aftercare, and relapse may be expected. The typical successful intervention achieves longer periods in which drug dependence is controlled and relapse periods are shorter. Because most abusers have had several years of dysfunctional drug use before coming to the attention of treatment or CJS system authorities, it is not unreasonable to expect that several more years will be necessary to control, reduce, and ultimately eliminate their drug use.

3. Community Aftercare

Upon completion of the inmate portion of their rehabilitation programs, probationers and parolees should be enrolled in community-based treatment programs. Even a lengthy period of treatment at the end of an incarceration term may be insufficient to ensure successful rehabilitation. With few exceptions, studies have generally shown that the longer an individual is retained in a treatment program, and the greater continuity of care during recovery, the more drug use and associated criminal activities are reduced and the greater the likelihood of successful employment (Anglin & Hser, 1989, 1990; McGlothlin & Anglin, 1979; Simpson, 1979, 1981).

All drug users on probation or parole should be given frequent urine tests for drugs, whether they are enrolled in a treatment program or not. Whether such monitoring affects treatment outcome has not been thoroughly studied, but considerable evidence points to its effectiveness when linked to aversive contingencies, such as those applied by CJS programs (McGlothlin et al., 1977). Urine testing in CJS settings, in combination with intensive legal or other supervision with sanctions for detected drug use, has been shown to be more effective than supervision without testing in reducing daily narcotics use and criminal activity by the narcotic addicts admitted to the California Civil Addict Program. This finding has been replicated in work with methadone maintenance admissions (Anglin, Deschenes, & Speckart, 1987). Other researchers have also found that effective monitoring of urinalysis results will help interrupt relapse to daily heroin and cocaine use and thus reduce the rate of criminality (Carver, 1986; Toborg et al., 1986).

The foregoing issues will require extensive changes in CJS philosophy and strategy. However, the corrections system is already extremely complex —and this complexity is not adequately resolving the problems now facing the correctional system. Coping with current and future needs will require changing the mission of corrections drastically, and the process will not be simple. But the techniques for treating drug abuse among CJS populations have been demonstrated to be effective, and implementing them on a wider scale should be well within the realm of possibility. If we are to make significant reductions in criminality due to drug use by offenders, we must implement more appropriate treatment programs within CJS and community environments. Reluctance to incur short-term costs, however, may compromise the goal of long-term benefits that would result from appropriate treatment interventions for CJS populations.

Furthermore, many of the misunderstandings surrounding CJS-based treatment programs arise because communication between the CJS and the drug treatment system has been almost nonexistent. Members of these systems need to move toward the realization that by collaborating to produce the desired behavior changes, they can significantly improve outcomes for individuals under their care and for society as a whole.

Concluding Comments

Knowledge of the size and characteristics of the criminal population is important for criminal justice system planning. Many studies show that most heavy drug users, particularly heroin and cocaine abusers, are involved with the criminal justice system at some time during their lives. The present study also demonstrates that dependent drug users are decidedly concentrated within the criminal justice system. The vast numbers of drug-using arrestees and criminals accentuate the tremendous disparity between treatment needs, availability, and utilization.

Counting drug users is a crucial first step toward learning more about their backgrounds and how they interact within the CJS and with various treatment systems. Estimates are necessarily crude, given available data, and further improvements in methodology are needed to improve the accuracy of the estimates. The number and characteristics of juvenile drug users involved with the CJS must also be determined to complete the assessment of resource requirements for CJS-based treatment interventions.

Determining treatment need is a necessary second step for the provision of services to drug-using offender populations in order to mitigate some of the social consequences of drug use. These needs have been shown to be extensive in the analyses presented above and by findings of other research studies. The suggested considerations for system modification and the necessary elements to be included will require careful planning and implementation. Without the proposed changes, the crisis in the CJS caused by current levels of offender drug use will not abate.

Notes

1. Ten drugs are objectively tested for in DUF: cocaine, opiates, PCP, marijuana, methadone, Valium, methaqualone, Darvon, barbiturates, and amphetamines. Specimens are analyzed by EMIT, which can detect heroin or cocaine use within the previous 2 to 3 days, marijuana use within the previous 1 to 4 weeks, and use of other drugs for varying lengths of time (Gerstein & Harwood, 1990). Positive results for amphetamine use are confirmed by gas chromatography to screen out arrestees who have used over-the-counter drugs. Our application examples include use of cocaine, heroin, any illicit drug use (i.e., any of the 10 drugs tested), and, because of its relevance to AIDS/HIV, any drug use by injection (injection is based on self-report).

2. DUF interviewers code each arrestee's ethnicity from information on the jail booking slips. The record is revised during the interview if, as rarely happens, the booking slip record is manifestly wrong.

3. Types of offenses are classified into violent crime, income-generating crime, drug violations, and other crimes. The correspondence of these crime categories with BCS and DUF recorded charges can be obtained from the first author. Violent crimes, for example, include homicide, manslaughter, sex assault/rape, assault, extortion/threat, arson, weapons, and so on. Income-generating crimes include robbery, burglary, forgery, and so on. Drug violations include drug possession and sale. Other crimes are further distinguished into DUF-identified other crimes and those excluded from DUF sampling. DUF-identified other crimes include flight/escape/bench warrant, obscenity, and probation/parole violation. Examples of other crimes excluded from DUF are vagrancy, drunkenness, driving under the influence, and other minor offenses.

4. *Lambda* of the truncated Poisson model as applied to arrest data is equivalent to *mu*, which is a more common term used in the field of criminology (Blumstein, Cohen, Roth, & Visher, 1986).

Appendix A Estimated Number of Drug Users Among Arrestees in Los Angeles, 1989

	DUF Sample Size	Urine Positive (%) For Any Illicit				BCS-Estimated Arrestees	Estimated Number of Drug-Using Arrestees							
		Cocaine	Heroin	Drug	IVDU		Cocaine	S. E.	Heroin	S.E.	Any Illicit Drug	S. E.	IVDU	S. E.
Violent Crime														
Male		39.49	6.07	57.94	13.45	58,949	23,281		3,581		34,155		7,929	
Anglo	39	15.38	7.69	48.72	15.38	14,979	2,304	865	1,152	639	7,298	1,199	2,304	865
African-American	56	60.71	1.79	78.57	14.30	17,052	10,352	1,113	305	302	13,398	935	2,438	798
Hispanic/Other	76	39.47	7.89	50.00	11.84	26,918	10,625	1,509	2,124	832	13,459	1,544	3,187	998
Female		43.71	5.86	56.83	20.24	7,259	3,173		425		4,126		1,469	
Anglo	13	30.77	0.00	46.15	15.38	2,114	650	271	0	N/A	976	292	325	212
African-American	28	67.86	7.14	75.00	10.71	3,120	2,117	275	223	152	2,340	255	334	182
Hispanic/Other	10	20.00	10.00	40.00	40.00	2,025	405	256	203	192	810	314	810	314
Income-Generating Crime														
Male		57.86	14.65	72.56	30.40	74,277	42,978		10,882		53,893		22,581	
Anglo	61	52.46	16.39	75.41	49.18	16,672	8,746	1,066	2,733	790	12,572	919	8,199	1,067
African-American	138	78.26	10.87	84.78	26.81	24,314	19,028	854	2,643	644	20,613	743	6,519	917
Hispanic/Other	127	45.67	16.54	62.20	23.62	33,291	15,204	1,472	5,506	1,098	20,707	1,432	7,863	1,255
Female		67.29	29.13	81.32	44.37	25,026	16,841		7,291		20,351		11,103	
Anglo	43	67.44	30.23	81.40	51.16	7,355	4,960	526	2,223	515	5,987	436	3,763	561
African-American	91	80.22	12.09	82.42	27.47	9,393	7,535	392	1,136	321	7,742	375	2,580	440
Hispanic/Other	40	52.50	47.50	80.00	57.50	8,278	4,346	654	3,932	654	6,622	524	4,760	647
Drug Violations Crime														
Male		62.48	17.24	86.45	22.74	64,804	40,490		11,174		56,022		14,734	
Anglo	20	35.00	15.00	90.00	40.00	14,242	4,985	1,519	2,136	1,137	12,818	955	5,697	1,560
African-American	9	88.89	11.11	100.00	11.11	21,130	18,782	2,213	2,348	2,213	21,130	N/A	2,348	2,213
Hispanic/Other	44	56.82	22.73	75.00	22.73	29,432	16,723	2,198	6,690	1,860	22,074	1,921	6,690	1,860

Category	N													
Female		72.39	22.08	95.15	41.54	14,449	10,459		3,190		13,748		6,002	
Anglo	19	52.63	21.05	100.00	36.84	4,770	2,510	546	1,004	446	4,770	N/A	1,757	528
African-American	17	82.35	5.88	94.11	29.41	5,594	4,607	517	329	319	5,265	319	1,645	618
Hispanic/Other	11	81.82	45.45	90.91	63.64	4,085	3,342	475	1,857	613	3,714	354	2,600	592
Other Crime														
DUF Identified														
Male		38.39	16.10	58.93	19.24	16,635	6,386		2,678		9,803		3,201	
Anglo	21	28.57	28.57	71.43	33.33	5,172	1,478	510	1,478	510	3,694	510	1,724	532
African-American	13	61.54	7.69	69.23	7.69	4,832	2,974	652	372	357	3,345	619	372	357
Hispanic/Other	24	29.17	12.50	41.67	16.67	6,631	1,934	615	829	448	2,763	667	1,105	504
Female		59.00	13.63	59.00	27.06	3,028	1,787		413		1,787		820	
Anglo	8	75.00	12.50	75.00	50.00	1,085	814	166	136	127	814	166	543	192
African-American	6	83.33	0.00	83.33	0.00	835	696	127	0	N/A	696	127	0	N/A
Hispanic/Other	4	25.00	25.00	25.00	25.00	1,108	277	240	277	240	277	240	277	240
DUF Non-Identified														
Male						155,502								
Anglo						47,618								
African-American						20,081								
Hispanic/Other						87,803								
Female						16,184								
Anglo						8,497								
African-American						3,136								
Hispanic/Other						4,551								
Total (DUF-Identified)	918	54.98	14.99	73.32	25.66	264,427	145,395	4,833	39,633	3,909	193,883	3,875	67,839	4,427

References

Anglin, M. D., Deschenes, E. P., & Speckart, G. (1987, November). *The effect of legal supervision on narcotic addiction and criminal behavior*. Paper presented at the American Society of Criminology Annual Meeting, Montreal.

Anglin, M. D., & Hser, Y.-I. (1989). Legal coercion and drug abuse treatment: Research findings and social policy implications. In *Handbook of drug control in the United States*. Westport, CT: Greenwood.

Anglin, M. D., & Hser, Y.-I. (1990). Treatment of drug abuse. In M. Tonry & J. Q. Wilson (Eds.), *Drugs and crime* (Vol. 13, pp. 393-460). Chicago: University of Chicago Press.

Anglin, M. D., & Hser, Y.-I. (1991). Criminal justice and the drug-abusing offender: Policy issues of coerced treatment. *Behavioral Sciences & the Law, 9*, 1-25.

Anglin, M. D., & McGlothlin, W. H. (1984). Outcome of narcotic addict treatment in California. In F. M. Tims & J. P. Ludford (Eds.), *Drug abuse treatment evaluation: Strategies, progress, and prospects* (NIDA Monograph No. 51, pp. 106-128). Rockville, MD: National Institute on Drug Abuse.

Ball, J. C., Rosen, L., Flueck, J. A., & Nurco, D. N. (1981). The criminality of heroin addicts when addicted and when off opiates. In J. A. Inciardi (Ed.), *The drugs-crime connection* (pp. 39-65). Beverly Hills, CA: Sage.

Ball, J. C., Shaffer, J. W., & Nurco, D. N. (1983). Day-to-day criminality of heroin addicts in Baltimore—A study in the continuity of offense rates. *Drug and Alcohol Dependence, 12*, 119-143.

Blumstein, A., Cohen, J., Roth, J., & Visher, C. A. (Eds.). (1986). *Criminal careers and career criminals* (Vol 1). Washington, DC: National Academy Press.

Blumstein, A., Sagasi, P. C., & Wolfgang, M. E. (1973). Problems of estimating the number of heroin addicts. In *Drug use in America. Social responses to drug use, the technical papers of the second report of the National Commission on Marijuana and Drug Abuse* (Vol. 2, pp. 201-211). Washington, DC: Government Printing Office.

California Drug Abuse Data System (CAL-DADS). (1989). Maintained by the California Department of Alcohol and Drug Programs.

California Drug Abuse Data System (CAL-DADS). (1990). Maintained by the California Department of Alcohol and Drug Programs.

California State Census Data Center. (1991). *Newsletter*. Sacramento: California Department of Finance, State Census Data Center.

Carter, R. M., & Klein, M. W. (Eds.). (1976). *Back on the street*. Englewood Cliffs, NJ: Prentice-Hall.

Carver, J. A. (1986, September/October). Drugs and crime: Controlling use and reducing risk through testing. *NIJ Reports, 199*. Washington, DC: U. S. Department of Justice, National Institute of Justice.

Chaiken, J. M., & Chaiken, M. R. (1982). *Varieties of criminal behavior*. Santa Monica, CA: RAND.

Chaiken, J. M., & Chaiken, M. R. (1983). Crime rates and the active offender. In J. Q. Wilson (Ed.), *Crime and public policy*. New Brunswick, NJ: Transaction Books.

Chaiken, M. R. (1986). Crime rates and substance abuse among types of offenders. In B. D. Johnson & E. Wish (Eds.), *Crime rates among drug-abusing offenders. Final report to the National Institute of Justice*. New York: Narcotic and Drug Research, Inc.

Collins, J. J., Hubbard, R. L., & Rachal, J. V. (1985). Expensive drug use and illegal income: A test of explanatory hypotheses. *Criminology, 23*(4), 743-764.

Criminal Justice Profile. (1989). *Crime and delinquency in California* (Suppl.). Washington, DC: U.S. Department of Justice, Bureau of Criminal Statistics and Special Services.

De la Rosa, M., Lambert, E. Y., & Gropper, B. (Eds.). (1990). *Drugs and violence: Causes, correlates, and consequences* (NIDA Research Monograph No. 103). Rockville, MD: National Institute on Drug Abuse.

DeLeon, G. (1984). Program-based evaluation research in therapeutic communities. In F. F. Tims & J. Ludford (Eds.), *Drug abuse treatment evaluation: Strategies, progress, and prospects* (NIDA Research Monograph No. 51). Rockville, MD: National Institute on Drug Abuse.

DeLeon, G., Andrews, M. P. A., Wexler, H. K., Jaffe, J., & Rosenthal, M. S. (1979). Therapeutic community dropouts: Criminal behavior five years after treatment. *American Journal of Drug and Alcohol Abuse, 6*, 253-271.

Desmond, D. P., & Maddux, J. F. (1984). Mexican-American heroin addicts. *American Journal of Drug and Alcohol Abuse, 10*(4), 317-346.

Gendreau, P., & Ross, R. R. (1987). Revivification of rehabilitation: Evidence from the 1980's. *Justice Quarterly, 4*(3), 359-407.

Gerstein, D. R., & Harwood, H. J. (1990). *Treating drug problems.* Washington, DC: National Academy Press.

Goldstein, P. J. (1985, Fall). The drugs/violence nexus: A tripartite conceptual framework. *Journal of Drug Issues*, 493-506.

Greene, M. A., & Stollmack, S. (1981). Estimating the number of criminals. In J. A. Fox (Ed.), *Models in quantitative criminology* (pp. 1-24). New York: Academic Press.

Gropper, B. A. (1985). Probing the links between drugs and crime. *Research in Brief.* Washington, DC: U.S. Department of Justice, National Institute of Justice.

Hser, Y.-I., Anglin, M. D., Wickens, T. D., Brecht, M., & Homer, J. (1991). *Techniques for the estimation of illicit drug-use prevalence: An overview of relevant issues* (NIJ Research Monograph). Washington, DC: U.S. Department of Justice, National Institute of Justice.

Hubbard, R. L., Marsden, M. E., Rachal, J. V., Harwood, H. J., Cavanaugh, E. R., & Ginzburg, H. M. (1989). *Drug abuse treatment: A national study of effectiveness.* Chapel Hill: University of North Carolina Press.

Inciardi, J. A. (1979). Heroin use and street crime. *Crime and Delinquency, 25*, 335-346.

Innes, C. A. (1986). *Profile of state prison inmates* (Special report). Washington, DC: U.S. Department of Justice, Bureau of Justice Statistics.

Innes, C. A. (1988, July). *Drug use and crime. State prison inmate survey, 1986* (Special report). Washington, DC: U.S. Department of Justice, Bureau of Justice Statistics.

Johnson, B. D., Goldstein, P., Preble, E., Schmeidler, J., Lipton, D. S., Spunt, B., & Miller, T. (1985). *Taking care of business: The economics of crime by heroin abusers.* Lexington, MA: Lexington Books.

Lipton, D., Martinson, R., & Wilks, J. (1975). *The effectiveness of correctional treatment: A survey of treatment evaluation studies.* New York: Praeger.

Little, G. L. (1981). Relationship of drug of choice, race, and crime to entry in drug abuse treatment. *Psychological Reports, 48*, 486.

Longshore, D., Hsieh, S., & Anglin, M. D. (1991). *Race and gender differences in perceived need for drug abuse treatment.* Manuscript submitted for publication.

McGlothlin, W. H., & Anglin, M. D. (1979). Effects of closing the Bakersfield methadone clinic. In L. S. Harris (Ed.), *Problems of drug dependence* (NIDA Research Monograph No. 47). Rockville, MD: National Institute on Drug Abuse.

McGlothlin, W. H., Anglin, M. D., & Wilson, B. D. (1977). *An evaluation of the California civil addict program* (DHEW Pub. No. ADM 78-558). Washington, DC: Government Printing Office.

Rounsaville, B. J., & Kleber, H. (1985). Untreated opiate addicts. *Archives of General Psychiatry, 42,* 1072-1077.

Sells, S. B., & Simpson, D. D. (Eds.). (1976a). *The effectiveness of drug abuse treatment: Further studies of drug users, treatment typologies, and assessment of outcomes during treatment in the DARP* (Vol. 3). Cambridge, MA: Ballinger.

Sells, S. B., & Simpson, D. D. (Eds.). (1976b). *The effectiveness of drug abuse treatment: Evaluation of treatment outcomes for 1971-1972 DARP admission cohort* (Vol. 4). Cambridge, MA: Ballinger.

Sells, S. B., & Simpson, D. D. (Eds.). (1976c). *The effectiveness of drug abuse treatment: Evaluation of treatment outcomes for 1972-1973 DARP admission cohort* (Vol. 5). Cambridge, MA: Ballinger.

Simpson, D. D. (1979). The relation of time spent in drug abuse treatment to posttreatment outcome. *American Journal of Psychiatry, 136*(11), 1449-1453.

Simpson, D. D. (1981). Treatment for drug abuse: Follow-up outcomes and length of time spent. *Archives of General Psychiatry, 38,* 875-880.

Speckart, G. R., & Anglin, M. D. (1986a). Narcotics and crime: A causal modeling approach. *Journal of Quantitative Criminology, 2,* 3-28.

Speckart, G. R., & Anglin, M. D. (1986b). Narcotics use and crime: An overview of recent research advances. *Contemporary Drug Problems, 13,* 741-769.

Stevens, S., Arbiter, N., & Glider, P. (1989). Women residents: Expanding their role to increase treatment effectiveness in substance abuse programs. *The International Journal of the Addictions, 24*(5), 425-434.

Tillman, R. (1987). *The prevalence and incidence of arrest among adult males in California. Forum.* Washington, DC: Bureau of Criminal Statistics.

Toborg, M. A., Bellassai, J. B., Yezer, A.M.J., Carver, J., Clark, J., & Pears, E. (1986). *The Washington, D.C., urine testing program for defendants awaiting trial: A summary of interim findings.* Washington, DC: Toborg Associates.

Toborg, M. A., Levin, D. R., Milkman, R. H., & Center, L. J. (1975). *Treatment and alternatives to street crime (TASC): An evaluative framework and state of the art interview.* Washington, DC: Lazar Institute.

Tonry, M., & Wilson, J. Q. (Eds.). (1990). *Drugs and crime.* Chicago: University of Chicago Press.

U.S. Senate, Committee on the Judiciary. (1990, May 10). *Hard-core cocaine addicts: Measuring—and fighting—the epidemic* (Staff report). Washington, DC: Author.

Visher, C. A., & Roth, J. (1986). Participation in criminal careers. In A. Blumstein, J. Cohen, J. Roth, & C. A. Visher (Eds.), *Criminal careers and career criminals.* Washington, DC: National Academy Press.

Wexler, H. K., Lipton, D. S., & Foster, K. (1985, November). *Outcome evaluation of a prison therapeutic community for substance abuse treatment: Preliminary results.* Paper presented at the American Society of Criminology Annual Meeting, San Diego, CA.

Wexler, H. K., Lipton, D. S., & Johnson, B. D. (1988). *A criminal justice system strategy for treating cocaine-heroin abusing offenders in custody* (Doc. No. NCJ 108560). Washington, DC: U.S. Department of Justice, National Institute of Justice.

Wish, E. D. (1987). Drug use forecasting: New York 1984 to 1986. *Research in Action.* Washington, DC: U.S. Department of Justice, National Institute of Justice.

Wish, E. D. (1988). Identifying drug-abusing criminals. In C. G. Leukefeld & F. Tims (Eds.), *Compulsory treatment of drug abuse: Research and clinical practice* (DHHS Pub. No. ADM 88-1578, pp. 139-159). Rockville, MD: National Institute on Drug Abuse.

Wish, E. D. (1990). U.S. drug policy in the 1990s: Insights from new data from arrestees. *The International Journal of the Addictions, 25*(3A), 377-410.

4. Gangs and Crack Cocaine Trafficking

MALCOLM W. KLEIN
CHERYL LEE MAXSON

The concern for gang involvement in cocaine trafficking, and especially the distribution of crack cocaine, has been primarily with the drug and violence dimensions. This chapter attempts to redress the balance somewhat by amplifying the gang dimensions. We show that street gangs are qualitatively different from other forms of criminal groups, and as such will require interventions with policy implications different from those commonly associated with drug interventions. But even this assertion is dependent upon the degree to which street gangs are either involved in or in control of crack distribution. Thus we review data on the gang/crack connection as well.

When the nature and variety of street gangs is juxtaposed against data on the gang/crack connection, we show that this connection has generally been overstated by public officials, leading to some inappropriate policy directions. We suggest some new research questions, which may be more relevant to gang-related drug intervention policies, and discuss approaches to such research that would require the collaboration of justice system agencies.

Introduction

There has long been an association between street gangs and drugs, but not of the sort supposed by the general public. Prior research has revealed that gang members have been involved primarily in drug use rather than drug sales (Chin & Fagan, 1990; Short & Strodtbeck, 1965; Spergel, 1990; but also see Moore, 1978; Taylor, 1989). Further, it has been small gang cliques rather than large gang organizations that have evidenced drug involvement (Short & Strodtbeck, 1965; Spergel, 1964). The most parsimonious explanations for street gang involvement in drug sales have been that sales are part and parcel of the general versatility of gang member crime patterns (Klein, 1971; Robin, 1967; Tracy, 1979) rather than a special feature of gang activity.

Recent developments, however, have raised anew the questions of level and form of street gang involvement in drug sales, in particular with respect to cocaine. This chapter undertakes an assessment of the gang/cocaine connection, with an emphasis on the crack form of cocaine. Our data from the mid-1980s in Los Angeles, where street gangs are rampant and where the national explosion of crack distribution was first noted and documented (Klein & Maxson, 1985), indicate that the vast majority of the cocaine involved is in the crack form (92% of cocaine sales incidents, with at least one gang member arrested). Thus we concentrate here on gangs and crack.

The Los Angeles public was first alerted to the crack phenomenon through press reports in late 1984, some 2 years after police investigation reports first recorded its appearance. The immediate impression provided by press and police alike was that the crack was being distributed in large part by black street gangs in an unusually organized and violent context. The evidence, at best, was anecdotal. By the time the explosion had traveled across the country and reportedly had reached epidemic proportions in such cities as New York and Washington, D.C., anecdotes had become accepted as fact, with "confirmations" from various federal agencies. But independent research assessment was still lacking. Our own data from Los Angeles, suggesting that the gang/crack connection was being greatly exaggerated, was summarily rejected both by local enforcement agencies and by the National Institute of Justice (NIJ) as out-of-date (in 1986) and irrelevant to policy (in 1989).

But as of this writing, enough research has been reported from other cities, and enough questions raised about the policy implications of the gang/crack connection, that a reassessment is possible. Further, the hype around crack distribution has now been given a good deal of considered attention (e.g., Reinarman & Levine, 1989), and the appropriateness of street gangs for crack distribution has received the sort of dispassionate analysis that was missing in the mid-1980s (see, for instance, Moore, 1991).

Our purposes in this chapter are three: to assess the suitability of street gangs for crack (or any other drug) distribution, to review reports that pertain to the gang/crack connection, and to suggest directions for related policy and research considerations.

Hyperbole About Gangs and Crack

Among those who argued that the gang/crack connection was both close and dramatic, several themes emerged:

- Gang organization was tailor-made for crack distribution (California Council, 1989; Kleiman & Smith, 1990)
- Gangs controlled street-level distribution (Hayeslip, 1989; Kleiman & Smith, 1990)
- Gang entrepreneurs were prominent as well at the mid-level, taking their consignments from professional traffickers such as the Colombian cartels (Skolnick, 1988; Skolnick, Correl, Navarro, & Rabb, 1990)
- Gangs brought their own violence potentials to bear on sales territories, enforcement of deals, and retribution for bad deals and bad debts. The crack violence was in large part supplied by the gangs (California Council, 1989; McKinney, 1988; Moreno, 1987)
- Los Angeles gangs exported their crack organization to cities across the country, expanding their markets and creating new gangs to feed the organization (McKinney, 1988)
- "Instrumental gangs" or "drug gangs" emerged from the larger structures of traditional street gangs as a new form of crime-specific organization to combine the features of gangs and crack sales organization (Genelin & Coplen, 1989; Skolnick, 1988; Skolnick et al., 1990)

The vast majority of these assertions were not based on careful empirical research; most, in fact, were based upon the testimony of law enforcement officials using undocumented field reports. The spirit of these materials is perhaps best captured in the dramatically overwritten report of a California State Task Force on Drugs and Gangs:

> Today's gangs are urban terrorists. Heavily armed and more violent than ever before, they are quick to use terror and intimidation to seize and protect their share of the lucrative drug market. Gang members are turning our streets and neighborhoods into war zones, where it takes an act of courage simply to walk to the corner store. (California Council, 1989, p. viii)

Everyone got in on the act: local papers and broadcasters; *Time* and *Newsweek*; DEA, NIJ, and OJJDP; and of course politicians who could ride the wave of fear and police officials who could, at one and the same time, justify requests for additional funds and duck responsibility for an uncontrolled crime rampage. Much of this process is well-documented by Reinarman and Levine (1989), who conclude, " . . . the media and politicians ignored or misrepresented the evidence and instead provided propaganda for the drug war. Further, we suggest that all of the attention and hype—the crack 'scare'—have raced ahead of crack use and casualties" (p. 538).

These authors also conclude that "crack has come to dominate discourse about many public problems that existed years before crack or cocaine appeared on the American cultural scene" (1989, p. 539). Our contention in this chapter is that this characterization applies well to the problem of street gangs.

Street Gangs as Suitable Sales Organizations

For our discussion we deliberately ignore the fanciful writings of those who apply traditional commercial business terminology to the role of gangs in drug distribution: CEOs, sales forces, public relations, franchising, and similar analogues simply do not stand up to field realities. But one can speculate on organizational dimensions that would enhance drug distribution systems, and ask of each how the typical gang is located on the dimension. Those we cite here are the ones commonly suggested in media and enforcement agency descriptions, and are occasionally found as well in recent criminological writing.[1]

Group Structure. Street gangs are said to be well suited to drug distribution because of their internal structure, which is hierarchical and highly controlled. In fact, however, street gangs are normally loosely structured and ill-controlled. Turnover is heavy and relatively constant, so that experienced members wax and wane in their participation, while older members are rapidly replaced by new recruits. Only in *West Side Story* is control wielded effectively by the few: In real street gangs, multiple cliques, dyads, and triads are the common units of companionship, each responsive to its own age peers rather than to powerful (or older) leaders. For drug distributors, such a haphazard organizational structure does not provide the basis for an effective distributional system. Small cliques may be effectively employed, but it would be best to divorce them from the traditional street gang structure.

Cohesiveness. In like manner, the popular conception of the gang is that it is close-knit, with strongly shared norms, values, and organizational loyalties. But this, too, is generally not the case. Most empirical research on gangs reveals a rather low level of cohesiveness, with common norms and values evident more in rhetoric than in behavioral patterns. As to loyalty, professional police gang units take pride in the number of gang members they "turn," that is, establish as informants on gang activity. Drug dealers counting on gang member loyalty are unknowingly depending on a weak link.

Leadership. Several myths abound concerning gang leadership. It is said to be (a) strong; (b) hierarchical, with the oldest and strongest in control; and (c) ubiquitous over a wide range of activities. Many enforcement officials accept the myth and base their gang-busting strategies on arresting and incarcerating specially targeted gang leaders with extensive records of crime and violence. But despite the crackdowns on so-called leaders, most gangs persist precisely because the police are so accepting of the myth.

As with most youth groups, gang leadership is age-graded; young people are influenced more by their own age peers than by those several years older. This contributes to a rather weak gang structure. In addition, influence on leadership is often activity- or domain-specific. The most influential in sports activities may carry little weight in gang fighting or criminal escapades, and social leadership may reside in yet another set of hands. With age and type of activity yielding often different leadership patterns, the drug dealer, like the police gang unit, will have a hard time controlling gang organization by controlling a few gang influentials.

Violence. Finally, it is said that gangs are violent and can bring their violence to bear on the control of drug sales and territories. Here, there is more truth (than for structure, cohesiveness, and leadership), but we still must be cautious in applying the assumptions about violence.

It seems clear that gang violence has increased over the years, that gang members are proportionately more prone to violence than non-gang delinquents and criminals, and that violence (in the company of today's ready supply of firearms) is potentially useful to drug dealers with territorial and defensive imperatives. The problem we see is that most gang violence is expressive (i.e., usually spontaneous, impulsive, unplanned, responsive to immediate threats to self or status) rather than instrumental (i.e., usually planned, motivated by expected outcomes, rational, employed in service to delayed gain). One does not automatically or easily turn expressive into instrumental violence. Drug dealers don't need—indeed, may be unwilling to tolerate—the impulsive violence of the gang member who is overly sensitive to personal insult or status threat. A good drug sale should go down quickly and quietly. And by the same token, the hired gang member enforcer may prove impatient with the planful form of threat, real or implied, used by the drug dealer to run a smooth operation. Yes, the gang may be a ready source of violence, but it may also be a poor choice in the presence of alternatives.

In sum, the traditional street gang strikes us as ideal for drug distribution only in its journalistic form. The Criminal Justice Coordinator in the mayor's office of a large West Coast city commented at a gang conference in 1991, "Gangs have the absolutely perfect organization for distributing drugs because of their hierarchical leadership, their group loyalty, their violence, and their control of territory." Thus the myth gets perpetuated. But the head of the police gang unit in that very same city described his gangs as large and loosely organized, with only a minority exhibiting the gang/cocaine sales connection. The drug distributor's need for close-knit, controlled, dependable organizational forms will not ordinarily be met by the typical street gang whose form could bear the seeds for the destruction of its benefactor. If gangs and drug sales are to be combined, we would expect some major accommodations such as:

1. Gang cliques breaking off from traditional gangs to form sales groups;
2. Formation of new, small gangs for specific sales purposes, avoiding the versatile display of other criminal involvements associated with street gangs; and
3. Imported gang groups, as in the case of the Jamaican posses, capable of establishing themselves, for their own purposes, in virgin territory or territory without strong prior gang claims.[2]

Street Gangs and Crack in Various Cities

All of the above leads naturally to the question of whether there is evidence for a pattern of gang dominance of drug distribution, and of crack in particular. Here we review published research reports, the first of two sources of evidence. Further on we will report preliminary results from a new survey in which the authors have recently been engaged.

Although the literature tying gangs to crack is not extensive, it contains useful clues to the relationship. Our own work in Los Angeles is a case in point because the crack explosion was noted first in that city. Relying principally on police reports, and to some extent on news reports as well, we described the development of crack sales and the associated technology (Klein & Maxson, 1985). We were led to believe that gang infusion into crack sales was quite substantial, to the point of major domination, according to some of our informants. Furthermore, a demonstrably increasing level of gang violence and homicide was laid directly at the door of the crack trade.

Using as a data source 1,889 cocaine arrest events, in 1983 through 1985, in the hottest gang and crack areas of the Los Angeles Police and Sheriff's departments, we found an increase of gang involvement up to about 25% of all crack sales arrests in late 1985 (Klein, Maxson, & Cunningham, 1988, 1991). With a peak of 25% and *gang-related* defined as one or more gang members present, these data revealed gang involvement, but certainly not gang domination at the street-level or mid-level sales as recorded by the police. This does not of course refer to nondocumented sales; only good ethnography can do that.

A further finding from the Los Angeles research was that we could not document any increase in drug-related violence associated with gang involvement. Indeed, the only increase in drug-involved homicides in particular was in *non-gang* homicides. A replication of this inquiry, using 1988-1989 data, reveals that drug involvement in gang and non-gang homicides has remained quite stable. These sets of findings, those concerning gang involvement in crack sales and the violence associated with it, have supported our assertion (see also Quicker, Galeai, & Batani-Khalfani, 1991; Reuter, 1988) that street gangs were not well suited to crack distribution enterprises. What other evidence questions the gang/crack connection?

Fagan (1989) has looked at gangs, drugs, and violence in several cities and concluded, as we shall in our own summary, that the connections between them are found here but not there, now but not then, and under some circumstances but not others. There are gangs with drug sales connections and gangs without them. There are more violent and less violent gangs. Basically, Fagan's data reveal sufficient but not necessary contexts for the connections. This is essentially the same conclusion one could have drawn from the classic gang literature covering the 1960s (Klein, 1971; Short & Strodtbeck, 1965; Spergel, 1964), but extended from drug use and minor sales to the current situation with crack cocaine.

Waldorf (1990, 1991), in interim reports of his intensive ethnographic study in San Francisco, draws several preliminary conclusions:

- There are indeed some gangs (primarily black, as in Los Angeles) involved in crack sales
- Most gang drug sales are poorly organized

- Gang members who sell crack are usually not users
- Violence primarily concerns intergang rivalries rather than drug issues

In Los Angeles, Quicker et al. (1991) conclude:

Street dealers represent the bottom rung of the drug organizational hierarchy. While many of these individuals are street gang members, a significant proportion are not. Although the profits of individual sellers can be considerable, and rudimentary organization and cooperation are necessary to effect drug deals, we found no evidence of a transition to entrepreneurial street gangs taking place, or for that matter, of the existence of entrepreneurial street gangs. (1991, p. 34)

In gang studies in Cleveland and Columbus, Ohio, Huff (1989) reports several categories of gangs and some crack use, but no consistent evidence for organized gang crack distribution or sales.

In New York, Goldstein, Brownstein, Ryan, and Bellucci (1989) are singular among New York drug researchers in finding some crack-related violence—homicides specifically—with clear gang connections. The report, however, does not clarify the relevance of street gang versus drug gang conceptualizations—we cannot know which are involved.

This issue of street gangs versus drug gangs was raised most directly by Skolnick and his students (Skolnick, 1988; Skolnick et al., 1990), based on interviews with 39 incarcerated felons and a larger number of police officials in California. These data led Skolnick to conclude, especially for Northern California, that gang members were centrally involved in crack distribution. The Skolnick findings have been subjected to considerable criticism in the research community, but received ready acceptance in the enforcement community. Both reactions may be inappropriate, because Skolnick et al. have readily conceded the inadequacies of their research methods, and because the findings refer more to mid-level sales rather than the street-level sales that have been the subject of most research.

More important in the limited Skolnick study is the distinction made between *cultural* and *instrumental* gangs, terms that equate roughly to our use of *street* gangs and *drug* gangs. The classical gang literature had to do with cultural or street gangs. More recent research, reflecting the emergence of gangs in a vastly expanded list of cities (Klein, 1990; Spergel, 1989), suggests that traditional gang structures and forms may no longer be predominant, although they are still being reported (Hagedorn, 1988; Huff, 1989). The question for this discussion, arising from

Skolnick's (1988) distinction, is whether the new gang forms are in some way *cultural* in the sense of territorial, ethnically distinct, and criminally versatile, or *instrumental* in the sense of being formed for the purpose of monetary gain through drug sales (and, in particular, crack sales). The ethnographic work of Quicker et al. (1991) suggests, for Los Angeles, that Skolnick's distinction does not hold up.

Both Hamid (1990) for Caribbean gangs in Brooklyn and Harlem, and Taylor (1989) for black groups in Detroit, provide extensive descriptions of gang sales systems. However, neither depiction clarifies the street gang versus drug gang issue, because the issue itself had not clearly emerged while these researchers were collecting their data.

Similarly, McKinney (1988) and Hayeslip (1989) provide reports in U.S. Justice Department publications of street sales dominated by street gangs, depending heavily for documentation upon Los Angeles enforcement spokespersons. No attempt at corroboration was undertaken in either case, and no description of the form of gangs involved was offered. With so much of the gang drug sales picture being taken from Los Angeles reports (though not from *research* reports, we should note), it is pertinent to note a significant shift in the views of Los Angeles enforcement agencies. Gang experts in the Sheriff's department have been consistently skeptical of the separate existence of drug gangs, and increasingly skeptical as well of street gang domination of crack sales. A recent public pronouncement by Sheriff Sherman Block explicitly placed the blame for increasing gang violence on traditional gang rivalries rather than on gang/drug connections (Sahagun, 1990).

The official LAPD response to Block's conclusion was to reiterate the gang/crack connection; but within the department, senior officials have been backing away from that assertion. The existence of drug gangs is now being seriously questioned, and street gang domination of sales is no longer seriously suggested by many officials in both departments.

Interestingly, both the prior and the emerging positions are still based less on careful data analysis than on a slowly accumulating consensus. If Los Angeles street gangs are not dominating crack sales (undocumented other than by our own research), and if new instrumental drug gangs are not an explanation for the crack explosion (undocumented by any research in these jurisdictions), then one must conclude that crack distribution is controlled by traditional narcotics operatives (undocumented by any local research). For our part, we have indicated our conceptual and empirical reasons not to accept the street gang control hypothesis. However, we see no reason not to continue to entertain the drug gang hypothesis. We will, in fact, report limited supportive evidence for these groups in cities other than Los Angeles.

Crack Without Street Gangs

As this section heading suggests, another form of evidence on the connection between street gangs and crack sales may come from looking for negative instances; that is, street gangs may be a sufficient but not a necessary requirement for organized crack sales. On this point, the available research literature seems more definitive. Examples of very active crack markets with no clear indications of street gang involvement are reported in New York City by Fagan and Chin (1989); Chin and Fagan (1990); Bourgois (1989); Johnson, Hamid, Morales, and Sanabria (1987); Hamid (1990); and Dunlap, Johnson, Sanabria, Holliday, Lipsey, Barnett, Hopkins, Sobel, Randolph, and Chin (1990). For Miami, Inciardi (1988, 1989, 1991) similarly documents the crack problem without recourse to the gang hypothesis. Mieczkowski (1990) similarly describes the situation in Detroit, as does Rosenfeld (1991) for St. Louis.

In the absence of empirical research, the most dramatic case may nonetheless come from the nation's capitol. For several years, Washington, D.C., has reported one of the very worst crack situations, with wide-open street sales accompanied by so much violence as to earn that city the epithet of the nation's homicide capital. Yet by all reports, Washington, D.C., has never been, and according to our newest survey still is not, a gang city. Clearly, if major cities like New York, Miami, St. Louis, Detroit, and Washington can sustain major crack markets without the obvious involvement of street gangs, then we must be careful not to assume or assert a generalized gang/crack connection elsewhere.

Gangs and Crack in Major Cities

The authors completed a 1991 survey of the police departments in the nation's 100 largest cities (excluding the old, 1960s traditional gang cities of New York, Philadelphia, Boston, Chicago, El Paso, Seattle, San Francisco, and Los Angeles). All of the remaining 92 cities responded to the survey. Of various questions covered in the survey, several allow us to estimate the cross-city prevalence of gang/crack connections. The results are as follows:

- Twelve of the 92 cities reported no gang problem. For the original purposes of the survey, no questions about crack were asked.
- Four respondents[3] were so unclear about the gang situation in their city that no conclusion could be reached about gang/crack connections.
- Nine of the 76 responding gang cities reported *no crack* involvement at all.
- Thirty-three reported only a *weak connection*; their gangs were broadly criminal, with sales assuming no particular importance.
- Fifteen reported a *strong connection*; street gangs are heavily involved in crack sales (this does not mean all gangs—only that a substantial number are involved).
- Fifteen reported the *simultaneous existence* of street gangs and the more narrowly defined drug gangs (almost always involving crack as the drug of choice).
- Four reported the existence of *drug gangs only*, with no sign of street gangs.

There is no clear geographic pattern in these response groups, nor, with one exception, any other pattern that we can discern, such as a relationship to city size, year of gang emergence, or nature of the respondent. The one consistent exception is the appearance of crack among black gangs but not among Hispanic, Asian, or white gangs. In this era of newly emergent gang cities juxtaposed against the still new phenomenon of crack cocaine, it may be that the form and prevalence of the gang/crack connections simply have not had time to stabilize beyond this ethnic connection.

What the survey does suggest, however, is that the myths perpetrated by the media and some local and federal enforcement officials are in poor correspondence to likely fact. In addition, the survey suggests that the research literature published to date is quite constrained in location and recognition of the varieties of gang/crack connections to be found nationwide.

Finally, the survey results reveal the non-equation of street gangs and crack sales. Gangs may or may not be involved; crack sales take place with and without gang organization; and drug gangs have indeed evolved around crack sales, but not in the majority of cities. All possible combinations have appeared. Broad generalizations about gang/crack connections must be qualified or discounted at this point. Two evolving phenomena, *gang cities* and *crack cities,* are traveling parallel but only partly intersecting paths.

Selected Policy Questions

Out of a list of policy-relevant questions that one might raise in connection with the gang/crack issue, we have selected several that have been posed to us over the past few years, and to which our data and experience seem pertinent.

1. *Should interventions be of a sort that are relevant to gangs and drugs at the same time?* This was the strong suggestion of the California State Task Force (California Council, 1989). Clearly, the data just presented argue against the suggestion. To crack down on gangs dealing drugs will miss a lot of gangs and a lot of dealers. Working to prevent gang emergence and the spread of drugs in the same thrust will obviously miss the mark in many cases.

Further, our Los Angeles research took a close look at the way that gang and narcotics units worked together under the best of circumstances; that is, when the connection seemed close, and the department chiefs mandated such close working relationships. The close working relationship failed to develop, and this was to the surprise of no one who understood the turf protection needs and habits of both types of units (Klein, Maxson, & Cunningham, 1988).

Finally, one should recognize that although gang activity and crack sales may well coexist in many neighborhoods, their etiologies are very different. Prevention targets for the one must of necessity differ considerably from those for the other. Drug prevention programs, for example, will do little about the needs for identity, status, and belonging that underlie much gang formation. Conversely, gang prevention programs do not relate to the market mechanics of drug sales—especially those that arise in Central America or Southeast Asia. Rather, we are inclined to the view that gang and crack interventions will and must have many unique features, although there may be advantages of some coordination as well.

2. *Can drug suppression programs, such as those described in Massachusetts (Kleiman & Smith, 1990) and New York (Zimmer, 1987), or the massive street sweeps employed by the Los Angeles Police Department, be used for gang suppression at the same time?* Although a number of police officials are sanguine about these programs, we find in our police survey that a surprising number are not. From a theoretical standpoint, our view is that suppression benefits in the narcotics realm are quite likely to backfire in the gang realm. The low cohesive nature of most gangs, as described earlier, is most susceptible to direct, exterior challenges. Rival gangs comprise the single most effective source of increased gang cohesiveness. Next most effective are probably the confrontive reactions of public institutions such as the schools or the police. Police crackdowns and sweeps, declarations of "war" on gangs, and singling out of gang members for special attention specifically because of their gang affiliation may only heighten

gang identity and status. It will provide, for many members and would-be members, yet more of what gang membership offers them anyway (Klein, 1993). If drug sweeps prove to be effective enforcement tools, we would argue for their being labeled and carried out as such, with no explicit attention to any associated gang connection.

3. *Should we undertake a national gang identification roster system, and develop national or regional gang enforcement task forces?* First, the side effects of increased gang cohesiveness, as noted above, should be carefully considered. Second, our multicity survey suggests that gang types, gang definitions, and gang intelligence vary widely among cities (see also Spergel, 1990), making a common approach premature at best. Third, one of the rationales for a national data system is the exportation of gangs from such gang hubs as Los Angeles and Chicago, or *gang migration* in the terminology of the National Institute of Justice's 1991 requests for proposals. Our survey respondents, with very few exceptions, have determined that the purported gang migration has been greatly overstated; most emerging gangs have been of local origin, even when Los Angeles and Chicago gang members came to town. The migration issue seems more pertinent to the expansion of crack markets, a phenomenon now seen as far less entangled in gang affairs than had earlier been suggested by many officials. We would approach the suggestion of a national gang database with considerable caution. Encouraging the exchange of gang information between individual jurisdictions on an as-needed basis would appear to be a more useful and cost-effective contribution at the federal level.

4. *What are the limits of enforcement approaches to reducing the gang/crack connection?* We would suggest there are quite severe limitations. As already noted, the connections are ephemeral to begin with. In addition, few gang control programs operated by the police have demonstrated much effect (Spergel, 1989). Indeed the cities with the largest gang control and intelligence units—Los Angeles and Chicago—continue to experience increases in gang violence. The best they can probably do is "keep the lid on"; gang policing does not affect those factors leading to the formation of gangs.

Increasingly, police and prosecutors are coming to understand and appreciate the need to involve, indeed to help form and support, local community organizations of many types. Community groups can be appropriate intervenors in both the gang and drug arenas. Gangs and dealers flourish in the absence of controls; they recruit to their cause best in the absence of reasonable alternatives for those to be recruited; they grow bold when allowed to feel they represent, protect, and serve their communities, rather than when they are given to understand that their illegal activities are not tolerable. Enforcement programs that go it alone, that fail to engage legitimate neighborhood concerns, will find themselves in unfriendly territory, unnecessarily. We would urge, as have others, far more attention to efforts that are labeled as service-oriented or community policing. The issues are difficult and complex, but so-called new breed and crime-fighting models have not proved their case in the world of gangs and drugs.

Selected Research Questions

Despite the relatively narrow focus of this chapter on the relationship of street gangs to crack distribution, there are still many unanswered questions toward which research efforts should be directed. We suggest the following as particularly worthy of attention.

1. What are the structural differences between the criminally versatile street gangs and the narrowly instrumental drug gangs? Direct intervention efforts will be considerably more relevant if they can take these structural elements into account, including levels of cohesiveness; size and subgrouping; concentration or diffusion of leadership; ethnic mixing; and age and gender integration.

2. To what extent are drug-selling gangs composed of local youth, or initiated and influenced by gangs from major drug distribution hubs such as Miami and Los Angeles? The importation or migration models, if confirmed, would require more attention to cross-city identification systems and interdiction.

3. The early years of the crack epidemic are over, but most of our knowledge of the gang/crack connection is based upon them. We need some updating, for the mid-1990s, of the prevalence and form of these connections in a variety of cities.

4. According to published research and the multicity survey discussed earlier, crack is principally although not solely associated with black communities. No one, in writing or otherwise, has satisfactorily explained the absence of crack in urban Hispanic communities and gangs. Learning more about the reasons for this might provide preventive clues for the Hispanic groups and intervention clues for the black groups.

5. We made the point earlier that street gang structure and values flourish in the face of confrontation with public agencies. We have

learned from our multicity survey that many police departments have engaged in heavy suppression activities based, one presumes, on general notions of deterrence. Other departments have chosen not to engage in suppression programs, limiting themselves to various combinations of intelligence, prevention, and investigative functions. Research is certainly possible that would assess the results of engaging in extensive gang suppression programming on street gangs versus drug gangs. Contrasts with non-suppressive approaches could well prove illuminating for further intervention efforts.

In sum, the first decade of the crack epidemic has revealed a number of questionable assumptions about its nature, and about the place of street gangs in its initiation and spread. Similarly, assumptions about effective intervention strategies based on notions of gang structure have increasingly come into question. A new round of research, informed by the studies of the past 10 years but more planfully developed, is now an appropriate goal. Policymakers, funders, and researchers need to be mutually involved in designing the framework for such an effort.

Notes

1. For various citations of gang literature pertinent to these organizational dimensions, refer to Klein and Maxson (1989).

2. Each of these accommodations represents various points in the dynamic process of group formation and evolution. Whether it is appropriate or useful to view such groups as street gangs has not been addressed systematically by gang or drug researchers. This lack of consensus on gang definitions is also quite visible among gang and narcotics specialists in law enforcement, a point elaborated upon later in this chapter.

3. Respondents ranged from part-time intelligence officers, to gang unit commanders, to bureau commanders, to deputy chiefs and chiefs.

References

Bourgois, P. (1989). In search of Horatio Alger: Culture and ideology in the crack economy. *Contemporary Drug Problems, 16*, 619-649.

California Council on Criminal Justice. (1989). *State task force on gangs and drugs: Final report*. Sacramento: Author.

Chin, K., & Fagan, J. (1990). *The impact of crack on drug and crime involvement*. Paper presented at the meeting of the American Society of Criminology, Baltimore, MD.

Dunlap, E., Johnson, B., Sanabria, H., Holliday, E., Lipsey, V., Barnett, M., Hopkins, W., Sobel, I., Randolph, D., & Chin, K. (1990). Studying crack users and their criminal careers: The scientific and artistic aspects of locating hard-to-reach subjects and interviewing them about sensitive topics. *Contemporary Drug Problems, 17*, 121-144.

Fagan, J. (1989). The social organization of drug use and drug dealing among urban gangs. *Criminology, 27*, 633-667.

Fagan, J., & Chin, K. (1989). Initiation into crack and cocaine: A tale of two epidemics. *Contemporary Drug Problems, 16*, 579-618.

Genelin, M., & Coplen, B. (1989). *Los Angeles street gangs: Report and recommendations of the countywide criminal justice coordination committee interagency gang task force*. Los Angeles: Interagency Gang Task Force.

Goldstein, P. G., Brownstein, H. H., Ryan, P. J., & Bellucci, P. A. (1989). Crime and homicide in New York City, 1988: A conceptually based event analysis. *Contemporary Drug Problems, 16*, 651-687.

Hagedorn, J. (1988). *People and folks: Gangs, crime, and the underclass in a rustbelt city*. Chicago: Lakeview.

Hamid, A. (1990). The political economy of crack-related violence. *Contemporary Drug Problems, 17*, 31-78.

Hayeslip, D. W., Jr. (1989). Local-level drug enforcement: New strategies. *NIJ Reports*. Washington, DC: U.S. Department of Justice.

Huff, R. C. (1989). Youth gangs and public policy. *Crime and Delinquency, 35*, 524-537.

Inciardi, J. A. (1988). *Crack cocaine in Miami*. Paper presented to the NIDA Technical Review Meeting, Rockville, MD.

Inciardi, J. A. (1989). Trading sex for crack among juvenile drug users. *Contemporary Drug Problems, 17*, 680-700.

Inciardi, J. A. (1991). The crack-violence connection within a population of hard-core adolescent offenders. In M. De la Rosa, E. Y. Lambert, & B. Gropper (Eds.), *Drugs and violence: Causes, correlates, and consequences* (NIDA Research Monograph No. 103). Rockville, MD: National Institute on Drug Abuse.

Johnson, B., Hamid, A., Morales, E., & Sanabria, H. (1987). *Critical dimensions of crack distribution*. Paper presented at the meeting of the American Society of Criminology.

Kleiman, M.A.R., & Smith, K. D. (1990). State and local drug enforcement. In M. Tonry & J. Q. Wilson (Eds.), *Drugs and crime*. Chicago: University of Chicago Press.

Klein, M. W. (1971). *Street gangs and street workers*. Englewood Cliffs, NJ: Prentice-Hall.

Klein, M. W. (1990). *Having an investment in violence: Some thoughts about the American street gang*. Sutherland Award address to the American Society of Criminology.

Klein, M. W. (1993). Attempting gang control by suppression. *Studies in Crime and Crime Prevention: Annual Review, 1993* (Stockholm).

Klein, M. W., & Maxson, C. L. (1985). Rock sales in South Los Angeles. *Sociology and Social Research, 69*, 561-565.

Klein, M. W., & Maxson, C. L. (1989). Street gang violence. In N. A. Weiner & M. E. Wolfgang (Eds.), *Violent crime, violent criminals*. Newbury Park, CA: Sage.

Klein, M. W., Maxson, C. L., & Cunningham, L. C. (1988). *Gang involvement in cocaine "rock" trafficking. Final report to the National Institute of Justice*. Los Angeles: University of Southern California.

Klein, M. W., Maxson, C. L., & Cunningham, L. C. (1991). "Crack," street gangs and violence. *Criminology, 29*, 623-650.

McKinney, K. C. (1988, September). Juvenile gangs: Crime and drug trafficking. *Juvenile Justice Bulletin*. Washington, DC: U.S. Department of Justice, Office of Juvenile Justice and Delinquency Prevention.

Mieczkowski, T. (1990). Crack distribution in Detroit. *Contemporary Drug Problems, 17,* 9-30.

Moore, J. (1978). *Homeboys: Gangs, drugs, and prison in the barrios of Los Angeles.* Philadelphia: Temple University Press.

Moore, J. (1991). Gangs, drugs, and violence. In M. De la Rosa, E. Y. Lambert, & B. Gropper (Eds.), *Drugs and violence: Causes, correlates, and consequences.* Rockville, MD: National Institute on Drug Abuse.

Moreno, T. (1987). *Gangs/narcotic activity.* A presentation to the California Gang Investigators' Association, Los Angeles, CA.

Quicker, J. C., Galeai, Y. N., & Batani-Khalfani, A. (1991). *Bootstrap or noose: Drugs in South Central Los Angeles.* Draft report to the Social Science Research Council, cited with permission of the authors.

Reinarman, C., & Levine, H. G. (1989). Crack in context: Politics and media in the making of a drug scare. *Contemporary Drug Problems, 16,* 535-577.

Reuter, P. (1988). *Youth gangs and drug distribution: A preliminary inquiry.* Washington, DC: RAND.

Robin, G. D. (1967). Gang member delinquency in Philadelphia. In M. W. Klein (Ed.), *Juvenile gangs in context.* Englewood Cliffs, NJ: Prentice-Hall.

Rosenfeld, R. (1991). Anatomy of the drug-related homicide. In *The St. Louis homicide project: Local responses to a national problem.* St. Louis: University of Missouri at St. Louis.

Sahagun, L. (1990, September 20). *Los Angeles Times.*

Short, J. F., Jr., & Strodtbeck, F. L. (1965). *Group process and gang delinquency.* Chicago: University of Chicago Press.

Skolnick, J. H. (1988). The social structure of street drug dealing. *BCS Forum.* Sacramento: Bureau of Criminal Statistics.

Skolnick, J. H., Correl, T., Navarro, T., & Rabb, R. (1990). The social structure of street drug dealing. *American Journal of Police, 9*(1), 1-41.

Spergel, I. A. (1964). *Racketville, slumtown, haulburg: An exploratory study of delinquent subcultures.* Chicago: University of Chicago Press.

Spergel, I. A. (1989). *Survey of the gang problem and organized responses in 50 cities and sites.* Chicago: University of Chicago, School of Social Service Administration.

Spergel, I. A. (1990). Youth gangs: Continuity and change. In M. Tonry & N. Morris (Eds.), *Crime and justice: A review of research* (Vol. 12). Chicago: University of Chicago Press.

Taylor, C. S. (1989). *Dangerous society.* East Lansing: Michigan State University Press.

Tracy, P. E. (1979). *Subcultural delinquency: A comparison of the incidence and seriousness of gang and nongang member offensivity.* Philadelphia: University of Pennsylvania, Center for Studies in Criminology and Criminal Law.

Waldorf, D. (1990). *First year report of the home boy study.* Alameda, CA: Institute for Scientific Analysis.

Waldorf, D. (1991). *Don't be your own best customer—Drug use of San Francisco gang drug sellers.* Alameda, CA: Institute for Scientific Analysis.

Zimmer, L. (1987). *Operation pressure point: The disruption of street-level drug trade on New York's Lower East Side.* New York: New York University School of Law.

PART II

Police Initiatives

5. Defining the Street-Level Drug Market

DAVID WEISBURD
LORRAINE GREEN
with FRANK GAJEWSKI
and CHARLES BELLUCCI,
Jersey City Police Department

The drug problem in America's cities occupies a central place both in the public's perceptions of the crime problem and in the allocation of police resources (Church, 1988; IACP, 1988). Every year a growing number of reports about drug-related crime and violations of public order occurring at drug sale locations lead to calls for effective action to clean up the streets and rid the inner city of one of its most intractable problems. In response to public concern, police departments throughout the country have enlarged their narcotics units, established special strike forces, and developed new strategies for fighting street-level drug dealing. Nonetheless, most of these strategies and programs have developed without reference to systematic information on the nature of drug markets, and few have included any systematic evaluation of what works in combating the drug problem and under what circumstances (Hayeslip, 1989).

AUTHORS' NOTE: This research was supported by Grant No. 90-IJ-CX-K004 from the National Institute of Justice. Points of view or opinions expressed do not necessarily represent the official positions or policies of the U.S. Department of Justice, Rutgers University, the Hebrew University, Northeastern University, or the Jersey City Police Department. We would like to thank Al Andrews, Michael Maltz, Stephen Mastrofski, Albert J. Reiss, Jr., and Craig Uchida for their advice and assistance in developing the DMAP program in Jersey City.

The Drug Market Analysis Program (DMAP) in Jersey City, New Jersey, developed, in great part, as a response to these concerns about the effectiveness of police efforts to combat the drug problem. We sought to develop a systematic, location-based information system that would facilitate the identification of street-level drug markets and allow an experimental evaluation of innovative drug enforcement strategies. In the following pages we describe how this information system was used to define drug markets in Jersey City. We also present some preliminary findings on the distribution and nature of those markets.

The Data Sources

In developing our understanding of the distribution of street-level drug markets in Jersey City, we wanted to take into account the official police view of the location of market areas as well as the perceptions of citizens. The police view was provided by narcotics arrest information. For the purpose of market identification we examined 1,227 "sales arrests"[1] over a 6-month period, between June and November of 1990.

Although we suspected that the main areas of street-level drug distribution would be revealed by arrest information, we also wanted to allow for identification of places with street-level drug activity that had escaped police attention.[2] To do this we conducted a narcotics "phone-in" and a large-scale location-based community survey in the city. The less comprehensive of these citizen-based data sources was the phone-in conducted on July 25, 1990, between 10 a.m. and 10 p.m. The police department advertised the phone-in, using two local cable television stations, six radio stations (two Spanish-speaking), and two local newspapers, and by distributing 10,000 flyers throughout Jersey City during the week preceding the event. The advertisements emphasized that the police department wanted to hear from citizens about drug locations in their area, and that all callers would be guaranteed confidentiality. One hundred and fifty-two people called to identify 191 places as active drug sale areas.

A much more comprehensive view of citizen perceptions of drug markets in Jersey City was gained through a community survey conducted between July and September of 1990 (see Center for Crime Prevention Studies, 1991). The survey was designed to allow identification of more obscure drug locations, which we suspected were likely to be found in lower density residential areas. Accordingly, we did not take a traditional probability sample of Jersey City residents, which would have led us to oversample high-density neighborhoods. Rather, we randomly selected a maximum of two households on each occupied block,[3] a technique that allowed us to draw responses from each discrete area of the city.[4] The survey sample included 3,601 respondents from more than 2,120 occupied city blocks.[5]

All survey respondents were given the option of identifying a drug location on their block. If they did not know of a location on their block, they were then asked if they knew of a drug location nearby. Only 6% of the 3,601 citizens interviewed identified drug activity on their block, and an additional 8% identified a drug location off their block yet in their neighborhood.

These results were very different from what the Police Department expected when the survey was commissioned; namely, that drug dealing was spread throughout this densely populated city. Because of this we looked closely at the possibility that citizens feared reporting drug activity, and accordingly that the survey had seriously underestimated the extent and spread of the drug problem. We suspected that we were most likely to see evidence of such fear in crime-ridden areas of Jersey City that had been identified as serious drug locations through police arrest reports. When we examined survey responses in such areas, however, we found that citizens were very likely to report the presence of active drug locations. Although we recognize that some citizens are afraid to provide information about drug activity, these results suggest a surprising degree of openness, even in those areas where the risk of reprisal would appear to be most serious.

Identifying Active Drug Areas

The central aim of the DMAP system in Jersey City was to use the data sources described above to identify discrete drug markets that could be targeted for police enforcement efforts. Our first task was to choose a base unit of analysis for identifying drug markets. Although the street address is used to define the location of street-level drug activity in the arrest, phone-in and survey data, the link of information to specific addresses, was likely to include a number of small errors. Both for the police and for citizens, there is often little difference between addresses located next to or near each other. For this reason, the address was too specific a unit to begin the process of selecting drug markets. Alternatively, because much drug dealing is linked to intersections in Jersey City, and dealers often drift up and down the blocks connected to intersections, the block or street segment also provides a potentially misleading base unit for identifying areas with significant drug activity.

Recognizing these problems, we chose the *intersection area* as our base unit for identifying active drug locations. The intersection area linked each of the 1,553 intersections in Jersey City with its related four street segments or blocks. In contrast to the address, it is not sensitive to small coding errors or short movements of offenders. The intersection area unit of analysis also avoids predicting the direction of drug sales activity on a particular block, and thus allowed the DMAP system to link activity on different blocks that could reflect related movements of offenders away from central intersections.

Once we had defined these intersection areas on a computer map of Jersey City, we linked narcotics sales arrests and community survey and narcotics phone-in data to them. Of the total of 1,553 intersection areas in the city, almost one third (479) were linked to narcotics activity by at least one of the DMAP data sources. This, however, did not mean that such areas evidenced significant ongoing drug problems.

We understood that a lone narcotics arrest assigned to an intersection area was not a good indicator of ongoing activity. Even multiple arrests at a specific location over a week or two might be evidence of an isolated short-term problem. Similarly, one community respondent perceiving a place as a drug location does not provide solid evidence of this fact, especially given the concern of narcotics detectives that citizens often mistake teenagers hanging out on the street as people selling or using drugs. Six threshold criteria were used to restrict the number of such places that would be included in the DMAP system. Each of these, listed below, required that there be multiple indicators, either within or across the databases examined:

1. The presence of at least one drug sales arrest in 2 or more of the 6 months examined;[6]
2. The presence of at least one narcotics phone-in response and one drug sales arrest;
3. The presence of at least one community survey response and one drug sales arrest;
4. The presence of at least one community survey response and one narcotics phone-in response;
5. The presence of multiple community survey responses; and
6. The presence of multiple narcotics phone-in responses.

Some 15% (239) of the total number of intersection areas in Jersey City met one or more of these selection criteria.

Identifying Active Street Segments and Intersections

Use of the intersection area as a preliminary unit of analysis prevented the deletion of drug locations that might have resulted from slight deviations in arrest recording procedures or casual movement of offenders along street segments. However, the fact that single events were counted in more than one intersection area meant that we had to return to the level of street segments and intersections in order to define specific drug markets in the city. Drawing from the 239 active intersection areas, we identified 399 intersections and street segments as evidencing some degree of drug activity.[7] There was a total of 4,404 street segments and intersections in the city.

When we mapped these places we noticed that many of the segments and intersections defined only by the survey and phone-in data (what we termed *unofficial* locations) were adjacent to locations with narcotics sales arrest activity. We thought it unlikely that these adjacent segments or intersections were new points of drug distribution that had gone unnoticed by the police, a view that was strongly stated by Jersey City narcotics officers. Rather, we suspected that citizens identified the casual movement of offenders to or from drug areas as activity on their block. In these "close match" cases, we felt that the official data more accurately captured the specific location of drug sales. Therefore, we deleted unofficial sites that were adjacent to segments and intersections identified through narcotic sales arrest information.[8] These deletions left 322 active segments and intersections, representing 9% of all intersections and 7% of all street segments in Jersey City.[9] The "pipeline" that led us to these active intersections and street segments is summarized in Figure 5.1.

The final map of these 322 active intersections and segments is presented in Figure 5.2. As is apparent, the vast majority of the city landscape is free of ongoing drug activity as we have defined it. Even in the South District of Jersey City, which contains 45% of the segments and intersections identified as active, the majority of the street segments and intersections did not meet our inclusion criteria.

While Figure 5.2 provides a good view of where we believe drug activity is centered in the city, it also illustrates one of the major dilemmas confronted when trying to develop a location-based definition of drug markets. How does one treat continuous areas of drug activity? Given the clustering of street segments and intersections in Figure 5.2, we could conclude that Jersey City includes three or four very large drug markets, each covering 25 or more blocks. Alternatively, one might ask whether these large areas could be split up into distinct drug markets that

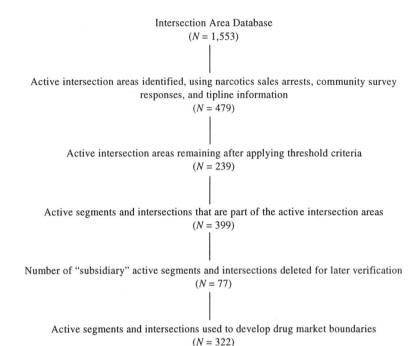

Figure 5.1. Pipeline for Choosing Segments and Intersections to Identify and Develop Drug Market Boundaries

are relatively close to each other, for example, a block or two away. The following section discusses these questions and presents the process that we used to define drug market boundaries.

Identifying Drug Markets

In economics, a *market* is defined by a set of arrangements in which buyers and sellers of a good or service are in contact to trade that good or service (Fischer, Dornbusch, & Schmalensee, 1988, p. 11). Examination of market activity can focus on either the consumer or the seller. For example, in the marketing literature the *market place* is often discussed in terms of the forces that result in a particular group of consumers converging in space and time to purchase a particular commodity (see Alderson, 1965). Alternatively, in examination of black market activities, the focus is often on the relationship between sellers and their

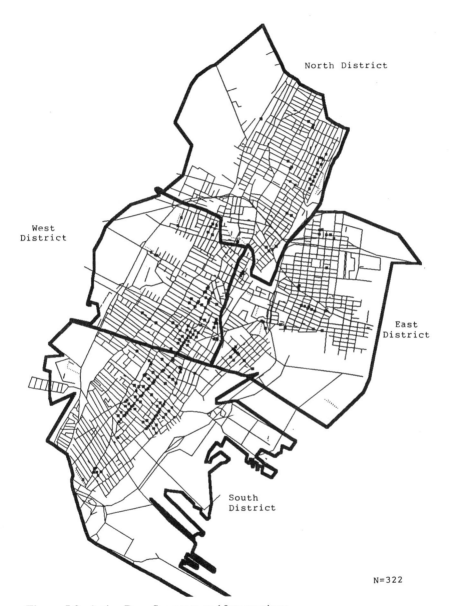

West
District

East
District

South
District

N=322

Figure 5.2. Active Drug Segments and Intersections

marketplace activities (see, e.g., Bookstaber, 1976; Karchmer, 1985; Reuter, 1983; Wisotsky, 1986). Consistently, the term *market* refers to a specific type of product and depicts some geographic concept of place, although the reference to a marketplace is often applied to different levels of analysis. Some markets are global, others national or regional. Other markets are identified as converging in local areas, or even limited to particular malls or stores.

In the criminological literature the term *drug market* is often used to describe aggregate market behavior in response to drug interdiction efforts (e.g., Reuter, 1989) or to elasticities of supply and demand (see Kleiman, 1988; Moore, 1977; Reuter & Kleiman, 1986). More recently, journalistic accounts have casually used the term *drug market* to describe small geographic areas where street-level drug activity is high (e.g., "Street Dealing," 1990; "Street Level Drug Markets," 1990). In developing a process to identify street-level drug markets in Jersey City, we sought to satisfy three main criteria. First, the process had to reflect the reality of drug distribution patterns in the city. Second, the process had to identify specific places that evidenced significant ongoing drug activity. Third, it was important that the identification system could be replicated at routine intervals by the police.

In developing a portrait of drug markets that met these criteria, we drew heavily from the perceptions of narcotics detectives about the ways in which narcotics sales are organized at the street level. Our decision was based in part on the fact that many of them had years of experience with the narcotics problem in the city, and thus their knowledge was a natural place for us to begin. Beyond this, the DMAP system was to define a group of places that would become the focus of their enforcement efforts. The operational dimension of DMAP made it essential that we construct drug market boundaries in a way that made sense to police officers, who would have the major responsibility for drug enforcement in the experimental phase of the project.

Although there are a number of neighborhoods in the city that appear to have continuous drug dealing across a large number of streets or intersections, narcotics detectives generally do not see these places as undifferentiated areas of drug activity.[10] For the detectives, a series of blocks, or sometimes even a single block or intersection, may be separated from others based on the type of drug that is being sold in that place. They argue that dealers tend to sell the same drug in the same area, providing a kind of specialization to market activities. These dealers do not drift considerably from one day to the next, because if they did, customers would not know where to find the market for the drug they are looking for. Although we were initially skeptical of this assumption of specialization at discrete places, our own analysis of narcotics arrest information generally confirmed their conclusion. In Jersey City only 15% of the intersections and street segments, in which information on type of drug was available for multiple narcotics arrests during 1990, evidenced two different drugs that each accounted for more than 30% of arrests.[11]

Detectives also distinguish areas that are market centers in the same neighborhoods, but are separated by a small number of blocks one from another. They argue that dealers tend to have a strong sense of territoriality, which provides a degree of insulation for market boundaries. This contention was also supported in our analyses. When we examined the pattern of arrests across the active segments and intersections, we found that only 15 out of the 448 people arrested more than once for *selling* narcotics during 1990 traversed an inactive segment or intersection to sell in an adjacent drug market. Further, 6 of these 15 people had to traverse more than four blocks to get to the adjacent market. Indeed, if a person was arrested in two separate areas, he or she was most likely to be arrested in two separate districts in the city.

In constructing the boundaries of drug markets in Jersey City, we followed two basic criteria drawn from these observations about the nature of drug distribution patterns in the city. Taking into account the importance of type of drug in determining a market's identity, we linked street segments and intersections that evidenced similar drug activity.[12] Recognizing that sellers seldom crossed inactive segments and intersections to participate in the drug trade, we separated areas where at least one inactive street segment and one inactive intersection existed between two active places. Using these criteria we identified 107 drug markets in Jersey City.[13]

Characteristics of Drug Markets in Jersey City

A key criterion used to identify drug markets in Jersey City was type of drug. As illustrated in Table 5.1, a majority of the *official markets* (those with information on type of drug derived from narcotics arrest data) were linked primarily to cocaine sales. Almost half of the markets identified comprised just one street segment or intersection, though 11% included more than 10 street segments and intersections. Almost one third of the markets identified were located in the South District of Jersey City, which includes the largest number of low-income and minority residents. Nonetheless, it is interesting that about one quarter of the

Table 5.1   Drug Markets Analyzed by District, Drug Type, and Size

Drug Markets	%	N
By Drug Type		
Cocaine	57.5	42
Heroin	11.0	8
Marijuana	9.6	7
PCP	1.4	1
Two or more drug types specified	12.3	9
No drug type	8.2	6
Total	100.0	73[*]
By Size[**]		
One segment or intersection only	45.8	49
2-4 segments and intersections	32.7	35
5-9 segments and intersections	10.3	11
10+ segments and intersections	11.2	12
Total	100.0	107
By District		
North	25.2	27
South	32.7	35
East	14.0	15
West	28.1	30
Total	100.0	107

[*] Number of markets that had official narcotics arrest police data.
[**] Includes all segments that fall within the market boundaries.

markets were found in the North District, which is primarily white and middle-class.

As part of our examination of the nature of drug markets in Jersey City, we sought to identify relevant physical and social characteristics of areas that fell in the market boundaries. The social descriptions of the markets derive from 1985 test census data from Jersey City. We collected physical data by videotaping and then systematically coding environmental characteristics of every street segment and intersection existing within our drug market boundaries.

The number of vacant lots and abandoned buildings characterizes the level of decay on the segments and intersections that fall within the boundaries of our drug markets. The data presented in Table 5.2 illustrate generally the level of dilapidation in the South District, even taking into account the larger number of markets that exist there. For example, 36 out of 2,108 buildings were abandoned in the markets of the South District. This was true for only 2 of the 704 buildings in the North District of the city. While 129 vacant lots were identified on the 80 street

Table 5.2 Selected Social and Physical Characteristics of Drug Markets (by District)

	North	South	East	West	All Drug Markets	Jersey City
Physical Characteristics (*N*)						
Schools	2	16	0	9	27	NA
Abandoned buildings	2	36	10	32	80	NA
Vacant lots	6	129	26	43	204	NA
Bars	7	4	7	10	28	NA
Graffiti*	37	138	18	84	277	NA
Number of street segments	22	80	24	66	192	NA
Number of buildings	704	2,108	508	1,337	4,657	NA
Median Housing						
Value ($)	50,197	46,172	34,250	47,252	44,468	62,509
Percent Non-White**						
Residents (district)	23.0	62.5	56.5	52.0	NA	48.5
Residents (markets)	26.0	81.1	57.1	64.3	57.1	NA
Arrestees (markets)	70.2	97.3	88.5	97.8	88.5	95.4

* Measured by the number of buildings that have graffiti on them that are within the market boundaries.
** Includes black, Hispanic, Asian, and other categories.

segments in the South District markets, there were only 6 on the 20 street segments in the North District markets. Differences among the city districts in the number of buildings with graffiti and bars in the markets were not as pronounced.

Census data provide one way of contrasting drug markets with other areas in the city. For example, the average median value of the houses in our 107 markets is significantly less than the median value for Jersey City houses as a whole. Examining the differences in the median value of the houses in the drug markets by district suggests that the markets reflect in great part the neighborhoods in which they are found. Markets in the primarily middle-class North District consistently show indicators of social well-being in comparison with the other, less well-off districts of the city. The median housing value in the North District markets is significantly greater than the values for the markets in the other districts.

The census data also indicate the racial and ethnic makeup of residents living in Jersey City. Overall, half of the city is defined as white by the census, with more than half of the remaining city population defined as black. While the proportion of *white* residents who live in the market areas is less than that found in the city generally, the drug markets reflect for the most part the racial makeup of the communities in which they are found (see Table 5.2). However, those defined as *non-whites* are very much overrepresented among narcotics arrestees in our drug markets in every district of Jersey City.

Overall, 9 out of 10 sales arrestees in the drug markets were males. Interestingly, women were overrepresented in the heroin markets and those defined as mixed-type drug markets. About 4 in 10 of sales arrestees were less than 20 years of age. This result concurs with perceptions of narcotics officers, who suggest that young people are actively recruited to sell drugs because they are cheap to bail out of jail and they generally receive more lenient penalties than older people arrested for similar offenses. Overall, the mean age of sales arrestees was 21.3 years. In comparison, the median age of people living in the markets in Jersey City was 30.7. The median age of Jersey City residents as a whole was 31.8.

Rengert and Wasilchick's (1990) portrayal of the evolution of drug markets suggests that particular details of activity at different drug markets, such as the quantity of sales and the range of hours that drugs are available, are indicators of its stage in the development process. Although we are just beginning to develop an understanding of this process in Jersey City, we have a number of initial indicators of the level and range of drug activity in the markets we identified.

One of these indicators is the number of arrests made in each of the markets. Although this measure reflects both the level of activity of the market and the vagaries of police enforcement efforts, it does illustrate the tremendous variety we find across the 107 drug markets we identified. Among those markets that evidenced arrest activity, 18 evidenced only 1 or 2 narcotics arrests. Twelve markets had more than 50 arrests for narcotics during the year we examined, and 3 markets had more than 200 arrests. The average number of narcotics arrests per official market was 37. Most of these arrests were of sellers, reflecting in great part a preference among narcotics officers to focus on those they define as key players in drug areas.

Another factor that Rengert and Wasilchick (1990) suggest as an indicator of the degree of development of the market is the range of hours that drugs are sold at the marketplace. They propose that the greater the number of hours a market is "open," the greater its degree of institutionalization. When we examined the hours that drug markets were active, we again found suggestive data on the importance of recognizing the wide variety of behaviors that make up the drug market problem (see Table 5.3). While arrests were found primarily in the afternoon and evening hours for cocaine, marijuana, and PCP markets, heroin markets were active at these times as well as in the morning hours. This suggests to us that recreational users play a much more important role in non-

Table 5.3   Percentage of Sales Arrests by Time of Day and Type of Drug[*]

	Morning	*Afternoon*	*Evening*	*Night*[**]
Heroin Markets	25.0	31.5	39.8	3.7
Cocaine Markets	5.7	36.2	48.9	9.2
Marijuana Markets	0.0	40.4	55.3	4.3
PCP Markets	0.0	53.3	46.7	0.0
Mixed Markets	14.7	31.1	44.4	9.8

[*] For $N = 73$ official markets only
[**] The time of day categories are as follows: morning = 6 a.m. to noon, afternoon = noon to 6 p.m., evening = 6 p.m. to midnight, and night = midnight to 6 a.m.

heroin drug markets. Conversely, the all-hours character of heroin markets would imply that a larger number of addicts are involved who need constant access to the drug.

Conclusions

We developed the drug market identification process described above to facilitate an experimental evaluation of drug enforcement strategies in Jersey City. Nevertheless, we believe that the decisions we made in developing a portrait of drug markets fits the reality of street-level drug distribution in the city. Our attention to the geographic character of markets, as well as our reliance on the types of drugs that predominate in an area for drug market identification, are consistent with our observations and analyses of drug market characteristics. They are also consistent with the perceptions of Jersey City narcotics detectives. Although we recognize that a fuller understanding and identification of drug markets would need to draw information from those who sell and buy drugs in these areas, the process we have defined provides a relatively straightforward method for distinguishing drug areas from one another and pointing out likely centers of drug distribution.

Looking at drug markets in this way, we are led to two preliminary conclusions about the nature of the drug problem in Jersey City, and we suspect in other cities as well. First, the drug problem is not endemic to the whole city, but is concentrated in relatively few discrete market areas. These areas are more likely to be found in poorer sections of the city, but there are also active markets, as we define them, in stable middle-class neighborhoods. Conversely, in more socially disorganized parts of Jersey City, there are large areas free of drug market activities. Second, there is wide variability in the intensity, size, and social character of drug markets. Some markets are active all day long, others just a few hours. Some span 10 or more blocks, others are concentrated on just one intersection. Some markets cater primarily to school-age youths, others to young working people, still others to hardened drug addicts.

The concentration of drug sales in market hot spots (see Sherman, Gartin, & Buerger, 1989; Weisburd, Maher, & Sherman, 1992) leads naturally to the conclusion that enforcement strategies should be geographically focused, taking into account the special combination of persons and environments that brings drug activity to certain points on the city map. Nonetheless, the fact that drug activity is tightly clustered in certain discrete areas does not mean that drug markets can be treated as a simple, uniform problem. The diversity of markets found in Jersey City suggests that strategies must be developed to approach a broad range of criminal activities and physical environments. They must, in this sense, be as complex as the phenomenon they seek to address.

Notes

1. In Jersey City the decision as to whether an arrest should be made under a "possession" or "sales" charge is made at the discretion of the officer, based on observations of the transaction. There is no legal threshold under which an offender must be charged for narcotics sales, or conversely a minimum possession amount that would prevent an officer from making an arrest for a narcotics sale.

2. Our efforts here were prompted by a substantial body of literature that stresses the need to look beyond the "official" view of criminal activity (see, for example, Chaiken & Chaiken, 1982; Collins, Hubbard, Rachal, Cavanaugh, Craddock, & Kristiansen, 1982). Nevertheless, our analyses suggest that more serious street-level drug markets are identified in official reports.

3. There was only one business or house on 15% of the street segments.

4. When households were not available, businesses were sampled. When someone was not at home, we chose the next randomly selected household on that same street segment.

5. The survey was conducted by the police department, under the supervision of staff from the Center for Crime Prevention Studies. Seven police officers (who worked in uniform because of departmental regulations and safety concerns) and one graduate student from Rutgers University acted as interviewers for the study. Although we were initially concerned that citizens would fear reporting drug activity to uniformed police officers, analysis of responses to the uniformed police, compared with the responses to 182 interviews conducted by the civilian interviewer, showed generally small and insignificant differences. The only areas of divergence were the reports of satisfaction with police services and the survey non-response rate. Citizens were less likely to give negative responses concerning satisfaction with the police to police officers, but they were more likely to let the police interviewers in the door to conduct the survey. The response rate for those who were identified at home by interviewers was more than 90%.

6. We examined the stability of using a threshold of 1, 2, 3, 4, 5, and 6 months for arrest data in conjunction with the other criteria to include intersection areas. If we had used just 1 month, we would have included 66% ($N = 316$) of the 479 active intersection areas. In contrast, by varying the number of sales arrest months from 2 through 6 months, the number of affected intersection areas only changed from 50% ($N = 239$) to 44% ($N = 211$) of the total active intersection areas. Therefore, we set the arrest threshold conservatively at 2 months.

7. At this stage we decided to include 11 rather than 6 months of narcotic sales arrest information. Although we initially wanted evidence only of recent narcotics activity (in identifying active intersection areas), at this step we wanted to be as inclusive as possible in identifying those segments and intersections linked with drug dealing within an intersection area.

8. We deleted street segments and intersections that were only identified by unofficial sources and were directly adjacent (within a block) to areas with official arrest histories. We then marked these sites as *subsidiary locations* for later verification.

9. Of these street segments and intersections, 19% were defined only by the *unofficial* data sources.

10. We suspect that the seeming continuity of drug activity in some areas reflects, in part, what Maltz and colleagues describe as the "clutter" resulting from mapping a large number of data points (Maltz, Gordon, & Friedman, 1991).

11. Type of drug information was coded for 68% of all narcotics arrests made in Jersey City during 1990. Nineteen percent of the officially defined active segments and intersections meeting our threshold criteria failed to reveal the type of drug that was seized.

12. Consistent with the way we linked officially defined places, we linked unofficial areas that were within a block and an intersection of one another. Recalling that we had deleted the unofficial locations that were adjacent to officially identified active places, the remaining unofficial locations were generally isolated from other drug areas and seldom went beyond two street segments.

13. Our base criteria led to the identification of 100 of these markets. The remaining market boundaries were created by applying two modifications. First, we linked places with missing drug information to the adjacent segment with type of drug data. These places were most often on the outskirts of an otherwise drug dominant market and did not include very many arrest events. In places with no drug type data that were more than a block and an intersection away from another market, we created a separate market that did not have a distinguishing type of drug.

References

Alderson, W. (1965). *Dynamic marketing behavior: A functionalist theory of marketing.* Homewood, IL: Irwin.

Bookstaber, R. (1976, Spring). Risk and structure of the black market for addictive drugs. *American Economist, 20*(1), 26-29.

Center for Crime Prevention Studies. (1991). *Drug market analysis program preliminary report: The Jersey City community survey.* New Brunswick, NJ: Rutgers University, School of Criminal Justice.

Chaiken, J. M., & Chaiken, M. R. (1982). *Varieties of criminal behavior: Summary and policy implications.* Santa Monica, CA: RAND.

Church, G. J. (1988, May). Thinking the unthinkable. *Time, 22,* 12-17.

Collins, J. J., Hubbard, R. L., Rachal, J. V., Cavanaugh, E. R., Craddock, S. G., & Kristiansen, P. L. (1982). *Criminality in a drug treatment sample: Measurement issues and initial findings.* Research Triangle Park, NC: Research Triangle Institute.

Fischer, S., Dornbusch, R., & Schmalensee, R. (1988). *Introduction to microeconomics* (2nd ed.). New York: McGraw-Hill.

Hayeslip, D. W., Jr. (1989). *Local-level drug enforcement: New strategies* (Report No. 213). Washington, DC: U.S. Department of Justice, National Institute of Justice.

International Association of Chiefs of Police (IACP). (1988, June). *Reducing crime by reducing drug abuse: A manual for police chiefs and sheriffs.* Gaithersburg, MD: Author.

Karchmer, C. L. (1985). Money laundering and the organized underworld. In H. E. Alexander & G. E. Caiden (Eds.), *The politics and economics of organized crime* (pp. 37-48). Lexington, MA: D. C. Heath.

Kleiman, M.A.R. (1988). Crackdowns: The effects of intensive enforcement on retail heroin dealing. In M. R. Chaiken (Ed.), *Street level drug enforcement: Examining the issues.* Washington, DC: U.S. Department of Justice, National Institute of Justice.

Maltz, M., Gordon, A. C., & Friedman, W. (1991). *Mapping crime in its community setting: Event geography analysis.* New York: Springer-Verlag.

Moore, M. H. (1977). *Buy and bust: The effective regulation of an illicit market in heroin.* Lexington, MA: Lexington Books.

Rengert, G., & Wasilchick, J. (1990). *Space, time and crime: Ethnographic insights into residential burglary.* Unpublished report to the U.S. Department of Justice, National Institute of Justice. Philadelphia: Temple University.

Reuter, P. (1983). *Disorganized crime: The economics of the visible hand.* Cambridge: MIT Press.

Reuter, P. (1989). *Quantity illusions and paradoxes of drug interdiction: Federal intervention into vice policy.* Santa Monica, CA: RAND.

Reuter, P., & Kleiman, M.A.R. (1986). Risks and prices: An economic analysis of drug enforcement. In M. Tonry & N. Morris (Eds.), *Criminal Justice: An annual review of research* (Vol. 7). Chicago: University of Chicago Press.

Sherman, L., Gartin, P., & Buerger, M. (1989). Hot spots of predatory crime. *Criminology, 27*(1), 27-56.

Street dealing. (1990, July 11). *The New York Times,* p. B7.

Street level drug markets. (1990, January 5). *The New York Times,* p. A16.

Weisburd, D., Maher, L., & Sherman, L. (1992). Contrasting crime general and crime specific theory: The case of hot spots of crime. *Advances in criminological theory* (Vol. 4). New Brunswick, NJ: Transaction Books.

Wisotsky, S. (1986). *Breaking the impasse in the war on drugs.* New York: Greenwood.

6. Controlling Street-Level Drug Trafficking: Professional and Community Policing Approaches

CRAIG D. UCHIDA

BRIAN FORST

This chapter discusses two models of policing that are subjects of debate within the research and police communities—the professional and the community policing models. The chapter lays out the elements of each model and shows how each is used in the context of street-level drug trafficking. By presenting information on the effectiveness of alternative drug enforcement strategies in Oakland, California, and Birmingham, Alabama, the chapter demonstrates the conflicts between the professional model and the community policing model.

Introduction

Two schools of thought have come to dominate the debate on law enforcement in a democratic society: the traditional *professional* form of policing and the more contemporary *community-oriented* approach. Although the two models can be construed as complementary in that a police chief may draw liberally from both paradigms in setting goals for the department, they are fundamentally different approaches to policing. The community policing approach stresses the importance of a police-citizen *partnership,* while the professional model emphasizes a *police* responsibility for

AUTHORS' NOTE: Supported under awards #87-IJ-CX-0058 and #88-IJ-CX-0015 from the National Institute of Justice, Office of Justice Programs, U.S. Department of Justice, to the Police Foundation. Points of view in this document are those of the authors and do not necessarily represent the official position of the U.S. Department of Justice, the National Institute of Justice, the Police Foundation, the Oakland Police Department, or the Birmingham Police Department.

crime control and order maintenance. As a result, different police departments are usually characterized as having leanings toward one or the
other school of policing, although their respective commitments to professionalism and to community policing are rarely made explicit.

This chapter primarily discusses models of policing as guides for
dealing with specific problems in various settings, but it also touches on
using models of policing as paradigms for departmental goal setting. By
focusing on the most serious problem in urban policing, street drug
trafficking, this chapter considers how tools associated with the professional and community-oriented schools of policing can be selected and
deployed to deal effectively with the problem. The problem of street-
level drug trafficking as it exists in various settings is described, and
specific tactics used by police to control the retail drug market are
reviewed. Evidence is examined from field experiments in two cities—
Oakland, California, and Birmingham, Alabama—for an empirical test
of various approaches to the control of street drug trafficking, approaches
that grow out of the community policing and professional policing
models. The implications of these evaluation findings are discussed.
Finally, the more general implications of policing models, their value
both for broad goal setting purposes and for determining appropriate
courses of action in dealing with specific problems under various circumstances is considered.

The Professional and Community-Oriented Models of Policing

HISTORICAL PRECEDENTS

The Professional Model. The professional model developed during the
early 1900s, largely as a reaction to an entrenched pattern of police
corruption and lawlessness that had evolved by the late nineteenth century. This reaction was an important aspect of the Progressive Era that
swept both the public and private sectors from 1890 to 1920. Progressive
reformers professionalized medicine, law, accounting, and engineering
with rules and standards to guide professional conduct. Policing was not
immune to this movement (Fogelson, 1977; Uchida, 1989; Walker, 1977).

Progressive Era professionalism transformed policing in several ways.
First, it produced police departments that were more centralized and less
prone to corruption. Under the decentralized structure of policing of the
1800s, police departments had become uneven in enforcing the law. The

resulting unevenness was rooted in the political ties between the precinct captain and the ward boss and other local powers.

Second, professionalism manifested itself in producing a better caliber of police officer. The recruitment and selection of officers shifted from a system of influence by local political powers to one of published selection requirements and standards.

A third feature of police professionalism was a narrowing of the role of the police officer—from a broad order-maintenance function (including the provision of services that ranged from ambulance to street-cleaning to the housing of homeless children) to a more sharply defined law enforcement role. Greater emphasis on laws meant less opportunity to exercise discretion arbitrarily.

Finally, a fourth feature of professionalism, one that is arguably more closely related to technological advances of the period than to Progressive Era ethics, was an emphasis on effectiveness and efficiency. Frederick Taylor's production management principles, Henry Ford's assembly line technology, and related private sector developments undoubtedly influenced August Vollmer (chief of the Berkeley Police Department), O. W. Wilson (chief of the Wichita Police Department), and other reformers who were innovators in the use of the scientific method in criminal detection and investigation, and in the efficient use of squad cars and other modern capital equipment.

The Community-Oriented Model. As discussed above, the foundation for the professional model is rooted in the Progressive Era and in technology breakthroughs of the early twentieth century. However, the community-oriented model, reactivated by the consumer movement of the 1980s, finds its roots in fundamental principles set forth some 150 years ago by the chief architect of modern policing, Sir Robert Peel (see Miller, 1977). The community-oriented approach was also inspired by growth in the social distance between the police and the public. This social distance, largely induced by virtually total replacement of the friendly foot patrol cop with the patrol car, was apparent in most large cities by about the mid-twentieth century. Sensitivity to this distance was surely increased by the popular movement for excellence in service delivery in the 1980s. Like the Peters and Waterman (1982) theory set forth in their *In Search of Excellence,* that corporate excellence is closely related to a focus on the needs of the customer, Skolnick and Bayley (1986) hypothesized that police innovation in six of the nation's leading police departments was closely related to a focus on the community (pp. 220-221).

CONTEMPORARY DIFFERENCES

The Professional Model. As stated earlier, the professional school of policing assigns responsibility for crime control and order maintenance to the police. The citizen is viewed primarily as a victim, witness, or offender, rather than as a partner. This model is generally characterized as rule-oriented, basic, and centralized, with an emphasis on rapid responses to calls for service and the effective handling of individual incidents.

The Community-Oriented Model. Contrasting with the professional model in emphasis, the community-oriented approach stresses the importance of a police-citizen partnership in the control of crime. With its aim focused on solving problems before they become criminal incidents, this model is generally described as flexible, decentralized, and more humane (see Wilson & Kelling, 1989).

A significant distinction between the two models of policing is the procedure the officer follows when *not* responding to a call for service. Under the professional model, the patrol officer is most often in the squad car, operating either in a proactive or a watching-and-waiting mode. Under the community policing model, the officer is more likely to be spending time solving problems (Goldstein, 1979; Spelman & Eck, 1987), or out of the car building bridges with the community, sometimes helping to organize it (Skolnick & Bayley, 1986, pp. 4-7; Weisburd & McElroy, 1988, pp. 97-98). Proponents of community policing view the movement as nothing less than revolutionary, a paradigm shift in policing (Skolnick & Bayley, 1988).

Advocates of community policing regard the approach as useful for a variety of reasons. Because the police officer has been moved from a position of anonymity in the patrol car to one involving direct engagement with the community, the department avails the officer of more immediate information about the problems that are unique to a neighborhood and insights into their solutions (Trojanowicz & Moore, 1988). The officer is thus freed from the emergency-response system to engage more directly in proactive crime prevention (Skolnick & Bayley, 1988). Police accountability to the public is increased by making operations more visible to the public.

By decentralizing operations, community policing can permit officers to shift emphasis from uniform application of department policy to greater familiarity with the specific workings and needs of various neighborhoods and constituencies in the community. In addition, the inducement of officers to view the citizens as partners will improve relations between the police and the public. Community policing may eventually work to cause citizens to be actually more initiative in preventing and solving crimes and helping the police to do so. Thus community policing may mean more crime control, not less.

Evidence from field experiments in Houston (Pate, Wycoff, Skogan, & Sherman, 1986), Newark (Kelling, Pate, Ferrara, Utne, & Brown, 1981; Pate et al., 1986), Flint, Michigan (Trojanowicz, 1982), and Baltimore (Pate & Annan, 1989) have served to validate the theory that closer ties between the police and the citizens of the community, especially in the form of door-to-door contact and foot patrols, raise levels of citizen satisfaction with police services and quality of life and lower their levels of fear of crime.

Advocates of professional policing are typically police executives, rather than criminal justice scholars; their arguments are more often oral than published, but they are no less sincere and are based on substantially more experience. Skolnick and Bayley (1988) observe that the professional model is less ambiguous than the community policing model. According to James Q. Wilson and George Kelling (1988), police chiefs are skeptical about community policing primarily because they see it as a movement that undermines centralized control and increases the risk of misconduct. Mastrofski (1988) notes that this skepticism is largely justifiable: "We are still faced with a reform that has been oversold" (p. 64). It may be worthwhile to recall that the police centralized their operations in the 1920s largely as an antidote to the corruption that was closely associated with Prohibition. Chiefs who move their officers into the community, without setting up effective safeguards against such corruption, could subject themselves and their officers to risks that are serious and avoidable. The prospect of community policing prompting a new era of police corruption may be far-fetched, but certain lessons of history cannot be ignored.

Street Drug Trafficking: A Modern Policing Problem

Drug trafficking is a serious problem in several respects: It corrupts virtually everyone involved, most notably the young; it contributes to decline in the health of the community; it is a bellwether of economic and social decline in the neighborhood; and it is clearly a major contributor to neighborhood decline, (Johnson, Williams, Dei, & Sanabria, 1990). Research has shown that the positive association between illicit drug abuse and trafficking and indicators of poor socioeconomic conditions and social disorganization in cities (e.g., poverty, crowding, unemployment, juvenile delinquency, adult crime, and illegitimate births) has been consistent over time (e.g., Johnson et al., 1990; Nurco, Shaffer, & Cisin, 1984).

Most important, drug trafficking is associated with other serious crimes as well. For example, Goldstein (1985) measured three ways in which homicides in New York may be drug-related. Evidence does indicate that drug use is a critical factor in robbery and other predatory crime (Chaiken & Chaiken, 1990; Greenwood, 1982), felonies and serious misdemeanors (Forst & Wish, 1983), school violence (Gold & Moles, 1978), and a variety of serious delinquent acts (Smith et al., 1979).

In recent years, law enforcement emphasis has shifted increasingly from wholesale to retail trafficking. The reasoning generally proceeds along the following lines:

> Should we concentrate our efforts on locking up the kingpins of the heroin trade or on protecting communities from the low-level dealers who have a direct and immediate effect on the life of a neighborhood? Ideally we should do both. But protection of our communities deserves far more attention than it has received. (Califano, 1989, p. 82)

Attempts to investigate and apprehend high-level drug distributors have been expensive and time-consuming, and too often futile. Interruptions in high-level distribution, moreover, have been all too temporary. Police have found their efforts to control drug traffic at the retail level to be more successful in terms of the sheer numbers of arrests and convictions, and more satisfying in terms of the ease in making each arrest.

Drug-related homicides, as noted earlier, are an indicator of the demand side of this growth. As the demand for drugs—especially cocaine—grew, sellers moved in to accommodate the buyers. Arrests for drug abuse violations increased by 55% from 1978 to 1987, a period that saw much smaller increases in arrests for violent crimes and property crimes: 25% and 16%, respectively (FBI, 1988, p. 168). Arrests for drug trafficking violations appear to have grown at an even faster rate. Juveniles and young adults make up the preponderance of this growth (Reuter et al., 1988).[1]

Controlling Street Drug Trafficking: Models and Tactics

Perhaps the most profound aspect of drug trafficking is its significant growth during the 1980s, despite a similarly significant growth in law enforcement attempts to control that growth, by both federal and local agencies (Reuter & Kleiman, 1986). Police departments have applied a variety of conventional and unconventional approaches to control street drug trafficking—from standard undercover, buy-and-bust operations to sophisticated stings—as well as programs that aim to eliminate drug abuse from the streets: targeting higher level dealing, enforcing laws against illegal possession and use, promoting prevention programs, and so on.

PROFESSIONAL POLICING METHODS

Law enforcement strategies against drugs can be considered in the contexts of the professional and community policing models. The random patrol and rapid response to calls for service aspects of professional policing are used to control street drug dealing by patrol officers. In addition, a variety of other programs have been created and used under the professional policing model: undercover drug operations including reverse buys, property confiscation, use of heavy construction equipment to enter crack houses, and drug sweeps or roundups. These programs are comfortably executed under the professional model; they are generally appreciated by the legitimate elements of the community, but they do not require partnership with those elements.

Undercover Operations. There are two basic undercover drug bust strategies: *buy-and-bust* operations that target the seller, and *reverse-buy* operations that target the buyer. Both tactics have been used with success for a number of years in New York (Moore, 1977), Miami, and elsewhere (see, e.g., Dickson, 1988; Will, 1988).

Property Confiscation. Government seizure of property used in the conduct of criminal activities is ancient practice. It continues today; virtually all states authorize forfeiture of assets associated with drug trafficking. Most states have provisions that confiscated property will go to state or local treasuries; law enforcement agencies in some states can keep all cash, property, and proceeds from the sale of forfeited assets (Stellwagen, 1985, p. 5).

Drug Sweeps. Some urban areas have been taken over by drug traffickers, to the dismay of most law-abiding people in those areas. A natural response of the police department is to declare war on drug traffickers and attempt to regain control of the area with sweeps or crackdowns, usually involving significant numbers of additional police resources.

Have these efforts been effective? The evidence suggests that they have been. This evidence, however, has not been definitive (Kleiman, 1988; Sherman, 1992; Zimmer, 1990). Drug sweeps generally succeed in the short run, elevating arrest rates and lowering calls for service in the immediate area, as well as making a police presence in the area visible. The short-term displacement effects (i.e., the shifting of crime and drug trafficking out to other areas) and the longer term effects in the immediate areas, on the other hand, have been the subject of both considerable debate and less than conclusive evidence to date.

The mixed evidence from the drug sweeps suggest that a variety of factors determine success under a particular policing approach, but that chief among them are three: (1) the orientation and commitment of the police department to the approach; (2) the will of the neighborhood to resist illegitimate activity; and (3) the strength of the offender population.

COMMUNITY POLICING METHODS

Community-oriented policing provides quite different opportunities to control street drug trafficking. This can be illustrated with an example from Weisburd and McElroy (1988), quoting an officer with a community-policing assignment in New York:

> People get to know you. They get to trust you a little bit, and if something's going on, they figure, if they tell you, you'll act upon it—because you'll have to answer back to them in a couple of days. . . . Well basically, I have people calling me up . . . and they say "Hey, this guy, he's dealing drugs right now in front of this address"—you would never get that on regular patrol. . . . They're also sending in anonymous letters, giving detailed descriptions of drug operations. (p. 99)

Such information is occasionally offered to patrol officers operating within a professional policing environment, generally by way of a 911 call. The above quote nonetheless exemplifies that the community policing model is capable of substantially increasing the flow of critical information about drug trafficking from citizens to the police.

The important problem-oriented aspect of community policing, noted earlier, has appeared in several law enforcement efforts to control drug trafficking. One of the best known examples of this is the Newport News (Virginia) Police Department's handling of burglaries, drug trafficking, and other drug-related crimes in the New Briarfield apartment complex in 1984. By conducting interviews in the New Briarfield complex, the Newport News Police discovered the real concerns of the residents: burglaries (the highest rate in the city), robberies, drug trafficking, and the physical deterioration of the project. In response, then-Chief Darrel Stephens worked with the city manager and other city agencies to fix up the project, pending its eventual demise; both the crime rate and the drug problem were noticeably lessened as a result of these efforts (Wilson & Kelling, 1989, pp. 46-47).

Currently, the problem-oriented approach is being used to combat drug trafficking in a number of cities across the country, including Tampa, Tulsa, San Diego, and Philadelphia (McPherson, 1988; Weisel, 1988).

Examining the Effectiveness of Policing Efforts

Tools associated with both the professional and the community-oriented schools of policing have been selected by police agencies and deployed to deal with the drug trafficking problem. To advocates of community policing, this hybridization or combination of tools detracts from the "true" definition of community policing, for police continue to focus on the use of efficiency and professionalism as guides, and arrests and seizures as outcome measures. Nonetheless, the realities of the drug problem have led chiefs and administrators to engage in both professional and community policing.

During the course of evaluating drug enforcement and community policing in two fairly large U.S. cities—Oakland, California, and Birmingham, Alabama—the authors experienced problems associated with combining professional and community policing (see Uchida, Forst, & Annan, 1992). The remainder of this chapter discusses those evaluations, focusing on the lessons learned and the implications for community policing.

THE OAKLAND EXPERIENCE

As in other cities, drug trafficking has been a serious problem in Oakland for more than a decade. Drug-related homicides created an aura of fear in some neighborhoods. The police reported that about 27% of the homicides committed in Oakland in 1984 were believed to be drug-related. In 1987 nearly 50% of the 114 homicides were drug-related.

Crack cocaine emerged at this time, with sellers and buyers openly dealing the substance in residential neighborhoods across the city. Controlling street-level drug trafficking became increasingly difficult for the police department.

Compounding these difficulties were the manpower problems faced by the department. Compared to the national average of cities with populations of more than 250,000, the Oakland Police Department is about 35% lower in the ratio of officers to resident population (1.8 per 1,000 versus 2.8 per 1,000 residents nationally). More important, compared to cities of similar size, Oakland ranked among the top five in reported homicides, robberies, and burglaries per officer.

To combat street-level drug traffickers, the Oakland Police Department put together a special unit of hand-picked, specially trained patrol officers who engaged in undercover buy-and-bust operations, aggressive patrol, and motor vehicle stops (Special Duty Unit 3—SDU3). The department also agreed to try a community policing approach, aimed at enlisting residents of the community to join with the police in controlling the retail trade of illegal drugs on the street. The department used *directed police citizen contacts,* or door-to-door interviews, to elicit support from the community. The application of this strategy was based on its success in the Newark and Houston police departments' fear reduction efforts (Pate et al., 1986).

BIRMINGHAM'S DRUG PROBLEM

In Birmingham, illicit street-level drug trafficking emerged as a serious problem around 1985. Birmingham's problem differed from Oakland's in a number of ways. First, rather than concentrating on crack cocaine, Birmingham drug traffickers sold and used powder cocaine and Dilaudid, a synthetic narcotic often used as a substitute for heroin. Second, street-level trafficking was confined primarily to public housing areas, rather than throughout residential neighborhoods, as occurred in Oakland. Third, drug enforcement was made solely the responsibility of vice-narcotics detectives, rather than allocating and distributing the responsibility to patrol, as was done in Oakland. Although patrol officers made arrests during the course of their duties, they did not have the training or ability to control drug trafficking in a systematic way. As few as a dozen narcotics officers were responsible for the entire city's drug problem.

In 1988 the Birmingham Police Department embarked on a multiphase program, called Operation 'Caine Break, aimed at street-level drug traffickers. The narcotics division targeted buyers and sellers through buy-and-busts and sting operations, while a captain in one precinct (of four) devoted a group of his patrol officers to a community-oriented approach.

RESEARCH METHODS

At both sites, the evaluation consisted of a pretest-posttest quasi-experimental design. In Oakland, the deployment of two aspects of the street drug trafficking prevention program (SDU3 and the door-to-door interviews) was structured so that each aspect could be evaluated within a 6-month field experiment in 4 of the city's 35 beats. Similarly, in Birmingham, three beats were selected for the evaluation of Operation 'Caine Break and the door-to-door contacts by police. At both sites, all the selected beats were noncontiguous and dispersed, to avoid problems of contamination.

Observational and official data were employed to ensure that the programs were implemented and that experimental conditions were followed. To evaluate the programs and determine their impact, the research team relied on both survey data and reported crime data. At both sites, a panel survey of residents in each beat was selected and interviewed at two different times. Citizens were asked a series of questions about drugs, police, and their neighborhoods, both before and after the treatments were imposed. Attitudes of the panel of citizens in each beat helped to determine the effectiveness of the programs. In Oakland, a sample of 1,668 residents was selected for the interviews. Fifty-eight percent of the residents were surveyed during the first wave of interviews. During the second wave, 75% of the desired sample were reinterviewed. In Birmingham, the response rates were higher. For the first wave, the general response rate was about 84% (758 residents were included in the sample). For the second wave, more than 77% of the desired sample were reinterviewed.

Monthly reported crime data were collected for each beat, and for each city as a whole, to determine whether the experimental treatments appeared to alter patterns of crime. These data were generated by the police department and included all Part I offenses known to the police.[2]

FINDINGS: OAKLAND

In Oakland, the combination of drug enforcement and door-to-door contacts was somewhat successful. These strategies, in tandem and separately, had effects on citizen perceptions of drug trafficking, property crime, satisfaction with police services, and neighborhood safety. In addition, crimes reported to the police declined substantially in one of the intervention areas where both enforcement and the door-to-door interviews were used.

Oakland's special enforcement unit was not that different from other squads that have been established in police agencies. Like the officers in Lynn and Lawrence, Massachusetts, and those in New York City's Operation Pressure Point and Washington, D.C.'s Operation Clean Sweep, this unit targeted street-level drug traffickers.

Unlike other programs, however, the special unit, with six officers and a sergeant, confined its activities to two experimental areas for 6 months. Through this intensified effort, drug trafficking virtually ceased in one beat and was noticeably reduced in the other area. More important, citizen reaction to these efforts was encouraging: Residents saw the decline in street-level buying and selling and continued to view the police in a positive way.

The implementation of the community-oriented aspect of the program was less than expected, but showed positive results. The execution of the police-citizen contacts was less than satisfying, showing that both the officers and the supervisors involved did not embrace the ideas or philosophies of community policing. Although officers eventually fulfilled the assignments allocated to them and interviewed a higher percentage of persons in households than in the Newark or Houston fear-reduction experiments (Pate et al., 1986), follow-ups with residents and problem-solving efforts never took hold in Oakland.

Despite these shortcomings, changes in citizen perceptions did occur. As indicated, residents perceived that property crime as a problem declined and that satisfaction with police services increased. Moreover, in the beats that received both the enforcement and door-to-door interviews, changes occurred in perceptions of drug trafficking and safety.

When all is said and done, however, positive assertions about the success of community policing in controlling drug trafficking cannot be made. The efforts of Oakland Police Department were less a form of community policing and more like a traditional police-community relations program. The effort fell short of the models established elsewhere regarding community policing. This occurred because of the focus on professionalism that pervades the department.

The chief's effort to bring community policing into his department was a noble idea. But it could not take shape fully because of the view that responding to calls for service was the most efficient way to serve the community. In addition, other biases worked against the community-oriented idea. One deputy chief remarked early in the program that he viewed door-to-door interviews as "merely social work." Watch commanders saw little value in sending officers into the neighborhoods to talk with citizens about problems when they could be answering calls for service. Furthermore, the commanders "knew" where the problems were and felt they could deal with them on their own.

Ironically and somewhat paradoxically, the attempt at the new wave of policing did have a positive effect on the community. Had the fullest efforts been attempted or even understood, the results would have been even more apparent. For now, however, the small step that was made will have to suffice.

Overall, the context for these efforts should not be ignored. Like other police agencies, the Oakland Police Department was confronted with severe drug and crime problems in 1987. In the past 3 years, however, the department has managed to control and perhaps stabilize the drug problem. In the long run, through the traditional, professional efforts of special duty units, vice-narcotics, and patrol officers, and with a concerned community, the City of Oakland appears to have controlled street-level drug trafficking. What remains untested, however, is the effect that community-policing, in its truest form, would have on drug trafficking as well.

FINDINGS: BIRMINGHAM

Like Oakland, Birmingham attempted to deal with the problem of drug trafficking by implementing two disparate approaches, deployed so that they could be assessed experimentally. The Birmingham Police Department implemented a buy-and-bust/sting operation it called Operation 'Caine Break. In addition, the door-to-door interviewing strategy was employed by patrol officers.

Arrests, reported crimes, and citizen surveys and observations were used to measure the effectiveness of the strategies. Operation 'Caine Break was deemed successful because of the positive press reports received and because the police were able to apprehend a high percentage (more than 90%) of the suspects they sought. The narcotics detectives involved in the program believed that they had sent a message to drug traffickers—that they fully intended to apprehend, charge, and convict both the dealers and the buyers of the drug trade.

Because of the nature of narcotics work, it was not anticipated that there would be significant changes in the attitudes of the residents in the area that received the treatment. For the most part, narcotics officers relied on a low-keyed approach to their undercover operations of stings and buy-busts. High visibility and aggressive buy-busts were not a part of the initial repertoire of the Birmingham narcotics detectives. As such, residents were not expected to see arrests on a regular basis, and, indeed, the impact on community attitudes was limited.

In Birmingham, community policing took two forms: police-citizen contacts through door-to-door interviews and the establishment of a police substation in a public housing development.

The findings from Birmingham show that these treatments had dramatic effects on citizen perceptions of quality of life, property crime, and satisfaction with police services. In addition, violent crimes reported to the police declined substantially in the area where the police-citizen contacts occurred.

THE EFFECTS OF THE BIRMINGHAM EXPERIENCE

Sting operations or reverse buys have become popular in a number of police agencies for targeting the buyers of illicit drugs. Making the user accountable for his or her actions has become another component of the war on drugs. Birmingham's Operation 'Caine Break was unique in that videotaping and audiotaping were important elements of the program. So was the presence of a deputy district attorney who oversaw the activities of the detectives.

As in the Oakland experiment, the officers and detectives in the Birmingham Police Department confined their activities to experimental areas. Through this effort, important determinations could be made about their work. Although drug trafficking itself was not noticeably reduced in the selected target areas, the door-to-door contacts in Gate City and the establishment of a substation in Kingston had a significant impact on citizen perceptions of property crimes, police services, quality of life, and safety.

In the door-to-door interviews, officers fulfilled the assignments allocated to them and interviewed a high percentage of persons in households. Unfortunately, neither follow-ups with residents nor problem-solving efforts were attempted in Birmingham.

The substation was also a success. The work of the housing authority and the residents in mobilizing support for the substation led to a relatively quick response by police.

As in Oakland, however, the efforts of Birmingham Police Department were less a form of community policing and more like a traditional police-community relations program. The efforts fell short of the philosophy and models established elsewhere regarding community policing. The transfer of the captain to Records and Communications, and the demand for action by the community when 11 people were shot, are indications that proactive policing that occurs with community-based approaches has some distance to go in Birmingham.

Just as in Oakland, the attempt at the new wave of policing did have a positive effect on the community. If the methods and philosophy of community policing are fully invoked, then there is no telling what can be achieved.

Summary

In this chapter we have discussed two models of policing, as they relate to the control of illicit street-level drug trafficking—the community policing model and the professional model. As we indicate, both models may be useful in providing guidance to the police as they cope with the burgeoning problem of drug trafficking.

Yet the tension between the two models has not been resolved. Part of the problem is the uneasiness among professional policing advocates toward the community-oriented model: that community policing shifts responsibility for crime control from the police to citizens and is, therefore, inherently weak and irresponsible. It is the job of the *police* to control crime; experiences in shared responsibility too often result in neither side carrying the load, thus police executives might feel uncomfortable with the community policing model.

On the other hand, proponents of the community-oriented school tend to view the appearance, if not reality, of elitism and autocracy under the professional approach as a force that alienates the police from the community. This distance can only limit the ability of the police to obtain information essential for crime prevention. Advocates of community policing hold that the basic approach of the professional model is, more fundamentally, inconsistent with quality-of-life needs of the community and democratic principles.

Regardless of the relative merits of the two camps as basic philosophical positions, both the professional and the community policing models may be useful as guiding lights, capable of illuminating specific approaches for dealing with specific problems under specific circumstances. The police can be productively guided by abstract goals and can be held accountable for dealing effectively with tangible problems—problems that have to do not only with preventing and solving crimes, but also with order maintenance and, more generally, problems in areas that involve the conditions that may tend to induce crime.

Notes

1. It should be pointed out, however, that the increase in arrests for drug trafficking crimes may, in part, be a function of increased police activity directed toward drug trafficking and away from other crimes.

2. For a detailed description of the data, sampling plan, and regression analyses used in both cities, see *Modern Policing and the Control of Illegal Drugs: Testing New Strategies in Two American Cities* (Uchida et al., 1992).

References

Califano, J. A., Jr. (1982). *The 1982 report on drug abuse and alcoholism*. New York: Warner Books.

Chaiken, J. M., & Chaiken, M. R. (1990). Drugs and predatory crime. In M. Tonry & J. Q. Wilson (Eds.), *Drugs and crime*. Chicago: University of Chicago Press.

Dickson, C. (1988, January). Drug stings in Miami. *FBI Law Enforcement Bulletin*.

Federal Bureau of Investigation (FBI). (1988). *Uniform crime reports: Crime in the United States—1987*. Washington, DC: U.S. Department of Justice, Federal Bureau of Investigation.

Fogelson, R. (1977). *Big-city police*. Cambridge, MA: Harvard University Press.

Forst, B., & Wish, E. (1983). Drug use and crime: Providing a missing link. In K. Feinberg (Ed.), *Violent crime in America*. Washington, DC: National Policy Exchange.

Gold, M., & Moles, O. C. (1978). Delinquency and violence in schools and the community. In J. A. Inciardi & A. E. Pottieger (Eds.), *Violent crime*. Beverly Hills, CA: Sage.

Goldstein, H. (1979, April). Improving policing: A problem-oriented approach. *Journal of Crime and Delinquency*, 236-258.

Goldstein, P. (1985). The drugs/violence nexus. *Journal of Drug Issues, 15*(4), 493-506.

Greenwood, P. W. (1982). *Selective incapacitation*. Santa Monica, CA: RAND.

International Association of Chiefs of Police. (1988). *Reducing crime by reducing drug abuse: A manual for police chiefs and sheriffs*. Washington, DC: U.S. Department of Justice.

Johnson, B., Williams, T., Dei, K. A., & Sanabria, H. (1990). Drug abuse in the inner city: Impact on hard-drug users and the community. In M. Tonry & J. Q. Wilson (Eds.), *Drugs and crime*. Chicago: University of Chicago Press.

Kelling, G., Pate, A. M., Ferrara, A., Utne, M., & Brown, C. E. (1981). *The Newark foot patrol experiment*. Washington, DC: Police Foundation.

Kleiman, M.A.R. (1988). Crackdowns: The effects of intensive enforcement on retail heroin dealing. In M. R. Chaiken (Ed.), *Street-level drug enforcement: Examining the issues*. Washington, DC: U.S. Department of Justice, National Institute of Justice.

Mastrofski, S. D. (1988). Community policing as reform: A cautionary tale. In J. R. Greene & S. D. Mastrofski (Eds.), *Community policing: Rhetoric or reality* (pp. 47-67). New York: Praeger.

McBride, D. C. (1976). The relationship between type of drug use and arrest charge in arrestee populations. In *Appendix to drug abuse and crime: Report of the panel on drug use and criminal behavior*. Research Triangle Park, NC: Research Triangle Institute.

McPherson, N. (1988, Summer). Posted: Keep out. *Problem Solving Quarterly*, 1-2.

Miller, W. R. (1977). *Cops and bobbies: The London metropolitan police and New York City police department*. Chicago: University of Chicago Press.

Moore, M. (1977). *Buy and bust: The effective regulation of an illicit market in heroin*. Lexington, MA: D. C. Heath.

Nurco, D., Shaffer, J., & Cisin, I. (1984). An ecological analysis of the interrelationships among drug abuse and other indices of social pathology. *The International Journal of the Addictions, 19*(4), 441-451.

Pate, A. M., & Annan, S. (1989). *The Baltimore community policing experiment*. Washington, DC: Police Foundation.

Pate, A. M., Wycoff, M. A., Skogan, W. G., & Sherman, L. W. (1986). *Reducing fear of crime in Houston and Newark*. Washington, DC: Police Foundation.

Peters, T. J., & Waterman, R. H. (1982). *In search of excellence: Lessons from America's best run companies*. New York: Warner Books.

Reuter, P., Haaga, J., Murphy, P., & Praskac, A. (1988). *Drug use and drug programs in the Washington metropolitan area*. Santa Monica, CA: RAND.

Reuter, P., & Kleiman, M.A.R. (1986). Risks and prices: An economic analysis of drug enforcement. In M. Tonry & N. Morris (Eds.), *Crime and justice: An annual review of research*. Chicago: University of Chicago Press.

Sherman, L. (1992). Police crackdowns: Initial and residual deterrence. In M. Tonry & N. Morris (Eds.), *Crime and justice: An annual review of research*. Chicago: University of Chicago Press.

Skolnick, J. H. (1988). The social structure of street drug dealing. *BCS Forum*.

Skolnick, J. H., & Bayley, D. H. (1986). *The new blue line*. New York: Free Press.

Skolnick, J. H., & Bayley, D. H. (1988). Theme and variation in community policing. In M. Tonry & N. Morris (Eds.), *Crime and justice: A review of research*. Chicago: University of Chicago Press.

Smith, C., et al. (1979). Definition, characteristics of incidents and individuals, and relationship to substance abuse. *National assessment of serious juvenile crime and juvenile justice system* (Vol. 2). Washington, DC: Government Printing Office.

Spelman, W., & Eck, J. E. (1987, January). Problem-oriented policing. *Research in Brief*. Washington, DC: U.S. Department of Justice, National Institute of Justice.

Stellwagen, L. D. (1985, July). Use of forfeiture sanctions in drug cases. *Research in Brief*. Washington, DC: U.S. Department of Justice, National Institute of Justice.

Trojanowicz, R. C. (1982). *An evaluation of the neighborhood foot patrol program in Flint, Michigan*. East Lansing: Michigan State University.

Trojanowicz R. C., & Moore, M. H. (1988). *The meaning of community in community policing*. East Lansing, MI: National Neighborhood Foot Patrol Center.

Uchida, C. D. (1989). The development of the American police: An historical overview. In R. Dunham & G. Alpert (Eds.), *Critical issues in policing: Contemporary readings*. Prospect Heights, IL: Waveland.

Uchida, C. D., Forst, B., & Annan, S. (1992). *Modern policing and the control of illegal drugs: Testing new strategies in two American cities*. Washington, DC: U.S. Department of Justice.

Walker, S. (1977). *A critical history of police reform: The emergence of professionalism*. Lexington, MA: D. C. Heath.

Weisburd, D., & McElroy, J. E. (1988). Enacting the CPO role: Findings from the New York City pilot program in community policing. In J. R. Greene & S. D. Mastrofski (Eds.), *Community policing: Rhetoric or reality* (pp. 89-101). New York: Praeger.

Weisel, D. L. (1988, Spring). Drug problem solving project picks up pace. *Problem Solving Quarterly,* 5.

Will, G. F. (1988, March 31). Miami sting. *Washington Post,* p. A23.

Wilson, J. Q., & Kelling, G. (1989, February). Making neighborhoods safe. *The Atlantic,* pp. 46-52.

Zimmer, L. (1990). Proactive policing against street level drug trafficking. *American Journal of Police,* 43-74.

7. Police Crackdowns on Drug Abuse and Trafficking

ROBERT E. WORDEN

TIMOTHY S. BYNUM

JAMES FRANK

A police crackdown entails an abrupt increase in police activity, especially proactive enforcement, which is intended to dramatically increase the perceived and/or actual threat of apprehension for specific types of offenses in certain places or situations, and so to produce a general deterrent effect. Police crackdowns on drug offenses might be expected to disrupt patterns of drug trafficking and to have other beneficial consequences. In this chapter, we first review the hypothetical impacts of crackdowns, and we summarize and critically evaluate the evidence about these hypotheses. Then we discuss issues to which future evaluative research should give more attention: the dimensions and characteristics of crackdown target areas and of drug hot spots; variation in the content of crackdowns—their tactics, intensity, and duration; and potential problems in implementing crackdowns. Finally, we describe some of the kinds of research efforts that might cast further empirical light on these issues, and we discuss the methodological problems that such research must surmount.

A police crackdown entails an abrupt increase in police activity, especially proactive enforcement, which is intended to dramatically increase

AUTHORS' NOTE: The preparation of this paper was supported by Grant No. 89-DD-CX-0049 from the National Institute of Justice, and it was enriched by our research on drug enforcement in Detroit, which has been conducted with the generous cooperation of the Detroit Police Department. We gratefully acknowledge the assistance of these agencies. Statements herein do not necessarily represent the position of either the U.S. Department of Justice or the Detroit Police Department.

the perceived and/or actual threat of apprehension for specific types of offenses in certain places or situations, and so to produce a general deterrent effect (see Sherman, 1990, pp. 7-8). As Hayeslip (1989, p. 3) observes, crackdowns are not new, but police crackdowns on drugs represent "refinements" of the older and more generic crackdown technology[1] to which American law enforcement agencies have increasingly turned. Crackdowns target police resources on specific problems (cf. Eck & Spelman, 1987) in providing for substantial increases in police visibility and sanctioning; they sometimes also coordinate these activities with the application of other tactics, such as asset seizure and forfeiture, or elements of community policing. Notwithstanding their promise, the effectiveness of police crackdowns in addressing the problems associated with drug sales and use is an issue on which little scientific evidence has accumulated. Furthermore, because substantial increases in the certainty of apprehension do not come cheaply, one must also ask—even if crackdowns are an effective enforcement tool—how crackdowns can be conducted most efficiently, and whether their benefits exceed their costs.

In this chapter, we first review the hypothetical impacts of crackdowns, and we summarize and critically evaluate the evidence about these hypotheses. Then we discuss issues to which future evaluative research should give more attention: the dimensions and characteristics of crackdown target areas and of drug hot spots; variation in the content of crackdowns—their tactics, intensity, and duration; and potential problems in implementing crackdowns. Finally, we describe some of the kinds of research efforts that might cast further empirical light on these issues, and we discuss the methodological problems that such research must surmount.

Police Drug Crackdowns: Theory and Evidence

The potential benefits of police drug crackdowns include reductions in the visibility of drug transactions, in the amount of drugs consumed, in the size of the user population, and in street crimes that are associated with drug use and drug trafficking, and improvements in the quality of life in targeted areas and in citizens' attitudes toward the police. Aside from the inescapable costs of personnel, equipment, and the benefits of forgone activities, the potential costs of drug crackdowns include increases in crime and in police abuse and/or subversion of their authority, and the erosion of citizen respect for and willingness to cooperate with police. Each of these potential benefits and costs corresponds to a plausible hypothesis about the impact of a drug crackdown.

THEORETICAL PROPOSITIONS

The hypothetical impact of a crackdown on the incidence and prevalence of drug consumption stems largely from enhancing the perceived risks of buying or (especially) selling drugs.[2] To the extent that street-level enforcement efforts make the sale or possession of drugs appear risky, they disrupt networks of retail drug distribution; dealers take steps to avoid detection by police—for example, they become more circumspect about where and to whom they sell—and in so doing also make themselves less accessible to buyers. Enforcement efforts may be able to so increase the nonmonetary costs of buying drugs—especially the costs of time and inconvenience, or "search time"—that experienced users reduce their consumption or desist, while novices refrain from (further) experimentation (Kleiman, 1988, pp. 11-12, 25-26; also see Moore, 1973, 1977, ch. 5). One can reasonably hypothesize, therefore, that the abrupt increases in police presence and sanctioning that drug crackdowns provide will affect both the aggregate level of drug consumption and, perhaps, the size of the user population.

Furthermore, by dispersing the market(s) for drugs, and perhaps by reducing drug consumption, police crackdowns might also reduce the levels of street crimes. Because a street drug market routinely attracts both "motivated offenders" and "suitable targets" (Cohen & Felson, 1979, p. 589) to the same area, the dispersal of that market is therefore likely to reduce the number of offenses that the former perpetrate on the latter (Kleiman, 1988, p. 27; Sherman, 1990, p. 35), including homicide, robbery, assault, and larceny. Furthermore, insofar as narcotic addicts' rates of offending vary directly with their levels of consumption (see, e.g., Anglin & Speckart, 1988; Nurco, Hanlon, Kinlock, & Duszynski, 1988), the numbers of street crimes might be expected to decline with reductions in their consumption.

Police drug crackdowns might directly and indirectly affect the quality of life in targeted areas. A crackdown could directly affect the quality of life by reassuring the citizenry through visible police activity, such as street sweeps, raids, and patrols. A crackdown could indirectly affect the quality of life by dispersing drug markets and by reducing street crime. Decreases in street crime diminish the likelihood of both direct and indirect victimizations, both of which contribute to fear of crime.[3] Further, a street-level drug market creates nuisances in the form of traffic, noise, and loitering users; it poses a potential for violence; and it exposes children (and others) to the temptations of using or dealing drugs. A crackdown that disperses the market also reduces or eliminates these problems. By enhancing the level of order that prevails in public places in this way, a crackdown might reduce fear of crime and promote the extension of informal social controls.[4] Hence improvements in the quality of life in target areas could represent short-term benefits that pay long-term dividends.

Finally, police crackdowns might enhance residents' confidence in and attitudes toward the police. Citizens may become more willing to report drug trafficking and other illegal activity, if they come to believe that police will respond to their complaints. Citizens may also feel empowered by police efforts, without which individual or collective action could seem futile.

Crackdowns also entail costs. The cost of personnel can be quite high: For example, Kleiman (1988, p. 16) estimates that Operation Pressure Point I, in New York City, cost roughly $12 million per year in salaries. Although personnel and other costs are inevitable, they are not beyond the control of police administrators, whose choice of crackdown elements—that is, the intensity and the duration of crackdowns—may affect the efficiency of this strategy (as we will discuss further below). But other potential costs must also be considered.

One potential cost is an increase in street crime. Street crime—especially larceny and robbery—could be expected to increase if enforcement efforts increase the monetary costs of narcotics without proportionately reducing consumption, and if users must consequently increase their rates of offending (Kleiman, 1988, p. 13). An increase in street crime seems theoretically unlikely because street-level enforcement is directed less toward the supply of drugs than toward the availability of drugs, and price is driven more by the former than the latter (see Kleiman & Smith, 1990); nevertheless, an increase in street crime is the kind of unintended consequence to which evaluative research must be sensitive.

Crackdowns might also entail costs in terms of police-community relations, as a result of either police abuses or merely the greater degree of intrusiveness. Conventional wisdom holds that aggressive police tactics may not be well received by the public (see, e.g., Wilson & Boland, 1978), even though empirical research has failed to detect a relationship between citizen attitudes toward the police and the frequency with which field interrogations are conducted (Boydstun, 1975; Whitaker, Phillips, & Worden, 1984). Drug crackdowns may be perceived as a more intrusive police tactic than field interrogations are, however, and one recent crackdown in Philadelphia apparently resulted in precisely the kind of community reaction that conventional wisdom would have predicted: The public was critical of what it saw (probably justifiably) as indiscriminate enforcement activity (Kleiman, 1988, p. 20). In view of the value of community involvement in controlling crime and maintaining order, which police officials are increasingly recognizing (see, e.g., Skolnick & Bayley, 1986; Sparrow, Moore, & Kennedy, 1990), it is important for research to ascertain whether crackdowns have negative impacts on citizens' attitudes (and if so, the circumstances under which they do).

Another potential cost is an increase in police abuse and corruption. The conventional technologies of drug enforcement generate pressures on officers to subvert and/or abuse their authority (see Manning & Redlinger, 1978; Skolnick, 1975). But one cannot assume that police departments or individual officers are equally susceptible to such pressures; neither can one assume that an increase in the level of drug enforcement will yield a commensurate increase in police abuse and corruption. Moreover, a drug crackdown typically entails not only (if at all) an increase in enforcement activity but also (or instead) the geographic concentration of enforcement effort. Inasmuch as concentrated activity may be more effectively monitored, the implementation of crackdown tactics might restrict corruption and abuse.

One important refinement of the theory on which police crackdowns rest has implications for the expected costs of crackdowns. Sherman (1990) builds upon a distinction between the perceived risk of apprehension and offenders' certainty about the likelihood of apprehension (cf. Reuter & Kleiman, 1986). Normal enforcement efforts, Sherman observes, provide for fairly stable and usually rather low risks. But a series of short-term crackdowns that are conducted intermittently, or what Sherman calls a "crackdown-backoff" strategy, makes the risks of apprehension uncertain. This uncertainty may make it possible to complement the initial deterrent effect, which is attributable to the increase in police presence and/or sanctioning, with a residual deterrent effect, which is attributable to the inability of offenders to predict the time of the next crackdown once the police have backed off. According to this theory, the risk perceived by offenders remains high (compared to that produced by normal enforcement efforts) due to offenders' uncertainty. The residual deterrent effect will inevitably decay, as offenders adjust their perceptions of risk, but as long as offenders overestimate the threat of sanctions, society enjoys a " 'free bonus' residue of deterrence" (Sherman, 1990, p. 3).

The intervals between crackdowns, that is, the duration of the backoff, can be as long as it takes for this effect to decay; the slower the rate of decay, the longer the intervals between crackdowns can be, and consequently the lower the costs of using the crackdown strategy.

If this theoretical analysis holds for drug dealers and drug users, it implies that resources for street-level drug enforcement could be used more efficiently if they were concentrated in particular areas for brief periods at unpredictable times, rather than dispersed across precincts or districts at levels that remain more or less constant over time. Thus departments that already conduct street-level enforcement could do so more effectively by following a somewhat different resource allocation strategy, while those that lack the resources to assign personnel to street-level enforcement units permanently, might be able to achieve similar results by making temporary assignments.

EMPIRICAL EVIDENCE

Unfortunately, few drug crackdowns have been the subjects of evaluation research; fewer still have been evaluated using research designs that provide a sound basis for inferences about impacts. Furthermore, research on drug crackdowns provides inconsistent results; on its face, the research suggests that crackdowns have worked in some cases but not in others.

Evaluations of drug crackdowns confront difficult problems in measuring outcome variables. The enumeration of drug offenses is even less reliable than that of other offenses. While efforts to measure the level of, say, auto thefts can rely to a large degree on reports by victims to the police, efforts to measure the level of drug offenses cannot draw on a comparably valid source of data. Neither can researchers make inferences about the level of drug offenses from the number of arrests for those offenses. Given the pervasiveness of drug offenses in many jurisdictions, and the fact that the principal police role in enforcement is one of discovery, it is not surprising to find that the number of arrests rises and falls with the level of enforcement activity, and not (necessarily) with the level of drug sales and consumption. As a result of these measurement problems, previous evaluations of drug enforcement rest, to some extent, on indicators of dubious merit, such as the street price of drugs or the demand for drug treatment.

It is technically feasible but costly to collect valid and reliable data about other conditions on which crackdowns may have an impact. Police records of reported crimes have well-known shortcomings (see Schneider & Wiersema, 1990; Skogan, 1975).[5] Victimization surveys can enumerate crimes that go unreported to police (Biderman & Reiss, 1967), but victimization surveys, which are not without shortcomings of their own, are expensive to conduct. So too are surveys about the quality of life, through which evaluations can measure perceptions of neighborhood problems, fear of crime, and self-protective behaviors. But in the absence of such survey data, evaluations must rely on much less systematic and reliable information (e.g., see Kleiman's [1988] assessments of the Lynn and Lawrence crackdowns).

Furthermore, when evaluations of drug crackdowns lack equivalent control groups, and when they examine only the immediately pre- and post-intervention levels of crime and other indicators, it is difficult to ascertain whether any changes that are observed are due either to the changes in enforcement activity or to some other circumstances. If the levels of drug and/or nondrug offenses in the vicinity of the crackdown decline, it might be as a result of, say, educational efforts, short-term fluctuations, or long-term trends. Extant evidence is open to alternative interpretations that either confirm or disconfirm the impact of drug crackdowns.

One interpretation to which virtually all evaluations of police crackdowns are open is that drug sales, crime, and other problems are merely displaced rather than deterred or solved. From the perspective of one jurisdiction or neighborhood, even a displacement effect is beneficial, of course; but from a broader perspective, a displacement effect alone offers no meaningful benefit. Unfortunately, discussions of displacement often cast the issue in either/or terms: Enforcement produces either a deterrent or a displacement effect. If drug enforcement displaces drug transactions, the displacement is probably partial rather than complete because even a temporary disruption of a drug market would prevent at least some drug offenses as the market relocates; in theory, the aggregate volume of sales and consumption would not remain constant (Caulkins, 1992; Kleiman & Smith, 1990, p. 89). The question is properly an empirical one, but because social scientists cannot tag drug sellers and buyers as biologists might tag birds or deer, a definitive answer could not be found even in the best empirical evidence. It is feasible to conduct analyses that are at least suggestive (see Caulkins, 1992), but most evaluations do not include such analyses.

The most encouraging evidence concerns a crackdown on street-level heroin dealing in Lynn, Massachusetts. The Lynn crackdown appears to have had all of the hypothesized impacts. First, casual observation and interviews with residents and merchants indicated that the volume of visible drug transactions decreased substantially. Second, interviews with treatment workers and with heroin addicts suggest that it became harder and riskier to buy heroin in Lynn; drug treatment centers experienced an 85% increase in the demand for treatment. Third, burglaries, robberies, and other crimes against persons all decreased—38%, 18.5%, and 66%, respectively—in the year after the crackdown began, and during the following year, burglaries remained at the lower level while robberies decreased further, down 30% compared with the base year. The absence of a control group, however, makes it difficult to attribute these outcomes to the crackdown: Some or even most of the decrease in street crime might have been observed in the absence of a crackdown.[6]

A later crackdown in Lawrence, Massachusetts, failed to produce the same results (Kleiman, 1988). Interviews with addicts indicated only a small reduction in the availability of heroin, and even though crimes against persons fell by 37% during the 28 months following the start of the crackdown, other crimes—burglary, larceny, and robbery—increased.

Similarly inconsistent results were reported for crackdowns in New York City. Operation Pressure Point, on the Lower East Side of Manhattan, reduced the amount of street dealing, increased the demand for drug treatment on the Lower East Side, and also appeared to reduce crime—robbery decreased 47%; burglary, 37%; grand larceny, 32%; and homicide, 62% (Kleiman, 1988, pp. 16-18; also see Zimmer, 1990, pp. 55-60). Furthermore, "the quality of life improved as citizens shopped at local stores, enjoyed neighborhood parks and playgrounds again and even took evening strolls" (Bocklet, 1987, p. 49). But according to a report in *The New York Times*, another crackdown in Harlem was largely unsuccessful in reducing street dealing, and it had little effect on crime (Sherman, 1990, p. 22).

An evaluation of Operation Clean-Sweep in Washington, D.C., reports mixed results (Reuter, Haaga, Murphey, & Praskac, 1988). This crackdown produced numerous arrests and, moreover, "good cases" that resulted in prosecution and conviction. It seems also to have reduced the number of street drug markets and to have enhanced the orderliness of some areas, although these conclusions must be qualified by the shortcomings of the indicators, as the authors acknowledge. These conclusions about neighborhood order are further qualified by the authors' speculation that intensified enforcement might have contributed to an increase in violence. An analysis of drug use failed to confirm the hypothesized decline, at least over the short term; in fact, drug use indicators rose after the crackdown began (Sherman, 1990, pp. 22-23).

An analysis of index crimes was inconclusive, owing partly to the lack of control groups.

Finally, crackdowns conducted by the Hartford (Connecticut) Police Department seem to have been no more than modestly effective in one targeted neighborhood and much more effective in another neighborhood (see Caulkins, Rich, & Larson, 1991). Both neighborhoods, Charter Oak Terrace and the Milner School area, were "considered major, open-air drug markets" (Caulkins et al., 1991, p. 5). The crackdowns commenced with 4 weeks of undercover work that produced 55 arrests, followed by intensive patrol by uniformed officers from the Crime Suppression Unit. Fewer arrests were made in Charter Oak Terrace (4.1 per month) than in the Milner School area (16.9 per month), and because the numbers of officer-hours spent in the neighborhoods were nearly equal, Caulkins et al. (p. 6) take this as an indicator of relative success in Charter Oak Terrace. This conclusion is also supported by retrospective surveys both of residents and of officers. After 5 months, more than 80% of the Charter Oak Terrace respondents, but only 30% to 40% of the Milner School area respondents, reported that there was less violent crime and fewer people selling drugs than there had been 3 months before. All of the 18 officers in Hartford's Crime Suppression Unit agreed that there was less drug dealing in Charter Oak Terrace and all but 2 believed that the neighborhood had become a more pleasant place to live; 12 of the officers reported that there was less drug dealing in the Milner School area, and only 3 believed that the neighborhood had become a more pleasant place to live. Once again, however, in the absence of control groups, the target areas can only be compared with each other.

Toward a Better Understanding of Police Crackdowns

It bears repeating that much of the empirical evidence about the effects of police drug crackdowns rests on studies with obvious and potentially serious methodological shortcomings. Our knowledge could be expanded enormously by executing more rigorous experiments or quasi-experiments, using control groups and systematic data on outcome variables. This is easy to say and difficult to do, of course, because such efforts require not only resources but also the unstinting cooperation of police departments in carrying out the crackdowns under controlled conditions.[7] Some of the most recent studies, including those reported in this book (see Sviridoff

& Hillsman and Uchida & Forst), have sought to overcome these difficulties, and their contributions are commensurate with the rigor of their designs.

The inconsistent findings produced by previous evaluations of drug crackdowns could be methodological artifacts, but there are sound theoretical reasons to expect that crackdowns will be more effective under some circumstances than they would be under others, and hence, that perhaps the research findings reflect the empirical reality. Consequently, future research on drug crackdowns could make still greater contributions by attending to these circumstances; some can be incorporated into the designs of individual studies, and information on others can be collected so that as findings accumulate, it might be possible to make inferences about the conditions under which crackdowns are more or less effective. These circumstances include characteristics of the neighborhoods that are the geographic targets of crackdowns, and characteristics of the crackdowns themselves. More attention should also be given to the administrative variables that may facilitate or impede the implementation of crackdowns.

CRACKDOWN TARGET AREAS

Police drug crackdowns are both offense-focused—enforcement activity is directed primarily or exclusively toward drug offenses—and geographically focused—enforcement is directed toward a targeted area. The sizes of crackdown target areas could vary from entire jurisdictions, in the cases of small municipalities, to police precincts or beats in larger cities, to still more narrowly defined areas of no more than several square blocks. Presumably, target areas are so designated by police departments partly on the basis of the severity of the drug-related problems therein; although for administrative convenience, the boundaries of target areas may coincide with those of beats or districts, thereby encompassing some smaller areas in which drug-related problems are less severe. The important points for evaluative research are, first, that if police crackdowns have impacts, those impacts are most likely to be felt (and detected) in those areas in which both drug transactions and enforcement activity are concentrated; and second, that the magnitude of the impacts may vary with the characteristics of the target areas.

Attention to the geographic focus of crackdowns usually takes the form of a discussion of drug markets. For example, Kleiman (1988) suggests that the impact of a crackdown is likely to depend on the size, concentration, and geographic isolation of the drug market: Small, concentrated, and isolated markets (like Lynn's) are more vulnerable to crackdowns than are larger, fragmented markets in proximity to other markets (like Lawrence's). Unfortunately, the term *drug market* is used rather loosely in the literature on drug enforcement, and market concepts have had far more value in developing theoretical propositions (e.g., Reuter & Kleiman, 1986) than in the empirical evaluation of drug crackdowns. To our knowledge, no one has even formulated a set of criteria on the basis of which boundaries could be drawn around an actual drug market.[8] For the present, however, it seems reasonable to suppose that any single drug market is larger in area than a single address and smaller than a major city (see the discussion in Bynum, Worden, & Frank, 1991).

For the purposes of evaluative research, it might be more useful to follow the lead provided by research on hot spots, locations in which illicit activity is concentrated or from which a disproportionate number of calls for police service originate (see Sherman, Gartin, & Buerger, 1989).[9] The sites of drug transactions are not randomly distributed across a jurisdiction, and thus it should be possible to identify drug hot spots as areas within which drug and drug-related problems are concentrated. A drug hot spot need not correspond to a single drug market. A single hot spot could encompass two or more markets, for example, one that caters to a local clientele and another that serves a more cosmopolitan clientele (suburbanites who drive in only to buy drugs), or one for heroin and one for crack. Furthermore, a drug hot spot need not correspond to the crackdown target area. If the target is, formally, an entire jurisdiction or even a single police precinct, the target area might encompass multiple drug hot spots. Evaluative research should seek to isolate one or more drug hot spots within crackdown target areas because crackdown impacts may be greatest in those hot spots.

A drug hot spot might be delineated on the basis of indicators of drug and drug-related problems: enforcement activity such as arrests and raids; citizen complaints about drug sales; reported levels of nondrug crimes such as larceny, robbery, and auto theft; and perceived levels of drug sales, violence, and disorder, as reported in surveys. No one of these indicators suffices by itself. Enforcement outputs are, of course, indicative of police activity as much as of drug activity; this is all the more true during a planned intervention. Citizen complaints are sometimes—perhaps, as many officers claim, often—inaccurate; a citizen might mistakenly believe that drugs are being sold out of a house down the block, or might phone in a fraudulent tip out of vengefulness or spite. Levels of nondrug crimes vary, spatially and chronologically, with many factors, of which retail drug outlets are but one (see Rengert & Wasilchick, 1990, pp. 64-94). Survey data suffer from one of the same problems from which citizen complaints suffer, namely, errors in perception. The best approach is to use multiple indicators, in the hopes that the strengths of some can compensate for the weaknesses of others.

Finally, if a drug hot spot is an area in which drug sales and related problems are concentrated, one must (implicitly or explicitly) establish a threshold above which the levels of these phenomena are such that the area is hot and not merely warm. There is no a priori basis for these judgments, and evaluations should test the sensitivity of the results to adjustments in the thresholds. Moreover, within any one jurisdiction the thresholds will be relative rather than absolute, and cross-jurisdictional comparisons of crackdown impacts should attend to these differences; a drug hot spot in Kansas City may seem no more than lukewarm in the context of New York or Miami.

Once we focus on drug hot spots, we can begin to empirically describe the characteristics of those areas and the conditions under which crackdowns are more or less effective. For example, the impacts of crackdowns are probably greater in those areas in which drugs are sold on the street than in areas in which transactions typically take place indoors (Kleiman & Smith, 1990, p. 85; also see Reuter et al., 1988, p. 32); drug transactions on the street are more vulnerable to enforcement action, and the disruption of such visible drug sales is more easily detected by residents. Most of the evaluated drug crackdowns have targeted open-air markets, so it remains to be seen whether crackdowns have comparable impacts when they target areas in which sales are made predominately at indoor locations.

Other characteristics of drug hot spots could condition the impact of a crackdown. For example, Caulkins et al. (1991) argue that the effectiveness of Hartford's crackdown in one neighborhood (Charter Oak Terrace) was enhanced by that area's well-defined physical boundaries (a river, a railroad track, and an interstate highway), which afforded limited access to the target area. Police could more easily observe those who entered the area, and they could establish more effective road blocks; patrons from outside the neighborhood were reluctant to drive in. Caulkins et al. further argue that these boundaries limited the opportunities for displacement to locations just outside the target area and highlighted the region of increased risk for both dealers and users. For another example, Zimmer (1990, p. 61) observes that New York City's Operation Pressure Point (OPP) was most successful in neighborhoods in which some gentrification preceded OPP. Zimmer (1990) attributes the disparate impacts to the makeup of the communities; in gentrifying neighborhoods, "a new group of people, themselves once intruders into a run-down, sparsely populated neighborhood, began to establish new standards of acceptable conduct and assist the police in enforcing them" (p. 63). Generally, one might expect that crackdowns would be more effective wherever enforcement action is complemented by community action.

CRACKDOWN CONTENT

Evaluative research must also recognize that crackdowns vary in their content, particularly in their tactics, their intensity, and their duration. Tactics are likely to vary with the methods of drug distribution and the nature and severity of drug-related problems (street crime, disorder), and perhaps with the skills and predilections of police. Some crackdowns consist of a uniformed police presence. Others rely largely on the use of observation-of-sale arrests and buy-bust tactics. Still others emphasize the execution of search warrants. Kleiman (1988, p. 18) offers the differences in police tactics as one explanation for the different results in Lynn and in Lawrence. The Lawrence crackdown, he points out, emphasized search warrants more and observation-sale arrests less than the Lynn crackdown. More generally, one could expect that different tactics have, by their nature, different impacts. A uniformed presence is as visible to law-abiding residents as it is to drug dealers and users, and thus it probably has a greater direct effect on the former than on the latter: It would reassure residents more than it would prompt dealers to take precautions. Undercover buy-bust tactics are more visible to drug dealers than to (other) residents, and thus probably affect the ease and hence the volume of drug transactions more than they affect residents' feelings of safety.

Another characteristic of a crackdown is its intensity, or the level of enforcement activity. Kleiman (1988, pp. 30-31) suggests that it may be necessary for a crackdown to exceed a "critical ratio" of officers to users and/or dealers in order to be effective. Furthermore, Sherman (1990) hypothesizes that the intensity of a crackdown affects both the extent to which offenders exaggerate the risk of apprehension and the duration of the residual deterrent effect. Intensity can be conceived and operational-ized in different terms: numbers of police personnel, levels of enforce-ment outputs (e.g., arrests, raids), or (in principle, at least) ratios of personnel or outputs to population, area, drug transactions, or points of drug sales. The appropriate conceptualization and operationalization will depend, of course, on the tactics: The intensity of a uniformed presence is better measured in terms of resources than in terms of outputs, but the intensity of a crackdown that emphasizes the execution of search warrants might be measured in terms of raids (i.e., an output). Each of these definitions has drawbacks, and no one of them will suffice for evaluation.

A third characteristic of crackdowns is duration. As Kleiman and Smith (1990, p. 89) point out, "The ideal focused crackdown strategy in a big city would move slowly from neighborhood to neighborhood. . . . " But for practice and for evaluation we must operationalize "slowly." Although theory predicts that "brief" crackdowns are more effective (and more efficient) than sustained crackdowns (Sherman, 1990), it does not specify the optimal duration of a crackdown; we can learn through empirical inference.

Where the jurisdiction is sufficiently large and the resources of the police department adequate, future evaluations of police drug crackdowns could seek to systematically vary the intensity and the duration of crackdowns. Treatment groups of target areas would receive a series of intermittent crackdowns of varying intensity and duration, while a control group would receive the normal level of enforcement effort.[10] Although for any one evaluation the number of treatment groups would be limited both by the number of potential target areas and by administrative practicality, such evaluations might tell us something about the intensity and duration that crackdowns must sustain in order to achieve a substantively significant impact, as well as the points at which greater intensity and longer duration begin to have diminishing marginal impacts.

IMPLEMENTATION

The intensity and duration of a crackdown depend not only on the intentions of police managers but also upon the extent to which the crackdown is actually implemented. Research on crackdowns has paid scant attention to the issue of implementation, even though a large literature makes it clear that policy directives are seldom translated readily into organizational action.[11] Sherman (1990, p. 10) observes that crackdowns suffer implementation "decay," which amounts to a decline in the intensity of enforcement: "Fewer arrests are made, fewer people are stopped, more officers are diverted to other duties, all of which could be planned by police commanders or just carried out by the lower ranks." At the limit, intensity may so diminish as implementation decays that the crackdown is effectively terminated.

But we should not presume that implementation decay is inevitable any more than we should presume full implementation. Crackdowns are delivered through organizational structures, and the degree of implementation probably depends upon organizational architecture. Although some impediments to full implementation are no doubt a fact of life in any organization, some administrative arrangements probably lend themselves more to successful implementation than others do. But previous research has seldom described in much detail the allocation of crackdown responsibilities, the competing goals and obligations of responsible actors, the structure of incentives, and the bases on which day-to-day enforcement decisions are made. These elements of process evaluation, accumulated across case studies of crackdowns, could form the basis for generalizations that link administrative structure to degrees of implementation, and for recommendations for administrative practice.

Future Research

Future evaluative research on police drug crackdowns should take advantage of the rich opportunities for theory-driven evaluation (Chen & Rossi, 1980). The theory that underlies police drug crackdowns (and street-level enforcement more generally) is fairly well developed. The empirical evidence is thin. Carefully designed and well-executed evaluations could yield valuable findings. If the theory is sound, then empirical validation would form the basis for strategic and tactical choices that enhance the effectiveness and efficiency of drug enforcement. If the theory requires modification, then the empirical results might highlight the weaknesses of the crackdown strategy and prompt further refinements in this enforcement technology. In either case, investments of evaluation resources promise substantial returns.

No one research design can be prescribed for evaluations of police drug crackdowns, which must be developed around the peculiarities of the jurisdiction and department under investigation and within available resources. The most comprehensive and powerful tests of the theory and practice of police drug crackdowns will require substantial amounts of resources, and the patient cooperation of police departments. Such evaluations would examine both processes—the enforcement activities of which crackdowns consist, and the organizational settings in which they occur—and outcomes, including immediate, intermediate, and ultimate outcomes.

Previous evaluations have paid scant attention to the most immediate of outcomes. The deterrent effect of any crackdown hinges on changes in offenders' perceptions of risk. Increases in police presence, raids, arrests, seizures, and the like, which are all part of the crackdown treatment, might be expected to increase the perceived risk of apprehension; this is the basis for an initial deterrent effect. The residual deterrent effect of a crackdown hinges on the ability of dealers and users to detect the withdrawal of police resources, that is, the backoff, and on the extent to which their perceptions of risk are affected by their uncertainty about subsequent crackdowns (Sherman, 1990). Hence we concur with Kleiman and Smith (1990, p. 103), who underscore the need to collect data that would drive "models of local drug sales activity as a function of local enforcement activity"; they call for "surveys, street ethnography, and the development of user, ex-user, and potential-user panels." Mieczkowski (1990) has employed surveys to learn more about drug distribution. Sviridoff and Hillsman (this volume) have used street ethnography to evaluate crackdown impacts. Such research can be incorporated into evaluations of police crackdowns to illuminate offenders' perceptions of risk as well as their behavioral responses to crackdowns.

Comprehensive and compelling evaluations of drug crackdowns would also examine the quality of life in targeted (and control) neighborhoods. Even if police efforts fail to reduce crime, they might reduce fear of crime and improve the quality of life (Police Foundation, 1981), and because the theory on which crackdowns rest suggests that the quality of life might be affected, the most comprehensive evaluations of police crackdowns will not fail to assess this proposition. Residential surveys are probably the best device for collecting systematic data on this outcome; in this, perhaps, one gets what one pays for.[12]

Less comprehensive and less costly evaluations, relying on process and outcome data that are readily available (or obtainable) through police or other sources, could nevertheless be well worthwhile, provided that due care is used in the interpretation of results (see, e.g., Campbell, 1969). For example, data on enforcement activity—for example, successful and unsuccessful attempts by informants and/or undercover officers to purchase drugs, and the quantities of drugs seized in raids—can provide clues about market adaptations to enforcement pressure—such as dealers refusing to sell to strangers, or keeping smaller amounts of drugs on hand. Crime levels in target and control areas can be measured, using officially recorded crime data, which are flawed, to be sure; but unlike victimization data, official data are available as a time series, in which crackdown impacts can be discriminated from short-term fluctuations and from long-term trends. Data on calls for service, and on calls to a police tipline, can also be used. Evaluations that exploit existing data need not be methodologically sloppy; if they are done carefully, they can make very substantial contributions to drug control policy.

Notes

1. Neither are crackdowns limited to enforcing against only one type of offense; as Sherman (1990) points out, a crackdown can instead focus principally on a geographic area, enforcing against a wide range of offenses in that area.

2. That theoretical treatments of crackdowns emphasize their general deterrent effects is not to deny that they might also have incapacitative effects. Kleiman (1988, p. 26) acknowledges, with reference to an apparently successful crackdown in Lynn, Massachusetts, that "given the extremely high crime rates characteristic of some heroin users, the incarceration of relatively small numbers of them might be responsible for substantial changes in crime rates in a city such as Lynn." But as Sherman (1990, p. 9) observes, "over short term periods with large enough numbers of offenders, it seems reasonably plausible for police to interpret a crime reduction as a deterrent effect."

3. An individual's fear of crime is affected not only by a crime of which the individual is a victim (i.e., a direct victimization), but also by crimes that the individual witnesses or about which the individual merely has some knowledge—"indirect" or "vicarious" victimizations; see, for example, Skogan and Maxfield (1981).

4. Wilson and Kelling's (1982) "Broken Windows" thesis holds that police actions that preserve or restore public order and that reduce fear of crime can, by reinforcing or reestablishing citizens' commitments to their neighborhoods, prevent or reverse neighborhood deterioration.

5. Moreover, these data do not permit researchers to distinguish drug-related offenses from other offenses in the same reporting category. One cannot, for example, disaggregate larcenies to enumerate only those committed in order to purchase drugs.

6. See Barnett (1988), whose analysis of a longer time period suggests that Kleiman's (1988) results may overstate the impact of the crackdown on street crime.

7. Even when police departments are willing to cooperate in this way, they can be overwhelmed by events beyond their control; see Uchida and Forst's account (this volume) of events in Birmingham.

8. One might seek to define a drug market on the basis of patterns of transactions among sellers and buyers, or on the basis of competition among sellers (e.g., sellers who do not compete with one another are not parts of the same market).

9. This is not to argue that we should abandon efforts to use market concepts in empirical research. More could be learned about market behavior by studying drug dealers and drug users through survey and ethnographic research, as we discuss below.

10. That is, the treatment would consist not of a single crackdown but a series of crackdowns/back-offs.

11. See, for example, Pressman and Wildavsky (1984) and Ripley and Franklin (1986). On problems peculiar to agencies such as police departments, see Prottas (1978).

For evaluative purposes, the implementation of a crackdown is equivalent to the implementation of the experimental treatment. But an analysis of the former directs attention to issues of administrative structure and managerial choices, while an analysis of the latter directs attention to issues of internal validity. Both types of analysis are important, to be sure, but we are concerned here with the former, because it has received too little attention in previous research on police crackdowns.

12. We would add that for this application of survey methodology, telephone interviews may be superior to—and less expensive than—face-to-face interviews. Both survey media will suffer non-response bias, but in the neighborhoods targeted for police crackdowns, the

proportions of households that lack phones may be no greater (and perhaps smaller) than the proportions unwilling to open their doors to strangers, especially strangers asking questions about drug dealing. The relative anonymity that phone interviews afford might produce higher response rates; it might also promote greater candor in discussing neighborhood problems.

References

Anglin, M. D., & Speckart, G. (1988). Narcotics use and crime: A multisample, multimethod analysis. *Criminology, 26*, 197-233.

Barnett, A. (1988). Drug crackdowns and crime rates: A comment on the Kleiman report. In M. R. Chaiken (Ed.), *Street-level drug enforcement: Examining the issues*. Washington, DC: U.S. Department of Justice, National Institute of Justice.

Biderman, A. D., & Reiss, A. J., Jr. (1967). On exploring the "dark figure" of crime. *Annals of the American Academy of Political and Social Science, 374*, 733-748.

Bocklet, R. (1987, February). Operation pressure point: Cleaning up a neighborhood. *Law and Order*, 48-52.

Boydstun, J. E. (1975). *San Diego field interrogation: Final report*. Washington, DC: Police Foundation.

Bynum, T. S., Worden, R. E., & Frank, J. (1991, November). *Hot spots of illicit drug sales: Implications for planning and evaluating enforcement programs*. Paper presented at the Annual Meeting of the American Society of Criminology, San Francisco.

Campbell, D. T. (1969). Reforms as experiments. *American Psychologist, 24*, 409-429.

Caulkins, J. P. (1992). Thinking about displacement in drug markets: Why observing change of venue isn't enough. *Journal of Drug Issues, 22*, 17-30.

Caulkins, J. P., Rich, T. F., & Larson, R. C. (1991). *Geography's impact on the success of focused local drug enforcement operations or "crackdowns."* Unpublished paper.

Chen, H.-T., & Rossi, P. H. (1980). The multi-goal, theory-driven approach to evaluation: A model linking basic and applied social science. *Social Forces, 59*, 106-122.

Cohen, L. E., & Felson, M. (1979). Social change and crime rate trends: A routine activity approach. *American Sociological Review, 44*, 588-608.

Eck, J. E., & Spelman, W. (1987). *Problem-solving*. Washington, DC: Police Executive Research Forum.

Hayeslip, D. W., Jr. (1989). Local-level drug enforcement: New strategies. *NIJ Reports, 213*, 2-6. Washington, DC: U.S. Department of Justice, National Institute of Justice.

Kleiman, M.A.R. (1988). Crackdowns: The effects of intensive enforcement on retail heroin dealing. In M. R. Chaiken (Ed.), *Street-level drug enforcement: Examining the issues*. Washington, DC: U.S. Department of Justice, National Institute of Justice.

Kleiman, M.A.R., & Smith, K. D. (1990). State and local drug enforcement: In search of a strategy. In M. Tonry & J. Q. Wilson (Eds.), *Drugs and crime: Vol. 13. Crime and justice: A review of research*. Chicago: University of Chicago Press.

Manning, P. K., & Redlinger, L. J. (1978). Invitational edges of corruption: Some consequences of narcotic law enforcement. In P. K. Manning & J. Van Maanen (Eds.), *Policing: A view from the street*. New York: Random House.

Mieczkowski, T. (1990). Crack distribution in Detroit. *Contemporary Drug Problems, 17*, 9-30.

Moore, M. H. (1973). Achieving discrimination on the effective price of heroin. *American Economic Review, 63*, 270-277.

Moore, M. H. (1977). *Buy and bust: The effective regulation of an illicit heroin market.* Lexington, MA: Lexington Books.

Nurco, D. N., Hanlon, T. E., Kinlock, T. W., & Duszynski, K. R. (1988). Differential criminal patterns of narcotic addicts over an addiction career. *Criminology, 26*, 407-423.

Police Foundation. (1981). *The Newark foot patrol experiment.* Washington, DC: Author.

Pressman, J. L., & Wildavsky, A. (1984). *Implementation* (3rd ed.). Berkeley: University of California Press.

Prottas, J. M. (1978). The power of the street-level bureaucrat in urban service bureaucracies. *Urban Affairs Quarterly, 13*, 285-312.

Rengert, G., & Wasilchick, J. (1990). *Space, time and crime: Ethnographic insights into residential burglary.* Unpublished final report submitted to the U.S. Department of Justice, National Institute of Justice.

Reuter, P., Haaga, J., Murphey, P., & Praskac, A. (1988). *Drug use and drug programs in the Washington metropolitan area.* Santa Monica, CA: RAND.

Reuter, P., & Kleiman, M.A.R. (1986). Risks and prices. In M. Tonry & N. Morris (Eds.), *Crime and justice: A review of research* (Vol. 7). Chicago: University of Chicago Press.

Ripley, R. B., & Franklin, G. R. (1986). *Policy implementation and bureaucracy* (2nd ed.). Chicago: Dorsey.

Schneider, V. W., & Wiersema, B. (1990). Limits and use of the uniform crime reports. In D. L. MacKenzie, P. J. Baunach, & R. Roberg (Eds.), *Measuring crime: Large-scale, long-range efforts.* Albany: State University of New York Press.

Sherman, L. W. (1990). Police crackdowns: Initial and residual deterrence. In M. Tonry & N. Morris (Eds.), *Crime and justice: A review of research* (Vol. 12). Chicago: University of Chicago Press.

Sherman, L. W., Gartin, P. R., & Buerger, M. E. (1989). Hot spots of predatory crime: Routine activities and the criminology of place. *Criminology, 27*, 27-55.

Skogan, W. G. (1975). Measurement problems in official and survey crime rates. *Journal of Criminal Justice, 3*, 17-32.

Skogan, W. G., & Maxfield, M. G. (1981). *Coping with crime: Individual and neighborhood reactions.* Beverly Hills, CA: Sage.

Skolnick, J. H. (1975). *Justice without trial: Law enforcement in democratic society* (2nd ed.). New York: John Wiley.

Skolnick, J. H., & Bayley, D. H. (1986). *The new blue line: Police innovation in six American cities.* New York: Free Press.

Sparrow, M. K., Moore, M. H., & Kennedy, D. M. (1990). *Beyond 911: A new era for policing.* New York: Basic Books.

Whitaker, G. P., Phillips, C. D., & Worden, A. P. (1984). Aggressive patrol: A search for side-effects. *Law and Policy, 6*, 339-360.

Wilson, J. Q., & Boland, B. (1978). The effect of the police on crime. *Law and Society Review, 12*, 367-390.

Wilson, J. Q., & Kelling, G. L. (1982, March). Broken windows: The police and neighborhood safety. *The Atlantic Monthly*, 29-38.

Zimmer, L. (1990). Proactive policing against street-level drug trafficking. *American Journal of Police, 9*, 43-74.

8. Assessing the Community Effects of Tactical Narcotics Teams

MICHELE SVIRIDOFF

SALLY T. HILLSMAN

In 1989 the Vera Institute of Justice began a quasi-experimental, multi-method study of the community-level effects of New York City's Tactical Narcotics Teams (TNT) in three Brooklyn precincts. TNT units provide short-term intensive street-level drug enforcement in designated target areas. The research included four components: a survey of residents; panel interviews with community leaders; process analysis of TNT implementation; and ethnographic analysis of effects on street-level drug markets. Preliminary analysis in the first target area showed some short-term impacts on the structure and intensity of street-level drug trafficking, but little effect on perceived quality of life or fear of crime.

Introduction

The litany of social ills associated with the urban crack epidemic of the late 1980s became one of the most pervasive media themes of the decade's end. Report after report focused on the emergence of visible, widespread street-level drug markets, drug-plagued neighborhoods, drug-related violence, shootings of children and other innocent bystanders, burgeoning rates of ancillary crime, drug-addicted mothers and babies, fear-ridden communities, and the general disorder associated with urban drug marketplaces.

AUTHORS' NOTE: This research was conducted with the support of the National Institute of Justice (Grant No. 89-IJ-CX-0056) and the New York City Police Department, neither of whom is responsible for the contents of this report. The authors wish to acknowledge the active collaboration in the data collection and analytic process of the following members of the Vera Institute of Justice research staff: Richard Curtis, Randolph Grinc, and Susan Sadd.

Although problems associated with the abuse of crack and other drugs in the inner city were widely reported, along with proposed solutions to those problems (law enforcement, public health, and/or community mobilization initiatives), there was somewhat less attention paid to questions about the efficacy of the various solutions. Law enforcement approaches in particular—the primary component of the war on drugs—were widely heralded and substantially funded at both the federal and local level. Throughout the nation, the arrest, prosecution, conviction, and incarceration of individuals arrested on drug-related charges commanded an increasingly large share of criminal justice resources, in response to the public demand that "something be done" about the drug problem.

Yet, within the criminal justice research and policy communities, debate has remained lively about the degree and type of impacts that various law enforcement approaches have on these problems. As the crack epidemic became more prominent, there was initial skepticism, rooted in empirical research, about the extent to which the dominant approaches of the 1970s and early 1980s—interdiction at the borders, drug eradication efforts in drug-producing countries, joint federal and local law enforcement efforts targeting "Mr. Big" at home—could affect the availability or price of drugs sold on the street, the amount of violence associated with local drug markets, or the quality of life in inner-city neighborhoods.

Increasingly, therefore, public policy attention in the late 1980s returned to the strategies of an earlier day, and law enforcement efforts focused once again on street-level crackdowns in highly visible, concentrated drug marketplaces (Kleiman, 1986; Mulgrav, 1985; Zimmer, 1990). Policymakers looked with growing interest on reported successes in Lynn, Massachusetts, and the Lower East Side of New York City (Operation Pressure Point) in designing new initiatives that attacked concentrated street-level heroin markets directly.

The advantages claimed for the "targeted crackdown" approach were several: increasing the nonfinancial costs of purchasing drugs (search time, hassles, and the like); reducing consumption among new drug users; reducing the ancillary crime that springs up in areas surrounding drug marketplaces; reducing perceived disorder and fear of crime in targeted neighborhoods; and improving relationships between the police and the community (see Worden, Bynum, & Frank, this volume).

Some reservations are voiced, however, about the appropriateness of the targeted drug crackdown approach in newer contexts, ones that differ significantly from the older, more concentrated heroin markets to which it was initially applied. Some theorists were skeptical about the potential of such efforts to have any effect on cocaine markets, which comprise a very large number of dealers and users of cocaine and crack—markets that were increasingly common in the late 1980s (Kleiman, 1986; Reuter & Kleiman, 1986). Indeed, knowledge is only now beginning to accumulate about how local markets for drugs other than heroin respond to enforcement efforts. Questions remain to be answered by research now ongoing and by future research about whether such marketplaces spring back up after enforcement efforts are relaxed, and if they do, how soon; whether drug selling and/or drug purchasing are readily displaced to existing, alternative marketplaces or to as-yet-undeveloped locations; whether new drug purchasers are deterred by visible enforcement, and if they are, whether local markets feel the effects of this; and whether community residents and local police can work together over time to maintain the gains achieved by the focused crackdown.

In addition, to the extent that recent focused drug crackdowns represent a conscious effort to win back the streets for specific communities, their structure and goals are outgrowths of the emerging philosophies behind both community-oriented policing (Kelling & Moore, 1988; McElroy, Cosgrove, & Sadd, 1990; Moore & Kelling, 1983; Police Foundation, 1981; Trojanowicz, 1983) and problem-oriented policing (Eck & Spelman, 1987; Goldstein, 1979; Spelman & Eck, 1987). In their goals and expectations, these crackdown initiatives share with community policing the belief that by reducing the level of fear and disorder in the community, the cycle of escalating disorder and criminality might be reversed (Skogan, 1986, 1990; Wilson & Kelling, 1982). In operational structure, these newer crackdown approaches attempt to draw upon partnerships with community residents and leaders (e.g., "drugbuster" hotlines) and with various public and private agencies.

There is also, however, some skepticism about the ability of the drug crackdown to have a broader community impact. Although there is some evidence that efforts of this type can reduce the levels of fear within a community (Pate, Wycoff, Skogan, & Sherman, 1986; Police Foundation, 1981; Trojanowicz, 1983), there is little evidence as yet that such efforts reverse the cycle of decline (Reiss, 1983).

Research on New York City's Tactical Narcotics Teams

TNT AS A STRATEGIC RESEARCH SITE

The development and expansion of Tactical Narcotics Teams (TNT) by the New York City Police Department provided a unique opportunity to examine the street-level effects of relatively short-term but intensive narcotics enforcement on crack cocaine markets and the urban neighborhoods in which they are most prevalent. TNT represents one of the most fully elaborated drug crackdown strategies in the country. Designed to provide a short-term concentrated overlay of street-level drug enforcement in a narrowly defined target area, TNT supplements existing narcotics operations with intensive buy-and-bust activity, focusing primarily on crack sales, but also addressing powdered cocaine and heroin trafficking. TNT operations are targeted primarily at street sellers, although some enforcement efforts have focused on interior drug sales operations as well (vacant city-owned buildings, taken over by drug dealers; the lobbies and hallways of apartment buildings; and so on).

Although TNT relies heavily on the tactics of rapid buy-and-bust to generate arrests, the initiative also draws upon the tools of problem-solving policing and community policing to address both quality of life and drug conditions. TNT has developed cooperative arrangements with a wide range of city, state, and federal agencies whose cooperation is needed to enhance drug enforcement and to address the quality-of-life problems that so often arise when neighborhoods are taken over by active drug markets.

There are currently seven TNTs (one in each of New York City's police patrol boroughs). They stay in a designated target area for approximately 90 days at a time (i.e., roughly four areas per team per year). In 1990 TNTs produced more than 24,000 narcotics arrests citywide; nearly two-thirds of those arrests were felonies.[1]

A Quasi-Experimental Multimethod Approach. Support from the National Institute of Justice, from the New York City Police Department itself, and from private foundations has provided the Vera Institute of Justice with a unique opportunity to study the community-level effects of TNT with a comprehensive design. The Vera research, begun in the fall of 1989, employs a quasi-experimental multimethod design, focusing on two relatively small TNT target areas and a comparison area (designated as a future TNT site), located in contiguous neighborhoods in Brooklyn. In addition to multiple-wave surveys of randomly selected households in the community, and analyses of statistical record data, the research employs a variety of qualitative techniques (in-depth panel interviews with community leaders and residents; operational analysis of TNT itself; and ethnographic interviews with drug users and sellers) to supplement information on community effects and to provide detailed information on the police intervention and its impact on local drug markets.

The research on TNT offers an opportunity to explore whether TNT can effectively reduce disorderly conditions related to drug trafficking in target areas, and if it can, whether there is a concomitant reduction among community residents in fear of crime. It is designed to provide information about perceived community conditions before, during, and after the implementation of TNT, the nature of the TNT intervention, the responses of community leaders to TNT, impacts on drug markets (including perceived displacement effects and effects on search time), impacts on ancillary property crime, the duration of impacts, and the court processing outcomes of TNT cases.

Within a quasi-experimental design, the multimethod approach has many advantages for this type of research. For example, conducting personal interviews with people representing different neighborhood groups helps bolster findings based on the household survey. This proved valuable because the rate of response to the survey during baseline interviews was disappointing (ranging from 13% to 27% in the three study areas; response rates were substantially higher in subsequent waves). The ethnographic component of the research, conducted by a seasoned research team, all of whom already had some connections with street-level users and dealers in the study neighborhoods, proved to be unusually fertile. Ethnographers carried out a substantial number of interviews with street-level traffickers and users in the first target area ($N = 59$) on subjects difficult to study, including the structure of local drug markets, responses to the threat of TNT, and displacement. Taken as a whole, the components of the research will ultimately permit an assessment of the community-level effects of TNT, reflecting a wide range of community voices—street people, ordinary residents, neighborhood leaders, local politicians, local precinct personnel, and TNT officers who participated in the initiative itself.

The Study Neighborhoods. The three research sites are relatively small concentrations of hot spots within the projected TNT target areas.[2] Because the experimental and comparison research areas were selected by asking the NYPD to define the three most likely TNT target areas in the Brooklyn South patrol borough (and to identify the hot spots of drug activity within those areas), it was important to determine whether and how they differed. At the start of the research, analysis of official data indicated substantial similarities among the study areas in terms of demographic composition, income levels, and drug and crime conditions. Police and ethnographic data indicated that all three study areas included active street-level crack markets. The three precincts within which the study areas are found were all characterized by a relatively high volume of crimes against the person, in marked contrast to other precincts in Brooklyn South.

In baseline research interviews, the large majority of community residents in all three areas reported that local drug trafficking was a "big problem."[3] Although baseline interviews with community residents pointed to significantly higher levels of fear and dissatisfaction among residents in the first experimental area, compared with the other study areas, these differences were relatively small. It is important to note, however, that although scales measuring physical deterioration, social disorder, and fear of personal victimization pointed to citizen concerns about quality of life, such problems in all three areas were not, on average, perceived as "big" problems. Levels of fear and disorder in the study neighborhoods were in the moderate range, a finding that reflects the TNT focus on reclaimable neighborhoods.

THE STATUS OF THE RESEARCH
AND PRELIMINARY FINDINGS

The collection of data in the three research precincts, begun in November 1990, is complete. Analyses of baseline community resident interviews, conducted before TNT entered any of the study precincts, have been conducted. A preliminary assessment of the impact of TNT on the community in the first experimental precinct has been carried out for all research components, except the survey of community residents: the analysis of TNT operations, ethnographic study of local drug sellers and consumers, and panel interviews with community residents and leaders. Research staff are currently analyzing the influence of TNT in the second experimental precinct and systematically comparing all the data from both experimental areas with the data from the comparison area. Analysis of the impact of TNT on ancillary crime in the study precincts and analysis of the criminal justice outcomes of TNT arrests are ongoing. Nevertheless, even at this preliminary stage in the analysis, some clear patterns, based primarily upon the first study area, are emerging.

TNT Activity. The TNT enforcement effort is sustained and intensive. In the first target area in 90 days, TNT officers made more than 1,000 arrests. Approximately half of these arrests involved felony-level drug sales, generally of crack. In addition, TNT personnel confiscated 70 vehicles from individuals who had driven to the neighborhood to buy drugs.[4] Both the ethnographic data and interviews with TNT officers pointed to a variety of responses to the implementation of TNT in the first experimental area. Police officers and traffickers both reported that street dealers quickly became aware of TNT's presence and learned to recognize the back-up teams that surrounded locations where undercover officers were operating. One officer, for example, reported that he was fairly sure that dealers recognized the unmarked cars investigators rode in, adding that if they were unable to do so in the beginning of the enforcement effort, "in a little while they definitely will. In the —th precinct it was the same as riding in a blue-and-white." Nevertheless, analysis reveals that TNT officers continued to make an undiminished number of arrests on charges of felony narcotics sales throughout the 90-day enforcement period.

Yet the TNT effort in the first study area appears to have been less intensive than other TNTs with respect to stimulating interagency enforcement initiatives. Although TNT has given rise to enhanced enforcement activity in other target areas by a variety of agencies with regulatory powers (e.g., the Department of Buildings, the Taxi and Limousine Commission, the Department of Consumer Affairs), there were comparatively few interagency enforcement initiatives directed at specific drug locations in the first target area studied. There appear to be structural reasons for this, arising out of the nature of the community rather than the implementation of TNT. This area contains few city-owned buildings. In other TNT target areas, where there were substantially more city-owned buildings, TNT worked actively with the New York City Department of Housing Preservation (HPD—the agency that manages city-owned property) and other city agencies in an effort to shut down active indoor drug locations. Yet even in these areas, the volume of interagency enforcement activities is relatively small, compared with the very high volume of street-level arrests of traffickers by TNT. In short, TNT appears to have implemented the street-level narcotics enforcement component of this initiative more fully than the longer term, problem-solving component.

Market Effects. A substantial number of street traffickers were arrested during the first few days of TNT operations, but ethnographic data indicates that they were quickly replaced by other street-level user-dealers. But this is not the whole story. Over the course of the TNT enforcement period, street dealers adapted to the intensive enforcement activity in a variety of ways, some of which directly affected the community: by moving selling locations indoors, by shifting selling hours to times when it was believed that TNT might not be operating, by devising schemes to reduce hand-to-hand exchanges, by moving out of the selling location after a sale, by using observers adept at spotting TNT vehicles, and by reducing the volume of outdoor sales for the duration of the intervention. As one dealer put it:

> One way to protect yourself is to just keep people from seeing you . . . just keep inside all the time. You got somebody outside, just lookin' out for you, tellin' the customers where you are. That's what most people are doin' now because they know that the cops are [around] . . . so nobody ain't doing no business outside. It's very hard now for the police to see who's dealing.

There was general agreement on some of the effects of TNT in this first target area in the qualitative data collected from street-level respondents, from TNT officers, from local precinct personnel, and from ethnographic observers. All the data indicate that TNT was able to virtually shut down street-level dealing on one block in the first research study area; this suggests the possibility that other such areas exist within the larger TNT target zone not studied by this research. However, data from the control area reveal similar locations that experienced a decline in drug trafficking during this period without the intervention of TNT, suggesting that broader market processes were at work alongside the effects of law enforcement. It appears likely, therefore, that TNT enhanced a process that was already under way and probably influenced where it happened most intensively. This conclusion is supported further by data that indicate that there were also specific locations within the first research area that experienced concentrated growth of drug activity in specific locations following the TNT intervention; this concentrated growth in specific locations was also found within both the second experimental area and the control area.

The data also indicate that, overall, drug trafficking became less blatant and less visible on the streets of the first experimental area than it had before the TNT enforcement period. Yet some movement of drug trafficking off the streets was evident in the control area as well. In the first two experimental areas, TNT appeared to be most effective in reducing the visibility of street markets in areas that were geographically separate from highly concentrated drug markets, and in areas that catered to purchasers from outside the neighborhood. TNT appeared to be less effective in areas that catered to recognized local purchasers, and in areas that provided ecological protection to traffickers (e.g., the courtyard of a self-contained apartment complex with a single entryway).

The data also support the general conclusion that this reduction in the blatant visibility of street drug markets was not the result of large-scale geographic displacement either within or outside the TNT target area. Although there were some small geographic shifts in the drug market (including the intensification of activity in some areas) and some temporal shifts, displacement was substantial only in the movement of drug activity from the street to indoor locations in the same geographic areas.

In addition, both ethnographic data and quantitative analysis of the time spent by TNT units before making a successful undercover drug purchase point to an increase in search time (the amount of time it takes to find a dealer and buy drugs) over the course of the enforcement period in this first study area. Ethnographic data also suggest, however, that the increased difficulty of finding drugs among established users was associated with more erratic consumption patterns—an increase in drug binges—rather than a reduction in their overall consumption. Although occasional users (known locally as "weekend warriors") and buyers from outside the neighborhood may have reduced consumption because of increased difficulty in finding distributors, ethnographic data reveal that daily crack users consumed at least as much, and possibly more, crack. For daily users, patterns of use during the enforcement period became characterized by episodes of binging, perhaps in response both to increased consumption taking place indoors and to occasional periods of enforced abstinence in response to law enforcement activity.

Some observed changes in drug market activity were evident in the comparison area as well as in the experimental area and, therefore, do not appear to be direct effects of the TNT intervention. Both ethnographic data and quantitative analysis of the cost of crack per unit of weight point to an increase in the cost of crack during the enforcement period.[5] A comparable wholesale price increase was widely reported both locally and nationally during the same period, although newspaper accounts suggested that higher prices for large quantities might not filter down to small-scale street markets. The TNT research reveals that there was indeed some filtering down of price increases. Although the unit cost of a vial of crack remained unchanged, the quantity of crack in those vials was reduced.

The ethnographic team found another characteristic of local drug markets to be common to both experimental and comparison areas. In developing an extensive network of contacts among street-level users and dealers, ethnographers came in contact with few new crack users during the year in which they actively observed the study areas. Most respondents had been using crack for at least 2 years. There appeared to be few new entrants into these markets and little evidence of recent crack consumption patterns among local teenagers. The ethnographic team believes these findings are related to a citywide leveling off in the demand for crack, even within inner-city markets. Therefore, it is difficult to distinguish any impact on overall demand, which may have been associated specifically with the TNT enforcement effort, from broader patterns of demand reduction that extended beyond the experimental area.[6] Although the period of TNT enforcement was associated with a variety of changes in drug market operations and structure, there was a strong perception among research respondents of all types (traffickers, police, community residents) that these market adaptations were temporary and that street-level drug trafficking would resume in full force once TNT was gone.[7] Subsequent interviews and ethnographic observations suggest that overall volume did not decline in the study area as a whole, and that a substantial volume of drug trafficking did return to some areas after the departure of TNT, although the specific locus of trafficking (particular street locations, shifts to indoors) and its intensity (concentrated growth in some areas, declines in others) appear to have changed. The data indicate that, even during the peak of the enforcement period, the overall level of drug trafficking remained steady throughout most of the target area, although patterns of trafficking did change to adapt to TNT's activities.

Community Effects. Although TNT's focus on street-level markets is designed to improve the quality of life in target neighborhoods, the adaptations of the drug market to this enforcement activity had both positive and negative effects on the community. Although some street locations improved, others did not. In a number of settings, a movement indoors reduced the volume of visible street drug traffic; yet, for some residents, this movement off the street brought drug conditions even closer to home. For different members of the community, therefore, the disruption of street-level drug markets appears to have had a different influence on quality of life; the degree of these impacts, however, whether positive or negative, is not as yet clear.

Because analysis of the survey of households in the target area during and after the TNT intervention is not complete, the research is not yet able to assess the broader impact of TNT on community perceptions and attitudes (e.g., fear of crime, perceptions of disorder, attitudes toward the police). Yet some information on these issues is available from in-depth panel interviews with community leaders and knowledgeable residents.[8] It should be recognized, however, that the awareness of TNT among such members of the community may differ from that of more typical, less involved community residents who are less familiar with public officials and local policy issues.

Community leaders in the first experimental area were generally aware of TNT's presence in the neighborhood, although they did not know very much about its structure or operations. As in the baseline household survey, they generally defined drug trafficking and addiction as the most important problems in the community. Those who knew about the police intervention generally believed TNT had a positive effect on the level of drug trafficking in the area and some influence on levels of public disorder.

Nonetheless, these respondents had reservations about the strength of this effect. They generally believed that local drug trafficking and substance abuse were structural problems that could better be addressed by educational and job opportunities than by police action; yet they were also anxious to ensure continued high levels of police attention, as a symbol of public disapproval and political commitment to the area. Still, TNT does not appear to have had an impact on this group's perceptions of personal safety or on their patterns of behavior (use of public amenities, using the streets at night, and so on). As one respondent put it:

> I haven't noticed any changes in the way people behave at all in the last 3 months. I didn't go out after dark before TNT got here and I don't plan to now either. The same people who always went out at night still do, but that's it. Most people won't do that.

There is also no evidence that the TNT initiative, in itself, encouraged the emergence of new grass-roots or community-based anti-drug efforts. Community leaders in this first research site generally attributed the lack of community-level response to the TNT intervention to the nature of the community itself. They characterized their area, in which a wide variety of recent immigrant groups (including Haitians, Jamaicans, Trinidadians) live in proximity to longer-term African-American residents, as marked by a general lack of solidarity and community organization, and by the presence of racial, ethnic, and economic conflict. Perhaps because of this fragmentation, these leaders were critical of what they perceived as insufficient outreach by TNT personnel to the neighborhood and community groups that do exist in the area.[9]

Community leaders in the first research area were generally skeptical about the possibility that even an improved TNT might have any long-term influence on drug markets or quality of life in their community. They saw the intervention as too short to accomplish these goals. They also voiced skepticism (echoed by police officers and even street-level respondents) about the ability of the criminal justice system to respond with sufficient severity to individuals arrested by TNT:

Most of the cops do their job. They take the dealers in and they do their paperwork and then turn them over to the prosecutors and judges and say, "It's up to you." They don't have enough lawyers and judges to handle this stuff and they don't have enough jail space to keep them all in. So what do they do? They turn them loose too quick.[10]

Nevertheless, community leaders generally supported the goals, tactics, and presence of TNT and welcomed the official recognition that "something must be done" about drug conditions in their community.

REMAINING QUESTIONS

One of the questions emerging from the research concerns which of the many segments that compose the target community are reached by law enforcement interventions of this type. Drug traffickers and users generally knew about the tactics and methods of TNT; many were arrested by it, often to be replaced by new (possibly less stable) entrants to the marketplace; others persisted in trafficking, without being arrested, by adapting their practices to the risks posed by TNT. Community leaders, particularly those who were most in contact with political officials, were also generally aware of TNT; yet most had limited knowledge of its goals and tactics, and few had seen it in action. The research awaits further analysis of the general survey of households to determine whether this level of awareness filters down to those who have less knowledge about official responses to community conditions, but who are an important audience for police efforts designed to affect the quality of life and levels of fear in a particular neighborhood.

Preliminary analysis of data from Vera's research on TNT suggests that the multimethod approach permits the perceptions of various groups to be matched against the perceptions of other groups within the relevant target community. The perspectives of various respondent groups differed; occasionally, similarities were striking and unexpected. For example, both community leaders and street-level respondents expressed a preference for a more community-oriented style of policing, in contrast to the enforcement-heavy TNT approach; not surprisingly, however, this community preference was not shared by TNT officers. There was, however, substantial agreement among street-level traffickers and police respondents about specific locations that were more or less resistant to TNT and about the nature and longevity of TNT's effect on local drug markets.

Future analyses will provide more information on the effects of TNT on ancillary crime, displacement effects, and the criminal justice outcomes of TNT arrests. Whatever these final analyses reveal, the general findings of the research on TNT must be understood in the context of recent local and national events. During the period in which the research was conducted, a number of incidents in New York City—"mushroom" shootings of innocent bystanders in the summer of 1990, the nationally publicized burning of a 14-year-old boy by a local bully because he refused to smoke crack[11]—affected levels of fear, community perceptions of disorder, and consciousness of risks to personal safety citywide.

Other events complicate the analysis in other ways: The implementation of an intensive, high-visibility foot patrol initiative in the second experimental area (Operation Takeback) during the summer of 1990—shortly after TNT left that area—brought both TNT officers and foot patrol officers back to the community. Thus during a period in which, according to the research design, there should have been a reduction in police presence, there was in fact a marked increase in enforcement activity. This variation in the implementation of the TNT initiative must be considered in the final analysis of research findings.

In addition, the analysis of the effect of TNT on neighborhood-based drug markets must take into account a widely reported national and local leveling off in the intensity of the crack epidemic during the research period. Without reference to the comparison area, it would be difficult to determine whether any apparent drying up of drug markets resulted from the enforcement initiative, or from the natural history of drug epidemics. Yet even at this preliminary stage, the advantages of the quasi-experimental design and the multimethod approach as a means of assessing the community-level effects of targeted street-level drug enforcement are evident.

Notes

1. Although the TNT strategy produces a large number of arrests, it differs from the traditional sweep strategy in several respects. It does not depend on a large, highly visible uniform presence, but relies upon a strategy of undercover purchases. The buy-and-bust strategy typically produces better quality (i.e., "convictable") arrests than the traditional sweep.

2. Because each study area is substantially smaller than the precinct (ranging from roughly one-third to roughly one-sixth of the precinct area), the study areas are not coterminous with geographical units for which relevant data are routinely maintained. Yet the sub-area strategy is appropriate to the TNT intervention, which focuses on specific hot

spots within a defined target area (itself a sub-area within a selected precinct). A community impact study would run the risk of failing to detect any effect of the intervention if the study area were too large; intervention effects can easily be diluted if the research is not narrowly focused on the area in which the intervention is concentrated.

3. To facilitate cross-site comparisons, the resident survey employed scales of demonstrated reliability that were developed by Pate and Skogan (1985) for the Police Foundation study of community policing and fear reduction in Newark and Houston.

4. The volume of enforcement activity in this research area was comparable to that of TNT units in other patrol boroughs, although a somewhat smaller proportion of TNT arrests in the research target area involved felony charges than in other target areas. The frequency of misdemeanor possession charges in this area may reflect the presence of a substantial marijuana market in this heavily Caribbean neighborhood.

5. Research staff collected data on the cost of drugs purchased by TNT and on the weight of those drugs, as measured by the police department lab. The data maintained by TNT on the weight and price of drug purchases constitute a unique database. Analysis of these data on a citywide basis would permit an assessment of local variation in price structure for small drug purchases of comparable type and weight, as well as variation in price over time across sites. According to media accounts and personal communications, there is growing ethnographic evidence of increased prices, although there is no parallel evidence that supplies declined.

6. Over the past year, media accounts have reported reductions in crack consumption both citywide and nationwide. It is difficult to determine the role played by any specific enforcement intervention, or increased enforcement generally, in these trends; clearly, multiple factors are at work, including the frequently observed cyclical nature of drug epidemics.

7. This belief was prevalent in spite of the fact that the TNT initiative is designed to return on a regular basis to target areas on specified maintenance days after the initial enforcement period has ended. In fact, in the first target area, this maintenance effort proved to be unusually intensive.

8. Panel interviews were conducted with leaders of block and building associations, local business people, church leaders, members of local community boards, and members of local police-community councils. In addition, a few panel interviews were conducted with informed residents who had few official links with community organizations, but were unusually knowledgeable about local issues and conditions.

9. Outreach between TNT staff and community groups was, in large measure, limited to formal presentations at scheduled community meetings at the beginning, middle, and end of the intervention in a given target area, although there were occasional interactions between TNT leaders and political figures in some areas. Respondents who represented smaller neighborhood groups expressed a preference for the more interactive collaboration afforded by New York City's Community Patrol Officer Program, in which officers trained in problem-solving methods patrol a regular beat.

10. Analyses, now under way, of an initial cohort of TNT arrests from the first experimental area will shed more light on this issue. Preliminary results suggest harsher outcomes for more TNT arrestees than their comments might suggest; however, the level of this impact—regardless of its severity—may not be observable to citizens, even those engaged in the drug traffic. Indeed, the continuity of drug market activity in general in the first TNT target area, as well as the continuous replacement of sellers, may mask the criminal justice outcomes of TNT arrests.

11. This incident took place in the first experimental precinct.

References

Eck, J. E., & Spelman, W. (1987). *Problem solving: Problem-oriented policing in Newport News*. Washington, DC: U.S. Department of Justice, National Institute of Justice.

Goldstein, H. (1979, April). Improving policing: A problem-oriented approach. *Crime and Delinquency, 25*(2), 236-258.

Kelling, G. L. & Moore, M. (1988, November). *The evolving strategy of policing: Perspectives on policing*. Washington, DC: U.S. Department of Justice, National Institute of Justice, and Harvard University, the John F. Kennedy School of Government.

Kleiman, M.A.R. (1986). *Bringing back street level heroin enforcement*. Program in Criminal Justice Policy and Management. Cambridge, MA: Harvard University, the John F. Kennedy School of Government.

Kleiman, M.A.R., & Smith, K. (1990). State and local drug enforcement: In search of a strategy. In M. Tonry & N. Morris (Eds.), *Crime and justice: An annual review of research* (Vol. 12, pp. 69-108). Chicago: University of Chicago Press.

McElroy, J., Cosgrove, C., & Sadd, S. (1990). *CPOP: The research—An evaluative study of the New York City community patrol officer program*. New York: Vera Institute of Justice.

Moore, M. H., & Kelling, G. L. (1983, Winter). To serve and protect: Learning from police history. *The Public Interest, 7*.

Mulgrav, J. (1985). *Operation pressure point: A community perspective* (Mimeo). New York: New York City Police Department.

Pate, A. M., & Skogan, W. G. (1985). *Coordinated community policing: The Newark experience. Technical report*. Washington DC: Police Foundation.

Pate, A. M., Wycoff, M. A., Skogan, W. G., & Sherman, L. (1986). *Reducing fear of crime in Houston and Newark*. Washington, DC: Police Foundation.

Police Foundation. (1981). *The Newark foot patrol experiment*. Washington, DC: Author.

Reiss, A. (1983, September/October). Crime control and the quality of life. *American Behavioral Scientist, 27*(1), 43-58.

Reuter, P., & Kleiman, M.A.R. (1986). Risks and prices: An economic analysis of drug enforcement. In M. Tonry & N. Morris (Eds.), *Crime and justice: An annual review of research* (Vol. 7). Chicago: University of Chicago Press.

Rosenbaum, D. P. (1988, September). Community crime prevention: A review and synthesis of the literature. *Justice Quarterly, 5*(3), 323-395.

Sherman, L. W. (1990). Police crackdowns: Initial and residual deterrence. In M. Tonry & N. Morris (Eds.), *Crime and justice: An annual review of research* (Vol. 12, pp. 1-48). Chicago: University of Chicago Press.

Skogan, W. (1986). Fear of crime and neighborhood change. In A. J. Reiss, Jr., & M. Tonry (Eds.), *Crime and justice: An annual review of research* (Vol. 8). Chicago: University of Chicago Press.

Skogan, W. (1990). *Disorder and decline*. New York: Free Press.

Spelman, W., & Eck, J. E. (1987, January). Problem-oriented policing. *Perspectives in policing*. Washington, DC: U.S. Department of Justice, National Institute of Justice, and Harvard University, the John F. Kennedy School of Government.

Trojanowicz, R. (1983). *An evaluation of the neighborhood foot patrol program in Flint, Michigan*. East Lansing: Michigan State University.

Wilson, J. Q., & Kelling, G. L. (1982, March). Police and neighborhood safety: Broken windows. *The Atlantic Monthly*, 29-38.

Zimmer, L. (1990). Proactive policing against street-level drug trafficking. *American Journal of Police, 11*(1), 43-74.

9. Drugs and Public Housing:
Toward an Effective Police Response

WESLEY G. SKOGAN

SAMPSON O. ANNAN

Introduction

Drug problems take on an added dimension in the special environment created by public housing. The 3.5 million people who live in public housing across the country are generally old or poor. Although local income requirements vary, to qualify for public housing most non-elderly public housing residents usually must be single, unemployed, and have children. In reality, this means that in the vast majority of cases the family is headed by a female and, in many cities, the families are disproportionately racial and cultural minorities.

Residents of pubic housing are highly vulnerable to crime. During the late 1950s and early 1960s, the Department of Housing and Urban Development (DHUD) permitted the construction of high-rise housing developments, and few were constructed with security in mind. They were often built in neighborhoods that were poor to start with and already had high crime rates. The problems this generated quickly became apparent, and by the 1980s most public housing units were in low-rise buildings of fewer than 5 stories. Only 7% of family public housing complexes are now composed of high-rise buildings (Bratt, 1986). Generally, high-

AUTHORS' NOTE: Prepared under Grant No. 89-DD-CX-0054 from the National Institute of Justice, Office of Justice Programs, U.S. Department of Justice. Points of view or opinions in this document are those of the authors and do not necessarily represent the official position of the U.S. Department of Justice.

129

rise public housing is reserved for the elderly and other special populations. Nationwide, slightly more than half of public housing developments are low-density, with fewer than 200 units. However, like high-rise
developments, these developments were constructed with multiple access
points that made it difficult to restrict unwanted visitors, and they remain
concentrated in inner cities.

Crime rates in public housing developments are often high, and their
community is difficult for residents to defend, especially on their own.
Too many developments are plagued by drug trafficking, violent and
property crime, and social disorder. This is frequently coupled with
distrust of the police and other public officials, including the local Public
Housing Authorities (PHAs) that manage the developments. Residents
often lack the capacity to defend themselves, be it against predators,
gangs looking for revenge, or drug dealers engaged in turf wars or
intimidation. Government, in the form of the local PHA, is the landlord,
and public housing is thus an arena in which it has a particular responsibility for order maintenance and crime control. It must use its powers to
ensure the health and safety of the residents.

What We Know

A number of studies have been conducted to help policymakers respond
to the perception that public housing developments are centers for especially
intense drug-related criminal activities. One study conducted by the RAND
Corporation (Dunworth & Saiger, 1992) identified drug problems and the
characteristics associated with different types of anti-drug initiatives in
public housing. The study focused on five sites: Los Angeles; Philadelphia;
Washington, D.C.; Phoenix; and Lexington, Kentucky.

A variety of drug control initiatives are under way in each of the five
cities. For example, Phoenix has implemented a walking beat program;
Los Angeles has conducted undercover investigations, social service
programs, passive security measures, and police sweeps. Records of
arrests and crimes over a 3-year period have been made available by each
of the cities in the study.

Preliminary findings from this study suggest that rates of both drug
and nondrug crime are considerably higher in public housing than in other
areas. In addition, the study suggests that there are variations between
the types of crimes occurring in public housing developments. Some
projects may have high rates of violent crime but low rates of drug crime,
or the reverse; the variation even between adjacent projects is noticeable

for violent crime. Two other evaluations, one involving problem-oriented policing in Philadelphia (Weisel, 1990), and the other community policing in a public housing neighborhood in Birmingham, Alabama, have examined methods of reducing crime in public housing (Uchida, Forst, & Annan, 1992). In the evaluation conducted in Philadelphia by the Police Executive Research Forum (PERF), the police initiated cleanup programs to tow abandoned cars and board up empty buildings, both of which served as drug trafficking locations; they launched two Narcotics Anonymous treatment programs for public housing residents; and they established Drug Free Zones around schools serving the targeted public housing development. Philadelphia has expanded this problem-solving approach to new neighborhoods (Weisel, 1990).

In Birmingham, an apartment was turned into a police mini-station after 11 shootings were recorded in an area during a 14-day period. The mini-station was established in one of the apartments within a local housing development, fortified by heavy wire mesh and a front door protected by iron bars. In a study of this effort, researchers found that residents perceived their neighborhood as a significantly improved place to live because of the police mini-station. Residents of the public housing community also perceived that the police were more responsive to their concerns, aided more victims, worked together with residents to solve local problems, spent more time in the neighborhood, and did a better job keeping order. Surveys indicated that 72% of the residents believed that the public housing mini-station was either somewhat effective or very effective in reducing drug-related crime (Uchida et al., 1992).

It has been argued that the involvement of the residents is a key factor in a successful crime reduction program. Kelling (1988) and others suggest that police, working in concert with local groups, can revitalize communities and help them devise their own defenses against drugs and crime. In the Fear Reduction Experiment conducted in Houston, an evaluation by the Police Foundation found that a police community organizing team, which organized an effective community group in a low-income neighborhood, scored a number of successes: They significantly reduced residents' perceptions of neighborhood social disorder, fear of personal victimization, and perceived neighborhood personal and property crime, and they increased the resident's satisfaction with police services (Pate, Wycoff, Skogan, & Sherman, 1986; Skogan, 1990b).

The conclusions that emerge from these studies suggest that the police focus must be wider than arresting drug traffickers. Studies of public housing have shown that many programs have misdefined the solution and generalized too much between developments. The PERF study in

Philadelphia noted that effectively dealing with enduring problems, such as gang violence and drug-related crime, requires a broader perspective. Drugs and related crime problems must be tackled together. The report concludes that solving these apparently overwhelming problems requires setting reasonable goals, and argues that progress will come from the "accumulation of many small hard fought victories" (Weisel, 1990, pp. 93-94). Although community-involvement programs can work, federal funds directed at innovative programs have not been fully implemented; instead, funds have been directed at financing and perhaps enhancing current programs.

A recent evaluation conducted by the authors for the Police Foundation highlighted some of these conclusions. We examined programs in New Orleans and Denver. In both cities the goal was to reduce the availability of narcotics and reduce levels of crime and fear in public housing. As they were implemented, the programs were enforcement-oriented and employed traditional policing methods, including conducting surveillance, developing informants, arranging controlled buys leading to later warrant arrests, and making buy-bust and on-view arrests. They focused new energy and resources on a problem that otherwise was not being squarely addressed in the two cities. This chapter reviews some of the lessons suggested by this evaluation. It summarizes what we learned about effective Narcotics Enforcement in Public Housing Units (NEPHU) operations, and raises some questions about enforcement as a response to drug and crime problems in public housing.

The Denver and New Orleans Programs

Special NEPHUs were formed in Denver and New Orleans, supported by grants from the Bureau of Justice Assistance (BJA). The goal of the Denver NEPHU program was to reduce the availability of narcotics in public housing areas and to reduce levels of crime and fear. Denver's NEPHU involved six full-time officers. NEPHU planned to use traditional enforcement methods: to conduct plainclothes investigations and gather intelligence that would lead to on-street arrests and searches of apartments in public housing. The Department also planned to increase levels of uniformed patrols and to maintain high visibility in the housing development areas in order to deter conventional crime. NEPHU also proposed to conduct drug awareness programs within the developments; one of their goals was to "educate citizens in . . . tenant responsibility, crime prevention, and drug identification and suppression." The unit was to meet regularly with Tenant Councils in the developments to improve community relations, and they operated a special telephone drug hotline. They also planned to cooperate with the Denver Housing Authority and the uniformed patrol division of the Denver Police Department.

The New Orleans program also had as its goals the reduction of violent crime and narcotics dealing in public housing. The unit hoped to increase the sense of security among public housing residents, increase the risk of apprehension among potential offenders in and around the developments, and increase residents' understanding of the severity of the narcotics problem and the ability of the police to tackle it. The unit also planned to develop intelligence files on individuals and gangs engaged in narcotics trafficking in public housing developments. The unit planned to seek resident input into their program through Tenant Advisory Councils that represent each New Orleans development. They advertised a special telephone drug hotline to encourage information sharing by the community. The police department proposed to augment the deterrent impact of undercover narcotics operations in the developments by assigning special uniformed patrols to those areas.

We conducted a process evaluation in both sites. We monitored the implementation of the program and observed it in operation. Observers gathered extensive information on levels of program effort and on the activities that took place in and around the developments. We made extensive site visits and gathered quantitative indicators of the extent of program activity. In Denver we were able to field three waves of survey interviews that gathered independent information on victimization, fear of crime, attitudes toward the police, and the perceived availability of drugs. Denver also provided a great deal of archival data on recorded crimes and arrests, both for selected target developments and for their surrounding areas. In New Orleans we conducted two waves of interviews with a panel of key local informants in three developments; they were positioned to be knowledgeable about the activities and experiences of many project residents.

Some Lessons About Enforcement

NEPHU WAS NECESSARY

Both NEPHUs focused their energies on public housing. This was easier in New Orleans, for almost 12% of the city's residents live in public housing developments. Sustaining their focus on public housing was a significant accomplishment for the NEPHUs, given the general disdain with which this sort of work was viewed by police in both cities.

In neither city were public housing developments being policed effectively before NEPHU. New Orleans's developments had not been effectively policed since the city's special Urban Squad was disbanded in the early 1980s for budgetary reasons. Other narcotics units in New Orleans avoided public housing developments because of the dangerous and unsavory conditions there and the seeming hopelessness of the task. Public housing residents appeared to them to occupy the lowest rung on the drug distribution ladder. As a result, drug and cash seizures there rarely equaled the statistical standards set in other areas. In both cities, PHA residents were frequently viewed with scorn by police officers, who perceived few signs of encouragement for their efforts in public housing areas.

After NEPHU was formed, arrests in and around public housing in Denver by non-NEPHU officers dropped off precipitously. It may have been that once NEPHU was created, other units in the department followed their natural inclination, which was to avoid working in public housing. Alternately, this decline might have been attributable to the "specialized unit problem"; the creation of a specialized policing unit like NEPHU sends a message to the remainder of the department that the unit's task is no longer their problem. Denver's NEPHU was continually rebuffed when they attempted to arrange for more frequent uniformed patrols in public housing areas, even when they proposed to pay for them from grant funds. The inability of NEPHU to secure the cooperation of district commanders in increasing the level of visible patrol in Denver Housing Authority (DHA) developments was indicative of the unit's relationship with the department. Many other narcotics officers and the Narcotics Bureau's management took a derisive attitude toward NEPHU and its task. There were a number of reasons for this, including jealousy over the unit's federally financed overtime compensation, vehicles, and occasional out-of-town travel.

Unlike the experience in Denver, there was no evidence that New Orleans' NEPHU was held in disrepute. They were very aggressive and productive detectives who made more arrests per officer than any other narcotics unit in the city. However, the unit was disbanded shortly after its federal funding dried up, and its staff and equipment were absorbed by various units of the New Orleans Police Department.

The NEPHUs in both cities operated relatively independently of their departments' narcotics divisions. This was probably a good thing, although it caused them problems in securing equipment, office space, and support from uniformed patrols. It is unlikely that their focus could have been maintained if the NEPHUs were more closely tied to citywide narcotics operations. They could easily have become paper organizations, officially charged with "concentrating" on public housing, but in reality ranging widely in search of opportunities for action elsewhere.

Our monitoring revealed that both NEPHUs conducted operations outside of public housing areas as well as in and around major public housing developments. It would have been unrealistic to insist otherwise, however. There were many good reasons for the NEPHUs to work elsewhere. Their job naturally expanded to include crack houses and dealers working in nearby neighborhoods, to scatter-site Section 8 housing as well as the developments, and to dealers and their suppliers who lived elsewhere but commuted daily into the developments. Both NEPHUs received help from other specialized units and law enforcement agencies, and the good inter-team cooperation that they needed from various SWAT, Crack, Drug Enforcement Administration, and nearby suburban jurisdictions demanded reciprocal action on their part. They did a good job when they were called upon.

FEDERAL FUNDING MADE A DIFFERENCE

In addition to encouraging their formation, federal funds made a difference in the effectiveness of these units. Confidential funds were needed to pay informants and buy drugs; the teams needed vehicles and sophisticated equipment; and the money for overtime work enabled them to focus their energies in a sustained way while compensating for the unwillingness of the cities to contribute more personnel to the NEPHU mission.

Informants were paid varying amounts, depending on the productivity of their leads and the value of the purchases that they made. This compensation was in addition to whatever arrangements they could make with regard to their initial arrest; although NEPHU in Denver made occasional use of a "revenge" informant, officers in both cities preferred to work with informants whose motives were more concrete. Virtually all of the officers we discussed the matter with (which included NEPHU members in both cities) agreed that their informants probably used the money to buy drugs themselves, but dismissed that issue as a reality of the world in which they worked. Both cities were generally strapped for cash during the evaluation period, and our informants judged it would have been difficult for the NEPHUs (and other narcotics teams) to secure adequate funding for informant compensation without federal support. In cash-strapped New Orleans, NEPHU's confidential funds played an important role in helping them to operate effectively and to occasionally penetrate middle-level drug markets. In Denver, financial considerations undercut NEPHU's effectiveness during the summer slump of 1990 when, due to corruption and mismanagement, the grant's confidential fund ran low on money. NEPHU ranged widely in search of more lucrative non-DHA cases in order to generate more currency seizures to finance their operations. This practice was institutionalized after the close of the evaluation period, when NEPHU was reorganized and merged with other units to form a somewhat larger unit; its formal area of responsibility was expanded to include a wide band around DHA developments so that NEPHU could generate more seizure money.

It is important to note the alternative to adequately funding narcotics operations. In other cities and at other times, it has been the practice of narcotics detectives to generate informant compensation on their own, by withholding money and drugs that they seize in the course of their operations, and then using that stockpile to reward informants (Manning, 1980; Moore, 1977). This is a dangerous practice, fraught with illegalities and opportunities for corruption. Moore and others have noted the importance of adequate confidential funds, in particular, for keeping narcotics operations free from corruption and financial abuse. Units like NEPHU require considerable operating capital. They generally can be expected to recover a substantial percentage of this investment. For example, between September 1989 and October 1990, New Orleans' NEPHU seized $34,000 in currency, while spending about $13,000 of their budgeted confidential funds. However, their confidential funds were always at risk on a monthly basis, and "it takes money to make money" in narcotics operations.

Both units made good use of the equipment they purchased, and would have had difficulty in securing any of it without their federal grant. Undercover officers need body transmitters to allow their partners to monitor the safety of street buys. New Orleans made good use of cameras, long-range binoculars, and other gear for conducting surveillance operations and building criminal intelligence files. The officers all used sophisticated pagers to keep in contact with one another and with selected informants. Undercover operations depend on unrecognizable vehicles, which are an expensive item. Denver's NEPHU leased Japanese cars, which were not stock police issue, but by the end of the evaluation period, they felt that their vehicles were "burned" (widely recognized) in a number of developments. New Orleans did not include vehicle leases in their grant budget, and it was only after some struggle that they got terrible cars, most of which were easily recognizable as police vehicles.

PERSONNEL POLICIES COUNTED

Several seemingly mundane but extremely important organizational considerations seemed to play an important role in the effectiveness of NEPHUs in Denver and New Orleans.

It was exceedingly difficult for Denver's NEPHU to sustain its activities because of the way in which it was organized. The officers all had accrued a great deal of vacation and sick leave before they joined the unit, and they were forced to use it during the evaluation year. Their overtime pay was limited to 25 hours per month, and they hit that limit by the middle of each month. The unit was too small to deal with the constant on-and-off-again scheduling this required, so operations were frequently canceled. The size of the unit also exacerbated its leadership and personality problems. The unit could not be subdivided so that sergeants were teamed with detectives they could work with, and so that partnerships could be formed of detectives who respected and trusted one another.

In New Orleans, on the other hand, the budget was carefully crafted so that each officer could work an extra 4 hours each day, every day. Because New Orleans police typically work a second job, this allowed the unit to focus its energies without demanding much more from the officers than they were already doing, and they could short-circuit these long days if they desired. Most delayed their vacations until after the end of the grant period, because they could make steady overtime money each week, and unlike Denver, New Orleans's NEPHU was virtually at full strength at all times. In addition, the unit's structure of a lieutenant, two sergeants, and nine detectives let officers form into working parties of various sizes. The team could easily adjust to the absence of several officers and still be at sufficient strength to conduct substantial operations, and partners and sergeants could be sorted out with the latitude that a 12-person team afforded.

NEPHU-PHA COOPERATION WAS NONEXISTENT

Although the proposals submitted by both cities envisioned close cooperation between NEPHU and local Public Housing Authorities (PHAs), they did not get along well. Some of their failure to cooperate may have

reflected personality conflicts between NEPHU leaders and PHA personnel, especially in Denver. However, it is apparent that the obstacles to
cooperation were multiple and complex.

Both PHAs were plagued by internal organizational problems. During
the evaluation period DHA was a besieged institution. Its director was
forced to resign after media investigations revealed widespread mismanagement and favoritism in hiring. The mayor replaced him with an
extremely political appointee, and DHA employees were fearful and
off-balance during much of 1990. One of the new acting director's
actions was to abolish DHA's security operations and lay off the security
director and his staff. The field managers of DHA developments often
disparaged their own top administrators to NEPHU members. To work
with NEPHU they sometimes had to conceal their actions from DHA's
central administration. The housing authority in New Orleans faced
continual charges of mismanagement, and its board was unable to find a
management team that could capture control of the agency. During the
evaluation period DHUD forced the Housing Authority of New Orleans
(HANO) to hire an independent management team following further
revelations of managerial incompetence. That team then came under fire
itself from DHUD and was in turn replaced. Corruption was endemic
among HANO's highly politicized administrators.

Not surprisingly, none of this endeared PHA management to NEPHU
members. In New Orleans, NEPHU members had initial problems explaining their mission to other police officers, who assumed that they
worked for the Housing Authority and would not trust anything that was
associated with HANO. Denver's NEPHU had continual problems scheduling meetings with DHA staff (who on key occasions failed to show up
for them), and found the staff attorney uncooperative when they tried to
mount an eviction program.

There were also turf problems. The executive director of HANO
initially believed that NEPHU would fall under his supervision, and
refused to cooperate once that mistake was clarified. The HANO board
was upset when they learned that NEPHU would conduct investigations
without consulting them. The security director of DHA was a former
Denver police officer, but NEPHU members still found ways to dismiss
his opinions and information, and believed that he did not understand
"real police work."

Finally, there was a conflict in the eyes of many PHA employees
between their mission of providing low-cost housing for the poor and the
expectation that they would become involved in enforcement activities.
In Denver, this was compounded by the fact that DHUD requirements

were read to require high monthly occupancy rates in order to justify DHUD rent subsidies. Development managers who were concerned about drug issues disregarded this constraint by aggressively moving against drug- and gang-involved leaseholders, but they risked higher vacancy rates as a consequence. Less dedicated managers emphasized keeping their units full, at the price of winking at lease violations. This posture may have contributed to the large variance that was observable in the frequency with which development managers complained to NEPHU about specific drug problems.

BE ALERT FOR CORRUPTION

Corruption plagues drug enforcement, for it is difficult to supervise plainclothes operations closely. Successful narcotics detectives encounter ample opportunities to steal cash and drugs from dealers, and to go into the business themselves. Corruption is fueled by frustration and cynicism among narcotics officers, who feel handcuffed by the rules of criminal procedure, who feel that they do not get the support they deserve from prosecutors and judges, and who believe that very little happens to those they arrest. They also do not get paid very much in comparison with those they pursue, and some officers inevitably are unable to resist the lure of stealing money from drug dealers, or even stealing and selling drugs themselves. NEPHU supervisors dealt with the threat of corruption by trying to recruit good officers. Supervisors monitored the dress and lifestyles of squad members, watching for gold chains and fancy shoes, and talk about new cars and expensive vacation plans. They searched squad vehicles for contraband, and in New Orleans narcotics officers were subjected to occasional urine tests.

However, corruption problems were quick to emerge in both the Housing Authorities and NEPHUs involved in this evaluation. The potential for corruption presented special problems in New Orleans, where police are poorly paid and the department has a reputation for corruption. Two NEPHU officers were transferred because of hints that they were involved in stealing money from drug dealers, and they later were indicted in federal court for selling cocaine by the kilogram. The indictments indicate they began their illegal activities in October of 1989, while they were assigned to NEPHU. The deputy executive director of HANO was indicted for cocaine trafficking shortly after our evaluation began.

The Denver department was rocked by the indictment of the lieutenant heading NEPHU, which was announced several months after the end of our evaluation period. He was accused of stealing $8,100 from confidential funds in Denver's BJA grant that were to be used to make drug purchases and pay informants. It now appears that NEPHU's shortage of confidential funds during the summer of 1990 was due to theft. The lieutenant's actions were uncovered when a new NEPHU sergeant reviewed the unit's accounts. He turned the books over to the department's Internal Affairs unit, who took their findings to the District Attorney. In a negotiated arrangement announced in July 1991, the lieutenant was allowed to retire from the department—and thus qualify for his pension—before he was formally charged; in return, he cooperated fully in the investigation.

BE PATIENT WITH POLICING

Despite their seemingly clear and limited mandate, it took a great deal of time for NEPHU operations in both cities to get off the ground. Some of the obstacles were bureaucratic. In New Orleans, there were no space or vehicles for NEPHU, so officers worked out of their own cars for almost 2 months. They repaired and painted an office that they secured in the train station, and scrounged for furniture. Few departmental administrators understood the unit's budget and what BJA would pay for. The City's Finance Office moved at a glacial pace, and it took the unit months to get a telephone. Larger purchases had to be processed through City Hall and submitted for formal bids, which meant that the more expensive items authorized in the grant were not available for almost a year. The unit obtained unmarked police cars that were in very poor condition and not very suitable for narcotics investigations. Creating the unit's infrastructure ahead of time would not only have avoided a great deal of frustration on the part of the street detectives but also saved a significant amount of grant money.

In both cities new NEPHU officers needed a great deal of training, and it took even longer for them to become effective narcotics detectives. Neither NEPHU was able to recruit experienced narcotics detectives, few of whom wanted to work in public housing. The new NEPHU officers had to learn the basics about writing search warrants, conducting interrogations, and organizing raids. They had to learn to identify many different kinds and forms of drugs, and how crime labs operated. In Denver they learned how to conduct a wiretap, and officers in both cities took advanced weapons training. In New Orleans they studied patterns of drug trafficking, evidence handling, and safety.

However, narcotics officers still spend years learning how to write incontestable warrants; how to develop and control their informants; how to perform fruitful surveillance; how to conduct productive interrogations; and how to piece together tight, legally defensible cases. Officers in both NEPHUs took some time to develop these skills.

Some Questions About Enforcement

WHAT HAPPENED TO COMMUNITY OUTREACH?

Since the 1980s there has been a great deal of interest in the role that voluntary efforts can play in dealing with drug and crime problems. The community approach to prevention emphasizes collaboration between the criminal justice system and neighborhood residents. It assumes that the police and other elements of the criminal justice system cannot effectively deal with crime on their own; rather, voluntary, organized community efforts to control crime and drug abuse must work in parallel with official programs if these goals are to be achieved within realistic budgetary constraints. Communities must learn how to defend themselves.

However, efforts by NEPHU in Denver and New Orleans to involve the community—or even the few council members representing them—in their campaign never got off the ground. One Denver officer attended a number of tenant council meetings in a particular housing development that we were monitoring closely, where he answered questions and occasionally spoke up on behalf of the program. Officers in New Orleans did even less, attending a few meetings with tenant council members at the beginning of the program. In both cities, NEPHU pointed to telephone drug hotlines as the preferred form of community input into their operations. NEPHU officers in both cities generally agreed that residents of public housing were the problem rather than a solution to it, although black officers in New Orleans expressed a great deal of compassion for the plight of children in the developments and the problems facing individual adults with whom they dealt (some of the officers lived briefly in public housing as children, but none grew up there). NEPHU members believed that PHA residents were not interested in halting the drug trade, that many of them had friends or relatives who were involved, that some found ways to profit from the trade, and that many other residents lived in terror of drug dealers.

On their side, the poor often fear the police and resent the way they exercise their authority. They may be as interested in monitoring police misconduct and pressing for police accountability as they are in increasing police presence in their community. Many residents of poor and minority neighborhoods have had antagonistic encounters with the police. The police are another of their problems; they frequently are perceived to be arrogant, brutal, racist, and corrupt. Groups representing these neighborhoods will not automatically look to the police for legitimacy and guidance in preventing drug abuse, or extend a welcome hand of cooperation if the police just appear at the door.

With survey data collected in Denver, we can explore the question of whether there is something distinctive about poor and minority residents of public housing developments that further undercuts the potential effectiveness of community outreach efforts by the police. There is reason to suspect that this may be the case. Most of the social and economic factors that are related to low levels of community participation are multiplied there, ranging from poverty and low levels of education to not having an automobile. Residents of public housing may also have extra reasons to be distrustful of the police. Officers are often suspicious and fearful of housing developments and enter only in armed groups. They do not like to patrol there, and they do not appear to be very effective at their job.

To examine the claims about the distinctively alienated character of public housing residents, we compared community commitment among residents of public housing in Denver with the responses of residents of "conventional" low-income and largely minority neighborhoods in Houston, Newark, Birmingham, Oakland, and Baltimore. The comparison was far from perfect, for these areas were policed by different forces, and the surveys were conducted at somewhat different points in time. However, we found that PHA residents in Denver were at least as committed to their community and to their neighbors. In terms of neighborhood satisfaction they stood above residents of Birmingham, Oakland, or Newark. They were at least as likely to feel a part of their community and to report that their neighbors help each other out, and they were more optimistic about the future. Denver PHA residents fell near the middle of the group in terms of their perceptions of the police.

Our data from Denver did not suggest that there were extra impediments to community outreach efforts by the police in public housing. Only 25% of residents thought the police in their area were "very fair," and less than one-third rated them as "very polite," which does not bode well for NEPHU's effort.[1] But residents of Curtis Park and Quigg Newton did not appear to be distinctively alienated; compared with poor and minority neighborhoods elsewhere, there seemed to be a firm basis for community involvement, and at least as much support for the police.

CAN PHAS DO MORE SELF-HELP?

PHAs doubtless could do more in their role as landlord to deal with crime and drug problems. However, we observed a number of physical, financial, and organizational obstacles to their taking action that seemed to inhibit the translation of seemingly good ideas in this regard into effective programs.

One widely discussed strategy is to improve tenant management. This involves instituting policies and procedures for screening initial applicants for housing, and evicting those who later break the rules. Around the nation there has been an increasing emphasis on enforcing the terms of PHA leases, and changes in DHUD regulations have made it easier in many jurisdictions to evict tenants whose apartments have been involved in drug-related activities. However, we saw in Denver and New Orleans how difficult it can be to implement this resolve. In New Orleans, HANO officials attributed their reluctance to evict residents to the belief that public housing was their last resort before homelessness. To forestall taking action, they took a narrow legal position that only actual leaseholders who were convicted of drug offenses could be evicted. In Denver, DHA was somewhat more successful in taking action against tenants whose units were involved in drug activities, but this was due more to the resolve of individual development managers than the Authority's attorney charged with monitoring this policy. Further, the adverse reaction by a vocal faction of residents to attempts by Quigg Newton's activist manager to take the initiative against drugs in that development illustrates how intensely political this kind of management tactic can be. In the end, the manager was "booted upstairs" and out of the development, and her chief supporters among the residents fled the development in the face of threats to their life.

The reality of life in many public housing developments also makes it difficult to impose draconian tenant management policies. It is hard to monitor exactly who is living in the units, which in New Orleans are often overcrowded with long-term "guests." In addition, while tenant rosters and even our household surveys indicate that the bulk of the adults living there are single women, there appeared to be no shortage of males in and around the housing developments we monitored, in either Denver or New

Orleans. This floating population of undocumented residents makes it more difficult to affix responsibility for drug involvement in public housing. Finally, at least in New Orleans it was clear that many, and perhaps most, adults involved in the drug trade did not live in public housing at all; rather, they were commuters who returned home on their off-hours.

To deal with these problems, there have been efforts to regain control of the apartments and corridors of PHA buildings, by locking all exits to a building and conducting unannounced warrantless searches of apartments. Then, while the building remains interdicted, new security doors and fences are thrown up; guard booths are erected in the central entrance area; legal residents are photographed and given identification cards; undocumented residents are evicted; and a special pass system is put in place to ensure that outsiders cannot stay in the building past midnight. In Chicago these sweeps are proceeding methodically, building by building, through the worst of the city's public housing areas, and similar sweeps are being conducted in New York City, Washington, D.C., Charleston, and other cities.

However, sweeps assume a style of physical design that does not characterize most public housing for poor families in the United States. PHA buildings in Denver and New Orleans are more typical: They are low-rise; many apartments have separate front and back doors (particularly in Denver); and they sprawl over large areas intersected by streets and parking lots. Research by Newman and Franck (1980), a modest evaluation of an early access control experiment in Chicago's Cabrini-Green project (Chicago Department of Planning, 1978), surveys by Burby and Rohe (1989), and related research lead us to believe that one of the most significant sources of the breakdown of social control in public housing is in fact its "public" character; anyone can enter, and no one has any particular legitimacy to challenge their presence. In this light, Clean Sweep-type programs indeed speak to a real problem. However, short of creating huge, walled compounds within which poor families must live, we cannot envision how they apply to most family public housing developments.

On the other hand, the dispersed, low-rise character of the family housing that we observed (especially in Denver) provides a better fit with elements of Crime Prevention Through Environmental Design (CPTED) theories of crime control. In addition to controlling access by nonresidents, a thoroughgoing crime prevention program would involve the physical redesign of PHA buildings to enhance their security by improving opportunities for surveillance and intervention by residents. This could extend their watchfulness and sense of territorial ownership beyond the front door. In some cases this might involve downsizing large developments and individual high-rises in order to reduce their density, encourage a sense of community in the area, and increase the manageability of the area.

However, more fundamental problems of deterioration dominate the construction budget of most PHAs, and few contemplate demolishing or even downsizing buildings when they have long lists of applicants for the space. Afflicted with buildings that were often poorly built and have frequently been ill-maintained, it would be difficult to convince most PHAs to invest in these subtle redesign efforts. In light of their generally deteriorating character, it can easily seem more important for PHAs to respond to vandalism and disrepair in a timely fashion. Moreover, it is not clear how much effect these redesign plans might have, compared with other forces that are at work in public housing areas. Even Newman and Franck (1980) concluded that most of the explained variance in measures of tenant victimization, fear, and residential satisfaction among public housing residents was accounted for by their economic and family status, rather than management, design, or building height factors; in the end, what predominated was the fact that PHAs frequently are the source of housing of last resort for the poor.

There is evidence that the physical deconcentration of public housing can reap positive returns. Prior to the enactment of the Civil Rights Act of 1964, PHAs placed almost all public housing in poor and minority neighborhoods. Since 1968 there has been legislative and judicial pressure to site this housing elsewhere, but a combination of local resistance and a dramatic decline in the rate at which new public housing has been constructed has limited the impact of this effort (Burby & Rohe, 1989). Research on both public housing placements and court-mandated moves by inner-city black families suggests that living in smaller, less dense, suburban developments or Section 8 housing leads to lower levels of victimization and fear (Burby & Rohe, 1989; Peroff, Davis, & Jones, 1979). However, given the resistance of many city and suburban communities to scatter-site public housing, it would be a bold move to pursue a deconcentration policy.

Finally, our experience in Denver leads us to be uncertain how much of a difference management policies can make, absent radical deconcentration or draconian management measures that are unlikely to be politically sustainable. For all of the problems in DHA's top management structure, the developments that we observed were manageable at the local level. They were well laid out and well maintained; they were small (none had more than about 400 units) and had solid doors and visible security arrangements. Broken windows got fixed, and there were not many of them because the leaseholders had to pay for the repair. The density of the housing developments approximated that of many private residential areas of Denver, and development managers generally were aggressive in enforcing DHA rules of conduct and keeping people who were not listed on the lease out of the apartments. And in our surveys in Curtis Park and Quigg Newton, about 70% of those interviewed said it was fairly easy or very easy to find a drug apartment in their development.

CAN ENFORCEMENT WORK, ABSENT OF SYSTEM REFORM?

The effectiveness of the rest of the criminal justice system plays an important role in enhancing or limiting the impact of special drug enforcement efforts. Significant policy changes have already been made in this regard by the states, including imposing longer sentences for drug offenses, making many of those sentences mandatory, limiting early release from prison on probation, and trying to constrain plea-bargaining practices that allow accused persons seemingly to be charged with lesser offenses in return for guilty pleas. However, in many jurisdictions prosecutors are overwhelmed with cases, and the jails are so full that arrestees for nonviolent offenses cannot be held until their cases are disposed of. There is great pressure to dispose of cases involving nonviolent offenses and persons with short criminal histories with sentences short of prison, because most state prisons are also at or above their capacity as well (cf., Skogan, 1990a). For example, the latest figures available for Louisiana indicate that the state's prisons were 99% full, and that Louisiana had to let out 1,541 prisoners under emergency release provisions in order to make room for new ones. In 1988 Louisiana housed 25% of its convicted felons in local jails because there was no room for them in state institutions. Colorado did not make any emergency releases in 1987, but that state's prison population stood at 109% of its rated capacity (BJS, 1989, Table 6.4; Skogan, 1990a, Table 10.3). These factors limit the effectiveness of the "arrest-prosecute-convict" model of deterrence that underlies crackdown strategies for controlling drug markets.

Drug treatment programs are at least as overloaded as the criminal justice system. In 1987 Louisiana was utilizing 97% of the budgeted capacity of its drug treatment units (BJS, 1989, Table 6.60). The limited availability of drug treatment programs for sentenced offenders is ironic, for they have been demonstrated to be effective. Drug treatment programs have been shown to inhibit drug use, reduce the likelihood that participants will be rearrested, and increase their ability to find and hold a job. The longer patients are involved in these programs, the more successful they are, although the programs are plagued by high dropout rates.

The enforcement end of the punishment cycle is also not inexpensive. In order to estimate how much it cost to move a typical case through the courts, our site observer in Denver followed the November 1989, NEPHU arrest of an illegal alien from Mexico. He was arrested for possession and sale of both cocaine and marijuana, tried before a jury, and found guilty on two possession and one sale (cocaine) charges; this took one full year. It cost the City and County of Denver almost $10,000 to move this case through the sentencing stage of the process, a figure that does not include the eventual cost of the accused's anticipated 5-year stay in the Colorado State Penitentiary, which certainly runs at or above the national average of about $15,000 per year.

Conclusion

Neither of the NEPHUs we monitored continued to operate in recognizable form once their BJA grants were discontinued. In New Orleans the unit was disbanded and its personnel scattered throughout the department. In Denver other units were merged into a new and larger "NEPHU," but its scope now extends far beyond DHA areas, and we suspect that its operations will refocus on other, more attractive and lucrative neighborhoods. Officers in both cities told us that it was difficult to mobilize community cooperation with NEPHU because "they've seen special programs come and go too many times before"; this proved to be an accurate prediction once again. Residents of public housing are especially poor and particularly vulnerable to exploitation, and their community is difficult to defend on their own. The government has special responsibility for protecting them, for it builds and manages the developments, decides who can live there, and plays a large role in shaping the quality of residents' daily lives. Public housing areas were being shortchanged in both Denver and New Orleans before the formation of the NEPHUs, but the national policy priorities that drive BJA made only a transitory difference in how the tremendous crime and drug problems facing PHA residents there were dealt with.[2]

Although there is a great deal of room for further research on the operation and effectiveness of NEPHUs, a closer analysis of local policy processes, which undermine the ability of government to shoulder their responsibilities effectively, also is called for.

Notes

1. In overwhelmingly white and well-off Madison, Wisconsin, by contrast, 55% of all city residents surveyed by the Police Foundation rated the police as "very fair," and 65% thought they were "very polite."

2. Almost one-quarter of those we interviewed in Denver had been victims of a burglary or attempted burglary during the 6 months preceding the first wave of interviews there. This is the highest neighborhood burglary victimization rate registered in 8 years of Police Foundation evaluation surveys of largely high-crime areas.

References

Bratt, R. (1986). Public housing: The controversy and contribution. In R. Bratt, C. Hartman, & A. Mayerson (Eds.), *Critical perspectives on housing* (pp. 335-361). Philadelphia: Temple University Press.

Burby, R. J., & Rohe, W. M. (1989). Deconcentration of public housing: Effects on residents' satisfaction with their living environments and their fear of crime. *Urban Affairs Quarterly, 25*(1), 117-141.

Bureau of Justice Statistics (BJS). (1989). *Sourcebook of criminal justice statistics*. Washington, DC: U.S. Department of Justice, Bureau of Justice Statistics.

Chicago Department of Planning. (1978). The Cabrini-Green high impact program. *Victimology, 3*(3-4), 334-338.

Dunworth, T., & Saiger, A. (1992). Narcotics enforcement in public housing. *Conference proceedings: Evaluating drug control initiatives*. Washington, DC: U.S. Department of Justice, Office of Justice Programs.

Kelling, G. L. (1988, June). *Police and communities: The quiet revolution*. Washington, DC: U.S. Department of Justice, National Institute of Justice.

Manning, P. (1980). *The narcs' game*. Cambridge: MIT Press.

Moore, M. H. (1977). *Buy and bust*. Lexington, MA: D. C. Heath.

Newman, O., & Franck, K. (1980). *Factors influencing crime and instability in urban housing developments*. New York: Institute for Community Design Analysis.

Pate, A., Wycoff, M. A., Skogan, W. G., & Sherman, L. (1986). *Reducing fear of crime in Houston and Newark: A summary report*. Washington, DC: Police Foundation and National Institute of Justice.

Peroff, K. A., Davis, C. L., & Jones, R. (1979). *Gatreaux housing demonstration: An evaluation of its impact on participating households*. Washington, DC: Government Printing Office.

Skogan, W. G. (1990a). Crime and punishment. In V. Gray, H. Jacob, & R. Albritton (Eds.), *Politics in the American states* (5th ed., pp. 378-410). Glenview, IL: Scott, Foresman.

Skogan, W. G. (1990b). *Disorder and decline: Crime and the spiral of decay in American neighborhoods*. New York: Free Press.

Uchida, C. D., Forst, B., & Annan, S. (1992). *Modern policing and the control of illegal drugs: Testing new strategies in two American cities*. Washington, DC: Police Foundation and National Institute of Justice.

Weisel, D. L. (1990). Playing the home field: A problem oriented approach to drug control. In *American Journal of Police: Drug enforcement* [Special issue] (pp. 90-94). Cincinnati: Anderson Press.

PART III

Judicial, Correctional, and Treatment Alternatives

10. Prosecuting Drug Offenders

JOAN E. JACOBY

HEIKE P. GRAMCKOW

This chapter examines the changing role of prosecution in the "war against drugs." Much like the rest of the criminal justice system, prosecutors' offices have been inundated with drug cases. However, new legislation, federal support for new programs, and new technologies enable the prosecutors not only to increase the capacity of their offices to fairly and efficiently adjudicate criminal cases, but also to employ strategies and tactics that affect drug crimes. Several innovative approaches are discussed, including new case management techniques, multi-jurisdictional task forces, asset forfeiture programs, and special strategies that interact with institutions outside the criminial justice system. It is concluded that a comprehensive strategy for prosecution should move beyond the traditional criminal justice responses, utilizing other powers such as civil sanctions and regulatory enforcement. The prosecutor has the potential to assume leadership in these areas through long-range planning and policy.

Background

The role of prosecution in the "war against drugs" has been less visible to the public than the widely publicized interdiction efforts of the police, the large number of offenders involuntarily released from overcrowded jails or prisons, and the long waiting lines at treatment centers. Nevertheless, as a result of this special emphasis on drug crime, and the new legislation that has been passed both at the state and federal level, prosecutors have been given power and tools not only to help reduce illegal drug activity but also to increase the capacity of the criminal justice system to fairly and efficiently adjudicate cases. The question of interest is, how can prosecutors best use this power to achieve these goals?

Federal support and major legislative changes profoundly affected criminal justice operations and activities and along with them, prosecution. The Anti-Drug Abuse (ADA) Act of 1988 provides major program support in dollars and resources to state and local jurisdictions to more effectively target drug offenders and reduce drug abuse in general. In the states, through block grant funds from the Bureau of Justice Assistance (BJA), these programs have reached deep into the local criminal justice system to improve the quality of its activities and services. Federal discretionary funds have been used in a similar fashion (Office of National Drug Control Policy, 1991). They supported new efforts such as multi-jurisdictional, or local task forces; asset forfeiture programs; the Comprehensive Adjudication of Drug Arrestees (CADA) programs; Differentiated Case Management (DCM); and Expedited Drug Case Management (EDCM) programs (BJA, 1990).

The ADA Act also extended its influence from the criminal into the civil courts. It created a different legal environment within which the stage was set for the development and use of new technology and programs, including DNA testing, hair analysis, and expert systems for crime-solving, profiling, and program development (Ratledge & Jacoby, 1989; Rau, 1991).

The changing legislative environment has also been instrumental in providing more sanctioning alternatives to the prosecutors and courts. At one end of the continuum, sanctioning has been increased at both the federal and state levels by statutes that deal with Racketeer Influenced and Corrupt Organizations (RICO), continuing criminal enterprises, kingpins, habitual offenders, career criminals, and mandatory minimums for an array of offenses, ranging from school zone sales to gun laws (Doyle, Klebe, Hogan, & Perl, 1989). At the other end, house arrests, alternatives to incarceration with conditional supervision, community service, and restitution, in addition to the use of shock probation and boot camps have been added to the sanctioning options in attempts to reduce overcrowded jails (Petersilia, 1987). The effect of this expanded range has been to increase the prosecutor's discretionary power in the area of plea negotiation and sentence recommendation. Other efforts have led to improvements in investigations and easier access to investigative assistance. Investigative assistance is offered by statewide and multi-jurisdictional task forces, by the state attorneys general offices, and by federal agencies such as the FBI, DEA, U.S. Postal Service, INS, and Customs (Gramckow, Martensen, & Jacoby, 1990). The effect is an increased capability to investigate and prosecute complex drug cases.

Despite all the tools, technology, and new programs, little attention has been given to the goals of prosecution (except insofar as they are shared by other agencies) that are directed at reducing crime and protecting the public. The goals of drug prosecution can be generally stated as: (a) to maintain or increase the capacity of the criminal justice system to fairly and efficiently adjudicate criminal cases, despite the special demands created by drug crimes; and (b) to employ strategies and tactics that reduce illegal drug crimes and trafficking and the other criminal activity associated with drug crimes.

The advent of mandatory minimums as a sentence of choice by many federal and state legislators has brought ambivalence to the criminal justice system. By taking away the prosecutors' discretion, there have been few options if the circumstances do not warrant the mandated sanction. On the other hand, the statutes have made incapacitation more certain and perhaps more effective for the professional drug trafficker.

To date, prosecutors have responded more as processors of cases than as planners and strategists capable of using their discretionary power and leadership to set the tone and quality of adjudication in a community. Yet, in those jurisdictions where prosecutors have taken a leadership role, either unilaterally or in conjunction with other federal, state, and local agencies, they have had a significant impact on controlling the flow of the high caseload of drug-related cases or even on the use and trafficking of illegal drugs. Due to the changing environment, the role of prosecution has taken on a new dimension that needs strategies for the future if it is to reach its full potential.

This chapter examines the role of prosecution in relation to the two goals that characterize much of the prosecutors' drug crime policies and practices. It examines prosecution as part of a system that requires improved coordination and communication and that is capable of attacking drug trafficking in the community.

Increasing the Capacity of the Criminal Justice System

The ability of prosecutors to make the criminal justice system more efficient and cost-effective is most obvious as they seek to manage caseloads and establish coordinated procedures among other agencies or programs.

MANAGING CASELOADS

There is no question that the high volume of drug crimes has strained the response capacity of many criminal justice systems (Goerdt & Martin,

1989; National Center for State Courts, 1988). Because of the high volume of drug arrests, and some inherent differences from other street crimes, drug crimes pose special problems for prosecutors. Their volume clogs the courts; strains relationships among prosecutors' offices, public defenders, and police agencies; and calls for more coordination and communication at the local, regional, state, and federal levels.

The number of estimated drug arrests made by state and local police has increased from 471,000 in 1980 to more than 1 million in 1988 (BJS, 1990a), reflecting a surge in both illegal drug activity and the responding allocation of law enforcement resources to this drug crime. From 1982 to 1987 the percentage of drug prosecutions rose in Washington, D.C., from 21% to 46%; in New York City, from 24% to 32%; in Los Angeles, from 21% to 40%; and in San Diego, from 18% to 26% (BJS, 1990b). In New York City, which has four elected prosecutors, each of whose jurisdictions exceeds 750,000, and an appointed citywide Special Narcotics Prosecutor, felony case filings have increased nearly 25% since 1987, almost all of the increase attributable to drug-related arrests (New York State Office of Court Administrators, 1990).

There is no evidence that the trend will ease up. Although the latest household studies (NIDA, 1990) and high school surveys (Johnston, O'Malley, & Bachman, 1991) indicate that recreational drug use is down, the results of the Drug Use Forecast (DUF) show that drug use in inner cities, which generates most of the arrests and related crime, remains at high levels (NIJ, 1991; O'Neil, Wish, & Visher, 1990). The traditional response of increasing the size of police departments results in more arrests and further strains the capacity of the system. For example, in New York City the government estimates that its planned increase in police strength will produce 50,000 additional arrests annually by 1994— an increase of more than 20% from the present. If present priorities persist, most of these arrests will be for drug crimes (New York Office of the Mayor, 1990). Delays in felony case dispositions resulting from case overload are a major cause of overcrowding and rising costs in pretrial detention facilities. New York City estimates that for every month added to the average time from arrest to disposition, its costs for detention increase by $9 million, draining the city's capacity to adequately fund other criminal justice activities.

Increases in crimes and arrests have forced adjustments and reforms to case management systems that affect all components of the adjudication process: the court, prosecutors, public defenders, the sheriff, and law enforcement agencies. DCM and EDCM represent major reforms in case management and have revolutionized procedures in the jurisdictions where they presently operate. Many of the practices and procedures developed and used here are all worthy of consideration for offices seeking to expedite a slow, backlogged court system.

The principles espoused by DCM and EDCM programs have the ability to significantly reform traditional methods for case management. Both of these programs are based on the assumption that the type of dispositional route followed by a case—whether by an early plea, a protracted negotiation, or a jury trial—can be predicted. Consequently, the adjudication process can be managed so as to allocate resources where they are needed, given the pattern of dispositions that can be expected. The adoption of this principle has led the DCM and EDCM courts to bring most of their resources to bear on the front end of the system, where the largest proportion of cases, those involving simple possession and use, can be disposed (Cooper, Solomon, Brakke, & Lane, 1991; Jacoby, Gramckow, & Ratledge, 1991b).

By focusing on the first dispositional outlet for cases (usually the first appearance or arraignment) and making dispositions possible at this point, substantial numbers of defendants and cases can be disposed. In Philadelphia's Court of Common Pleas, the introduction of EDCM in the first year affected almost 16,000 felony cases filed. The average time from indictment to sentence dropped from 210 days in prior years to 140 days; the jail population was reduced 36%; there was a 42% decrease in jury trials and a 32% reduction in the court's inventory by the end of the first year (Jacoby, Krisciunas, & Taylor, 1991d).

Much of this was possible because the largest proportion of felony drug cases can be adjudicated quickly once questions of law and fact are decided by judges. The fighting issues are almost always the legality of the search and seizure, and the results of the lab reports. Once these findings have been made, dispositions are the next step. The prompt disposition of drug cases is facilitated by having experienced prosecutors and public defenders assigned to the initial court appearance for plea negotiation, providing early discovery and open files, building capacity for pretrial release investigations or even abbreviated presentence investigations at the early stages of the court process, and expediting the transmittal of lab test results (Jacoby et al., 1991b).

Probation officers have been used in the Middlesex County, New Jersey, EDCM program to prepare mini-presentence investigation reports immediately after arrest. These reports, originally designed to assist in the pretrial detention decision, now have another use. They allow the judge to accept guilty pleas early in the process and use the probation report for sentencing in a selected group of cases (Jacoby, Krisciunas, & Taylor, 1991e).

These programs have shown remarkable results in enabling the courts to dispose of huge caseloads in a timely manner, without sacrificing equality and fairness. These programs also have demonstrated that communication and coordination among different offices and agencies are a crucial part of a not only more efficient but also more effective adjudication process.

IMPROVING CRIMINAL JUSTICE COORDINATION

The need for coordination exists on many levels: internal to the agency itself; within the local criminal justice system; and among agencies at the regional, state, and federal levels. The insurgency of drug trafficking has also created a special requirement for the coordination of highly complex drug prosecutions.

The traditional need for coordination between the police and the prosecutor has been intensified by the task forces and programs spawned by anti-drug legislation. Along with the new initiatives, however, emerged a different set of problems and issues. For example, the dual objectives of intelligence and incapacitation offer a potential for conflict between the police and prosecutor if there is no clearly stated and accepted policy about processing cases where the defendant offers to "roll over" in return for a reduced sanction. The conditions under which the needs for intelligence supersede those for incapacitation are a good example of the need for a clear delineation of policy and procedure.

Police/prosecutor teams offer a powerful strategy to overcome persistent problems. The strength of this relationship is demonstrated by the success of repeat offender and career criminal programs that are coordinated between prosecutors and police (Buchanan, 1989; Feeney, 1981; Forst, 1981; Jacoby, 1981; McDonald, 1982). They also show that, to achieve this type of cooperative success, the relationships between police and prosecutors need a structure or organization within which activities occur (Crawford, Giordano, Goldsmith, Jacoby, Martensen, Phillips, & Sonner, 1989).

The different goals and strategies applied by prosecutors can be implemented in various organizational settings. A program's success can depend on these differences, not only in terms of actual outcome but especially in relation to efficiency and effectiveness measures. Task forces and specialized units are the typical organizations created to maximize the impact of the investigative and apprehension goals of the law enforcement agencies, as well as the successful prosecution goals of the state. Although a specialized unit might be the most successful approach to deal with special complex cases, a jurisdiction that encounters few complex cases and has limited resources may be forced into either participating in a task force or looking for a federal adoption of the case.

The purpose of task forces is to bring together resources from various agencies and direct them at specific drug problem areas. Task forces make efficient use of existing resources and information by reducing uncoordinated and overlapping activities. Primarily as a result of the Anti-Abuse Act, more than 700 multi-jurisdictional task forces and drug units have been either created or expanded (Coldren, Coyle, & Carr, 1990). These cooperative efforts have been organized and used in various ways: for example, as ad hoc or permanent units, including a variety of different criminal justice agencies and involving various jurisdictional levels. The nuclei of many task forces are representatives from law enforcement agencies and prosecutors; their scope and range of activities vary widely. The role of the prosecutor in a task force varies according to its goals and priorities, which can cover a range from money laundering to street trafficking and distribution.

The Pima County Attorney's Office, for example, is part of a regional drug enforcement effort in the Tucson, Arizona, metropolitan area called MANTIS (Metropolitan Area Narcotics Trafficking Interdiction Squad). The members of MANTIS, working in teams and with an attorney detailed from the Pima County Attorney's Office, identify, arrest, and actively prosecute drug offenders and operate a drug asset forfeiture program within the organization (Jacoby, Gramckow, & Price, 1991a).

A different approach was taken in Colorado Springs, Colorado, where the Metro Vice and Narcotics Investigations (VNI) Task Force contracted, through its governing board, with the district attorney to provide an attorney for their asset forfeiture operations. A contract was used both to avoid the appearance of conflicts of interest and to maintain the independence of criminal and civil case processing (Jacoby, Martensen, Gramckow, Leverenz, & Draa, 1991g).

Whether federal agencies are involved also sets the nature and focus of the investigation and prosecution. Because many offenses fall under both federal and state jurisdiction, and with increased legislation supporting the investigation and prosecution of complex cases, local prosecutors may also be members of a federal task force. Communication and coordination are keys to the varying degrees of success experienced in the operations of Law Enforcement Coordinating Committees (LECC), multi-jurisdictional task forces, the cross-designation of attorneys, and joint intelligence-sharing operations (Office of National Drug Control Policy, 1991).

Some of the results are very impressive. For example, the state and local task force programs under DEA direction were responsible in 1988 for more than 6,800 arrests (about one-third were major violators) and seizures of about $110 million in traffickers' assets (U.S. Attorneys and the Attorney General, 1989).

The LECCs within the U.S. Attorney's offices lead coordinated activities involving task forces. One of many examples is the formation of a multi-jurisdictional Drug Gang Task Force by the U.S. Attorney, through the LECC in the Northern District of Georgia, to combat the growing problem of drug gang activity in the Atlanta area and throughout Georgia (U.S. Attorneys and the Attorney General, 1989).

Organized Crime Narcotics Trafficking Enforcement (OCNTE) projects utilize the concept of shared management of state, local, and DEA resources and operational decision making to target, investigate, and prosecute major drug enterprises. In 1988, 4,626 high-level drug traffickers were arrested and close to $205 million in cash, drugs, and property was seized (BJA, 1989).

Prior research indicates that pooling resources in task forces is cost-effective and efficient under certain circumstances (Chaiken, Chaiken, & Karchmer, 1990; Coldren et al., 1990). But organizing any cooperative operation is complicated by many internal and external factors. Task forces composed of personnel detailed from other agencies present problems and conflicts that would not occur within a single agency. How personnel relate to their respective organizations and its policies and procedures, and what role they play vis-à-vis their own and other agencies, are important considerations. Even the role of the prosecutor will vary depending on where the direction and leadership are lodged. If the prosecutor's role is advisory to law enforcement, the focus will be on investigations; if the prosecutor has policy control, then the requirements of the adjudication process will take priority.

Prior experiences have shown that working relationships that require coordination, communication, and collaboration are most likely to succeed if they focus on special programs, such as repeat offenders or asset forfeiture; have a clearly identifiable target population; and have goals that can be stated simply and a rationale that is understood and accepted by all participants (Crawford et al., 1989; Jacoby, Gramckow, & Ratledge, 1992). It is essential for success to establish procedures and techniques that avoid conflict and try to resolve problems in advance.

It is not easy to establish organizations and programs within criminal justice environments that share a common mandate but have varying objectives and priorities and different procedures, philosophies, and personalities. It is especially difficult if prosecutors must choose between participating in a task force and creating their own program. The choice is difficult because there are few guidelines or models to follow (Jacoby, Martensen, Gramckow, Bertucelli, & Saugit, 1991f).

Specialized units or programs to organize a prosecutorial response to drug crimes can also be established within a prosecutor's office. This avoids many difficulties with coordination that might result from task forces, and also allows for a more directly controlled allocation of resources to special drug prosecutions. However, these programs or units may be more costly than cooperative shared programs. Nevertheless, several notable programs have been established throughout the United States.

The Wayne County (Michigan) Prosecuting Attorney's Office formed a four-attorney drug unit that focuses on traffickers charged with delivery or the intent to deliver. The unit coordinates drug search warrants countywide through a database that is also available for intelligence gathering. The unit also works closely with the prosecutor's civil forfeiture unit, which is staffed by eight attorneys and one investigator. In addition, the drug unit attorneys are cross-designated with the U.S. Attorney's Office. The impact on the criminal justice system during the unit's first year of operation was quite phenomenal, producing a 140% increase in the issuance of felony narcotics warrants, from 550 in 1987 to 1,327 in 1988.

Many prosecutors have established dedicated drug prosecution units, sometimes operating jointly with one or more police agencies, sometimes in cooperation with federal agencies, and sometimes in specially designated drug courts. The "Rockefeller Drug Law," enacted by the New York State Assembly, established a Special Narcotics Prosecutor for New York City with citywide jurisdiction over drug cases. And the District Attorney in Bronx County, New York, developed a special program to prosecute illegal gun traffickers who sell guns to drug dealers in his county.

Sometimes successful drug prosecution requires special strategies to interact with sources outside the criminal justice system. To facilitate cooperation with the banks and other private sector businesses in money laundering investigations, the Arizona Attorney General's Office grants civil immunity to banks and financial institutions if they provide the investigating agency with information requested about a case (Jacoby et al., 1992).

One of the most ingenious legislative initiatives fueled by the need for funds to support the war on drugs can be found in Kansas City, Missouri. There the Jackson County voters, under the leadership of Prosecuting Attorney Albert Riederer, added ¼ of a cent to the sales tax for 7 years to fund the war against drugs. It is estimated that this will amount to approximately $14 million in tax revenues annually; $7 million or half of the collections, whichever is greater, is directly allocated to the Jackson County Prosecuting Attorney's office for law enforcement, prosecution, and deferred prosecution programs. The effect has been to extend the influence and involvement of the prosecutor's office into other criminal justice areas, most notably community treatment and deferred prosecution (Jacoby, Johnson, & Johnston, 1991c).

Maximizing the Impact of Prosecution to Reduce Drug Crime

Securing the effective prosecution of rising caseloads driven by increasing numbers of drug arrests is not the only goal of prosecution. The fabric of control exerted by the criminal justice system is weakened if the capacity of the court to process high caseloads sets prosecutorial priorities. No society can condone the blatant criminality that occurs in public view when an open drug market flourishes, without suffering serious erosion of the crucial role of criminal justice in reinforcing norms and maintaining respect for and obedience to the law.

However, there is an equally important need to reduce illegal drug activities and other crimes associated with drug abuse. The search for innovative practices, employed by prosecutors to respond to drug crime, extends beyond mechanisms that address only the ability to prosecute drug offenders. It reaches into all facets of criminal justice and even into the community.

It is apparent from experience so far in the war against drugs that arrest, conviction, and incarceration rates are inadequate measures of success in reducing the incidence of illegal drug trafficking, drug use, or related crime. Numerous studies have indicated that only a very low percentage of drug sales and other crimes committed by drug abusers resulted in arrest (see, e.g., Inciardi, 1986; Inciardi & Pottieger, 1991). And there is little empirical or scientific evidence that criminal prosecutions act to deter the criminal activity of specific offenders, despite persistent policies that seem to be premised upon the assumption that they can (Manning, 1980; Nagin, 1978; Paternoster, 1987). The criminologist Leslie Wilkins (1984) writes of an inflationary spiral of increased crime rates, followed by increases in prison sentences, followed by more crime increases and so on.

The futility of measuring success in terms of increases in arrest and conviction rates is clear. As long as contraband drugs are available and buyers are willing, the potential profits of drug dealing override the fear of even the most certain arrest and incarceration over a relatively short period of time (Adler, 1985; Reuter, MacCoun, & Murphy, 1990). Deterrence may be effective on middle-class, middle-aged users; but for the young and impoverished, the fear of arrest and imprisonment is not enough. Whenever one offender is incapacitated, others stand quite ready to fill that space, keeping intact the drug trafficking network (Reuter et al., 1990; U.S. Attorneys and the Attorney General, 1989).

Prosecutors and other criminal justice policymakers who want to reduce the plague of illegal drugs in their jurisdictions must develop strategies and tactics with the specific characteristics of the drug trafficking culture in mind. For state and local law enforcement unable to control the flow of drugs into their jurisdictions, this means trying to disrupt local drug markets and reducing demand in order to reduce the opportunity for profitable drug trafficking (Bocklet, 1987; Eck, 1989; Kleiman, 1988). Also, the characteristics of different drug offenses have to be recognized to identify the prosecutorial issues relevant to them and to outline specific strategies and procedures that enhance their prosecution, not only in terms of system capacity but also in terms of availability of adequate treatment and sanctions.

Of all the legislation enacted by Congress over the past decade, the most powerful are those that are directed at taking the profits out of trafficking and incapacitating the distributors. Included in this set are the RICO Act; the drug kingpin Continuing Criminal Enterprise (CCE) statute; civil and criminal forfeitures; and the laws governing money laundering, firearms, tax evasion, and public corruption. The task of tracing hidden assets benefits from the Bank Secrecy Act, which requires the reporting of financial transactions of more than $10,000 and allows investigative agencies to trace money flow. Many states have modeled legislation after the federal statutes, especially with regard to asset forfeiture and money laundering (APRI, 1989).

To date, the financial and legal complexity of some of these cases, and their international scale, have deterred state and local agencies from targeting major drug ring operations, or building financially oriented cases against drug trafficking and money laundering operations. Because state and local agencies often lack the information and investigative resources to address complex cases involving financial fraud, money laundering, drug trafficking conspiracies, and drug-related banking crimes, the federal government has taken the lead, and the state and local jurisdictions have concentrated on problems that are closer to home (Karchmer, 1988).

More appropriate for local prosecutions are activities that are based on the concept of selective prosecution, which underlies the structure of career criminal/repeat offender programs (Crawford et al., 1989; Feeney, Dill, & Weir, 1983; Forst, Lucianovic, & Cox, 1977; Garofalo & Neuberger, 1987; Jacoby, 1977). These offer techniques that are suitable for the local prosecution of more complex drug cases and drug traffickers because the short-term goals are compatible with the targeted population groups. They include increased convictions and incarceration with longer terms, pretrial detention, and speedier dispositions (Greenwood, 1980).

Another powerful weapon for local prosecutors is asset forfeiture, the taking by the government of property illegally used or acquired, without compensating the owner (*U.S. v. Eight Rhodesian Statutes*, 499 F. Supp. 193; CD CAL. 1978). In targeting the motive behind most drug distribution and money laundering cases, that is, profit, asset forfeiture provides a powerful tool in the war against drugs (Preston, 1990).

Forfeiture has a long history in the United States. Colorado, for example, has had forfeiture statutes against bawdy houses and public nuisances since the 1890s. However, until the 1970s federal forfeiture legislation was available only in the civil courts. In 1970 the RICO Act and the Controlled Substance Act authorized criminal forfeitures for racketeering and CCE offenses. Despite the authorization of these new statutes, few forfeitures were conducted until the mid-1980s. In 1984 asset forfeiture was redefined as a crime-fighting weapon against illegal drug activities with the enactment of the Comprehensive Crime Control Act; in 1988 it was further strengthened by the Anti-Drug Abuse Act.

Even though the federal government has given priority emphasis to asset forfeiture, and despite the impressiveness of federal forfeitures of $460 million in 1990 alone (Office of the Attorney General, 1991), state and local governments have not utilized asset forfeiture at their expected levels. A recent state-of-the-art survey indicates that this powerful strategy in the war against drugs is either mostly unknown or incompletely known to most state and local law enforcement and prosecutorial agencies (Jacoby et al., 1991f).

Part of this is due to the fact that most asset forfeiture statutes are based on civil law, whose procedures and principles are unfamiliar to many prosecutors and criminal courts. And it is partly due to the complexity of the procedures involved, which require different investigative techniques to trace hidden assets and develop net worth analysis as evidence. But perhaps the largest impediment is the public and media sentiment opposed to the seizing of assets. The headline stories about an innocent owner losing assets have done more to reduce the effectiveness of these programs than any other single factor. Although the concept of depriving criminals of their ill-gotten gains, and thereby also impeding subsequent illegal activities (no business without money), is a sound response to profit-oriented crimes, legislators and the judiciary often view asset forfeiture procedures with criticism and skepticism (Jacoby et al., 1991f). If asset forfeiture programs are to succeed, several changes will be needed. First, there needs to be education about what asset forfeiture really is; second, communication and coordination must be established with the public, the legislatures, the courts, and not the least, law enforcement.

Also contributing to the vagueness that surrounds these programs is the role of the prosecutor, which can range from being inconsequential to having command authority. Because the essential nature of asset forfeiture is civil, it is sometimes difficult for the prosecutor to participate in this non-criminal program. As a result, in Florida, forfeitures are generally handled by police legal advisors; in Colorado Springs, the attorney is a prosecutor employed under contract by the oversight board for the program; while in Prince Georges County, Maryland, the prosecutor controls, directs, and operates a prosecution-based asset forfeiture program.

Many of the special tasks associated with these programs—such as financial search warrants, asset protection and insurance, property management and disposition—create unfamiliar activities in addition to the civil notification procedures and their different standards of proof and evidence. Nevertheless, where asset forfeiture has been successful, the results are stunning. Of the three demonstration programs funded by BJA in 1990, each has not only recovered the amount of its initial investment (at about $140,000 per site), but has also demonstrated that this is a powerful, but underrated strategy. By seizing and forfeiting illegal assets, these programs were able to make a considerable dent in the drug trafficking market (Jacoby et al., 1992). Some states have extended this potential to new limits. Most notable are Arizona, Florida, and Michigan, where the capacity to successfully investigate and prosecute other complex drug cases has also developed. Favorable state legislation, extensive coordination with federal agencies, and smoothly operating processes make these agencies models for the country.

Other responses have been initiated to reduce the market for drugs, by emphasizing user accountability or concentrating on minor trafficking cases. These programs include treating and rehabilitating drug abusers, educating the public, and making more use of civil sanctions, such as forfeiture statutes, not only to take the profits out of trafficking but also to serve as a deterrent for the recreational user. Some of these activities, such as pretrial diversion and deferred prosecution programs, are wholly under the prosecutor's control. Others may require coordination with a number of agencies, such as participating in drug education programs in the schools, developing protocols for the private sector response to drug trafficking in the workplace, or working with the community or neighborhood to target specific problem areas.

The mobilization of the community is often crucial to success in this area. Massive community support was developed as part of the Middlesex County, New Jersey, EDCM program, where volunteers monitored the conditions of offender release and attendance at drug treatment programs, and assisted offenders in obtaining education and employment (Jacoby et al., 1991b).

A coalition among neighborhood policing, the citizens, and the prosecutor was formed in Multnomah County, Oregon, to target specific neighborhood problems in response to citizens' demand for safety. Through the use of regulatory and public nuisance statutes, the full force of the coalition resulted in the boarding up of crack houses. The Multnomah County experience is an example of the access that prosecutors have to a variety of statutes and laws that may play a crucial role in reducing drug crimes (Bea, 1990; NAAG et al., 1988; NDAA et al., 1989).

An integral part of this reform movement is also the expansion of alternative interventions starting at the pretrial level, such as treatment, diversion, and supervised release programs, in addition to the adoption of the full range of sanctions, which includes many new options for consideration after conviction in the form of intermediate sanctions. Increasing the types of options provided by legislation and used by the courts makes the criminal justice system more responsive to the circumstances of individual offenders (MacKenzie, 1990; OJP, 1990).

In retrospect, as one views the ability of the American prosecutor to reduce crime, the disturbing conclusion is that the attempts are still fragmented, often incompletely planned, and implemented on a less than systematic basis. Yet the potential for success still exists, and without the often recommended, but ill-advised solution in the form of national standards. As James Wilson expressed it: "I am struck by what we know and what we do not know . . . " and "In fact, we do not know what to do in any comprehensive way . . . " (Wilson, 1990, p. 543).

Strategies for the Future

The ability of the prosecutor to achieve the goals of efficiency and effectiveness within the criminal justice system, and reduce crime in the community, has been spotty and uneven. The innovative practices and strategies previously discussed support the claim that the goals can be met. Where funding has been made available and a vehicle established to demonstrate the effectiveness of programs and practices, they have tended to be adopted by prosecutors. However, wholesale acceptance is not possible. This is primarily because the environment and tradition within which American prosecutors operate make it difficult to success-fully transfer programs to other jurisdictions.

A profile of prosecutorial efforts to deal with the drug epidemic in the United States shows a variety of policies, strategies, and tactics operating quite differently at the federal, state, and local levels. A large part of this diversity is due to differences in state legislative environments, case law, and judicial interpretation. And it also stems from differences in local cultures. State and local criminal justice systems have demonstrated considerable immunity to innovation. Local legal cultures tend to absorb and neutralize any change that interferes with accepted and comfortable arrangements for doing business. Inertia is especially dominant when prosecutors propose new practices that involve changes in more than just their offices, and may create apprehension about the prosecutor's lead-ership role (Jacoby, Mellon, & Smith, 1982).

A few programs have been evaluated and documented, but most have never been assessed in a way that would allow either an estimate of their success or a judgment about their transferability to other jurisdictions. Still, it is difficult to assess the effectiveness of new programs; the areas where they can have a significant impact; and the areas where their impact is impeded by other factors, such as lack of resources, poor management, or ineffective controls and operations. As a result, prosecutors who are inter-ested in implementing a program to prosecute drug cases or reduce drug trafficking are confronted with a variety of choices, but little knowledge about the important factors that make them successful.

Furthermore, demonstrating success is easier for projects that attempt to enhance prosecutions, but more difficult for those that aim at control-ling or reducing these drug crimes. Prosecutorial responses to drug crime are usually only one of many actions that the criminal justice system and society take in an attempt to change the volume of drug crime. Positive results can rarely be attributed to a special effort. The disruption of one trafficking network might open the market for another organization; complicating the use of bank accounts for illegal financial transactions can lead to the development of other laundering activities, or a relocation of the activities to another state or country (Uchida, 1990). Just like decreasing indicators of drug crime and abuse (e.g., arrest rates, calls for services, percentage of arrestees tested positive, emergency room data, overdose death rates), the results might only represent a displacement of the problem (Office of National Drug Control Policy, 1990).

Another problem arises when information from a program is to be used to extract the necessary components of a project, indicate the type of conditions that support or impede its development, and suggest how these barriers might be overcome. This is not so easily done. If crucial factors are not identified, the future credibility of the program may be jeopardized. Collecting information about new approaches for processing drug cases or reducing drug crime has to be more than just program description. If the experiences gained from pilot projects and demonstrations are to be of use to others, then the information has to inform them about the sensitive issues and the goals of the program, how success was achieved, the resources required, and the results obtained. Transferring programs requires access to in-depth information and assistance. It seems important, therefore, that the search for ways to assess and document successful programs or strategies be continued and supported, and that the results be made available to others less advanced in their quest.

Another major deficiency exists, however, in a means for communication, assessment, and dissemination of information about new and "successful" programs that should be considered for transfer to other jurisdictions. Part of this deficiency is due to the local nature of prosecution, and part is due to the relatively low level of management and administrative support within a prosecutor's office.

Management and administration have not been seen by American prosecutors as major parts of their function. Consequently, when prosecutors have attempted to improve either their own offices or some other criminal justice function, their efforts often suffer from lack of access to the skills involved in planning, implementing, and assessing public sector programs and innovations (Jacoby, 1982, 1987). Prosecutors have staff to support their investigative and litigation functions, but rarely do they have adequate staff to support their role as chief executives of their criminal justice systems. No recognized professional administrative corps exists for prosecution that is comparable to that of the court administrator position, which was developed just 25 years ago. Leaving policy development and planning to operational staff only means that innovation tends to get put off by the pressure of the day-to-day work of investigations and litigation and tends to be intuitive and ad hoc, rather than informed and disciplined by relevant social science research and skills.

The dissemination of knowledge is further impeded by the local, autonomous nature of the urban prosecutor. In national prosecution systems, such as our federal system and most European systems, research, policy, and program development are usually functions of a central office. In England and Wales, for example, the newly organized Crown Prosecution System includes a Policy and Information Division at its London Headquarters, with criminologists on staff (Rozenberg, 1987). Because American prosecutors do not have this centralized structure, it is all the more important that each office has a capacity to communicate with other prosecutors' offices, to compare their activities and have access to the latest knowledge emerging from criminology and public administration.

Some recognition of the need American prosecutors have for communication was given by the Edna McConnell Clark Foundation, who requested that the Prosecuting Attorneys Research Council (PARC) assist prosecutors in addressing issues of sentencing policy, and prison and jail overcrowding. Similarly, the Program in Criminal Justice Policy and Management at the Kennedy School of Government, and the American Prosecutors' Research Institute (APRI), have convened several seminars related to specific policy issues and have published short analyses of research publications that are of interest to prosecutors.

But none of these efforts has successfully addressed the policy and management changes and operational steps that have to be undertaken to translate new ideas into reality. Prosecutors return from policy discussions inspired, but are again soon mired in the day-to-day operations of case management.

What is missing, to guide prosecutors around the pitfalls and problems mentioned above, is a comprehensive strategy that explicates the full range of prosecutorial activities and functions within a goal-setting environment that looks 10 to 20 years into the future. This strategy should provide a conceptual frame for prosecution as it seeks system efficiency and effectiveness and as it attempts to reduce crime. Within each of these areas, strategic plans need to be developed that will take into consideration differences in external environments, and within these environments, most important, the policy of the prosecutor. By specifying the full range of prosecutorial activities possible (such as pretrial diversion, early pleas, and the like), prosecutors will not only be able to respond more adequately to the crime problems in their jurisdiction but will also be able to identify what facet or program might be lacking in their jurisdictions. Someday the emphasis on drug crimes will be replaced by some other form of illegal or deviant behavior; and although the subject may change, the needs and issues will be constant. If prosecution is to move into the twenty-first century as a powerful innovator and force in the arena of social control, then well-informed, long-range planning efforts should be advanced now.

References

Adler, P. A. (1985). *Wheeling and dealing: An ethnography of upper-level drug dealing and smuggling communities*. New York: Columbia University Press.

American Prosecutors Research Institute (APRI). (1989). *The uniform controlled substance act*. Alexandria, VA: NDAA.

Bea, K. (1990). *State and local narcotics control assistance*. Washington, DC: Congressional Research Service.

Bocklet, R. (1987. February). Operation pressure point. *Law and Order*, 48-52.

Buchanan, J. (1989). Police-prosecutor teams: Innovations in several jurisdictions. *Research in Action*. Washington, DC: U.S. Department of Justice, National Institute of Justice.

Bureau of Justice Assistance (BJA). (1989). *FY 1988 report on drug control*. Washington, DC: U.S. Department of Justice, Bureau of Justice Assistance.

Bureau of Justice Assistance (BJA). (1990). *Evaluating drug control initiatives. Conference proceedings*. Washington, DC: Criminal Justice Statistics Association.

Bureau of Justice Statistics (BJS). (1990a). *Drugs and crime facts, 1989*. Washington, DC: U.S. Department of Justice, Bureau of Justice Statistics.

Bureau of Justice Statistics (BJS). (1990b). *Felony defendants in large urban counties, 1988*. Washington, DC: U.S. Department of Justice, Bureau of Justice Statistics.

Chaiken, J., Chaiken, M., & Karchmer, C. (1990). *Multijurisdictional drug law enforcement strategies: Reducing supply and demand*. Washington, DC: U.S. Department of Justice, National Institute of Justice.

Coldren, J. R., Coyle, K., & Carr, S. (1990). *Multijurisdictional drug control task forces 1988: Critical components of state drug control strategies*. Washington, DC: U.S. Department of Justice, Bureau of Justice Assistance.

Cooper, C. S., Solomon, M., Brakke, H., & Lane, T. (1991). *BJA pilot differentiated case management (DCM) and expedited drug case management (EDCM) program. Overview and program summaries: Vol. II*. Washington, DC: U.S. Department of Justice, Bureau of Justice Assistance.

Crawford, F., Giordano, P., Goldsmith, S., Jacoby, J., Martensen, K., Phillips, J., & Sonner, A. (1989). *Guidebook for the establishment of career criminal programs*. Washington, DC: U.S. Department of Justice, Bureau of Justice Assistance.

Doyle, C., Klebe, E., Hogan, H., & Perl, R. (1989). *Anti-drug abuse act of 1988 (P.L. 100-690): Summary of major provisions*. Washington, DC: Congressional Research Service.

Eck, J. E. (1989). *Police and drug control: A home field advantage*. Washington, DC: Police Executive Research Forum.

Feeney, F. (1981). *Case processing and police-prosecutor coordination*. Davis: University of California, Center on Administration of Criminal Justice.

Feeney, F., Dill, F., & Weir, A. (1983). *Arrests without convictions: How often they occur and why*. Washington, DC: Government Printing Office.

Forst, B. (1981). *Improving police-prosecutor coordination: A research agenda*. Washington, DC: Institute for Law and Social Research.

Forst, B., Lucianovic, J., & Cox, S. J. (1977). *What happens after arrest? A court perspective of police operations in the District of Columbia*. Washington, DC: Institute for Law and Social Research.

Garofalo, J., & Neuberger, A. (1987). *Reducing felony case attrition through enhanced police-prosecutor coordination*. Washington, DC: U.S. Department of Justice, National Institute of Justice.

Goerdt, J. A., & Martin, J. A. (1989, Fall). The impact of drug case processing in urban trial courts. *State Court Journal*, 4-12.

Gramckow, H., Martensen, K., & Jacoby, J. (1990). *Asset forfeiture programs. Directory of resources*. Washington, DC: Jefferson Institute for Justice Studies.

Greenwood, P. (1980, Summer). Career criminal prosecution: Potential objectives. *The Journal of Criminal Law and Criminology, 71*(2), 85-88.

Inciardi, J. A. (1986). *The war on drugs: Heroin, cocaine, crime, and public policy*. Palo Alto, CA: Mayfield.

Inciardi, J. A., & Pottieger, A. E. (1991). Kids, crack, and cirme. *Journal of Drug Issues, 21*, 257-270.

Jacoby, J. E. (1977). *The prosecutor's charging decisions: A policy perspective*. Washington, DC: Government Printing Office.

Jacoby, J. E. (1981). *Working paper on police-prosecutor relations*. Prepared for the U.S. Department of Justice, National Institute of Justice.

Jacoby, J. E. (1982). *Basic issues in prosecution and public defender performance*. Washington, DC: U.S. Department of Justice, National Institute of Justice.

Jacoby, J. E. (1987). *Caseweighting systems for prosecutors: Guidelines and procedures*. Washington, DC: U.S. Department of Justice, National Institute of Justice.

Jacoby, J. E., Gramckow, H., & Price, E. J. (1991a). *Survey of asset forfeiture programs in 1990*. Washington, DC: Jefferson Institute for Justice Studies.

Jacoby, J. E., Gramckow, H., & Ratledge, E. C. (1991b). *Expedited drug case management program. Final report* (Draft report). Washington, DC: U.S. Department of Justice, National Institute of Justice.

Jacoby, J. E., Gramckow, H., & Ratledge, E. (1992). *Issues and implications of asset forfeiture programs. Draft report*. Washington, DC: U.S. Department of Justice, National Institute of Justice.

Jacoby, J. E., Johnson, T., & Johnston, D. (1991c). *Management appraisal of the Jackson County prosecuting attorney's office*. Washington, DC: Jefferson Institute for Justice Studies.

Jacoby, J. E., Krisciunas, R., & Taylor, R. J. (1991d). *The expedited drug case management programs in the Philadelphia court of common pleas*. Washington, DC: Jefferson Institute for Justice Studies.

Jacoby, J. E., Krisciunas, R., & Taylor, R. J. (1991e). *The expedited drug case management programs in the Middlesex County superior court*. Washington, DC: Jefferson Institute for Justice Studies.

Jacoby, J. E., Martensen, K., Gramckow, H., Bertucelli, S., & Saugit, W. (1991f). *Asset forfeiture program evaluation. Program description: Metropolitan area narcotics tactical investigative squad (MANTIS) Tucson, Arizona.* Washington, DC: Jefferson Institute for Justice Studies.

Jacoby, J. E., Martensen, K., Gramckow, H., Leverenz, M., & Draa, J. (1991g). *Asset forfeiture program evaluation. Program description: Metro vice, narcotics and intelligence task force (Metro VNI) Colorado Springs, Colorado.* Washington, DC: Jefferson Institute for Justice Studies.

Jacoby, J. E., Mellon, L. R., & Smith, W. F. (1982). *Policy and prosecution.* Washington, DC: U.S. Department of Justice, National Institute of Justice.

Jacoby, J. E., Ratledge, E. C., & Allen, R. (1988). *Building an expert system for Baltimore County police department.* Washington, DC: Jefferson Institute for Justice Studies.

Johnston, L. D., O'Malley, P. M., & Bachman, J. G. (1991). *Drug use among American high school seniors, college students and young adults.* Rockville, MD: National Institute on Drug Abuse.

Karchmer, C. (1988). *Illegal money laundering: A strategy and resource guide for law enforcement agencies.* Washington, DC: Police Executive Research Forum.

Kleiman, M. (1988). Crackdowns: The effects of intensive enforcement on retail heroin dealing. In M. Chaiken (Ed.), *Street level drug enforcement: Examining the issues.* Washington, DC: U.S. Department of Justice, National Institute of Justice.

MacKenzie, D. L. (1990, August). Boot camp prisons: Components, evaluations, and empirical issues. *Federal Probation.*

Manning, P. (1980). *The narc's game: Organizational and informational limits on drug law enforcement.* Cambridge: MIT Press.

McDonald, W. F. (1982). *Police-prosecutor relations in the United States: Executive summary.* Washington, DC: Government Printing Office.

Nagin, D. (1978). General deterrence: A review of the empirical research. In A. Blumstein, J. Cohen, & D. Nagin (Eds.), *Deterrence and incapacitation: Estimating the effects of criminal sanctions on crime rates.* Washington, DC: National Academy Press.

National Association of Attorneys General, National District Attorneys Association. (1988). *Toward a drug-free America: A nationwide blueprint for state and local drug control strategies.* Washington, DC: Authors.

National Center for State Courts. (1988). *On trial: The length of civil and criminal trials.* Washington, DC: U.S. Department of Justice, National Institute of Justice.

National District Attorneys Association with National Association of Attorneys General. (1989). *The uniform controlled substance act.* Alexandria, VA: American Prosecutors Research Institute.

National Institute of Justice (NIJ). (1991). *Drug use forecasting. Drugs & crime 1990 annual report.* Washington, DC: U.S. Department of Justice, National Institute of Justice.

National Institute on Drug Abuse (NIDA). (1990). *National household survey on drug abuse: Population estimates 1989.* Rockville, MD: National Institute on Drug Abuse.

New York Office of the Mayor. (1990). *Safe streets—Safe city.* New York: Author.

New York State Office of Court Administrators. (1990). *Caseload activity report.* New York: Author.

Office of Justice Programs. (1990). *Survey of intermediate sanctions.* Washington, DC: U.S. Department of Justice, Office of Justice Programs.

Office of National Drug Control Policy. (1990). *Leading drug indicators. White paper, September 1990.* Washington, DC: Government Printing Office.

Office of National Drug Control Policy. (1991). *National drug control strategy.* Washington, DC: Government Printing Office.

Office of the Attorney General. (1991). *Annual report of the Department of Justice asset forfeiture program, 1990.* Washington, DC: U.S. Department of Justice, Office of the Attorney General.

O'Neil, J. A., Wish, E. D., & Visher, C. A. (1990). *Drug use forecasting, July to September 1989.* Washington, DC: U.S. Department of Justice, National Institute of Justice.

Paternoster, R. (1987). The deterrent effect of the perceived certainty and severity of punishment: A review of evidence and issues. *Justice Quarterly, 42,* 173-217.

Petersilia, J. (1987). *Expanding options for criminal sentencing.* Santa Monica, CA: RAND.

Preston, J. E. (1990). *International and domestic money laundering: A strategy for enforcement.* Washington, DC: Police Executive Research Forum.

Ratledge, E. C., & Jacoby, J. (1989). *Handbook on artificial intelligence and expert systems in law enforcement.* New York: Greenwood.

Rau, R. M. (1991). Forensic science and criminal justice technology: High tech tools for the 90's. *NIJ Reports, 244,* 6-10. Washington, DC: U.S. Department of Justice, National Institute of Justice.

Reuter, P., MacCoun, R., & Murphy, P. (1990). *Money for crime. A study of the economics of drug dealing in Washington, DC.* Santa Monica, CA: RAND.

Rozenberg, J. (1987). *The case for the crown. The inside story of the director of public prosecutions.* Wellingborough, UK: Equations.

U.S. Attorneys and the Attorney General of the United States. (1989). *Drug trafficking. A report to the president of the United States.* Washington, DC: U.S. Department of Justice.

Uchida, C. (1990, Summer). NIJ sponsors system to speed information to police on drug hotspots. *NIJ Reports, 221,* 8, 36. Washington, DC: U.S. Department of Justice, National Institute of Justice.

Wilkins, L. T. (1984). *Consumerist criminology.* Totowa, NJ: Barnes & Noble.

Wilson, J. Q. (1990). Drugs and crime. In M. Tonry & J. Q. Wilson (Eds.), *Drugs and crime* (Vol. 13, pp. 521-546). Chicago: University of Chicago Press.

11. Classifying Drug Offenders for Treatment

JOHN R. HEPBURN

Classification for treatment is an effort to discover enough information about the needs of offenders to accurately determine the most appropriate treatment modality for each class of offenders. This effort has had only limited success to date, however, and the debate continues over the relative merits of objective versus subjective assessments. The most relevant factors to consider in selecting an instrument are highlighted by a review of several classification instruments currently in use.

Decisions in the criminal justice system are typically made on the basis of incomplete and irrelevant information, often in an effort to achieve ambiguous or even contradictory objectives, and are frequently influenced by political pressures and organizational constraints. Even in the best of environments, decision makers seldom have information about how they or their colleagues have responded previously to similar offenders. As a result, inconsistent and haphazard decisions occur as similarly situated persons are treated differently, and differentially situated persons receive the same treatment.

The classification of drug-using criminal offenders for treatment is a conscious effort to group offenders into two or more separate categories or classes on the basis of one or more observable traits or characteristics thought to be relevant to the desired treatment outcome. As such, classification for treatment rests on the scientific assumption of an underlying order and regularity in human behavior and on the use of science to increase our ability to understand, predict, and control human behavior (Clear, 1988; Sechrest, 1987).

Most attempts at classification within the criminal justice system address the question of *risk*: the risk of absconding while awaiting trial or sentencing, the risk to security within the jail or prison, and the risk of recidivism while on probation or parole. Classification for treatment introduces the element of *need*. There is a presumed discrepancy between the offender's current state and the desired state for that offender—between what is and what ought to be—and this discrepancy represents a need that can be met by habilitation or rehabilitation. Classification should identify the appropriate treatment for the need(s) of the offender.

Treatment is not equally effective for all offenders. Some types of drug users do better in treatment than others do, regardless of the type of treatment provided. Further, the competing philosophies and modalities of treatment underscore the fact that not all treatments are equally effective. That is, some types of treatment work better than others, regardless of differences among the clients treated. Because some treatments are effective for some offenders (Anglin & Hser, 1990a; Brown, 1990; Finney & Moos, 1986; Hser, Anglin, & Chou, 1988; McLellan, Woody, Luborsky, O'Brien, & Druley, 1983; Palmer, 1976; Ross & Gendreau, 1981), the task of classification is to determine which offenders will profit most from which treatment.

Limitations in the Use of Classification

Classification promises more uniform and consistent decision outcomes, that is, increased rationality. However, certain assumptions are necessary if we are to achieve such outcomes. Implicit in the process is the assumption that complete and accurate information is available to the decision maker. Another assumption is that we can identify the important characteristics or traits among drug-using offenders that will signify which level and type of treatment program is optimal to achieve the desired outcome. Finally, there is the assumption that the accuracy of any classification strategy will increase efficiency and reduce costs. At present, these assumptions are not wholly warranted.

QUALITY OF INFORMATION

Because rational decisions occur when all pertinent information is used to make the optimal choice, classification can only be as good as the quality of the information on which it is based. Currently, the available information often is very inadequate. At the level of case-specific information required for routine classification, improvements are needed in the current level of our information about the offenders' history of arrests and convictions, drug use, employment, residential stability, and personal relationships. Agency files and archives inevitably contain inaccurate, incomplete, sketchy, and missing information, and self-reported information from offenders may contain purposeful as well as inadvertent errors and omissions.

Relatedly, there is an inadequate theoretical framework about the relationship among offender characteristics, treatment modalities, and outcomes from which to derive a better classification instrument. Compared to empirically derived frameworks, theoretically based classification decisions provide a better understanding of the factors at work. They also create a conceptually parsimonious model of behavior. As the amount of information about the etiology and treatment of drug-using criminal offenders increases, theoretical models will become more sophisticated and refined (Brennan, 1987; Sechrest, 1987).

VARIATIONS IN DRUG USE AND AMONG DRUG USERS

Efforts to classify drug-using offenders for treatment are necessarily slowed by the complexities of the problem. For instance, drug use is not a unitary phenomenon (Battjes & Jones, 1985; Brown, 1990; Carlin & Stauss, 1977). Most drug users do not become drug abusers. The types of drugs available, the social meanings attached to drug use, and the social and psychological factors associated with drug use vary over time and place. Similarly, there are important differences among drug users in such relevant characteristics as the patterns of onset, escalation, and cessation; the amount and type of drug(s) used; and the criminal, social, and treatment histories of the users.

Frequently, classifications are so unidimensional that they fail to take into consideration other salient characteristics of the offender. Drug-using offenders need to be distinquished on the basis of the type, intensity, and duration of their drug use, but classification should also recognize that drug-using offenders may also be violent offenders or sex offenders, may be dually diagnosed with a mental illness, may be HIV-positive, and/or may experience sexual dysfunction, depression, or suicidal thoughts. The extent to which drug users have other medical and mental problems needing attention, and the availablity of other social services and supports, must be considered in assessing the type of treatment needed.

VARIATIONS IN TREATMENT

Classification of offenders for treatment is also limited by the many variations in the type, structure, and flexibility of treatment programs (see Anglin & Hser, 1990a, 1990b; Brown, 1990; Hubbard, Marsden, Rachal, Warwood, Cavanaugh, & Ginzburg, 1989). The interaction between offender class and treatment types compels us to determine the most appropriate treatment for each specific offender class to achieve the desired outcome. As the number and variety of treatment programs increase, the classification must become more refined and sophisticated. Some programs exist for offenders during confinement, but most deal directly with drug-using offenders in the community. Because most drug users are not drug abusers, outpatient programs are more approriate than residential programs for most offenders. Outpatient programs are also cheaper.

Residential programs are of two general types (Anglin & Hser, 1990b; Brown, 1990; DeLeon, 1990). Detoxification programs are of short duration, rarely exceeding 3 weeks, and are usually administered in an inpatient hospital or clinical residential setting. The immediate goal is withdrawal from narcotic addiction, and methadone is the favored medication. Detoxification is not likely to provide lasting effects, but it often is the prelude to other treatment strategies. Long-term residential treatment programs, including such widely publicized therapeutic community programs as Daytop Village, Gateway House, and Phoenix House, attempt to effect more permanent changes in the offender's behavior. During treatment, which may extend from 6 to 24 months in duration, each offender receives a variety of medical, psychological, and social services.

Outpatient programs are of three general types. Random urine monitoring may be more surveillance and threat than treatment, but it is thought to be an effective intervention to deter continued drug use among casual or occasional users of marijuana, cocaine, and some other drugs (Visher, 1989). For those addicted to opiates, methadone clinics allow addicts to lead a socially productive life. The addict is not drug-free, however, because methadone is a drug-maintenance program. Finally, there is a broad spectrum of drug-free outpatient treatment programs, which range from unstructured drop-in centers to highly structured counseling and therapy programs (Hirschel & Keny, 1990). Drug-free outpatient treatment programs may be the initial placement for persons who have no prior treatment experience, but they are also used to provide transitional care following incarceration or residential treatment.

Not only are there variations among treatment modalities, but there also are variations in desirable treatment outcomes, as determined by the question, "Treatment for what purpose?" There is no consensus on what constitutes a realistic treatment outcome (Cole & James, 1975; Graff &

Ball, 1976; Hubbard et al., 1989). For some, treatment should offer adaptive programs, through which drug users might continue indefinitely on methadone while developing the vocational and social skills necessary to be self-supporting. Others advocate programs that eliminate drug use altogether. Still others argue for change-oriented programs that lead to both abstinence from drugs and a resocialization of the user. Differences in desired outcome should be reflected in differences in the nature, intensity, and duration of the treatment program, and differences in the type of clients who enter the program.

The outcome criterion is important for three reasons (Clear, 1988). First, the classification and treatment of offenders cannot be very meaningful and effective in the absence of a clear and precise statement of the desired outcome criterion. Second, a classification or treatment designed to achieve one objective should not be expected to be equally likely to achieve another objective. Third, the outcome selected will affect the accuracy of the classification instrument. The greater the rate at which the desired outcome is expected to occur in an untreated population of offenders, the greater the accuracy of the classification. Drug use while on probation, for example, has a lower base expectancy rate than drug use during one's lifetime, thus making it more difficult to accurately predict the former than the later.

Finally, any differences in the degee to which the treatment is received voluntarily do not seem to affect the outcome. The limited evidence available indicates that treatment is equally effective with those clients who volunteer for treatment and those clients who are mandated to treatment by the criminal justice system (Anglin, Brecht, & Maddahian, 1989; Anglin & Hser, 1990b; Dunham & Mauss, 1982; Simpson, 1984). In fact, the threat of legal sanctions appears to improve the drug user's willingness to continue with the program. Because length of participation in treatment has been found to be positively associated with the likelihood of success (Allison & Hubbard, 1985; Kofoed, Kania, Walsh, & Atkinson, 1986), coercion to treatment may actually aid in achieving the desired outcomes.

DEFINITIONS OF SUCCESS

The treatment program's ability to achieve its desired outcome may be approached from different perspectives. "Success" may be viewed in one light by the criminal justice system and in quite another by treatment specialists. For the criminal justice system, the objective of treating the drug-using offender is to prevent future criminal activity, especially theft, fraud, and other crimes related to drug use. Treatment professionals, on the other hand, may feel they have accomplished their goal if they can extinguish the offender's use of drugs, regardless of subsequent criminal behavior. Moreover, treatment professionals know that most drug users will relapse occasionally as a part of their recovery, so the occurrence of a relapse is not a sign of failure as long as the offender continues with the treatment program. Yet, these same sporadic and intermittent episodes may be defined by criminal justice professionals as instances of recidivism, and the treatment is considered a failure (Hirschel & Keny, 1990).

ACCURACY

Classification instruments have a limited ability to predict outcomes correctly. Their accuracy is determined by their ability to correctly classify the potential for failure among a large group of offenders, not the potential for failure of each offender individually (Clear & Gallagher, 1983). Each treatment class to which offenders are assigned, not unlike the categories of actuarial tables used by insurance companies, has a known probability of failure. Each treatment class will have a different probability of failure, but each offender assigned to the same treatment class is assumed to have the same probability of failure. These probabilities represent class-specific *group rates* of failure when untreated. Group rates may be very accurate, but within each group there is likely to be variabilty among individual offenders.

Classification results in two types of error. Offenders predicted to fail without treatment, but who actually succeed when left untreated, are considered "false positives." In such cases, money, personnel, and other resources that could have been devoted to other offenders have been wasted on persons who would have succeeded without these interventions. The other error of classification, the "false negative," occurs whenever offenders predicted to succeed without treatment are left untreated and then fail. These are misssed opportunities. Any immediate savings in treatment are offset by the future costs of failure to the offender, to individual victims and their families, and to the community, which could have been prevented or reduced with accurate prediction.

Clearly, not all errors in classification have the same consequences. False positives are a largely invisible group. Because we rarely withhold treatment from offenders predicted to fail without treatment, seldom do we know which, or how many, offenders fall into this group. In stark contrast, false negatives are a very visible, and often embarrassing, classification error. Every judge, parole board, or treatment specialist is made aware of the failures among offenders classified as likely to succeed.

This differential visibility between false positive errors, which generate little public concern, and false negative errors, which can lead to a public outcry, can produce more conservative classification decisions (Clear, 1988). Adjustments in classification are made, decision rules are toughened, and a "when in doubt" approach is called for, resulting in fewer cases for which treatment is unnecessary. As more cases are assigned to treatment to reduce the possibility of these embarrassing false negative errors of classification, however, the probability of false positives increases and more persons are receiving unnecessary treatment. Clearly, the goal of classification is to balance the two types of errors.

Objectivity and Subjectivity in Classification

All decisions affecting the treatment of drug-using offenders are based on a classification of offenders. Early efforts have been very subjective— that is, they have been individualized assessments based on inferences and interpretations drawn from a wide and varying spectrum of possible indicators. *Subjective classification* is often based on a pattern recognition process in which the clinician/interviewer seeks information sufficient to place the offender into one or another informal typification. By use of interviews, psychological profiles, and other means, clinicians come to know each offender and the appropriate treatment for each offender.

Subjective classification has come under increasing criticism for a number of shortcomings. One source of criticism is that subjective classification is open to abuse—that is, that discretionary decisions may become politicized or may be unscientific value judgments. Another criticism is that, although the clinical judgments are assumed to be based on technical/medical information, such as a personality disorder or the offender's insights into problems, the diagnosis may in fact be affected by such nontechnical and objective factors as marital status, employment history, and criminal history (Ashford, 1988).

Moreover, because the indicators used in subjective classification are not standardized, the indicators used are not necessarily consistent across offenders (with the same clinician) or among clinicians (with the same offender). Unless classification is based on a limited, known, and consistent set of factors, critics argue, it is impossible to conclude that similar offenders will be classified similarly. Assessments based in whole or part on clinical judgment are not systematic and reliable (Finney & Moos, 1986).

In contrast, *objective classification* decisions are based on their ability to compel the decision maker to base all decisions on only a prescribed set of known factors for which complete and accurate information is available on all offenders. If those factors are then weighted differentially in determining the class appropriate for each offender, the classification gains greater refinement and precision. In general, the more the classification instrument relies on objective measures, the greater its reliability. Furthermore, objective criteria have the advantage of reducing uncertainty in classification and increasing accountability for the classification decisions.

Yet no objective classification instrument will be able to take into account all the unusual circumstances and special situations that arise (Clear, 1988). Indeed, the very infrequency and idiosyncrasy of these events preclude their inclusion in a classification instrument. Because these subtle individual differences are important, clinicians assert, classification must allow for modifications and adjustments on the basis of the clinician's more intimate knowledge of and subjective intuition about the offender.

In light of these arguments, it is not suprising that the level of subjectivity in classification varies widely. In some classification instruments, the decision maker's subjective assessment is included as an independent and contributing factor—perhaps the sole contributing factor in the classification decision. In other instruments, objective indicators are used to make a preliminary or general classification decision, but the clinican's subjective assessments may be used to override the objective indicators altogether. In such cases, any departures from the objectively determined classification should be noted and explained as a means of holding the decision maker accountable. Finally, there are some classification instruments that rely entirely on objective criteria.

Available Classification Instruments

These and other differences in classification instruments are highlighted by a brief summary of seven instruments widely used with drug-using offenders.

ASI. The Addiction Severity Index, developed by Thomas McLellan and his associates (McLellan, Luborsky, O'Brien, & Woody, 1980), assesses the level of treatment needed by drug-using adults. It is designed to be administered (and interpreted) by a highly trained technician in a 60-90-minute interview with the client. The interview stresses seven potential problem areas: medical, employment/support, alcohol, drug, legal, family/social, and psychiatric. Largely objective information is obtained from the offender about each problem area, which then is supplemented by two subjective scores. One is the client's rating scale (How troubled have you been by problems in this area?); the other is the interviewer severity rating (How would you rate the patient's need for treatment with this problem?). A preliminary assessment of the overall drug severity problem is made on the basis of only the objective information, but the subjective ratings may modify or supercede the objective information in determining the final assessment of the client's need for treatment.

CMC. The Client Management Classification was developed by the Wisconsin Department of Corrections (see Lerner, Arling, & Baird, 1986) to identify the human service needs and supervision strategies for adult probation, parole, and institutionalized populations. The instrument is designed for use with all criminal offenders, and the offender's drug use becomes salient only if it is revealed by the offender. Both objective and subjective information is obtained in a 45-60-minute interview conducted by highly skilled and specially trained staff. The Client Management Classification consists of four components: (1) the offender's social, educational, work, and criminal history; (2) the offender's attitudes about this history (e.g., attitudes toward teachers, motivation for current offense, acceptance of responsibility for current offense, satisfaction with interpersonal relationships, and feelings toward both father and mother); (3) the interviewer's assessment of the offender's behavior during the interview (i.e., cooperation, candor, and receptivity); and (4) the interviewer's impressions of contributing factors. The interview results are analyzed to determine offender-specific goals, services, and treatment strategies.

CMRS. Developed by George DeLeon and his associates (see DeLeon & Jainchill, 1986), this totally subjective instrument consists of a series of attitudinal questions designed to measure the likelihood that the offender will remain in residential treatment. The Circumstance, Motivation, Readiness, and Suitability for Substance Abuse Treatment scale is a self-administered questionnaire that can be completed by most offenders in less than 30 minutes; trained clinicians are needed for interpretation, however. Circumstance refers to such treatment-inducing external pressures and conditions as family support, health risks, and employment status. Motivation examines the internal pressures for treatment, including such feelings as guilt, despair, and fatigue. Readiness touches on the offender's acceptance of the problem and the need for treatment, while Suitability addresses the offender's willingness to change and determination to succeed in treatment.

OPI. The Offender Profile Index is a needs assessment instrument developed by the National Association of State Alcohol and Drug Abuse Directors. It is a highly structured interview schedule that can be administered in 45-60 minutes. Because it is totally objective, highly trained technicans or clinicians are not needed to administer or interpret the OPI. Each offender is scored on two factors: drug use severity and stakes in conformity. Drug use severity is determined by onset, persistence, and patterns of drug usage. Conformity stakes are determined on the basis of reported family, education, school, work, home, criminal justice, psychological, and treatment stakes. More weight is given to drug use severity, but both scores are used to assess the offender's need for one of five possible intervention strategies: (1) random urinalysis only, (2) outpatient treatment with urinalysis, (3) intensive outpatient treatment with urinalysis, (4) short-term residential care, and (5) long-term residential care. A short, subjective "readiness for treatment" scale also is used with the OPI, but its results are not considered in the assessment.

RAS. The Risk Assessment Scale has been developed by TASC of Arizona, a member of the national consortium of Treatment Alternatives to Street Crime (TASC) programs. Very similar to the Offender Profile Index, the Risk Assessment Scale uses a highly structured interview that can be administered in about 45 minutes, by staff without advanced skills or training. The objective items form six subscales: the equally weighted social history, education/employment, and psychological/social profile scores; and the double-weighted criminal justice involvement, substance abuse background, and drug history scores. Combined, these scores produce the RAS Score used for placing the offender in one of four intervention modes: (1) random urinalysis only, (2) outpatient treatment with urinalysis, (3) short-term residential, and (4) long-term residential. In addition, however, the RAS includes four subjective Interviewer Assessment items, which address the offender's cooperation, motivation, honesty, and likelihood of completing treatment. When, as frequently occurs, the RAS Score places the offender on the border between two intervention modes, the subjective Interviewer Assessment Score is used to make the final placement decision.

DOPERS. The Drug Offender Profile Evaluation/Referral Strategies, developed by the Texas Department of Criminal Justice, combines objective and subjective measures of drug use and criminal behavior to determine specific strategies of treatment for probationers. It is administered in an interview setting, in about 30 minutes, by staff who have received special training with this instrument. Personal drug use, drug use and criminal behavior, consequences of use, treatment history, offender's reality, and interviewer's impressions are scored. When combined, these scores are used to develop a probationer profile to aid in selecting referral and supervision strategies.

POSIT. The Problem Oriented Screening Instrument for Teenagers has been developed by the National Clearinghouse for Alcohol and Drug Information for use with youths aged 10-19. It is a self-administered questionnaire that can be completed in less than 30 minutes and interpreted by untrained staff. The items are heavily subjective in nature, and each offender is then scored on 10 domains: substance use/abuse, physical health, mental health, family relations, peer relations, educational status, vocational status, social skills, leisure and recreation, and aggressive behavior/deliquency. POSIT is a preliminary screening device only, used to identify persons in need of more thorough assessment. Accordingly, those offenders whose score in any of the domains exceeds a preestablished cutoff, or who endorse any of the "red flag" items within the questionnaire, are identified for further and more comprehensive assessment.

Selecting a Classification Instrument

Important differences exist among these and the many other classification instruments currently in use. Instruments differ in their purpose, ease of administration, number of classes, validity, and objectivity. The choice of the "right" instrument will depend on the specific needs of the agency.

PURPOSE

The first question to be asked is, "What trait do we hope to classify among which client group?" Some instruments (e.g., ASI) classify the degree of the client's addiction to drugs and alcohol, some (e.g., CMRS) classify the client's readiness for treatment, and still others (e.g., CMC) classify the client's need for treatment. In addition, some of these instruments (e.g., OPI) are designed to provide a substantial profile of the client and a recommended treatment; but others (e.g., POSIT) are to be used only as a preliminary screening device to identify persons for further and more comprehensive assessment by other means. Finally, the choice of an instrument must take into consideration the age (adult versus juvenile) of the clients and the client group's stage in the criminal justice system (e.g., pretrial, probation, incarceration).

In addition, the instrument to be used must be examined in the context of the philosophy and goals of the organization, and the nature of the drug-treatment program it offers. Programs oriented toward the total life context of the offender outside of treatment, which are prepared to provide an array of social, psychological, educational, vocational, and other outpatient services as a part of their treatment program, may benefit from a classification instrument that incorporates personal, social, and environmental circumstances, such as the CMC or the OPI. In contrast, the CMRS is designed to be used for residential therapeutic community programs.

EASE OF ADMINISTRATION

The ideal instrument will be inexpensive, will require little time, and will be simple to administer, score, and interpret. Further, it should be dependable—that is, the classification of an offender should be the same regardless of who administers the instrument, when it is administered, or under what conditions it is administered. Highly educated and trained staff are required for some classification instruments (e.g., ASI and CMC), while others can be administered by persons with minimal levels of skill and training (OPI and RAS). Even if the instrument includes very detailed and complex questions requiring skilled clinicians, consistency and accuracy require that it should be fairly simple to score and interpret. The CMRS, for instance, is easy to administer but rather complex in its scoring procedures.

NUMBER OF CLASSES

Any device or instrument used to classify drug-using offenders must create two or more homogeneous classes of offenders. These classes must be mutually exclusive and exhaustive, such that each offender can be placed in one, and only one, class. By differentiating the offender population into two or more classes, the treatment can be varied according to the specific characteristics of each class. The greater the number of classes, and hence the greater the homogeneity of the offenders within classes, the more the treatment can be varied and refined, according to the unique characteristics of each class of offender. The RAS classifies offenders' treatment needs into four treatment categories, including that of "Outpatient Treatment," but the OPI creates five treatment need categories by distinguishing between that of "Outpatient Treatment" and that of "Intensive Outpatient Treatment." In choosing an instrument, then, it is important to seek one that provides maximum differentiation among the offender population served.

VALIDITY

A classification instrument should have predictive validity. Unfortunately, little is known about the accuracy with which these or other instruments identify the treatment needs of drug-using offenders. The early returns are favorable (Andrews, Bonta, & Hoge, 1990; DeLeon, 1990; Finney & Moos, 1986; McLellan et al., 1983), but more rigorous and substantive research is needed before any classification instrument can claim predictive validity. Until an acceptable level of predictive validity can be documented, all classification instruments should be viewed as an important aid to treatment, but they should not be used as the sole determinant of treatment.

Even when predictive validity is reported for an instrument, its applicability to a different client population or program is questionable. Any instrument, no matter how reputable and valid, should be "calibrated" for the local population. Perhaps it will be necessary to eliminate some items or subscales; it is possible that different weights will be assigned to existing items and subscales; maybe different cutoff points will be necessary. However, because any change in scoring will affect the relative balance between false positives and false negatives, such changes must be based on an evaluation of the instrument's predictive validity with that particular population of offenders.

Face validity also is very important, particularly when the practitioners and staff who will be using the instrument greet it with suspicion, resistance, or hostility. There must be an obvious correlation between the items that form the instrument and the instrument's purpose, and there must be some correlation between the intuitive knowledge and under-standings of the practitioners and the outcomes of the instrument. If, for instance, the objective instrument calls for outpatient treatment for offenders whom the staff believe should be placed in long-term residential care, then the staff will question the validity of the instrument.

OBJECTIVITY

A final factor in selecting a classification instrument is the preferred degree of objectivity. On the one hand, objective instruments such as the OPI and POSIT tend to be quicker and easier, to require less skillful staff, and to be more reliable. On the other hand, the CMRS and other instruments that call for totally subjective assessments permit staff to feel that their professional knowledge and skills are being utilized and that the treatment is being individualized to some degree. These same staff may undermine objective instruments by freely using overrides of objective scores, or even by manipulating the scoring format so as to arrive at an objective score that matches their subjectively derived assessment.

Some of these problems are avoided by combining objective and subjective assessments in the same instrument. Both the CMC and the DOPERS instrument mix and weigh both objective and subjective items to arrive at a final classification. The ASI and RAS instruments, in contrast, use objective items to arrive at a preliminary classification, but then allow for a possible modification in the final classification on the basis of subjective items.

Conclusion

A broad array of formats and instruments is available to assist in the classification of drug-using offenders for treatment. Some are better than others; a few are terrible; not one is perfect. Behavioral scientists seek an efficient and reliable classification instrument with great predictive accuracy, and so does the practitioner. But the practitioner is more concerned than the behavioral scientist with problems of implementation at the local level. Agencies need a classification that is easy, cheap, and quick to use. It should have clearly defined classes and treatments, and the location of offenders into each should be unambiguous and decisive. Also, agencies are looking for breadth of coverage. They want a single classification that can be used with a large number of offenders, that can be used with offenders at different stages in the criminal justice system, and that can be transferred across jurisdictions with no adverse consequences.

Clearly, more work is needed. Research has yet to discern which types of offenders receive which benefits from which treatment modalities. Without such information, a definitive classification of offenders for treatment is impossible. As Sechrest (1987) summarizes the issue, it is not a matter of which comes first, adequate classification or adequate treatment; it is a matter of developing an overall classification/treatment scheme. That is the goal of behavioral scientist and practitioner alike.

References

Allison, M., & Hubbard, R. (1985). Drug abuse treatment process: A review of the literature. *The International Journal of the Addictions, 20*, 1321-1345.

Andrews, D., Bonta, J., & Hoge, R. (1990). Classification for effective rehabilitation. *Criminal Justice and Behavior, 17*, 19-52.

Anglin, M., Brecht, M., & Maddahian, E. (1989). Pretreatment characteristics and treatment performance of legally coerced versus voluntary methadone maintenance admissions. *Criminology, 27*, 537-557.

Anglin, M., & Hser, Y. (1990a). Legal coercion and drug abuse treatment. In J. Inciardi (Ed.), *Handbook of drug control in the United States* (pp. 151-176). New York: Greenwood.

Anglin, M., & Hser, Y. (1990b). Treatment of drug abuse. In M. Tonry & J. Wilson (Eds.), *Drugs and crime* (pp. 393-460). Chicago: University of Chicago Press.

Ashford, J. (1988). Assessing treatability in drug offenders. *Behavioral Sciences and the Law, 6*, 139-148.

Battjes, R., & Jones, C. (1985). Implications of etiological research for preventive interventions and future research. In C. Jones & R. Battjes (Eds.), *Etiology of drug abuse: Implications for prevention* (pp. 269-276). Rockville, MD: National Institute on Drug Abuse.

Brennan, T. (1987). Classification for control in jails and prisons. In D. Gottfredson & M. Tonry (Eds.), *Crime and justice: Vol. 9. Prediction and classification* (pp. 323-366). Chicago: University of Chicago Press.

Brown, B. (1990). The growth of drug abuse treatment systems. In J. Inciardi (Ed.), *Handbook of drug control in the United States* (pp. 51-69). New York: Greenwood.

Carlin, A., & Stauss, F. (1977). Descriptive and functional classifications of drug abusers. *Journal of Consulting and Clinical Psychology, 45*, 222-227.

Clear, T. (1988). *Statistical predictions in corrections.* Washington, DC: National Institute of Corrections.

Clear, T., & Gallagher, K. (1983). Screening devices in probation and parole. *Evaluation Review, 7*, 217-234.

Cole, S., & James, L. (1975). A revised treatment typology based on the DARP. *American Journal of Drug and Alcohol Abuse, 2*, 37-49.

DeLeon, G. (1990). Treatment strategies. In J. Inciardi (Ed.), *Handbook of drug control in the United States* (pp. 115-138). New York: Greenwood.

DeLeon, G., & Jainchill, N. (1986). Circumstance, motivation, readiness and suitability as correlates of treatment tenure. *Journal of Psychoactive Drugs, 18,* 203-208.

Dunham, R., & Mauss, A. (1982). Reluctant referrals: The effectiveness of legal coercion in outpatient treatment for problem drinkers. *Journal of Drug Issues, 12,* 5-20.

Finney, J., & Moos, R. (1986). Matching patients with treatments: Conceptual and methodological issues. *Journal of Studies on Alcohol, 47,* 122-134.

Graff, H., & Ball, J. (1976). The methadone clinic: Function and philosophy. *International Journal of Social Psychiatry, 22,* 140-146.

Hirschel, J., & Keny, J. (1990). Outpatient treatment for substance-abusing offenders. *Journal of Offender Counseling, Services, and Rehabilitation, 15,* 111-130.

Hser, Y., Anglin, D., & Chou, C. (1988). Evaluation of drug abuse treatment: A repeated measures design assessing methadone maintenance. *Evaluation Review, 12,* 547-570.

Hubbard, R., Marsden, M., Rachal, J., Warwood, H., Cavanaugh, E., & Ginzburg, H. (1989). *Drug abuse treatment: A national study of effectiveness.* Chapel Hill: University of North Carolina Press.

Jaffe, J. (1984). Evaluating drug abuse treatment. *Drug abuse treatment evaluation: Strategies, progress, and prospects* (NIDA Research Monograph No. 51, pp. 13-28). Rockville, MD: National Institute on Drug Abuse.

Kofoed, L., Kania, J., Walsh, T., & Atkinson, R. (1986). Outpatient treatment of patients with substance abuse and coexisting psychiatric disorders. *American Journal of Psychiatry, 143,* 867-872.

Lerner, K., Arling, G., & Baird, S. (1986). Client management classification strategies for case supervision. *Crime and Delinquency, 32,* 254-271.

McLellan, A., Luborsky, L., O'Brien, C., & Woody, G. (1980). An improved evaluation instrument for substance abuse patients: The addiction severity index. *Journal of Nervous and Mental Disease, 168,* 26-33.

McLellan, A., Woody, G., Luborsky, L., O'Brien, C., & Druley, K. (1983). Increased effectiveness of substance abuse treatment: A prospective study of patient-treatment "matching." *Journal of Nervous and Mental Disease, 171,* 597-605.

Palmer, T. (1976). Martinson revisited. *Journal of Research in Crime and Delinquency, 5,* 133-148.

Ross, R., & Gendreau, P. (1981). *Effective corrections.* Toronto: University of Toronto Press.

Sechrest, L. (1987). Classification for treatment. In D. Gottfredson & M. Tonry (Eds.), *Crime and Justice: Vol. 9. Prediction and classification* (pp. 293-322). Chicago: University of Chicago Press.

Simpson, D. (1984). National treatment system evaluation based on the drug abuse reporting program (DARP) followup research. *Drug abuse treatment evaluation: Strategies, progress, prospects* (NIDA Research Monograph No. 51). Rockville, MD: National Institute on Drug Abuse.

Visher, C. (1989). Linking criminal sanctions, drug testing, and drug abuse treatment. *Criminal Justice Policy Review, 3,* 329-343.

12. Do Criminal Sanctions Deter Drug Crimes?

JEFFREY A. FAGAN

The mobilization of legal institutions in response to drug crises of the 1980s led to legislative activism to increase the deterrent effects of criminal prosecution. The result was sharp increases in the number of arrests and harsher treatment of drug offenders at all stages of the legal system. New statutes increased the likelihood and length of incarceration for arrestees charged with drug offenses. However, the drug crises that fueled the legal response unfolded in social and economic contexts where the drug economy grew in the wake of deindustrialization and the decline of the formal economy. Analyses of sanctions and recidivism for 6,800 drug arrestees in New York City in 1983-1986 showed that neither the prevalence nor the rates of recidivism were associated with sanction severity. The deterrent effects of harsh punishment were mitigated by the devaluation of legal work and the weakening of informal social controls. Punishment was not a threat worth avoiding for drug sellers in a social context of severely constrained opportunities for legal work and widespread demand for drugs. Efforts to increase the deterrent effects of criminal sanctions should address both the costs of punishment and motivations for its avoidance.

INTRODUCTION

Since the 1880s social and legal responses to successive drug crises have viewed each new drug as different and more severe than its predecessors. In each instance, policies have been developed within the context of a moral crusade (Gusfield, 1975; Reinarman & Levine, 1989) to mobilize

AUTHOR'S NOTE: The author is grateful to Steven Belenko and Ko-lin Chin for their efforts in compiling the data for this effort, and to the New York City Criminal Justice Agency for generously making it available for this research. Data collection was supported by Grant No. 87-IJ-CX-0064 from the National Institute of Justice. The opinions are solely those of the author.

188

legal institutions to control the use of intoxicants. Responses to mari-juana in the 1930s and again in the 1960s (Silver, 1979), heroin in the 1960s and 1970s (Epstein, 1977; Kaplan, 1983; Trebach, 1982), PCP in the late 1970s (Feldman, Agar, & Beschner, 1979), and several cocaine crises in the 1980s (Office of National Drug Control Policy, 1989 [here-after, ONDCP, 1989]; Zimmer, 1987; Zimring & Hawkins, 1992) each have regarded the drug of the day as a gateway to violence, addiction, and a variety of destructive effects on families and communities.

Throughout each of these crises, law and policy have increasingly relied on criminal sanctions to control drug use and drug selling. In September 1989 the publication of the *National Drug Control Strategy* formalized the nation's policy response to the most recent drug crisis (ONDCP, 1989). It called for an "unprecedented" expansion of police, prosecutors, courts, and prisons to "[make] streets safer and drug users more accountable for their actions" (ONDCP, p. 24). It also called for stronger punishment for drug offenders, and greater resolve by judges and prosecutors to incarcerate them.

By stating drug problems in *moral* terms, or *mala in se* (Hughes, 1983), the ONDCP policy defines drug use and selling as dual problems of legal transgressions. First, the ONDCP policy assumes that all drugs are bad, and that none is more dangerous than any other. Taking or selling illegal drugs is a socially deviant act whose social and health consequences are sufficiently harmful to merit state control and intervention. Second, because drugs are illegal, taking or selling them undermines the law and, by extension, the social order of laws.[1] Every illegal drug user has violated societal norms and must be held accountable for doing so.

These assumptions fueled a mobilization of legal and political institutions throughout the past decade and repeated a cycle that has been evident in American social and political life for more than a century (Myers, 1989; Reinarman & Levine, 1989).[2] For example, police crack-downs on street-level drug trafficking have been widely implemented since the mid-1970s (Chaiken, 1988; Moore, 1977; Sherman, 1990). By 1982 a cycle of congressional activism began, which lengthened prison sentences and made incarceration mandatory for specific federal of-fenses, placed restrictions on bail, and limited the use of the exclusionary rule (Zimring & Hawkins, 1992).

States quickly followed suit. In 1985 Georgia legislation increased mandatory minimum sentences for cocaine trafficking, permitted fines up to $500,000, and restricted judicial discretion in sentencing.[3] New Jersey's 1987 drug legislation, considered a "model for the nation" (New Jersey Supreme Court, 1990), mandated imprisonment for selling drugs within 1,000 feet of a school, and increased penalties for all drug posses-sion and sale offenses. In 1988 New York legislators reduced the thresh-old for a felony cocaine possession charge from one-eighth ounce (3.5 grams) to approximately one gram, or six vials of crack.[4] Penalties for felony sale convictions were set equal to mandatory minimums for armed robbery, aggravated assault, and manslaughter. Both New York and Georgia passed laws mandating incarceration for second drug convic-tions. These statutes typified legislative efforts to strengthen punishment and increase its certainty.

One obvious result of the war on drugs has been vast increases in drug arrests, both for possession and selling, and a dramatic change in the composition of defendant and prison populations. Between 1980 and 1988, drug arrests in New York City increased from 18,521 (40% for heroin or other opiates) to 88,641 (44% for crack) (Belenko, Fagan, & Chin, 1991). The proportion of drug arrestees increased from 11% of the arrestee popu-lation in 1980 to 31% in 1989 (New York City Police Department, 1990).

Drug arrestees have also received harsher treatment at all stages of case processing, compared with both nondrug arrestees and drug arrestees during earlier drug epidemics.[5] Since 1983 drug offenders in New York City have a higher probability of felony charges at arrest, are less likely to make bail, and are more likely to be held in pretrial detention without bail (Belenko et al., 1991). In the courts, drug caseloads increased by 56% between 1983 and 1987 in a sample of 26 cities nationwide (Goerdt & Martin, 1989).

In New York, California, and the federal prison systems, drug offend-ers are now the largest inmate group (Bureau of Justice Statistics, 1992). In the federal prisons in 1990, more than 50% of the 1990 inmates were drug offenders (BJS, 1992). In 1988 drug offenders comprised more than 20% of New York State prison population, exceeding all other offense and offender types and outpacing rapid prison expansion (Division of Criminal Justice Services [hereafter, DCJS], 1988); within one year, drug offenders comprised more than one third of the prison inmates (DCJS, 1990). In California 43% of the admissions to state prison were parole violators returned to prison by the Parole Board without a conviction for a new charge, due in large part to the increased use of drug testing by parole officers (Messinger et al., 1988). This situation was evident in other large states nationwide, including Texas and Florida (BJS, 1989). As investments in treatment and other sentencing alternatives have lagged behind the growth in arrests and convictions, prison populations have grown sharply.

Obviously, efforts to mobilize legal institutions to respond more harshly to drug crimes have been successful. Arrests, prosecutions, convictions, prison sentences, and parole revocations all have increased sharply in a relatively short time (Goerdt & Martin, 1989; Zimring & Hawkins, 1992). Both legislative activism and the political salience of drug cases increased the likelihood that drug offenders will be incarcerated, regardless of their criminal histories or the comparative risks they posed to public safety (Belenko et al., 1991).

Mobilizing the Law for Deterrence

The mobilization of the criminal law to deter drug crimes has both symbolic and substantive components. Certainly, the passage of legislative mandates for lengthy prison terms "symbolizes public contempt for the actions of persons who sell, manufacture, or possess large quantities of drugs" (Myers, 1989, p. 296). Such responses are particularly appropriate when drug use is defined as a "moral problem" (ONDCP 1989, p. 53). The symbolic component of drug policy may be intended as a general deterrent, by conveying the message that legal consequences are likely and severe if one uses or sells drugs.

However, no such clarity is evident regarding the substantive bases of criminal punishment for drug offenders. Apart from conveying societal outrage at drug offenders, we expect the law to "do something" about drug problems. Yet the intent of the criminal law and the precise meaning of criminal sanctions is rarely stated with such precision. Although federal policy calls for the use of "tough and coherently punitive anti-drug measures" (ONDCP, 1989, p. 5) that call for more police and more prisons (ONDCP, cited in Zimring & Hawkins, 1992), we are not told why criminal sanctions are appropriate: to retributively punish drug offenders, to incapacitate them, or to deter them from further involvement with drugs.

The substantive component evidently is a specific deterrent: to stop people from using drugs, to stop users who are "highly contagious" (ONDCP, 1989, p. 8). Such laws may also reflect incapacitative intents: The ONDCP strategy mentions "a short-term reduction in the number of . . . casual and regular users" and "future reductions in [those who] are recruited" (ONDCP, 1989, p. 7). In either view, the use of criminal sanctions is intended to reduce the extent and severity of drug problems by incarcerating drug offenders.[6]

Sanctions and Deterrence

Commonsense notions guide the deterrence doctrine: Most individuals would rather avoid prison and, accordingly, are discouraged from criminal behavior (Miller & Anderson, 1986). For advocates of deterrence, punishment has greater utility than the indirect effects of decreasing criminal participation through increasing legitimate opportunities or individual treatment: Punishment is less expensive and more direct. Yet, despite a growing body of literature on general deterrence (for reviews, see, Blumstein, Cohen, & Nagin, 1978; Cook, 1980; Tittle, 1985; Williams & Hawkins, 1986), there has been virtually no research on the general or specific deterrent effects of criminal sanctions for drug offenders.

General deterrent effects depend on the probability that offenders view their behaviors as likely to be detected and severely punished. That is, the threat of punishment will regulate perceptions of crime costs and the marginal gains from crime opportunities (Kramer, 1990). Specific deterrent effects suggest that offenders, having received some pain or deprivation from punishment, will choose not to pay that penalty or cost again. Our focus in this chapter is on the specific deterrent effects of punishment.

There is little experimental evidence that punishment deters future crimes. Farrington (1983) and Farrington, Ohlin, and Wilson (1986) found no evidence of deterrent effects in a review of the results of randomized experiments. The Provo experiment found no differences in recidivism among delinquent males who were assigned to a community program under threat of incarceration, compared to regular probation supervision (Empey & Erickson, 1972). Sherman and Berk (1984) found evidence of the deterrent effects of arrest and a night in jail for wife assault, but replications that corrected biases in the original experiment failed to confirm the results (Dunford, Huizinga, & Elliott, 1990; Hirschel, Hutchison, & Dean, 1992).

Evidence of deterrent effects were found in experiments on tax compliance (Schwartz & Orleans, 1967, cited in Zimring & Hawkins, 1973), and enforcement of child support orders (Lempert, 1981). However, these involved relatively weak sanctions, such as threats of further legal action. Few studies have examined whether deterrent effects vary by sanction strength or severity; in fact, most experimental research has examined relatively weak sanctions (Farrington, 1983).

Farrington et al. (1986) found evidence that punishment may actually have iatrogenic effects that produce increases in offending rates. Grau, Fagan, and Wexler (1984) found that abused women who obtained restraining orders against their assailants were more often and more severely battered after the orders were issued, compared to women seeking other remedies. And consider Fagan's (1990b) finding that recidivism rates were higher among youths in weak experimental correctional treatment programs, compared to those in mainstream juvenile corrections. In that study, experimental interventions were iatrogenic in poorly implemented programs, but significantly effective in well-implemented programs. Evidently, deterrent effects vary by the strength and integrity of the sanction.

Other research suggests that sanction severity may interact with offender and offense types to influence specific deterrent effects. That is, the strength or severity of a criminal sanction may interact with offender backgrounds or behaviors to produce or inhibit deterrent effects. For example, the deterrent effects of arrest were greater for spouse assailants with fewer prior contacts with the police, and were weaker for assailants who had low "stakes in conformity" (Sherman, 1992).[7] The salience of sanctions seemed to interact with ecological factors that influenced the social or economic costs of conformance or continued law violation. Evidently, both situational factors and cognitive processes influence individual thresholds for sanction sensitivity.

Zimring and Hawkins (1973) point out that specific deterrence requires social actors to rationally calculate the costs and benefits of crime, a notion that Akers (1990) has explicitly linked to social learning processes. In other words, specific deterrence is likely to depend on the individual actor's social context and prior experiences to calculate the opportunity costs of legal behavior, the perceived costs and likelihood of punishment, and the marginal benefits of illegal monetary gains. However, these processes have not been examined under the skewed economic and social conditions in inner cities, where drug arrests have been concentrated for more than a decade (Chaiken & Chaiken, 1990).

In particular, two factors may influence the deterrent effects of criminal sanctions for drug offenders in the context of legal mobilization against drug crimes: the social context of sentencing that determines the likelihood and severity of sanctions for drug offenders, and the economic context where the costs of punishment and benefits of continued participation are weighed.

DETERRENCE AND THE ECONOMIC CONTEXT OF SANCTIONS

The expansion of the drug economy in the 1980s created opportunities for income and drug use that have been well exploited by inner-city residents. Participants in drug use and selling were people who were not well matched to the rapidly changing formal labor market, either spatially or in their job skills (Case & Katz, 1990; Fagan, 1992; Freeman, 1991). And they were very well matched to the labor market for drug distribution (Fagan & Chin, 1990). Drug selling evidently has not drawn people away from the formal labor market (Fagan, 1992), and for many already employed, drug selling offers greater rewards (but with greater risks) than formal income (Fagan, 1992; Reuter, MacCoun, & Murphy, 1990).[8]

Although drug sellers in Washington, D.C., acknowledged the legal, physical, and social risks of their work, criminal punishment was not high among them (Reuter et al., 1990). The risk of physical harm was more salient for this group than arrest or incarceration. Freeman (1991) found similar trends for risk assessments and the deterrent effects of perceived sanctions among disadvantaged inner-city youths in Boston. Fagan (1992) and Padilla (1992) showed the strong economic incentives for drug selling compared to licit income among young drug sellers, and the independence of drug selling from prior incarceration experiences.

For those outside the formal and/or licit economy, the high returns from drug selling may raise their reservation wage (the base wage at which they will enter the formal labor market) and further distance them from legal economic activities (Bluestone, Stevenson, & Tilly, 1991; Moss & Tilly, 1991). For participants in the illicit economy of drug selling, punishment is an opportunity cost (i.e., lost income); but so is participation in the formal economy at relatively lower wages (Fagan, 1992). For punishment—imprisonment or probation supervision—to be an effective deterrent, it must be coupled with changes in the perceived marginal gains from continued drug selling, compared to licit economic activities.

Accordingly, the deterrent effects of criminal sanctions are likely to vary with labor market conditions generally, and with specific individuals' positions within the licit or illicit labor market. For drug sellers, the role of financial gain was evident in the calculation of the likelihood of continued drug selling (Case & Katz, 1990; Freeman, 1991; Reuter et al., 1990). Sanctions are unlikely to be effective if they address only the costs of criminal activity. Sanctions also must either discount or neutralize the gains from participation in drug selling, or change perceptions of monetary opportunities and rewards for renewed participation following punishment. If deterrent effects are contingent on the conditions under which punishments are applied (Tittle, 1969, 1980), these conditions will determine the motivations and perceptions of actors within specific contexts (Zimring & Hawkins, 1973).

DRUG CRIMES AND THE ORGANIZATIONAL CONTEXT
OF SENTENCING

Beginning in 1985 legal institutions in New York expanded rapidly to accommodate the unprecedented numbers of drug arrests. To cope with the expansion of their calendars and caseloads, criminal justice agencies created new legal institutions and renovated existing ones. Prosecutors created special units for drug cases, special court units (N Parts) were created to handle drug cases exclusively, and a new court was created that consolidated lower and superior court functions (arraignment, felony indictment, trial, and sentencing) to expedite processing of drug cases (Belenko, Nickerson, & Rubinstein, 1990). Judges were reassigned from civil and other courts to preside in the special courts. Public defense counsel and administrative staff also expanded quickly to service the new courts and defendants.

This expansion occurred at the same time that judicial responses to drug offenses grew more severe. From 1984 to 1986, decisions in drug cases became harsher: Higher bail amounts were set; bail was denied more often; charges were more severe; and as a result, cases more often were disposed in superior courts where longer sentences were available (Belenko et al., 1991). The emergence of crack cocaine during a moral panic over substance use (Reinarman & Levine, 1989), and rapid expansion of the judicial system during an era of declining societal tolerance for drug crimes, further hardened judicial responses.[9]

As the courts expanded rapidly, new actors were assembled quickly in working groups within each court and confronted with unprecedented drug caseloads (Belenko et al., 1990).[10] To the extent that sentencing reflects holistic and work group processes (Eisenstein & Jacob, 1977; Emerson, 1983), the new working groups did not have the time to form shared perceptions and a consensus of crime seriousness (relative severity) to determine the "going rates" of imprisonment for drug offenses. They rarely saw cases other than drug cases, limiting their perceptions of which in the "stream of cases" (Emerson, 1981) were more serious and thus deserving of the last resort sanction of imprisonment. The volume of cases offered little time or incentive for differentiation of cases that were most deserving of the last resort punishment of prison, while legislative activism to stiffen sentences further limited judicial discretion as to how much time was merited by what types of drug offenders.

Faced with few treatment options for users or intermediate sanctions, sentencing also was constrained by demands for organizational efficiency and resource limitations. The special courts for drug offenders in New York City (N Parts) exerted irresistible pressure on defendants to accept pleas or face trials with the barely concealed threat of lengthy sentences for more serious charges (Belenko et al., 1990). With ritual or symbolic pressure to implement punitive sentences, sentencing alternatives were unlikely to be considered, even if widely available. There was little political or discretionary margin for risk taking.

Although historically there has been a calculus or threshold for incarceration among offense and offender types, the influx of a large number of new cases with high political salience, but little correspondence to other cohorts of arrestees, complicated the efforts of the hastily assembled working groups to establish their importance relative to other types of cases. Factors that influenced sentencing decisions for other cases (for example, victim injury and prior records for robbery offenders) became less important in this context in sorting drug cases for use of last resort sanctions (see, Emerson, 1981, on the concept of last resorts). Accordingly, sanctions were determined more by the charges attached to the case than normative legal and social dynamics in the courtroom.

Evaluating Drug Policy:
Research Questions About Deterrence and Drug Crimes

Despite the mobilization of the law and legal institutions to combat drug crimes, there has been virtually no research to assess the effects of punishment on drug offenders, either users or sellers.[11] There also has been little research on the implementation of deterrent effects for drug offenders. Has the mobilization of legal institutions increased the certainty and severity of punishment? If so, are the targets of most legislative activity, drug traffickers, more likely to receive the most severe forms of punishment? Finally, because drug use, drug selling, violence, and other crimes are closely related (Fagan, 1990a), we might expect that sanctions would deter criminality in general. Are deterrent effects for drug offenders limited to drug crimes, or are they generalized to law violations more broadly?

These questions are addressed in this chapter. The specific deterrent effects of incarceration are compared to other criminal sanctions for drug offenders in New York City, arrested during two successive cocaine crises in the 1980s: the expansion of street-level cocaine markets in the early 1980s (Zimmer, 1987), and the emergence of crack in 1985 (Fagan & Chin, 1989). During this era the ritual world of public statements was translated into legal interventions through increased efforts to detect drug activities and penalties to sanction them. Street-level enforcement was vastly expanded through programs such as Operation Pressure Point

(Zimmer, 1987) and the Tactical Narcotics Teams (TNT) (see Sviridoff & Hillsman, this volume). Penal code definitions and penalties were modified to stiffen punishment for crack possession and sale.[12] Legal institutions were mobilized further through the creation of special narcotics courts and special prosecution teams (Belenko et al., 1990). These combined efforts created conditions that made possible the implementation of specific deterrence for drug offenders.

But the unique context in which drug problems unfolded in the past decade suggests that social and economic contexts may mediate the effects of criminal sanctions for drug crimes. The specific deterrent effects of criminal punishment for drug offenses are contextually embedded in two ways. First, the economic lives of defendants and the labor market and economic conditions of the community combine to subjectively influence perceptions of risks and opportunities. Thus deterrent effects must account not only for the certainty of punishment, but also for whether prison is a threat worth avoiding. Second, the social and organizational context of sentencing influences the probability and logic of sanctions, especially the last resort sanction of imprisonment. Accordingly, if sanctions are reactive with offenses and offenders, the contextual processes that shape the "going rates" of punishment will also influence the effectiveness of sanctions.

A Case Study

In this chapter, these propositions are examined for drug offenders in the criminal justice system of New York City during the mid-1980s, a period of rapidly changing contexts both in the courts and in the neighborhoods where drug activity was concentrated.[13] Official records were recorded and analyzed from 3,424 cocaine hydrochloride (HCL, or powdered cocaine) arrestees[14] and 3,403 crack arrestees[15] between 1983 and 1986. The samples were drawn from the New York City Police Department (NYPD) computerized on-line booking system (OLBS). Drug cases were identified from "special events codes," or "flags," on booking forms that indicated whether their arrest involved possession or sale of cocaine powder or crack.[16] Case outcomes and criminal history information were obtained from the state's Department of Criminal Justice Services. For details on the samples and other methodological issues, see Belenko et al. (1991) and Fagan and Chin (1989).

The defendants were hardly newcomers to the criminal justice system. More than two-thirds of the felony arrestees had prior records. Nearly one-fourth of the felony possession cohorts, and 40% of the misdemeanor arrestees, had at least four prior arrests. About 40% of arrestees charged with felony possession, 50% of those charged with felony sale, and 60% of the misdemeanor arrestees had one or more prior felony or misdemeanor convictions. More than one-third had prior jail sentences, and 10% had prior prison records.

Few defendants were young; less than 20% were below 21 years of age. There were significant racial differences by drug offense and type of drug. Latinos were disproportionately present in the arrest cohorts, especially for crack selling. Misdemeanor arrestees differed from felony arrestees in several ways: They were younger, more often African-American, and for cocaine HCL arrestees, less stable residentially and more often out of the labor force. These distinctions between misdemeanor and felony will become important in explaining the differential effects of criminal sanctions for this group that we observe later on.

We compared recidivism by the type of sanction imposed at sentencing: (a) prison terms of more than one year, (b) jail terms of less that one year, (c) probation sentences, (d) fines and continuances, and (e) discharges (conditional and unconditional). We also examined the effects of actual sentence length.[17] Recidivism rates for several types of nondrug and drug offenses were computed, after controlling for time at risk through September 30, 1989. The annual rate was computed from the ratio of arrests to time at risk. The number of incarceration terms and total time served were retained as additional recidivism measures.

SANCTIONING DRUG OFFENDERS

Pretrial Decisions

For many defendants, pretrial detention was the sole punishment they received; their guilty pleas resulted in sentences to split sentences, with the incarceration portion suspended pending probation outcomes. Others were sentenced to time served (in detention) rather than further jail or prison sentences. This reliance on front-end punishment was an unofficial policy that was acknowledged by prosecutors in private conversations and public forums.[18]

Defendants charged with felony drug sales had the highest rates of pretrial detention (82.2%). Bail amounts also were consistently higher for drug selling charges, controlling for other charges in the case. Evidently, felony drug sale charges were regarded more seriously by the courts in their pretrial decisions than were other drug charges. These patterns reflect judicial views about the severity of crack selling: In interviews, 125 lower court and superior court judges in New York ranked crack selling as equal in seriousness to violent crimes, and more serious than felony property offenses or drug possession offenses (Belenko et al., 1990).

Punishment Certainty

Conviction rates were consistently high: More than 80% were convicted on the original charge or a reduced charge. Conviction rates were highest (83%) for those originally charged with misdemeanors. Most of these occurred through guilty pleas, and fewer than 1% went to trial. Dismissals occurred in 12.3% of the cases, and were virtually nonexistent in misdemeanor drug cases. The residual were cases that either transferred to other jurisdictions or courts, or those where defendants absconded.

Table 12.1 shows that more than one in three convicted defendants were sentenced either to prison or jail. The likelihood of incarceration was higher for misdemeanor drug defendants (46.1%) than felony drug defendants, and higher when the most serious case charge was a misdemeanor (44.4%) than felony drug or nondrug cases. The greater likelihood of jail (compared to prison) terms may reflect either greater comfort among judges with the shorter sentences for misdemeanor crimes, or their reticence to use scarce prison spaces for drug offenders. The higher incarceration rates for misdemeanor convictions may also reflect the dependence on plea bargaining during arraignment to cope with the glut of drug cases and move calendars swiftly.

The special N Parts (drug courts) in New York were developed to cope with the mass production of arrests from street-level enforcement programs to attack drug selling, and may have contributed to the routinization and standardization of sentencing decisions. The organizational demand to maintain calendars in the face of unprecedented numbers of arrests created dependence on plea bargaining and may actually have increased the base rate of plea acceptance (Belenko et al., 1990). The pressure from N Part judges on defense attorneys and defendants to accept pleas at arraignment, or face more drastic sentences in superior court, provided inadequate time for defendants to digest plea offers or to enter into more detailed plea negotiations.

Punishment Severity

The average sentence was 11.4 months.[19] Contrary to expectations, defendants charged with drug sales were not punished more severely than

Table 12.1 Sanction Probability and Severity by Drug Charge and Most Serious Case Charge

| Drug Charge | Most Serious Case Charge | | | All Cases |
	Felony Drug	Nondrug Felony	Misdemeanor	
Felony Possession				
N	906	112	324	1,342
% Dismissed	14.1	15.4	10.3	14.4
% Convicted	74.6	81.8	74.7	75.2
% Incarcerated[a]	35.3	28.3	39.8	36.7
Avg. Minimum Term[b]	10.4	28.3	2.1	9.8
Felony Sale				
N	3,232	23	250	3,504
% Dismissed	12.3	17.4	13.6	12.4***
% Convicted	82.2	73.9	74.0	81.6***
% Incarcerated[a]	33.9	39.1	35.6	34.0
Avg. Minimum Term[b]	20.0	13.6	6.5	18.9
Misdemeanor Drug Charge				
N	26	130	1,730	1,886
% Dismissed	3.8	14.2	10.7	10.8*
% Convicted	76.9	77.2	83.2	82.7*
% Incarcerated[a]	46.2	40.8	46.5	46.1
Avg. Minimum Term[b]	3.3	13.0	1.3	2.1
All Cases				
N	4,163	265	2,304	6,723
% Dismissed	12.6***	14.2	11.6***	12.3
% Convicted	80.5***	78.8	81.0***	80.6
% Incarcerated[a]	34.3	39.6	44.4***	38.0***
Avg. Minimum Term[b]	17.7	19.3	1.9	11.4[c]

a. Percentage of those convicted or pled guilty,
 $p\chi^2$: *$p \le .05$
 ***$p \le .001$
b. In months
c. ANOVA for sentence:

	F	p	β
Drug Charge	247.7	.000	
Case Charge	70.1	.000	
Drug × Case Charge	9.9	.000	
Age	2.1	.143	.061
African-American	133.1	.000	−7.542
Prior Drug Arrests	9.9	.002	1.101
Prior Time Served	19.6	.000	1.904

other defendants. Most felony offenders were sentenced to 3-year terms, with little variation for sales versus possession charges. Figure 12.1 illustrates the significant interaction between drug charges and other case

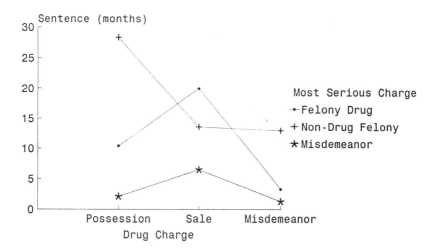

Figure 12.1. Sentence Length by Drug Charge and Most Serious Case Charge
Drug Charge × Case Charge: $p(F) = .000$

charges for sentence length. Possession cases involving nondrug felonies received the longest sentences, but defendants with only possession charges received more lenient sentences. Felony sales cases with no other charges resulted in more severe sentences than sales cases involving other felony charges.

Overall, there appeared to be weak logic guiding sentencing decisions. Maximum likelihood estimates for detention (probit models) and sentencing decisions (probit, tobit models) were weak and inconclusive. Neither offense nor offender characteristics combined with charges to influence sentencing outcomes. Prior record was the only factor that influenced incarceration decisions, but it was a weak predictor in an overall weak model and appeared to be independent of the type of drug charge in its effects on sentencing outcomes. Perhaps factors not measured were salient in sentencing decisions, but any such factors would have been social markers, not legally relevant information. Uniformity, even homogeneity, characterized sentencing decisions. The most severe sentences were not reserved for the defendants with the most serious charges. Lacking a calculus for assigning punishments, sentencing of drug offenders appeared to be a random process.

Table 12.2   Percentage Rearrested for Five Offense Types by Sanction Severity
(One Year or More Years at Risk)

| | | Rearrest Offense Type | | | |
Sanction	Drug Sale	Drug Possession	Felony Violence	Felony Property	All Offenses
Incarceration > 1 Year (N = 156)	14.1	15.4	10.3	9.0	41.0
Incarceration < 1 Year (N = 1,389)	18.4	26.3	12.4	22.3	56.0
Probation (N = 551)	15.6	14.0	6.4	9.6	39.0
Fine/Continuation (N = 2,293)	18.8	30.3	10.0	16.4	52.2
Dismissed/Discharged (N = 418)	23.4	23.4	9.8	17.0	49.5
Statistics					
χ^2	13.47	46.26	16.53	56.76	91.32
p	.097	.000	.035	.000	.000
Gamma	.069	−.0002	−.059	−.047	−.006

THE EFFECTS OF SANCTIONS ON RECIDIVISM

Recidivism measures were computed for all defendants who had at least one year of street time. Those with less than one year at risk either had lengthy minimum prison sentences or were rearrested quickly and reincarcerated. Accordingly, defendants sentenced to prison more often were excluded from the recidivism analysis because they did not have any street time and therefore had no opportunity to commit new crimes. Statistical corrections were introduced to address this problem.[20]

The percentage of defendants rearrested was calculated separately for each offense type. Table 12.2 shows that the percentage of offenders rearrested for drug possession, felony violence, felony property crimes, and total arrests differed significantly by type of sanction. However, the deterrent effects of more serious sanctions were not necessarily greater than less serious punishments, and they varied by type of rearrest charge. In particular, drug selling and drug use appear to be persistent and somewhat intractable behaviors that are as likely to be deterred by probation as by imprisonment.

Defendants with the most severe sentences had lower recidivism rates for drug sales and property offenses. But for drug possession, felony violence, and total rearrests, defendants sentenced to probation had the lowest recidivism rates. Recidivism rates for defendants with no sanctions were highest for drug sales, but lower than defendants sentenced to jail for drug possession, felony violence, felony property, and total rearrests. Sentences to short incarceration terms seem to be particularly ineffective in deterring future offending. Punishment may be effective in deterring some crimes, but it appears to be no more effective than probation in controlling drug sales, drug use (possession), or violence.

Certain offender types had lower rearrest rates for specific types of rearrests. The highest rates were found for sellers rearrested for selling. For this group, the probability of rearrest increased with sanction severity. Conversely, rearrests of drug users for violence were uniformly rare, regardless of the severity of sanction. Both sellers and users (possession charges) were more likely to be rearrested for violence when their cases were continued, but were equally likely to be rearrested for violence if their cases were dismissed (no sanction) or if they were sentenced to state prison.

The likelihood of rearrest for the five offense categories was not influenced by combinations of type of sanction, arrest charges, and offender characteristics. Maximum likelihood estimates of rearrest prevalence (logit) and incidence (tobit) were weak and inconclusive. Neither sanction severity nor length of incarceration were influential in the likelihood of rearrest after controlling for offense and offender characteristics. Having prior drug sale arrests increases the probability of a subsequent drug arrest, and having prior felony possession arrests increases the likelihood of rearrest for drug possession. Prior time served in prison or jail increases the likelihood of future arrest. Crack defendants were more likely to be rearrested for felony drug sales and felony violence.

We also examined offending rates for defendants with at least one year of street time. The results were similar to the previous recidivism analysis. Table 12.3 shows that, after controlling for background factors and prior record, there were only weak effects of sanction severity on rearrest rates after controlling for prior sanctions. Rearrest rates for drug selling and possession were comparable, regardless of whether the case was dismissed or the defendant imprisoned. Rearrest rates for violent and property crimes were lower for probationers than for those imprisoned. Prior behaviors were strongly associated with rearrest rates, independent of sanction severity. There were also no significant interactions between sanction severity and type of drug charge, suggesting that sanctions were not more effective for certain types of drug offenses. Once again, drug crimes appear to be intractable, persistent behaviors that are insensitive to the severity of criminal sanction.

Table 12.3 ANOVA on Adjusted Annual Reoffending Rates for Five Offense Types by Sanction Severity, Controlling for Background Factors (One Year or More Years at Risk)

	Drug Sale	Drug Possession	Felony Violence	Felony Property	All Offenses
			Offense Type		
Sanction					
Incarceration > 1 Year	.83	.77	.84	.95	1.09
Incarceration ≤ 1 Year	.79	1.15	.84	1.09	1.66
Probation	.70	.78	.74	.69	.92
Fine/Continuation	.81	1.03	.78	1.00	1.43
Dismissed/Discharged	.81	1.04	.71	1.09	1.62
ANOVA Results[a]					
Main Effects					
Sanction	.96	.85	.68	.98	2.34
Drug Charge	.43	8.29***	2.44	3.83*	1.05
Interactions					
Sanction × Drug Charge	1.63	.97	.08	.62	.85
Covariates					
Age	7.61**	.16	4.42*	1.96	5.94
	(.005)	(.002)	(-.006)	(.007)	(-.006)
African-American	.64	15.47***	.86	3.31	3.18
	(.027)	(.242)	(.039)	(.122)	(.066)
Prior Time Served	.40	21.90***	12.67***	19.68***	30.91***
	(.000)	(.001)	(.001)	(.001)	(.001)
Prior Arrest Rate	12.84***	54.58***	1.02	23.87***	9.40**
	(.070)	(.217)	(.019)	(.161)	(.061)
df	889	1,092	488	804	2,429

[a] ANOVA: F, Significance of F, Regression coefficients for covariates
$p(F)$: *$p \leq .05$
**$p \leq .01$
***$p \leq .001$

Conclusions

The anti-drug crusades of the 1980s translated into laws and policies that relied heavily on criminal sanctions, especially incarceration, to control the use and trafficking of illicit drugs. Sentences for drug offenders in New York City between 1983 and 1986 reflected ideological trends that regarded punishment as important symbolic and substantive components of anti-drug sentiment. The enactment and popularization of laws mandating incarceration, regardless of their enforcement, symbolized public contempt for both users and sellers (Myers, 1989), while the mobilization of legal institutions to punish drug offenders reflected public will to wage war against drug users.

Whatever the successes of the symbolic component of drug policy, its specific deterrent effects evidently were quite limited for drug offenders in the large and active drug markets in New York in the 1980s. The limited effects of incarceration for all types of drug offenders call into question the assumptions about punishment that mandate or encourage prison sentences for drug offenders. Reductions in the participation and frequency of rearrest among drug offenders were unrelated to the severity of the criminal sanction they received.[21] The same results might easily be achieved by chance. Despite the considerable risks of incarceration if arrested, the marginal reduction in rearrest rates for those imprisoned, compared to probationers or those not sanctioned at all, suggests little utility in the widespread use of incarceration as a crime control measure for drug offenders.

Why wasn't recidivism influenced by sanction severity? The explanations have policy implications for drug policy in a changing economic and legal context.

RAISING THE "GOING RATE"

The mobilization of legal institutions to respond to drug epidemics occurred during overlapping cocaine epidemics, beginning in the early 1980s and continuing through the appearance of crack. The courts expanded rapidly and new actors were thrown together in working groups and confronted with unprecedented caseloads. Prevailing formulas for sentencing and plea bargaining were challenged: Most drug crimes rarely involved violence or property loss (Fagan & Chin, 1989), yet prosecutors and sentencing judges linked drug selling with violence (Belenko et al., 1990). There was little differentiation of cases that were most deserving of the last resort punishment of prison, nor how much time was merited by what types of drug offenders.

In this climate, sentencing evidently became a monolithic process that focused on one dimension—the severity of the drug offense—and offered few options short of incarceration. In raising the "going rate" for drug crimes, factors that might have influenced a more strategic and rational sentencing scheme were no longer salient dimensions for sentencing. It is not surprising that this climate produced sentencing decisions where offenders and punishments were not well matched, and the differential reactions of offender types to sanctions were not considered.

DETERRENCE AND THE ECONOMETRICS OF DRUG SELLING

The high rate of incarceration suggests that the risk component of deterrence was well implemented in New York; yet offenders were not sensitive to these sanctions. Experienced offenders in particular seemed unfazed by punishment. For them, punishment is likely an accepted hazard of their chosen work that is inconsequential compared to the potential yields of drug crimes.

This raises doubts about the implied econometric model of specific deterrence that does not consider nonlegal factors.[22] As long as demand for drugs remains high, and the likelihood of marginal gains from drug selling are sufficient to neutralize motivations to avoid crime or participate in licit work, offenders in socially and economically marginal neighborhoods may continue to perceive strong economic benefits from participation in the drug economy. They also are likely to perceive little threat of punishment because there are few costs attached to its consequences. That is, their decisions may be independent of the certainty of punishment or its costs if no other choices are perceived. Deterrent effects reflect more than actual or perceived risks—marginal risk and marginal gain from avoidance of risk also are factors that some individuals seem to weigh in deciding that prison is not a threat worth avoiding.

HOW DO PEOPLE STOP USING OR SELLING DRUGS?

The natural history of drug use and selling offers some insight into the reasons why criminal punishment may have equivocal deterrent effects. Desistance from drug use (Biernacki, 1986; Waldorf, Reinarman, & Murphy, 1991) and selling (Adler 1985; Padilla, 1992; Williams 1989) is a lengthy, elaborate social psychological process that involves complex changes in definitions of self and management of one's social interactions. Desistance is a process, with many starts and failures, where relapses are common. For sellers, temporary returns to the material pleasures and excitement of the "life" are not unexpected when the mundane straight life may lead to boredom or financial problems.

Deterrence is not likely to result from a single punishment or any particular event in a sequence of encounters with the law. Together with pressures from the law and other highly valued sources (e.g., family), deterrence seems to be a process that unfolds over time. The low return from legal work may discount the rewards of stopping. Arrest, jailing, the hassle of court appearances, and perhaps a term in prison are part of a familiar cycle for drug offenders that is repeated several times in their careers. The deterrent effect of legal intervention is more likely to derive from maintaining a steady pressure over time that interacts with other social pressures to raise the risks/costs of drug involvement.

If desistance is a social psychological process, what are the potential contributions of criminal punishment in advancing the process? Are the marginal gains in deterring future drug crimes worth the costs of mounting a credible deterrent? The redirection of public resources from other areas that also contribute to desistance—treatment, economic and labor policies, education—implies a marginal cost for deterrence. The funds may be better spent on neutralizing the discount for legal financial gain and reducing the demand side of the equation. The weak deterrent effect of incarceration, compared to probation, suggests that similar marginal deterrent effects might be gained from less expensive alternative sanctions and legal pressures that interact with the social processes of desistance.

BALANCING POLICY

The exclusive focus on specific deterrence in the demand side of drug policy discounts important factors that are part of the natural process of desistance from drug use and selling. This focus also discounts the economic context of decisions to persist or desist from drug involvement. Mounting a specific deterrent effect in the face of widespread drug involvement may be an insurmountable challenge for legal institutions. The relocation of sentencing discretion from judges to the legislature, and in turn to prosecutors through their charging decisions, has achieved a uniformity in sentencing that serves political goals but adds little to the deterrent effect of punishment. Can we reasonably expect to jail all drug offenders? And with what effects on crime rates?

The weak effects of punishment may have counter-deterrent effects that breed disrespect for the laws and institutions that the punishments are designed to uphold. The challenge for policy is to contribute to the processes that motivate drug offenders to stop using and selling. This requires a balanced policy that addresses both punishment for law violation and efforts to revalue the gains from legal behaviors.

The limited choices for punishment present an opportunity for balanced policy. The current reliance on the extremes of incarceration and probation offer little substantive choice for judges and policymakers. Instead of questioning the underlying assumptions of specific deterrence, we respond to the limited effects of punishment with more serious punishment. A range of sanctions makes more sense, as does diversifying the substantive elements of sanctions to include "exits" from drug use or selling. For users, linking punishment with expanded treatment options would provide the types of pressures and alternatives that are implied in the desistance literature. For both users and sellers, so would treatments that increase human capital—job skills and education—that are part of the mix of pressures and escape paths that also characterize desistance. The creation of intermediate punishments would respond to the inadequacies of (de facto unsupervised) probation and provide pressures to stop, while limiting uses of incarceration. Expanding the options for sentencing might restore a more rational allocation of punishments that recognizes the varying thresholds and reactivity of offenders to sanctions.

Finally, the deterrent effects of sanctions may benefit from related policies that emphasize the conditions in which deterrence becomes effective—conditions that both provide and revalue legal opportunities for financial gain, increase the costs of illicit gain, and reduce the opportunities for drug use.

Notes

1. This position is termed "legalism" by Zimring and Hawkins (1992), who distinguish it from other views that are more functional regarding the public health and econometric (cost-benefit) consequences of drugs. The principle harm that accrues, apart from any harm from the drug itself, is the "threat . . . to the established order and political authority structure" (p. 10). Zimring and Hawkins characterize the federal (and most state) policy as legalist.

2. For comprehensive reviews, see Gusfield, 1975; Myers, 1989; Siegel, 1989; and Trebach, 1982.

3. Judges were no longer allowed to suspend or defer sentences, nor could they impose split sentences without the offender serving the mandatory minimum in prison (Myers, 1989). The 1985 bill (*1985 Ga. Laws 552, 1*) also lengthened minimum sentences for cocaine trafficking from 5-15 years to 10-25 years, and allowed life sentences for manufacturing or selling opiates, heroin, or hallucinogens.

4. This was an accommodation to the transformation of the cocaine market to primarily a crack market in New York City. One-eighth ounce of cocaine HCL powder converted to 40 to 55 vials of crack, depending on the size of the rocks and the contents of each vial (Fagan & Chin, 1988). Legislators reasoned that possession of six or more vials of crack indicated intent to sell rather than personal use of the drug.

5. Classification of drug offenders was problematic in New York and other locales. For obvious reasons, many arrestees charged with nondrug crimes are excluded from this classification, despite their possible involvement with drugs. But an audit of arrest reports by Fagan and Chin (1988, 1989) showed that many cocaine and crack arrestees actually did not possess or sell cocaine products. Instead, they were flagged as "drug" offenders but were charged with loitering and other nondrug crimes.

6. Some observers contend that the justification for deterrence should not depend on the deterrent effects of punishments. This argument most often has been advanced in the case of firearms control (Heumann & Loftin, 1979; Loftin & McDowall, 1984) and drunk driving (Ross, 1982).

7. Sherman (1992) reviewed the results of six experiments on the specific deterrent effects of arrest for spouse assault, and found that deterrence was weakest for assailants who were unemployed or not married. He concluded that deterrence was undermined when informal social controls were weak, or when attachments and commitments to conventional social activities were compromised by ecological contexts where marriage and work were devalued.

8. Much of this discussion applies to drug use as well. Among adult sellers in New York, nearly all were extensive users (Bourgois, 1989; Fagan, 1992; Fagan & Chin, 1989). Similar results were reported among probationers in Washington, D.C. (Reuter et al.. 1990) and adolescents (Altschuler & Brounstein, 1991). Others have reported strict codes of non-use among sellers (e.g., Williams, 1989).

9. See Gusfield (1975, p. 15) for an analysis of the moral component behind political fervor over drug problems. In the ONDCP (1989) strategy, crack was the substance that symbolized America's drug problems (p. 3). Its high potential for addiction and the violence associated with its distribution made crack a symbol of the moral argument in favor of bans against all drug use. Crack was said to be "the most dangerous and quickly addictive drug known to man" (ONDCP, 1989, p. 3). Casual use of crack and other drugs was deemed "highly contagious" (p. 11) and "degrad[ing to] human character" (p. 7). In a 1989 survey of judges in New York, nearly all believed that crack was more powerful and addictive than cocaine HCL (powder), and more closely associated with violent crime than any other drug (Belenko et al., 1990). Few (18.3%) believed that effective treatment exists for crack, while most believed that the public wanted harsher sentences for drug sellers and users.

10. See Eisenstein and Jacob (1977) and Emerson (1981, 1983) for a discussion of the importance of the social organization of the court in reaching consensus within informal working groups, for processing court cases and establishing the expected rates and types of punishment.

11. Research on deterrence has emphasized the perception of future detection and punishment for crime commission. Its applications to drug crimes generally have been limited to drunk driving (Lanza-Kaduce, 1988; Ross, 1982; Shapiro & Votey, 1984), and marijuana use (Paternoster, 1988). Research on the "Rockefeller" drug laws in New York in the 1970s found little evidence of general or specific deterrent effects for heroin users or sellers (Trebach, 1982, citing National Institute of Drug Abuse monographs). For comprehensive reviews, see Grasmick and Bursik, 1990; Klepper and Nagin, 1989; Kramer, 1990; Miller and Anderson, 1986; Paternoster, 1988; and Williams and Hawkins, 1986.

12. Under the New York State Penal Law, felonies are classified into five categories (A, B, C, D, E, in descending order of severity). B-felony drug sale or possession carries a maximum prison sentence of 25 years. B-felony sale is charged for the sale of any amount of a "narcotic" drug (the Penal Law definition includes cocaine and its derivatives). In 1987 the threshold for B-felony possession of any amount of a "narcotic" drug with intent to sell, was reduced from one-half ounce or more (aggregate weight) of a substance containing "narcotics" to one-eighth ounce.

13. See Fagan, 1992; Johnson, Williams, Dei, and Sanabria, 1990; and Sullivan, 1989, 1991; for analyses of the relationship between drug markets and structural changes in New York City neighborhoods throughout the 1970s and 1980s.

14. The cocaine HCL arrest cohort included all defendants arrested for a cocaine-related offense during 1983-1984, the period of intensive street-level enforcement responses to cocaine (Zimmer, 1987), and preceding the appearance of crack in New York City.

15. The crack arrest cohort included all arrests that occurred between August 1, 1986, and October 31, 1986. This represents a period shortly after vigorous anti-crack enforcement efforts began, with the creation of a special Anti-Crack Unit within the NYPD Narcotics Division (see Fagan & Chin, 1989, for details on this unit).

16. To validate the crack or cocaine HCL flags, incident descriptions on arrest reports were examined. Cases meeting one of the following criteria were included in the analysis: (a) the defendant was arrested for drug possession, drug sale, drug sale and possession, or possession of drug paraphernalia; (b) the arrest report mentioned a controlled substance, cocaine, crack, narcotic, or paraphernalia; (c) drugs or drug paraphernalia were confiscated; or (d) the defendant was arrested for loitering for the purpose of using drugs. Loitering arrests were screened for the specific mention of drugs or paraphernalia to avoid inclusion of spurious arrests from street sweeps (see Fagan & Chin, 1988, for details on the case evaluation procedures).

17. Because time served was unavailable, actual prison time was estimated as the minimum sentence. Because of crowding in New York State prisons, the majority of defendants serve only the minimum term after becoming eligible for parole at two-thirds of the minimum sentence. For jail terms, the sentence was used as the actual incarceration term.

18. Kings County (Brooklyn) Prosecutor Leslie Snyder stated, in a debate on public television, that the glut of drug offenders made it impossible to adequately punish all who were convicted. She went on to say that front-end punishment was a necessary goal for cases whose severity did not require scarce prison space.

19. Data for time served were not available. For jail sentences of less than one year, the time served was assumed to be equal to the sentence. For prison sentences, the time served was assumed to be the minimum sentence. Inmates first become eligible for parole at two-thirds of the minimum sentence. Assuming that parole releases occur at first hearing for only a percentage of defendants, the time served was estimated at the minimum term.

20. This type of sample selection bias poses a number of risks in accurately estimating the effects of sanctions (Berk, 1983; cf. Weisburd, Waring, & Wheeler, 1990; Stoltzenberger & Relles, 1990). Using probit models to estimate the selection process, the recidivism models were corrected by including a new variable that represents the effects of variables that were significantly associated with the model for sentence length (see Berk, 1983; Myers, 1989; Smith, Wish, & Jarjoura, 1989). The solution involved eliminating explanatory variables that were not significantly associated with whether a defendant has any free time in which to commit new offenses. Because lengthy incarceration was more likely for drug sellers with prior histories of drug selling and current offenses that included nondrug felonies, these factors were used to approximate the bias in the analyses in which some cases were censored by not having sufficient street time. Despite these efforts, no discernible differences were found in the results after the correction.

21. Considering unreported and undetected crimes by drug offenders, the deterrent effects were likely to be even weaker.

22. See, for example, Klepper and Nagin, 1989; Kramer, 1990; Miller and Anderson, 1986.

References

Adler, P. (1985). *Wheeling and dealing: An ethonography of an upper-level drug dealing and smuggling community.* New York: Columbia University Press.

Akers, R. A. (1990). Rational choice, deterrence, and social learning theory in criminology. *Journal of Criminal Law and Criminology, 82*(2), 653-676.

Altschuler, D. M., & Brounstein, P. M. (1991). Patterns of drug use, drug trafficking, and other delinquency among inner city adolescent males in Washington, D.C. *Criminology, 29*(4), 589-622.

Belenko, S., Fagan, J., & Chin, K. (1991). Criminal justice responses to crack. *Journal of Research in Crime and Delinquency, 28*(1), 55-74.

Belenko, S., Nickerson, G., & Rubinstein, T. (1990). *Crack and the New York City courts: A study of judicial responses and attitudes. Final report* (Grant No. SJI-88-14X-E-050). Albany, NY: State Justice Institute.

Berk, R. A. (1983, June). An introduction to sample selection bias in sociological data. *American Sociological Review, 48*, 386-398.

Biernacki, P. (1986). *Pathways from addiction.* Philadelphia: Temple University Press.

Bluestone, B., Stevenson, M. H., & Tilly, C. (1991 March). *The deterioration of labor market prospects for young men with limited schooling: Assessing the impact of "demand side" factors.* Paper presented at the Eastern Economics Association Meetings, Pittsburgh.

Blumstein, A., Cohen, J., & Nagin, D. (1978). *Deterrence and incapacitation: Estimating the effects of criminal sanctions on crime rates.* Washington, DC: National Academy Press.

Bourgois, P. (1989). In search of Horatio Alger: Culture and ideology in the crack economy. *Contemporary Drug Problems, 16*(4), 619-650.

Bureau of Justice Statistics (BJS). (1989). *Criminal cases in five states.* Washington, DC: U.S. Department of Justice, Bureau of Justice Statistics.

Bureau of Justice Statistics (BJS). (1992). *Prisoners in 1991* (BJS Bulletin NCJ-134729). Washington, DC: U.S. Department of Justice, Bureau of Justice Statistics.

Case, A., & Katz, L. F. (1990). *The company you keep: The effect of family and neighborhood on disadvantaged youths.* Unpublished manuscript. Cambridge: Harvard University, Kennedy School of Government.

Chaiken, J. M. (Ed.). (1988). *Street-level drug enforcement: Examining the issues.* Washington, DC: U.S. Department of Justice, National Institute of Justice.

Chaiken, J. M., & Chaiken, M. R. (1990). Drugs and predatory crime. In M. Tonry & J. Q. Wilson (Eds.), *Drugs and crime* (Vol. 13, pp. 203-240). Chicago: University of Chicago Press.

Cook, P. J. (1980). Research in criminal deterrence: Laying the groundwork for the second decade. In N. Morris & M. Tonry (Eds.), *Crime and justice: An annual review of research* (Vol. 3). Chicago: University of Chicago Press.

Division of Criminal Justice Services. (1988). *New York State: Trends in felony drug offense processing, 1983-87.* Albany: Author.

Division of Criminal Justice Services. (1990). *New York State: Trends in felony drug offense processing, 1985-89.* Albany: Author.

Dunford, F., Huizinga, D., & Elliott, D. S. (1990). The role of arrest in domestic assault: The Omaha domestic violence experiment. *Criminology, 28*, 183-206.

Eisenstein, J., & Jacob, H. (1977). *Felony justice: An organizational analysis of criminal courts.* Boston: Little, Brown.

Emerson, R. (1981). On last resorts. *American Journal of Sociology, 87*, 1-22.

Emerson, R. (1983). Holistic effects in social control decision making. *Law and Society Review, 17*, 425-455.

Empey, L. T., & Erickson, M. L. (1972). *The Provo experiment.* Lexington, MA: D. C. Heath.

Epstein, E. J. (1977). *Agency of fear*. New York: Putnam.

Fagan, J. (1990a). Intoxication and aggression. In M. Tonry & J. Q. Wilson (Eds.), *Drugs and crime* (Vol.13, pp. 241-320). Chicago: University of Chicago Press.

Fagan, J. (1990b). Treatment and reintegration of violent delinquents: Experimental results. *Justice Quarterly, 7*(2), 233-263.

Fagan, J. (1992). Drug selling and licit income in distressed neighborhoods: The economic lives of street-level drug users and dealers. In G. Peterson & A. Harrell (Eds.), *Barriers to urban opportunity*. Washington, DC: Urban Institute Press.

Fagan, J., & Chin, K. (1988). *Validation of arrest flags for crack and cocaine arrests, 1983-86* (Internal memorandum). New York: New York City Criminal Justice Agency.

Fagan, J., & Chin, K. (1989). Initiation into crack and cocaine: A tale of two epidemics. *Contemporary Drug Problems, 16*(4), 579-618.

Fagan, J., & Chin, K. (1990). Violence as regulation and social control in the distribution of crack. In M. De la Rosa, E. Lambert, and B. Gropper (Eds.), *Drugs and violence* (NIDA Research Monograph No. 103). Rockville, MD: National Institute on Drug Abuse.

Farrington, D. P. (1983). Randomized experiments on crime and justice. In N. Morris & M. Tonry (Eds.), *Crime and Justice: An annual review of research* (Vol. 4). Chicago: University of Chicago Press.

Farrington, D. P., Ohlin, L. E., & Wilson, J. Q. (1986). *Understanding and controlling crime: Toward a new strategy of research*. New York: Springer-Verlag.

Feldman, H., Agar, M., & Beschner, G. (1979). *Angel dust: An ethnographic study of PCP users*. Lexington, MA: Lexington Books.

Freeman, R. B. (1991). *Crime and the economic status of disadvantaged young men*. Presented at the Conference on Labor Markets and Urban Mobility. Washington, DC: The Urban Institute.

Goerdt, J. A., & Martin, J. A. (1989). The impact of drug cases on case processing in urban trial courts. *State Court Journal*, 4-12.

Grasmick, H. G., & Bursik, R. J., Jr. (1990). Conscience, significant others, and rational choice: Extending the deterrence model. *Law and Society Review, 24*(3), 837-861.

Grau, J., Fagan, J. A., & Wexler, S. (1984). Restraining orders for battered women: Issues in access and efficacy. *Women and Politics, 4*, 13-28.

Gusfield, J. R. (1975). The futility of knowledge: The relation of social science to public policy toward drugs. *Annals of the American Academy of Political and Social Science, 417*, 1-28.

Heumann, M., & Loftin, C. (1979). Mandatory sentencing and the abolition of plea bargaining: The Michigan felony firearm statute. *Law and Society Review, 13*, 393-428.

Hirschel, J. D., Hutchison, I. W., III, & Dean, C. W. (1992). The failure of arrest to deter spouse abuse. *Journal of Research in Crime and Delinquency, 29*, 7-33.

Hughes, G. (1983). The concept of crime. In S. Kalish (Ed.), *Encyclopedia of crime and justice*.

Johnson, B. D., Williams, T., Dei, K., & Sanabria, H. (1990). Drug abuse and the inner city: Impacts of hard drug use and sales on low income communities. In M. Tonry & J. Q. Wilson (Eds.), *Drugs and crime* (Vol. 13). Chicago: University of Chicago Press.

Kaplan, J. (1983). *The hardest drug: Heroin and public policy*. Chicago: University of Chicago Press.

Klepper, S., & Nagin, D. (1989). The deterrent effect of perceived certainty and severity of punishment revisited. *Criminology, 27*(4), 721-746.

Kramer, S. (1990). An economic analysis of criminal attempt: Marginal deterrence and the optimal structure of sanctions. *Journal of Criminal Law and Criminology, 81*(2), 398-417.

Lanza-Kaduce, L. (1988). Perceptual deterrence and drinking and driving among college students. *Criminology, 26*(2), 321-341.

Lempert, R. (1981). Organizing for deterrence: Lessons from a study of child support. *Law and Society Review, 18*, 5-10.

Loftin, C., & McDowall, D. (1984). The deterrent effects of the Florida firearms law. *Journal of Criminal Law and Criminology, 75*, 250-283.

Miller, J. L., & Anderson, A. B. (1986). Updating the deterrence doctrine. *Journal of Criminal Law and Criminology, 77*(2), 418-438.

Moore, M. H. (1977). *Buy and bust.* Lexington, MA: Lexington Books.

Moss, P., & Tilly, C. (1991). *Why black men are doing worse in the labor market: A review of supply-side and demand-side explanations.* Paper prepared for the Social Science Research Council, Committee on Research on the Urban Underclass, Subcommittee on Joblessness and the Underclass. New York: Social Science Research Council.

Myers, M. A. (1989). Symbolic policy and the sentencing of drug offenders. *Law and Society Review, 23*(2), 295-315.

New Jersey Supreme Court. (1990). *Proceeding of the 1990 New Jersey State judicial conference.* Trenton: Administrative Office of the Courts.

New York City Police Department. (1990). *Statistical report: Complaints and arrests, 1989.* New York: Office of Management Analysis and Planning.

Office of National Drug Control Policy (ONDCP). (1989). *National drug control strategy.* Washington, DC: The White House, Office of National Drug Control Policy.

Padilla, F. (1992). *The gang as work.* New Brunswick, NJ: Rutgers University Press.

Paternoster, R. (1988). Examining three-wave deterrence models: A question of temporal order and specification. *Journal of Criminal Law and Criminology, 79*(1), 135-179.

Reinarman, C., & Levine, H. G. (1989). Crack in context: Politics and media in America's latest drug scare. *Contemporary Drug Problems, 16*(4), 535-578.

Reuter, P., MacCoun, R., & Murphy, P. (1990). *Money from crime* (Report R-3894). Santa Monica, CA: RAND.

Ross, H. L. (1982). *Deterring the drunk driver: Legal policy and social control.* Lexington, MA: Lexington Books.

Shapiro, P., & Votey, H. L., Jr. (1984). Deterrence and subjective probabilities of arrest: Modeling individual decisions to drink and drive in Sweden. *Law and Society Review, 18*(4), 583-604.

Sherman, L. W. (1990). Police crackdowns. In N. Morris & M. Tonry (Eds.), *Crime and justice: An annual review of research* (Vol. 12). Chicago: University of Chicago Press.

Sherman, L. W. (1992). The influence of criminology on criminal law: Evaluating arrests for misdemeanor domestic violence. *Journal of Criminal Law and Criminology, 83*, 1-45.

Sherman, L. W., & Berk, R. (1984). The specific deterrent effects of arrest for domestic assault. *American Sociological Review, 49*, 261-272.

Siegel, R. K. (1989). *Intoxication: Life in pursuit of artificial paradise.* New York: Dutton.

Silver, G. (1979). *The dope chronicles: 1850-1950.* San Francisco: Harper & Row.

Smith, D., Wish, E., & Jarjoura, R. (1989). Drug use and pretrial misconduct in New York City. *Journal of Quantitative Criminology, 5*, 101-126.

Stoltzenberger, R. M., & Relles, D. A. (1990). Theory testing in a world of constrained research design. *Sociological Methods and Research, 18*, 395-415.

Sullivan, M. L. (1989). *Getting paid: Youth crime and unemployment in the inner city.* Ithaca, NY: Cornell University Press.

Sullivan, M. L. (1991). Crime and the social fabric. In J. H. Mollenkopf & M. Castells (Eds.), *The dual city: Restructuring New York.* New York: Russell Sage.

Tittle, C. (1969). Crime rates and legal sanctions. *Social Problems, 16*, 409-423

Tittle, C. (1980). *Sanctions and social deviance: The question of deterrence.* New York: Praeger.

Tittle, C. (1985). Can social science answer questions about deterrence for policy use? In R. Shotland et al. (Eds.), *Social science and social policy.* Beverly Hills, CA: Sage.

Trebach, A. (1982). *The heroin solution.* New Haven: Yale University Press.

Waldorf, D., Reinarman, C., & Murphy, S. (1991). *Cocaine changes: Cessation from habitual cocaine use.* Philadelphia: Temple University Press.

Weisburd, D., Waring, E., & Wheeler, S. (1990). Class, status, and the punishment of white collar criminals. *Law and Social Inquiry, 15*(2), 223-243.

Williams, K., & Hawkins, R. (1986). Perceptual research on general deterrence. *Law and Society Review, 20*, 545-568.

Williams, T. (1989). *Cocaine kids.* Boston: Addison-Wesley.

Zimmer, L. (1987). *Operation pressure point.* An occasional paper of the Center for Crime and Justice, New York University School of Law, New York.

Zimring, F., & Hawkins, G. (1973). *Deterrence: The legal threat in crime control.* Chicago: University of Chicago Press.

Zimring, F., & Hawkins, G. (1992). *The search for rational drug control.* Berkeley: Cambridge University Press.

13. Shock Incarceration as an Alternative for Drug Offenders

DORIS LAYTON MacKENZIE

Our criminal justice system is in a state of crisis. From 1980 to 1989 the national incarceration rate grew from 139 (per 100,000) to 271, a more than 82% increase (U.S. Department of Justice, 1990). Prisons are filled to capacity, and probation caseloads have grown so large that agents can give many offenders only nominal supervision.

In part, this phenomenal growth in offender populations is a result of drug law violations. Arrests for drug offenses increased by more than 125% during the 1980s (U.S. Department of Justice, 1990). Many of these arrestees are recent drug users. For example, in 1990, 67% of the arrestees in 21 U.S. cities tested positive for some illegal drug; 83% of those arrested for drug sale or possession tested positive (NIJ, 1991).

The criminal justice system was not equipped for this growth in the number of sentenced offenders. Nor were there appropriate techniques for managing the drug offenders within the correctional system. Frequently there were no available places for offenders to obtain appropriate treatment either in prison or in the community. Identification of inmate risks and needs, and matching these with appropriate security, custody, and treatment also presented difficulties.

Correctional jurisdictions searched for ways to manage the increased numbers of offenders being sentenced—a large percentage of whom were

AUTHOR'S NOTE: This investigation was supported in part by Grant No. 90-DD-CX-0061 from the National Institute of Justice, Office of Justice Programs, U.S. Department of Justice, to the University of Maryland. Points of view in this document are those of the author and do not necessarily represent the official position of the U.S. Department of Justice.

young and drug-involved. Until relatively recently there were few options to deal with these offenders; either they were sent to prison or they were supervised on probation. The growth in the probation caseloads frequently meant that a sentence of probation was equivalent to "doing nothing" (Morris & Tonry, 1990). On the other hand, prison and jail crowding prohibited locking up all offenders. These problems led decision makers to focus their attention on alternative punishments that would be less than full prison sentences but more than standard probation. Intensive supervision in the community, financial penalties, electronic monitoring, house arrest, and increased conditions of probation were some of the intermediate or alternative punishments developed.

The intermediate sanctions seemed ideal to manage some of the young, nonviolent, and frequently drug-involved offenders (Morris & Tonry, 1990). However, the climate of the time was not conducive to intermediate sanctions that would reduce the structure and control over offenders. Too often the intermediate sanction was seen as a "soft" alternative, inappropriate for a prison-bound offender. Judges appeared to want options short of prison that would offer an alternative to probation, would be sufficiently harsh, and, at the same time, would have a chance of changing offenders so they would acquire the skills, ability, and desire to live law-abiding and satisfying lives.

The general public also seemed to want alternatives that were sufficiently harsh. In one survey 80% of the respondents said that "criminals are let off too easy," and 83% believed that "courts don't deal harshly enough with criminals" (U.S. Department of Justice, 1991). Policymakers were caught between the pressure from the public for increased punishment for offenders and the enormous expense of constructing and operating prisons and jails.

In addition to wanting criminals to be punished, the public also believes that offenders should receive appropriate treatment. In one public opinion survey, a higher percentage of the respondents felt that prisons should be used for rehabilitation (48%) rather than for punishment (38%) (U.S. Department of Justice, 1991). And they felt that treatment programs would do more to reduce illegal drug use than punishing the users (57% versus 33%, respectively).

In this climate, one intermediate sanction that became increasingly popular was shock incarceration or boot camp prisons. Shock programs began in Georgia and Oklahoma in 1983, and the idea quickly spread to other jurisdictions. By 1992, 25 states and the Federal Bureau of Prisons (FBOP) had programs for adult offenders, and additional programs were being developed for juveniles and for inmates in local prisons and jails.

The boot camp prison differed from earlier shock probation by separating participants from other inmates, and by the military boot camp atmosphere.

The appeal of these programs may be that they are intermediate sanctions with "teeth" in them, which combine punishment with elements that people believe will be effective in rehabilitating offenders. The programs are designed to be similar to boot camps and include strict discipline, rigid rules, military drills, and physical training.

The boot camp prisons seem to have strong public appeal (MacKenzie & Parent, 1992). In the minds of many the structure and discipline of such programs address the very problems that are characteristic of young, nonviolent offenders. One survey found that 49% of the respondents thought even occasional drug users should be sent to military-style boot camps as punishment (43% responded "no") (U.S. Department of Justice, 1990).

Shock Incarceration Programs

The earliest shock prisons emphasized the structure and discipline aspect of the programs. As new programs developed they incorporated more therapy and treatment into the daily schedule of activities (MacKenzie, 1990b). And it became clear that many of the offenders who were entering the programs were drug-involved. The issue then became, how to make the programs appropriate for these young, drug-involved offenders.

SURVEY OF SHOCK PROGRAMS

In 1992 we surveyed all state correctional systems and the Federal Bureau of Prisons in order to identify shock incarceration programs for adults and to examine the characteristics of the programs then in existence.[1] We were particularly interested in obtaining information on whether drug treatment was incorporated into the programs.

At the time of the survey there were 41 programs in 26 jurisdictions, holding approximately 5,814 inmates. New York, with 1,500 inmates, had the largest number of offenders in boot camps. Most programs (56%) were much smaller and were designed to hold between 100 and 300 inmates at one time. In five programs fewer than 100 beds were allotted for boot camp inmates.

Although all programs had some components in common, there were wide variations in other components. For example, programs differed in the amount of supervision given to offenders released from shock prisons. Some programs intensively supervised all shock parolees (38%), some gave all releasees moderate supervision (8%), and others varied supervision (50%), frequently based on a risk score.

Programs also differed in length. Illinois, New York, and Wisconsin, with 180 days, had the longest programs. The shortest programs were 45 days in two Oklahoma prisons, and the average overall was approximately 107 days. Thus although the number of offenders in boot camps was relatively small (5,814) in comparison to the total number of incarcerated offenders, the number of offenders that could potentially complete the programs in a year was much larger (e.g., $365/107 \times 5,814 = 19,833$).

The daily activities of offenders in boot camps varied substantially. In some programs offenders spent 8 to 10 hours working or in physical training and drill, and then participated in rehabilitation or educational activities in the evening. In other programs the work and physical training time was reduced, and more time was spent in rehabilitative activities.

DRUG TREATMENT AND EDUCATION

All 26 responding jurisdictions reported having some type of drug treatment or education for inmates in their shock programs (Table 13.1). Seven (30.4%) provided only drug education, while the remaining 19 (76%) had treatment or a combination of education and treatment. All inmates were required to attend the treatment activities in 84.6% of the programs. Forty-one percent of the programs were legally required to provide treatment.

The amount of time spent in drug programs (treatment and/or education) while in the shock programs varied greatly. For instance, the Florida program had only 15 days of treatment and education; in contrast, in the New York program all offenders received 180 days of treatment. Inmates in 38% of the shock programs had less than 50 days of treatment or education while in prison, 20% had 50 to 99 days, and 23% had more than 100 days of treatment. Drug use during the program was monitored by urine testing in 62% of the shock programs.

The average length of time served in the programs was not substantially different for the seven programs with drug education only (111 days), in comparison to the average time served in the programs with treatment (116 days). The drug education programs did spend fewer days in education, 62 days, compared to 73 for the treatment or combination

Table 13.1 Drug Treatment and Education in Shock Incarceration Prisons for Adult Felons in 26 States and in the Federal Bureau of Prisons in 1992

State	Number of Days of Drug Treatment/ Education	Emphasis on Treatment or Education	Treatment Legally Required	Drug Use Monitoring Method (in prison)	Drug Use Monitoring Method (follow-up)
Federal Bureau of Prisons	*	Combination	No	Urinalysis	Urinalysis
Alabama	40	Treatment	No	Observation	*
Arkansas	105	Combination	Yes	Urinalysis	Urinalysis
Arizona	20	Education	Yes	Observation/ Strip Searches	Urinalysis
Colorado	4 days/week	Combination	Yes	None	Urinalysis
Florida	15	Combination	Yes	None	Urinalysis
Georgia	64	Education	No	Urinalysis	Urinalysis
Idaho	21	Combination	No	None	Urinalysis
Illinois	120	Combination	Yes (Counseling)	None	Urinalysis
Kansas	*	Education	No	Urinalysis/ Observation	None
Louisiana	112	Education	No	None	Urinalysis
Maryland	233 hrs.	Combination	No	Urinalysis	Urinalysis
Michigan	24	Education	No	Urinalysis	Urinalysis
Mississippi	60	Combination	No	Urinalysis	Urinalysis
Nevada	150	Combination	Yes	Urinalysis	*
New Hampshire	12	Combination	No	Urinalysis/ Supervision	Urinalysis
New York	180	Treatment	Yes	Urinalysis/ Supervision	Urinalysis
North Carolina	20	Combination	No	Urinalysis/ Observation	Urinalysis/ Observation
Ohio	2 days/week	Combination	No	Urinalysis	Urinalysis
Oklahoma	26	Combination	No	Urinalysis	Urinalysis
South Carolina	16 hrs.	Education	No	Observation	Urinalysis
Tennessee	24	Combination	Yes	Urinalysis	Urinalysis
Texas	70	Combination	Yes	Observation	Urinalysis
Virginia	90	Education	No	Urinalysis/ Observation	Urinalysis/ Observation
Wisconsin	180	Treatment	Yes	Urinalysis	Urinalysis
Wyoming	78	Combination	No	None	Urinalysis

* No resonse to this question

programs. However, as mentioned, there was a wide variance among programs in days of treatment.

Drug use monitoring during follow-up was available during community supervision for all shock programs. Most programs also reported that drug use was monitored during community supervision. However, the schedule and frequency of this monitoring is unknown.

In visits to programs we discovered differences in the way drug treatment was incorporated into the shock programs. For example, the New York program used a therapeutic community model for the shock program, and all offenders were given a similar regimen of drug treatment while they were incarcerated (see also New York Department of Correctional Services, 1992). Each platoon in the New York program forms a small community and meets daily to problem solve and discuss their progress in the shock program. They also learn decision-making skills as well as life skills through the therapeutic community or Network Program. In addition, inmates spend approximately 200 hours during the 6-month shock program attending Alcohol and Substance Abuse Treatment (ASAT) program activities. This program consists mainly of substance abuse education and group counseling, and is based on the Alcoholics Anonymous (AA) and Narcotic Anonymous (NA) model of abstinence and recovery. All inmates participate in ASAT, regardless of substance abuse history.

The Illinois program also targets substance abusers; but in contrast to the New York program, the counselors evaluate offenders and match the education or treatment level to the identified severity of the offenders' substance abuse problems (see also Illinois Department of Corrections, 1991). There are three levels of education and treatment. Level-one inmates have no history of substance abuse problems and therefore receive only 2 weeks of education. The second-level inmates are identified as probable substance abusers and receive 4 weeks of treatment in addition to drug education. For this group, treatment consists of group therapy, focusing predominantly on denial and family support issues. Level-three inmates are considered to have drug addictions. They receive drug education and 10 weeks of drug treatment. In addition to denial and family support issues, the group therapy sessions include the following topics: substance abuse relapse, co-dependency, behavioral differences, and family addiction and roles within the family.

In yet another model, Texas gives all participants drug education for approximately 5 weeks (see also Texas Criminal Justice Policy Council, 1990). During this phase inmates may also receive individual counseling and attend 12-Step fellowship meetings. Offenders must volunteer for phase two of the substance abuse treatment. (The substance abuse counselors in Texas believe that treatment should be voluntary.) Offenders

Table 13.2 Goals of Shock Incarceration Prisons as Rated by Program Officals

Goals	Very Important % (N)	Important/ Somewhat Important % (N)	Unimportant/ Not a Goal % (N)	Mean Score[a]
Rehabilitation	69.2 (18)	26.9 (7)	3.8 (1)	3.5
Reduce Recidivism	57.7 (15)	42.3 (11)	0.0 (0)	3.4
Drug Education	53.8 (14)	42.3 (11)	3.8 (1)	3.4
Work Skills	50.0 (13)	38.5 (10)	11.5 (3)	3.1
Safe Prison Environment	48.0 (12)	36.0 (9)	16.0 (4)	3.0
Drug Treatment	42.3 (11)	30.8 (8)	26.9 (7)	2.6
Education	38.5 (10)	38.5 (10)	23.0 (6)	2.7
Reduce Crowding	34.6 (9)	65.4 (17)	0.0 (0)	3.2
Deterrence	30.8 (8)	46.2 (12)	23.1 (6)	2.6
Vocational Education	3.8 (1)	26.9 (7)	69.2 (18)	.9
Punishment	0.0 (0)	60.0 (15)	40.0 (10)	1.7

a. Very Important = 4, Important = 3, Somewhat Important = 2, Not Important = 1, and Not a Goal = 0

who volunteer spend approximately 4 hours per week in drug treatment. Meetings are held during free time, so inmates are not released from work to attend. Treatment consists of group therapy (12 offenders per counselor) and focuses on social values, self-worth, communication skills, self-awareness, family systems, self-esteem, and setting goals. Inmates may also receive individual counseling and attend 12-Step meetings during this phase.

PROGRAM GOALS

We asked respondents to the survey to rate the importance to their program of 11 goals (Table 13.2) (see also MacKenzie & Souryal, 1991). The goals with the highest importance ratings were rehabilitation (69% rated it very important) and reduce recidivism (58% very important). Less important were the goals of safe prison environment (48% very important), reduce crowding (35% very important), and deterrence (31% very important). No one rated punishment as a very important goal.[2]

Five of the 11 goals the respondents were asked to rate were rehabilitation-type goals, such as drug treatment, education, and work skills. Of these the most important, in the view of the respondents, were drug education (54% very important) and work skills (50% very important). Education and drug treatment were rated less important, and relatively few considered vocational education important.

In part, the ratings of the goals of the programs reflect the daily activities—few programs include any vocational training, and only one respondent considered this to be a very important goal. Forty-two percent of the programs rated drug treatment as an important goal, but none of the programs that had only drug education (no treatment) rated treatment as very important. The seven programs without drug treatment in the curriculum did not see this as a very important goal of the program, six responded that it was unimportant or not a goal, the other rated it as an important or somewhat important goal.

The Effectiveness of Shock Incarceration in Changing Offenders

The major focus of studies examining the effectiveness of shock programs has been the recidivism rates, including a comparison of these rates to the rates for similar offenders serving different sentences. Overall, studies comparing shock completers to similar offenders who served different types of sentences have found no significant differences in recidivism as measured by arrests, return to prison, or reconvictions (Flowers, Carr, & Ruback, 1991; MacKenzie, 1991; New York Department of Correctional Services, 1991). However, as shown in Table 13.3, when returned to prison rates are examined, there is some consistency in results, with the shock parolees being less likely to be returned to prison, or arrested or convicted of new crimes. The one exception is for the Louisiana offenders, who are arrested and returned to prison more often than other offenders for technical violations, but not for new crimes. That is, in Louisiana the shock offenders were more likely to be arrested or revoked for technical violations, and less likely to be arrested or returned to prison for new crimes.

The Louisiana program consists of two phases: an in-prison phase followed by intensive supervision in the community. The researchers concluded that the differences between shock parolees and others in technical violations and new crimes is most likely a result of the intensive supervision that the offenders received.

In another study of the Louisiana offenders, the positive social activities of parolees, probationers, and shock parolees were compared (MacKenzie et. al, 1992). Researchers found that shock parolees engaged in more positive social activities (work, drug treatment). However, like the new crimes and technical violations, this appeared to be related to the intensity of supervision. That is, offenders did participate in positive

Table 13.3 Estimates of Recidivism Rates of Shock Incarceration Releasees and Comparison Groups of Parolees and Probationers at End of 24 Months of Community Supervision

	Arrests			Returned to Prison			New Convictions		
	Shock	Parol-ees	Proba-tioners	Shock	Parol-ees	Proba-tioners	Shock	Parol-ees	Proba-tioners
Louisiana[a]									
New Crimes	34	40	37	18	19	13	9	15	15
Technical Violations	32	10	15	29	14	10			
New York[b]									
New Crimes				17	19	20			
Technical Violations				23	25	27			
Georgia[c]				36	44	44			
Florida[d]				19	21				

[a] MacKenzie & Shaw, 1993
[b] New York Department of Correctional Services, 1991
[c] Flowers et al., 1991
[d] Florida Department of Corrections, 1989

activities as long as this was required as a condition of supervision. When the supervision intensity decreased, the performance also declined.

The finding that offenders will participate in positive activities when they are required to is interesting in regard to drug offenders, because it is consistent with the results of research examining compulsory treatment for drug offenders. That is, drug offenders who are forced to attend drug treatment as a condition of community supervision are less likely to drop out of the treatment program (Leukefeld & Tims, 1988).

Researchers in New York investigated the differences among shock graduates who were returned to Department of Corrections custody (e.g., the failures) and those who were not (e.g., the successes) (New York Department of Correctional Services, 1991). Those who were returned were younger, had more extensive criminal histories, had shorter sentences, and were convicted of less serious crimes. A similar study in Louisiana found that the failures (arrested, revoked) during the first year of community supervision were younger, had more past criminal history, were less likely to be employed, and were involved in fewer positive activities during the first month of supervision (MacKenzie et al., 1992). For both the New York and the Louisiana shock graduates, the characteristics associated with failure during community supervision are similar to those found in numerous prior recidivism studies examining other correctional programs. Younger offenders with more past criminal history have the highest failure rates.

The results of this research must be interpreted with caution. Large differences among programs make it difficult to generalize from one program to another. A multisite study of boot camp prisons in eight states, currently in progress, will give more information of the effectiveness of a wide variety of programs (MacKenzie, 1990a). The studies have been based on comparison groups, not experimental designs. The studies from Louisiana and Georgia did employ survival analysis techniques that permit statistical controls for differences among groups. However, a more rigorous design, with random assignment of offenders to groups, would permit clearer interpretations of the results of the research.

Furthermore, all of the studies have used official statistics to measure recidivism. There is some indication that these figures may differ substantially from the true number of criminal acts, and might be better thought of as indicators of involvement with the criminal justice system. In the future, studies using self-report data might greatly add to our knowledge of the impact of these programs on drug use and recidivism.

DRUG OFFENDERS IN SHOCK PROGRAMS

To date, there is very little information on how drug-involved offenders fare in shock programs. In many programs, a large percentage of entrants to shock drop out of the programs (30% to 50%) prior to completion (MacKenzie, Gould, Riechers, & Shaw, 1989; New York Department of Correctional Services, 1992). This is also a problem in drug treatment programs (Chaiken, 1989). One study of the Louisiana shock program examined the dropout rates for two groups of drug-involved offenders: (a) those who had a legal history of drug-involvement (an arrest or conviction), and (b) those who were identified as drug abusers on the basis of self-report. These rates were compared to the dropout rates of offenders who were not drug-involved. Surprisingly, the drug-involved offenders were *less* likely to drop out of the program, in comparison to those who were not drug-involved (Shaw & MacKenzie, 1990).

In another study of the Louisiana shock program, 20% of the offenders in the program were identified as problem drinkers on the basis of self-reported alcohol use and problems associated with use (Shaw & MacKenzie, 1991). In comparison to others, the problem drinkers were no more likely to drop out of the prison phase of shock.

Drug-involved offenders appear to do poorer during community supervision in comparison to offenders who have no drug involvement. Shaw and MacKenzie (1990) found this was true of shock parolees as well as parolees from traditional prisons and probationers. In this study drug-involved offenders were identified as either (a) having a legal history of drug involvement, or (b) being identified by the department of probation and parole as drug abusers who were in need of community substance abuse counseling. During one year of community supervision, the drug-involved offenders were more likely than others to have a positive drug screen.

There were differences between the drug abusers and those who have a legal history of drug use. The drug abusers were more likely to be arrested and to be jailed or revoked during community supervision. Furthermore, those who were judged by their parole agents to be making satisfactory progress in treatment were less likely to be arrested, while those who were not making satisfactory progress were arrested more often.

In contrast, those with a legal drug history were less likely to be arrested, jailed, or revoked. However, these results were true for those released from shock and others—shock incarceration was unrelated to performance during community supervision.

Problem drinkers who graduated from the Louisiana shock program were found to perform better, as measured by positive activities during community supervision (Shaw & MacKenzie, 1991). However, their performance was found to be more varied than that of non-problem drinkers. The researchers concluded that this may indicate the importance of support and aftercare for these offenders.

In interpreting these results, it is important to remember the wide variation among shock programs. The research reported above on the performance of problem drinkers and drug-involved offenders comes from the Louisiana shock program (MacKenzie et al., 1989). At the time of the research, the program included a short drug education course and had AA and NA meetings with volunteers from the community. The program did not have intensive treatment programs for those with sub-stance abuse problems. It is unknown whether the performance of the shock offenders would be similar if the program incorporated a drug treatment component.

The New York shock programs do provide intensive treatment for all offenders in shock. New York researchers compared shock graduates who were returned to custody to those who were not (New York Depart-ment of Correctional Services, 1992). The research revealed that those who were returned were more likely to be alcoholic, but less likely to be convicted for a drug crime (including both selling and using). This is consistent with the results from the Louisiana study, that a legal history of drug crimes was associated with better performance during community supervision. On the other hand, in New York those with higher alcoholism scores did poorer (as measured by recidivism rates) in the community, while in Louisiana they did better (measured by positive social activities).

In a more intensive survey of a subset of graduates from the New York shock programs, researchers interviewed samples of offenders who were still in the community, and compared their responses to another sample of offenders who had been returned to custody. A majority of both groups reported that they were not under the influence of drugs at the time of their crime, and there were no significant differences between the groups. However, those who had returned to prison, and who said they were under the influence of drugs, were more likely to report using marijuana, cocaine, or heroin prior to the crime, while the shock successes who were under the influence reported using crack. Additionally, although there were no differences among failures and successes in the proportion who had attended drug treatment prior to shock, the failures were younger when they first attended treatment. The failures were also more likely to have family members with substance abuse problems, and they either did not attend or quit substance abuse treatment.

THE ADEQUACY OF SHOCK PROGRAMS
FOR DRUG OFFENDERS

What becomes clear from the survey of shock programs is that the boot camp prisons are not a unitary phenomenon. There are large differences among programs in goals, activities, and aftercare. These differences would be expected to have an impact on the success of the programs in reducing the drug use and criminal activities of offenders who complete the program.

Most programs do provide a significant level of structure in a controlled setting, which is, according to Anglin and Hser (1990), a characteristic of successful treatment programs. However, it is questionable whether the structure and discipline, although possibly beneficial in some ways, could give offenders enough to enable them to successfully confront the problems that drew them into criminal activities in the first place. This is particularly true for drug-involved offenders. If a drug treatment component is not incorporated into the schedule of daily activities, offenders will return to the community without having worked on the problems that led to drug use and associated criminal behavior (see Hser & Anglin, this volume).

It might be tempting for policymakers to view shock incarceration itself as a potential treatment for substance abuse. For example, it may be seen as a program capable of instilling in drug offenders the discipline, or whatever else they are thought to lack, that "caused" them to become involved in drug use. The research did not support this idea. Substance abusers who had attended the shock program did not do better upon release from prison than offenders who were serving different sentences (Shaw & MacKenzie, 1991).

One problem in designing a program for drug-involved offenders is the length of time of the programs. It is generally accepted that successful drug treatment programs must be lengthy. Drug dependence is a chronically relapsing condition, and it may take years to control or eliminate the drug dependence (Anglin & Hser, 1990). The boot camp programs are relatively short, and therefore, some follow-up drug treatment will be crucial for these offenders. Drug treatment is not considered a goal of some programs. This might be reasonable if the targeted offenders do not have substance abuse problems. However, given the large numbers of arrested offenders who test positive for illegal drugs, and the large increases in the numbers of drug offenders entering prison, it would be surprising if many of these offenders were not drug-involved. To fail to initiate treatment during the in-prison phase means that this period is not used to begin addressing the problems of the drug-involved offenders. This is time in a structured setting that could be advantageously used to begin therapy and treatment.

On the other hand, the shock programs are relatively short—offenders spend less than 4 months in the prison phase. There is some evidence, from more traditional prisons, that the optimal program length for a prison drug treatment program is 9 to 12 months (Rouse, 1991). Some have proposed that it is neither therapeutically wise nor cost-effective to begin a program of treatment that cannot be completed. This might be an argument for providing only drug education during the incarceration phase of shock, and initiating treatment upon release. This might work well for programs that require a relatively short period of incarceration.

However, if we assume that many of the offenders admitted to shock are drug-involved, it seems less than optimal not to begin treatment during the in-prison phase of shock.

All programs reported that drug treatment was available for offenders during community supervision. More information is necessary to determine the links between treatment programs and supervision, and how the transition is made from the prison phase to the community supervision phase. Some programs attempt to facilitate this transition through group meetings for boot camp graduates in the community (Arizona, New York), or by having parole agents meet with inmates while they are in prison (New York, Illinois). A planned transition for drug treatment might be particularly helpful for offenders who have substance abuse problems.

Obviously, programs should be carefully designed to meet the desired goals. If one of the goals of the program is to provide drug treatment to substance abusing offenders, sufficient time must be available for treatment in the program, or the transition must be carefully planned so that treatment initiated in the program is not disrupted when the inmate is released. There is little available data to help jurisdictions make decisions about whether to introduce drug education only during the in-prison phase, or to begin drug treatment.

Offenders with drug abuse history who were released from the Louisiana shock program had more difficulty adjusting to community supervision. This is not necessarily true of those with a legal history of drug involvement. These results may indicate differences among users and sellers of drugs (sellers may be those with a legal history). Users may need additional help to adjust to the community. They will most likely benefit from being coerced to attend treatment.

Differences among users and sellers may also mean that they should be managed differently during the in-prison phase of shock. Some counselors have reported that sellers are disruptive or inattentive in group treatment sessions, possibly because their needs are so different from the needs of users (MacKenzie, 1992). This may be a rationale for differential treatment for users and sellers. It may also be the case that this is very dependent on the type of program. For example, in New York's therapeutic community atmosphere, it may be effective to combine users and sellers in the treatment program, while combining them in the Illinois model using group therapy may not be effective.

Summary

What becomes clear from this discussion of boot camp prisons is that we do not know how appropriate these programs are for drug-involved offenders. Boot camp prisons differ in aspects that are expected to have an impact on how effective they will be in reducing the drug use and criminal behavior of drug-involved offenders. There is no evidence from past research of drug treatment programs that structure and discipline will reduce drug use, although it may be valuable during the initial phase of drug treatment.

Given the facts that boot camp prisons continue to develop, and that a large percentage of the participants are drug-involved, there are many questions that remain about these programs and how to address the needs of drug-involved offenders.[3] Among these are: (a) Should treatment be initiated during the in-prison phase of the program, and if so, how long should the program be? (b) What type of treatment program is most effective, and for whom? (c) How can the transition from treatment in prison to treatment in the community be coordinated so that treatment is not disrupted? (d) What type of aftercare is most effective in reducing the drug use and criminal behavior of releasees from shock?

Notes

1. It should be noted that we did not survey either juvenile or local jurisdictions.

2. It must be noted that the respondents were those responsible for developing and/or overseeing the boot camp prisons. We would expect very different responses from other individuals (e.g., judges, the public).

3. It is assumed that these programs are developing for a variety of reasons, and that research will continue to examine their effectiveness in obtaining the desired goals.

References

Anglin, M. D., & Hser, Y.-I. (1990). Treatment of drug abuse. In M. Tonry & J.Q. Wilson (Eds.), *Drugs and crime: Vol. 13. Crime and justice.* Chicago: University of Chicago Press.

Chaiken, M. R. (1989). *In-prison programs for drug-involved offenders.* Washington, DC: U.S. Department of Justice, National Institute of Justice.

Florida Department of Corrections. (1989). *Boot camp evaluation.* Tallahassee: Bureau of Planning, Research and Statstics.

Flowers, G. T., Carr, T. S., & Ruback, R. B. (1991). *Special alternative incarceration evaluation.* Atlanta, GA: Department of Corrections.

Illinois Department of Corrections. (1991). *Overview of the Illinois Department of Corrections impact incarceration program.* Springfield: Author.

Leukefeld, C. G., & Tims, F. M. (1988). Compulsory treatment: A review of findings. *NIDA Research Monograph No. 86,* 239-240. Rockville, MD: National Institute on Drug Abuse.

MacKenzie, D. L. (1990a). Boot camp prisons: Components, evaluations, and empirical issues. *Federal Probation, 54*(3), 44-52.

MacKenzie, D. L. (1990b). "Boot camp" programs grow in number and scope. *NIJ Reports, 22,* 6-8. Washington, DC: U.S. Department of Justice, National Institute of Justice.

MacKenzie, D. L. (1991). The parole performance of offenders released from shock incarceration (boot camp prison): A survival analysis. *Journal of Quantitative Criminology, 7*(3), 213-236.

MacKenzie, D. L. (1992). Personal communication at Georgia boot camp.

MacKenzie, D. L., Gould, L. A., Riechers, L. M., & Shaw, J. W. (1989). Shock incarceration: Rehabilitation or retribution? *Journal of Offender Counseling, Services & Rehabilitation, 14,* 25-40.

MacKenzie, D. L., & Parent, D. (1992). Boot camp prisons for young offenders. In J. Byrne, A. Lurigio, & J. Petersilia (Eds.), *Smart sentencing: The emergence of intermediate sanctions.* Newbury Park, CA: Sage.

MacKenzie, D. L., & Shaw, J. W. (1993). The impact of shock incarceration on technical violations and new criminal activities. *Justice Quarterly, 10.*

MacKenzie, D. L., Shaw, J. W., & Souryal, C. C. (1992). Characteristics associated with successful adjustment to supervision: A comparison of parolees, probationers, shock participants, and shock dropouts. *Criminal Justice and Behavior, 19,* 437-454.

MacKenzie, D. L., & Souryal, C. C. (1991). States say rehabilitation and recidivism reduction outrank punishment as boot camp program goals. *Corrections Today, 53,* 90-96.

Morris, N., & Tonry, M. (1990). *Between prison and probation: Intermediate punishments in a rational sentencing system.* New York: Oxford University Press.

National Institute of Justice. (1991, November). *National institute of justice—Research in action—Drug use forecasting.* Washington, DC: U.S. Department of Justice, National Institute of Justice.

New York Department of Correctional Services. (1991). Shock incarceration in New York State: The corrections experience. *The third annual report to the legislature, department of correctional services and division of parole.* Albany: Author.

New York Department of Correctional Services. (1992). *The fourth annual report to the legislature on shock incarceration and shock parole supervision.* Albany: Department of Correctional Services and Division of Parole.

Rouse, J. J. (1991). Evaluation research on prison-based drug treatment programs and some policy implications. *The International Journal of the Addictions, 26*(1), 29-44.

Shaw, J. W., & MacKenzie, D. L. (1990). *Boot camps: An initial assessment of the program and parole performance of drug-involved offenders.* Paper presented at the Annual Meeting of the American Society of Criminology, Baltimore, MD.

Shaw, J. W., & MacKenzie, D. L. (1991). Shock incarceration and its impact on the lives of problem drinkers. *The American Journal of Criminal Justice, 16,* 63-96.

Texas Criminal Justice Policy Council. (1990). *Special alternative incarceration program enhanced substance abuse component.* Austin: Author.

U.S. Department of Justice. (1990). *Sourcebook of criminal justice statistics.* Washington, DC: U.S. Department of Justice, Bureau of Justice Statistics.

U.S. Department of Justice. (1991). *Sourcebook of criminal justice statistics.* Washington, DC: U.S. Department of Justice, Bureau of Justice Statistics.

14. The Implementation and Effectiveness of Drug Testing in Community Supervision: Results of an Experimental Evaluation

SUSAN TURNER

JOAN PETERSILIA

ELIZABETH PIPER DESCHENES

Intensive supervision coupled with drug testing has become a popular mechanism for monitoring and controlling drug offenders in the community. This chapter presents results on the implementation and effectiveness of five randomized intensive supervision programs (ISP) that incorporated drug testing. Background and one-year follow-up data were gathered for offenders, using official record data, and telephone interviews were conducted with probation/parole staff in each site.

Results reveal that during the one-year follow-up, more than half of ISP offenders in all sites tested positive for drugs, primarily for cocaine and marijuana. However, system responses to positive drug tests varied across the sites, with some placing more emphasis on referrals to treatment and others on increased punitive sanctions. Drug testing in the context of intensive supervision did not reduce officially recorded recidivism, as measured by technical violations and arrests. In three of the sites, ISP increased the percent of offenders who received technical violations.

Although drug testing appears a popular tool in the supervision of drug offenders in the community, the technology appears to have moved faster than some agencies' ability to utilize the information effectively in the treatment and surveillance of offenders.

AUTHORS' NOTE: We would like to thank the Intensive Supervision staff in Contra Costa, California; Seattle, Washington; Santa Fe, New Mexico; Des Moines, Iowa; and Winchester, Virginia; for their collaboration in the research project. We would also like to thank our grant monitor, Dr. Bernard Gropper, formerly at the National Institute of Justice, for his support over the course of the study. This research was supported by Grant 89-IJ-CX-0044 from the National Institute of Justice, Office of Justice Programs, U.S. Department of Justice. Points of view or opinions in this document are those of the authors and do not necessarily reflect the position or policies of the U.S. Department of Justice.

Introduction

Drug-involved offenders have inundated the criminal justice system, particularly community corrections. Not only have the number of offenders on probation and parole reached record levels, but professionals in the field believe that the composition of caseloads has become more serious, particularly with respect to drug involvement. It is estimated that more than half the 3 million persons on probation or parole are drug-involved, either as users, sellers, or both (Nurco, Hanlan, & Kinlock, 1990).

Performing probation/paroles' dual responsibilities—of controlling offenders in the community and facilitating their growth to crime-free lives—seem particularly challenging when applied to drug offenders. Research has shown that many probationers continue to use drugs while on probation and parole (Petersilia & Turner, 1990; Petersilia, Turner, Kahan, & Peterson, 1985; Wish, Cuadrado, & Martorana, 1986), and that drug use (particularly heroin and cocaine) is associated with higher rates of committing crimes (Anglin, 1988; Chaiken & Chaiken, 1982).

On the other hand, research has shown that the effectiveness of drug abuse treatment can be enhanced with criminal justice involvement (Anglin & Hser, 1990; Gerstein & Harwood, 1990) and that probation/parole programs that combine treatment with strict surveillance can reduce recidivism by as much as 15% over surveillance-oriented probation alone (Petersilia & Turner, 1990).

Thus the ultimate challenge is for probation/parole staff to manage drug offenders so that they receive the maximum exposure to rehabilitation programs, while at the same time closely monitoring their behavior so that violations are quickly detected and, if serious enough, result in the offenders' removal from the community.

In many communities, officials have been meeting this challenge by implementing Intensive Supervision Probation/Parole (ISP) programs with periodic drug testing. Although there is no standard ISP program, these programs generally utilize smaller caseloads and more intensive contacts than traditional probation/parole programs. It is hoped that smaller caseloads will allow officers to maintain close surveillance of, and work more closely with, each offender (Petersilia, 1987). In addition to increased contact levels and drug testing, ISP programs often include a variety of other program features including job placement, electronic monitoring and house arrest, community service, and referrals for drug and alcohol treatment (Petersilia & Turner, 1993a; Petersilia & Turner, 1993b).

The utility of drug testing while under supervision is based upon several premises. Knowledge that one may be tested for drugs may deter persons from use.[1] In addition to deterrence, testing can be used to identify the drug-abusing offender for special handling by the criminal justice system. Identification may lead to treatment. And in this case, drug testing can provide a more reliable indicator of recent drug use than self-reports (Wish, 1988).[2] Drug testing can also be used as a tool for identifying the most active of the predatory offenders—those offenders who commit offenses for material gain, such as robbery or burglary. Research has shown that predatory offenders who frequently and persistently use large amounts of multiple drugs commit crimes at higher rates than do less drug-involved offenders (Chaiken & Chaiken, 1982). Once identified, high-rate predatory offenders can be targeted for more intensive monitoring.

In summary, drug testing holds promise both as a deterrent and as a diagnostic technique. However, little empirical study has been done of drug testing's implementation and effectiveness for probationers and parolees, although this is undoubtedly its largest use in the justice system.[3] Anecdotal evidence suggests, however, that drug testing has not been unanimously endorsed by community corrections staff. Many complain that the court orders too many drug tests, mandating testing schedules that are unreasonable and costly. Staff often note that when they do implement drug testing orders, and return to the court requesting revocation for a positive test, judges often fail to revoke to custody, heeding pressures to use incarceration for the truly dangerous. Equally frustrating is the lack of treatment in many communities, thus further limiting the usefulness of the test to coerce drug-using offenders into treatment.

Given the widespread use of testing in community supervision, it is important to ask:

- How do probation/parole agencies implement drug testing orders?
- How many drug dependent offenders have testing conditions ordered?
- How many offenders are actually tested, with what frequency and results?
- How does the justice system respond to positive drug tests?
- Do such tests result in added probation/parole conditions, referrals to treatment programs, or revocation?
- What impact does ISP with drug testing have on offender recidivism, as measured by official records of technical violations and new arrests?
- How do jurisdictions differ on these dimensions?

STUDY DATA

This article uses information collected from five sites that participated in the Bureau of Justice Assistance's "Intensive Supervision Program for Drug Offenders."[4] The BJA Demonstration program funded sites to implement intensive supervision programs for drug offenders, following a general ISP model developed in Georgia (Erwin & Bennett, 1987). The Demonstration program ran from 1987 through 1990. The five sites used in the current analyses are: Contra Costa, California; Seattle, Washington; Des Moines, Iowa; Santa Fe, New Mexico; and Winchester, Virginia. These sites were similar in that each of them:[5]

- Designed an ISP program specifically for adult drug offenders.
- Incorporated urinalysis testing as one of the major ISP components (although the actual frequency of tests varied, from less than one to almost three per month).
- Implemented ISP as a probation/parole enhancement program (as opposed to prison diversion).
- Faithfully implemented an experimental design in which eligible offenders were randomly assigned to either the ISP program or routine probation/ parole supervision, thus permitting a strong test of the effectiveness of ISP contrasted with routine supervision.[6]

RAND served as the evaluator of the ISP Demonstration: randomly assigning offenders, designing the data collection instruments, training the data coders, assembling the coded information, and analyzing the data. Three separate data collection forms were recorded for each study partici- pant. A *Background Assessment* was completed shortly after study assign- ment. It recorded demographics, prior record, and current offense informa- tion, as well as information about the offender's prior drug dependence and treatment history. The *6- and 12-Month Review* forms recorded the nature and type of services received, program participation, and recidivism (as measured by technical violations and arrests) during the 12-month follow- up.[7] Specifically related to drug testing, the forms also recorded for each month of the follow-up the number of tests ordered and taken, and the types of drugs for which the offender tested positive. In addition, the most serious sanction imposed for a positive drug test during the review period was also recorded. Data for all three forms were abstracted from official record files. The offender's presentence investigation (PSI) supplied most of the neces- sary information for the background form; officer chronological notes were used for the 6- and 12-month reviews.[8]

In addition to the individual offender data, semistructured phone interviews were conducted with ISP staff on questions relating to the implementation of drug testing in ISP, goals for testing, and ISP staff perceptions of the impact of testing on offender drug use and criminal behavior.

An important caveat to the current analysis is that drug testing, as implemented by these ISP programs, was only one component of a more intensive package of services. As we describe below, the ISP programs were more intensive in other monitoring activities as well as drug testing. Thus it is not possible to disentangle the independent contribution of drug testing over and above the other ISP services offered, or alternatively, the independent impact of drug testing over and above the services offered on routine supervision. We return to this issue again in the Conclusions section of this chapter.

Intensive Supervision With Drug Testing: Site Descriptions

All five sites were similar in that they included drug testing as a component of enhanced probation/parole targeted at drug offenders. However, each site tailored the ISP program to its local clients' needs and risks, its own financial resources, and internal and external political constraints. Thus although the programs shared common characteristics, they often differed on other dimensions. Elsewhere we have discussed more fully individual site characteristics (see Petersilia & Turner, 1990; Turner, Petersilia, & Deschenes, 1992). Table 14.1 presents the key program and offender characteristics relevant to the current analysis.

Individual sites were responsible for defining who would be eligible for ISP participation. The BJA initiative stated that the ISP programs were to target *drug offenders.* The operationalization of drug offender, however, differed across sites. For example, in four of the sites, offenders could be eligible for ISP based on a current drug conviction. In three of the sites, drug dependency or drug abuse could qualify an offender as ISP eligible. Only in Seattle were both drug dependency and a drug-related conviction required for offender eligibility.

ISP program protocol also varied in terms of the emphasis on surveillance and treatment, although all did encompass both in their programs.[9] Santa Fe stressed a strong therapeutic approach, emphasizing counseling and job development. In contrast, the Seattle ISP program was the most surveillance-oriented, utilizing close cooperation with local law enforcement and strict sanctions for positive drug tests. The Des Moines ISP

Table 14.1 Program and Offender Characteristics

			Site		
	Contra Costa	Seattle	Des Moines	Santa Fe	Winchester
Study Group Size (ISP and control combined)	170	173	115	58	53
Offender Status	Probation	Probation	Probation/ Parole	Probation/ Parole	Probation/ Parole
Target Group	Adult F/M convicted of drug or drug-related offense	Adult F/M convicted of drug or drug-related offense and drug dependent	Adult F/M convicted of drug offense or drug-involved burglars	Adult felons with high-risk/needs and drug dependent	High-risk adult felons with drug/ drug-related conviction and/or drug abuse history
Sex					
% Male	81	73	75	88	81
Race					
% White	18	29	63	12	66
% Black	79	64	34	0	34
% Hispanic	3	5	1	83	0
Average Age	23	31	30	30	27
Prior Record					
Avg no. arrests	6	9	7	8	9
Avg no. felony convictions	1	1	2	2	2
% with prior prison	5	21	47	33	25

program was also more surveillance-oriented than treatment-oriented. ISP programs in Contra Costa and Winchester fell in between these two extremes.

Differences were also evident in the basic demographics and prior record characteristics of participants.[10] The vast majority of study participants in all sites were males in their late twenties and early thirties, although about one-quarter of offenders in Seattle and Des Moines were female. Most offenders had lengthy prior records: The average number of prior arrests ranged from six in Contra Costa to nine in Seattle and Winchester. However, offenders in some sites had more serious prior records than in others. For example, almost half of the offenders in Des

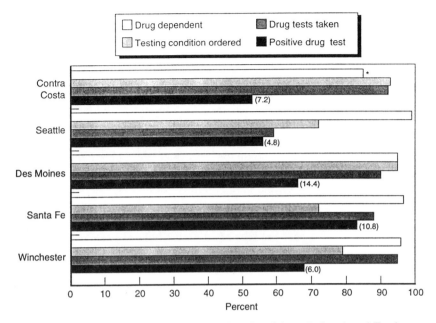

Figure 14.1. Prior Drug Dependency, Testing Conditions Ordered, and Testing Outcomes During 12-Month Follow-Up for ISP Offenders Only

NOTE: Numbers in parentheses represent the number of positive tests during 12-month follow-up.
*Data on dependency unavailable for Contra Costa. For this site, we present the percentage of offenders who have drug treatment needs.

Moines had served a prior prison term, contrasted with 5% of offenders in Contra Costa. Sites also varied widely on the racial composition of the study samples, as shown in Table 14.1.

RESULTS

The Implementation of Drug Testing in ISP

Despite the different operationalization of drug offender, the resulting samples were highly drug-dependent, as seen in Figure 14.1.[11] More than 95% of offenders in Seattle, Des Moines, Santa Fe, and Winchester were dependent upon one or more types of drugs. In results not shown here, it was also true that drugs had previously impacted offenders' lives in important ways. More than one-third of offenders in Des Moines and Santa Fe, and approximately half of offenders in Winchester and Seattle, had been involved in drug sales and dealing. In addition, substantial percentages of offenders had participated in prior drug treatment: About one-third of offenders in Seattle and Winchester had previously received drug treatment. Percentages were higher in Santa Fe and Des Moines, where 43% and 65%, respectively, had previously been in treatment. Treatment episodes included not only outpatient, but residential placements as well. Between 42% and 93% of those offenders with prior drug treatment had been placed in a residential/therapeutic setting.

In designing their ISP programs, each site decided what contact and drug testing schedules would be implemented. Their decisions were driven mostly by local preferences and resources, as opposed to empirical data, because no empirical data currently exist as to the most effective testing schedules.

All sites used the Syva EMIT test.[12] Reported costs ranged between $8 and $12 per full screen, and the results were obtained anywhere between 24 hours and 2 weeks. Sites generally requested a screen of drug tests for multiple drugs, as opposed to single substances. Not all sites requested the same drugs in the screens, but cocaine, amphetamines, barbiturates, marijuana, PCP, and opiates were generally included.[13]

Most ISP supervisors had evaluated different types of testing technologies and chose the EMIT test because they believed in its accuracy. GC/MS was available for confirmatory tests in Contra Costa, Santa Fe, and Winchester. However, the use of confirmatory tests varied across sites. In Santa Fe, ISP supervisors reported that all positive tests were confirmed by GC/MS. The ISP supervisor in Seattle reported that the court never required the use of confirmatory tests.

Each ISP program decided how to implement drug testing. In Contra Costa and Santa Fe, offenders were notified by phone the day before they were to be tested to come in and provide a urine sample.[14] In the other programs, testing was conducted during regular office visits, although the offender was usually unaware of whether he or she would be tested on any given visit.

Most studied offenders had court-ordered testing conditions; however, the meaning of these testing conditions varied across sites. In Contra Costa and Seattle, the judge controlled whether offenders would receive drug testing; only offenders for whom the judge specifically ordered drug testing were required to submit to drug testing in the ISP program. In Winchester and Santa Fe, testing conditions could be ordered by the court, but probation and parole staff could test offenders regardless of the court-imposed condition. In Des Moines, although drug testing was often imposed by the court, the more important factor was that drug testing was a requirement of the ISP contract while the offender was under probation/parole superision. Thus in this site, all ISP offenders were subject to testing.

Despite the differences in the meanings of court-ordered testing conditions, a high percentage of offenders in all sites were tested. As Figure 14.1 shows, with the exception of Seattle, more than 90% of all ISP offenders were tested at least once during the one-year follow-up period.[15] The average total number of tests taken during the year ranged from just under 5 in Seattle to just under 35 in Santa Fe and Des Moines. The average number of positive drug tests during the year ranged from a low of 4.8 in Seattle to a high of more than 14 (more than once per month) in Des Moines.[16] As Figure 14.1 shows, more than half of all ISP offenders tested positive at least once during the one-year follow-up period. However, these percentages are based on all ISP offenders, not just those who were tested. If we consider only those offenders who were tested, these data suggest that about three-quarters of tested offenders tested positive for drug use during the year on ISP probation/parole. Offenders in Santa Fe were the most likely to test positive, with 86% of tested offenders testing positive at least once during the one-year follow-up (they were also the most frequently tested offenders). In contrast, 58% of tested ISP offenders in Contra Costa tested positive during the one-year follow-up.

To bring the ISP drug testing and other program components into focus, Figure 14.2 compares ISP and routine probation/parole on three key dimensions: monthly face-to-face contacts, monthly drug tests, and the percentage participating in any counseling during the one-year follow-up.[17]

ISP programs were significantly more intensive than routine probation/parole in terms of face-to-face contacts, drug testing, and participation in counseling. Face-to-face contacts for ISP ranged from 2.7 per month in Contra Costa to more than 10 in Santa Fe. These are contrasted with routine supervision rates of between .5 per month in Contra Costa and 3.8 in Des Moines. ISP participation in counseling ranged from 32% in Winchester to 100% in Santa Fe. Counseling participation for routine supervision ranged from a low of 12% in Winchester to a high of 41% in Des Moines.

In contrast to drug testing in the ISPs, urinalysis testing in routine supervision was much less frequent, averaging between .1 and 1.1 tests per month. In Seattle, with the lowest rate of drug testing for routine probationers, drug testing had traditionally been difficult to implement. Occasional testing was arranged by local TASC personnel, or the individual offender might pay for tests.[18]

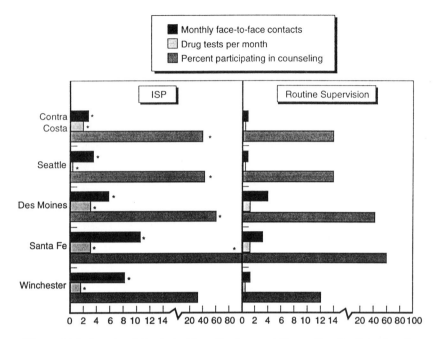

Figure 14.2. Levels of Contacts, Drug Testing, and Counseling Participation for ISP and Routine Supervision During 12-Month Follow-Up

* indicates that ISP and routine supervision are significantly different, $p < .05$. Face-to-face and drug tests are calculated as monthly rates; counseling is calculated as percent with any counseling during 12-month follow-up.

In contrast, drug testing in the other sites had been used with routine supervision caseloads for years. In Contra Costa, ISP staff recalled that some form of drug testing had been conducted by the probation department for nearly 30 years. Routine supervision in Des Moines, Santa Fe, and Winchester also incorporated drug testing, utilizing the same drug tests and labs as for the ISP demonstrations. Policies in Des Moines specified that offenders under routine supervision would be tested once per month; policies were not as specific in Santa Fe, Winchester, and Contra Costa, where probation/parole officers used their discretion in ordering tests.

Despite the differences in testing policies, once offenders were tested, the results for routine supervision cases were similar to those for ISP cases. More than 50% of tested routine supervision offenders tested positive, primarily for cocaine and marijuana.

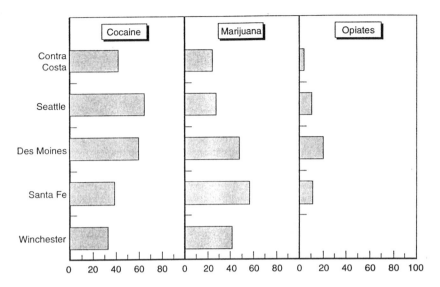

Figure 14.3. Percentage of ISP Offenders Testing Positive for Different Drug Types During 12-Month Follow-Up (Tested Offenders Only)

As we have seen, most ISP offenders tested positive for drugs during the follow-up year. But what were they testing for? Figure 14.3 presents the percentage of tested ISP offenders testing positive for cocaine, marijuana, and opiates. Across the different sites, positive tests most frequently occurred for cocaine and marijuana use. More than one-third of all tested offenders in the ISP sites tested positive for cocaine; between 24% and 57% tested positive for marijuana. Opiate use (primarily heroin) was less frequent, although almost 20% of offenders in Des Moines tested positive for opiates. And as other studies have found (Carver, 1986; Goldkamp, Gottfredson, & Weiland, 1990; Toborg, Bellassai, Yezer, & Trost, 1989), many offenders are not users of a single drug type. Between 25% and 50% of the ISP offenders were poly-drug users, testing positive for two or more drugs during the follow-up period—the most common combination being cocaine and marijuana use.

An obvious question is whether the results from the drug ISP sites mirror drug use patterns that have been reported in other offender samples.[19] Levels of use uncovered in the drug ISP sites were similar to those uncovered in other contexts. In a study of intensive supervision probationers in New York, 68% tested positive by urinalysis, primarily for cocaine and marijuana (Wish et al., 1986). Results from the National

Institute of Justice's Drug Use Forecasting (DUF) Program have provided information on drug use on samples of arrestees in major cities across the United States since 1986. Recent results show that with few exceptions, between approximately 50% and 80% of male offenders test positive for any drug, with cocaine being the most prevalent drug in many sites (National Institute of Justice, 1991). Marijuana is also used by a large percentage of offenders. Like the DUF data, the drug ISP sites also differ from one another in the mix of drugs for which offenders tested positive. Similar to the DUF results, in our study, the West Coast sites (Seattle and Contra Costa) evidenced more amphetamine use than the other Drug ISP sites. Of the drug ISP sites, Santa Fe stands out as an unusual site. This site evidenced one of the lowest rates of cocaine use, but was characterized by some of the highest rates of barbiturates, heroin, and marijuana use. The ISP supervisor suggested that these rates are a product of the long-standing drug subculture in the local area.

What Was the System Response to Dirty Tests?

Urinalysis has generally been included in community supervision for the purposes of identifying and monitoring offender drug use and determining the need for treatment. Urinalysis provides an objective measure of drug use and is often more desirable than self-reports, which often underreport drug use.[20] In our conversations with the ISP staff, we found similar reasons for their use of urinalysis as well. In addition, many ISP staff felt that the drug testing would help deter drug use and reduce criminal behavior. How did system officials utilize positive drug test information? Were their responses mainly to refer to treatment, or to impose punitive sanctions?

ISP programs generally included guidelines for the response to dirty tests. However, the structure and formality of the guidelines differed across sites. The Contra Costa ISP program protocol included no formal guidelines for responding to positive tests. Individual officers had wide discretion for dealing with positive drug tests, although treatment was generally used as the first option. Several sites utilized graduated sanctions in response to dirty tests. Winchester's graduated sanctions approach included treatment as the first option. Initially all ISP offenders were referred to a local mental health agency for evaluation and preparation of a treatment plan. If an offender continued to test positive, testing would be increased, followed by more intensive surveillance (increased contacts with probation/parole officer, travel restrictions). Partial revocation (to jail) and finally full revocation to prison were used as ultimate sanctions. Des Moines also utilized a graduated sanctions approach in which offenders were placed on electronic monitoring for the first cocaine positive test. After three positives, offenders were referred to inpatient treatment. In Santa Fe, warnings were issued for the first two dirty tests. After the third positive test, the court was notified, and offenders were often sent to jail for a few days or to shock incarceration. After the fourth dirty test, the offender would be revoked, although occasionally the court would decide to place the offender in long-term residential treatment. In contrast to the graduated response in Des Moines, Santa Fe, and Winchester, each time an offender had a positive test in Seattle, he or she was charged with a violation and taken to court, where a short (15-day) jail sentence was often imposed. The more positives, the longer the jail term recommended to the court.[21] In conjunction with the jail term, however, officers would also try to work with the offender to get him or her into treatment. Despite the existence of guidelines in the ISP programs, many ISP staff stressed that the specific response would often depend upon the individual offender and his or her progress in the program.

Our data provide the opportunity to examine system responses to positive drug tests for offenders on ISP supervision. Figure 14.4 presents the most serious system response to a positive urine test for the ISP offenders during the 12-month follow-up period.[22] We categorized the responses into four major types: (1) minimal (no action, warning, warrant issued); (2) added treatment conditions (referral to outpatient/inpatient treatment); (3) added control conditions (increased testing, new conditions added); and (4) placed in custody (jail, prison).

Similar to the previous analyses, there is a great deal of variation among the sites. Figure 14.4 shows that in Seattle, 71% of the offenders who tested positive on a drug test were placed in custody as a result. This is consistent with the policy outlined above regarding jail sentences for positive drug tests. More than the other sites, Des Moines and Santa Fe used positive drug tests to refer offenders to treatment, about 25% of offenders testing positive received treatment referrals as the most serious system response. In Winchester, more than half of offenders who tested positive received no formal action against them.[23]

We queried ISP staff concerning restrictions on their choice of responses, particularly treatment resources. ISP staff in Contra Costa and Santa Fe were often unable to obtain inpatient beds for the ISP offenders. ISP staff in Seattle, Des Moines, and Winchester, on the other hand, felt they were not greatly hampered by the availability of treatment slots. ISP staff acknowledged that treatment slots were less available than in the

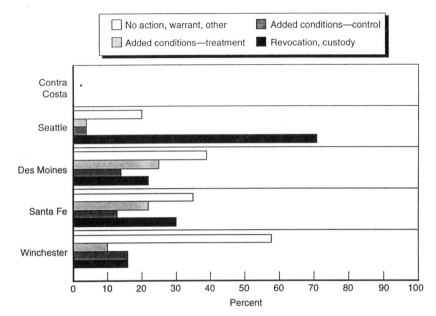

Figure 14.4. "Most Serious" System Response to Positive Drug Tests for ISP During 12-Month Follow-Up
*Data unavailable for Contra Costa.

past; however, the three sites felt they could get their ISP offenders into inpatient treatment. This perception may have been the result of the latter sites' working with treatment "brokers" to find beds. In Seattle and Des Moines, ISP staff worked closely with TASC staff to locate treatment beds. In Winchester, ISP staff worked with a local mental health agency that performed drug evaluations for ISP offenders.

How Did Testing Impact Offender Recidivism?

We turn now to the question of impact. Is there evidence that ISP programs with drug testing—as implemented and responded to in these five sites—affects recidivism? We are interested in whether the ISP programs were associated with increased (a) technical violations, (b) arrests for new offenses, and (c) return to custody (jail and prison).[24] The hope of ISP programs is that more frequent testing and contacts will serve to deter offenders from new crimes.

Two important points should be kept in mind as we discuss impact. First, the ISP programs were actually packages including several components, one of which is urinalysis. In this respect, they do not provide us with a definitive answer about the impact of urinalysis testing alone on offender behavior. Second, this analysis draws upon the strength of the random assignment component of the evaluation. Because offenders were randomly assigned to ISP or routine supervision, in a clear sense, the outcomes we observed are the direct causal result of the ISP programs.

Figure 14.5 presents recidivism measures for ISP and routine supervision offenders. This figure shows that:

- ISP significantly increased the level of technical violations, particularly drug technicals in three of the five sites.
- ISP did not affect officially recorded arrests, generally, or drug arrests in particular.
- ISP increased the percentage of offenders going to jail for technical conditions in two sites, and in one site increased the number of offenders going to prison.

In no instance did ISP reduce recidivism, as measured by officially recorded technical violations and arrests. As some have pointed out, however, ISP offenders may be committing fewer crimes, but their probability of detection has been increased by the more intensive ISP supervision. Thus we observe similar officially recorded arrests, when in fact, underlying behavior has been affected by the ISP program. We have discussed this issue more fully in Petersilia and Turner (1990).[25]

Conclusions and Policy Recommendations

Our analysis of the drug ISP programs has provided a number of important findings. True to their original design, the ISP programs were more intensive in terms of providing more face-to-face contacts, counseling, and drug testing than the routine supervision programs. Drug testing revealed high percentages of offenders using illegal drugs, primarily cocaine and marijuana. System responses to positive drug tests varied across sites. However, despite differences in drug testing schedules, system responses, and offender characteristics, offender recidivism results were surprisingly similar: In no instance did the drug ISP reduce officially recorded recidivism. On the contrary, the impact of the drug

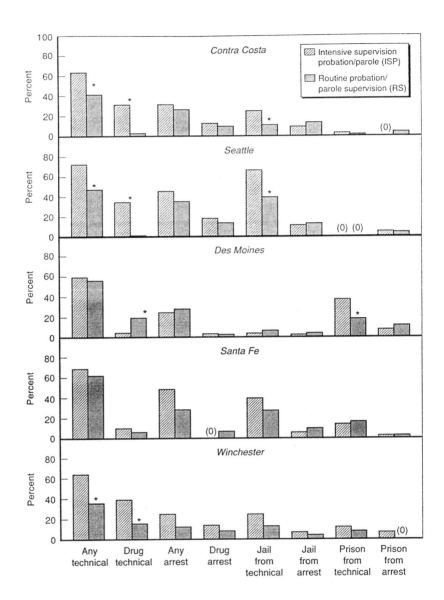

Figure 14.5. Drug ISP Impact on Recidivism During 12-Month Follow-Up
* indicates ISP significantly different from routine supervision, *p* < .05.

ISP programs was to increase technical violations and their resulting pressure on jail and prison commitments.

Given these findings, what can we say about the success of the drug-testing ISP programs? The officially recorded measures suggest ISP, as structured in the programs studied, was not effective in reducing recidivism, but this is not the only measure of success. Most ISP staff considered it a valuable tool for monitoring drug use and most believed that drug testing reduced drug use and criminality for some of the offenders under ISP supervision. All five jurisdictions have plans to continue with drug testing and many have expanded it to other offender populations.

ISP programs that incorporate drug testing can also be evaluated in terms of their ability to provide an intermediate sanction. All five sites screened their current populations to identify those they felt were most in need of additional services and supervision offered by a drug ISP program. These offenders were then provided with more intensive testing and monitoring than offenders on routine supervision. From this standpoint, all programs were successful in providing an intermediate sanction for serious drug-involved offenders.

However, it is also obvious from the current study that there is no clear sense of how best to use drug testing with serious offenders. We do not know which testing frequencies are the most effective, the relative advantages of testing alone versus testing combined with treatment, or which sanctions are best employed to reduce drug use and crime.[26] Fortunately, recent research is beginning to address these issues. With funding from the National Institute of Justice, RAND is collaborating with the Maricopa County Probation Department in an experimental evaluation designed to test the impact of the frequency of drug testing alone, and testing combined with treatment and sanctions. Results from this study should help us understand and better target services for drug-involved offenders under community supervision.[27]

Although drug testing appears to be a popular tool in the supervision of drug offenders in the community, the technology appears to have moved faster than some agencies' ability to utilize the information effectively in the treatment and surveillance of offenders. However, as community corrections awaits the results of empirical studies, such as the one noted above, useful and practical advice on how to implement drug testing is available on several fronts. In 1991 the Bureau of Justice Assistance released the *American Probation and Parole Association's Drug Testing Guidelines and Practices for Adult Probation and Parole Agencies* (BJA, 1991). The guidelines, compiled from information from 125 state and local probation and parole agencies, provide the best practices available for agencies either developing a new program or updating an already existing program. The guidelines address issues such as agency mission, purposes of testing, and offender selection, to help clarify why drug testing is being conducting. Practical advice on the implementation of drug testing policies and procedures, authority to test, selecting technologies, and so on provide concrete guidance for the operationalization of drug testing within a jurisdiction. However, as the APPA guidelines aptly point out, drug testing is not a panacea for resolving the drug problem in any particular jurisdiction; it is a tool that should complement other probation and parole operations (BJA, 1991, p. 2).

In addition to these formal guidelines, research findings can inform drug testing policies. Current drug testing technologies allow for accurate and reliable detection of illegal drugs in an offender's system. Drug testing alone, however, may not be sufficient to deter offender drug use and crime; combining treatment and criminal justice sanctions in a coordinated fashion appears to be critical. Longer periods of treatment, and treatment combined with legal sanctions, are associated with more positive outcomes (Anglin & Hser, 1990; Hubbard, Marsden, Rachal, Harwood, Cavanaugh, & Ginzburg, 1989; Visher, 1990a). To accomplish these aims, close supervision of drug-involved offenders, including the use of strict monitoring and graduated sanctions for program violations, appear to be necessary (Nurco et al., 1990; Visher, 1990b). Lengthy treatment and close supervision, however, come at a high price. Individual jurisdictions need to balance the costs of such programs against their utility and effectiveness.

Notes

1. This belief has not yet received empirical support. Testing itself may not be enough to deter drug use and attendant criminality. Wilson (1990) suggests that testing coupled with sufficient supervision and credible sanctions may be sufficient to reduce drug use and related crime (p. 541).

2. Self-reports can provide reliable estimates of drug use if they are collected in a safe, nonthreatening environment. However, this is often not the case in the criminal justice system (Wish, 1988).

3. Most studies in criminal justice have explored the utility of drug testing for identifying chronic users, screening for recent use, and tracking drug-use trends (Wish & Gropper, 1990).

4. The Bureau of Justice Assistance is an agency within the U.S. Department of Justice. One of its functions is to provide financial support to local criminal justice agencies that wish to implement new ideas.

5. Three additional sites also participated in the ISP program for drug offenders. They were Atlanta, Macon, and Waycross, Georgia. We did not include these in the current

analysis because their control programs were another form of ISP, rather than routine probation/parole.

6. Other reports have examined overall ISP results (see Petersilia & Turner, 1990; Petersilia & Turner, 1993; Petersilia, Turner, & Deschenes, 1992; Turner & Petersilia, 1992).

7. The 12-month follow-up was defined individually for each offender. The 6-month form recorded events from the point of assignment through month 6 of the follow-up. The 12-month form recorded events during months 7 through 12.

8. Some of the data items regarding drug history and drug testing outcomes are not available for Contra Costa. This is because the Contra Costa program started a full year earlier than the other four sites included in the current analysis in conjunction with nondrug ISP sites (Los Angeles and Ventura, California; Marion County, Oregon; and Milwaukee, Wisconsin). These earlier sites used data collection forms that were not specifically geared toward drug-testing ISPs.

9. Our source is the program descriptions provided by the sites. Our characterization of sites using these dimensions is necessarily subjective.

10. Differences between sites are descriptive only. No tests of significance were performed between sites because randomization was conducted *within*, and not *across* sites.

11. The item in the data collection form was worded, "At the time of the offender's arrest, (indicate) evidence of dependency on the following substances. . . . " Response choices were none; marijuana/hashish; LSD; PCP; Uppers; Downers; Quaaludes; cocaine; heroin; other. Coders circled all that applied.

12. The EMIT (Enzyme Multiplied Immunoassay Test) is the most popular immunoassay test currently used. Other urine tests include TLC (Thin-Layer Chromatography); Gas Chromatography; and Gas Chromatography/Mass Spectrometry. The latter two are often used for confirmatory tests, when an initial screen (by EMIT) shows positive. Hair analysis was not used in any of the sites. See Wish and Gropper (1990) and Visher and McFadden (1991) for a review of drug testing techniques.

13. In some cases, full screens were ordered early in the program. After an offender's drug use pattern had been established, fewer drugs were included in the screen.

14. Contra Costa utilized a drug testing hotline. Offenders were given numbers and were required to call the hotline 6 days a week to listen to their number on a prerecorded message. If the offender heard his or her number, he or she was to report for urinalysis testing by the end of the following day. ISP staff placed numbers on the hotline message based on their perceptions of the offender's possible drug use and ISP program requirements. In Santa Fe, urinalysis tests were generally conducted on a weekly basis on a random schedule (with the day changing each week). Offenders were called and told which day of the week they were to report to get tested. If offenders tested positive often, random tests would be increased to twice a week.

15. Far more so than any other sites, the Seattle ISP program was constrained in the types of conditions imposed on offenders. Washington's Sentencing Reform Act (SRA) strictly limited the conditions the court can impose, including drug treatment, employment, drug testing, and so on. In addition, probation staff were unable to modify the court-imposed conditions.

16. Each positive drug test in a drug screen was considered a "drug positive." Thus if an offender tested positive for both marijuana and cocaine on a test, we counted this as two positives.

17. Comparisons of ISP and routine supervision on other program measures can be found in Petersilia and Turner, 1990; Petersilia, Turner, and Deschenes, 1992.

18. TASC stands for Treatment Alternatives to Street Crime, a program designed to bridge the criminal justice and treatment communities (see Cook, Weinman et al., 1988).

19. A difficulty in comparing the current results with those obtained by others is that we present the percentage of offenders who tested positive *at any time* during the follow-up. Thus results are based on multiple tests per person. Most other reports use single test results to categorize drug use among offenders. Thus our rates are likely to be somewhat higher than the percentage testing positive for a single test.

20. The validity of self-reports has been found to be conditional on the subject's perception of threat (Wish, 1988).

21. In Seattle, ISP offenders, by law, could not be revoked to prison.

22. This analysis excludes Contra Costa. As noted earlier, Contra Costa did not have data relevant to some of the drug testing items.

23. One of the primary reasons why referrals to treatment were low in Seattle was that fewer than 30% of offenders received treatment orders on their terms and conditions. As noted above, conditions for offenders were not subject to modification by probation staff, and only those who received treatment conditions could be mandated to treatment.

24. A technical violation occurs when the offender fails to abide by one or more of the terms and conditions of his supervision (such as curfews, reporting to the probation/parole officer, absconding, testing dirty). Violations of these conditions are not generally considered law violations.

25. One of the potential remedies for addressing this issue is to collect confidential self-reported offense information from offenders.

26. The Drug ISP data does not allow us to answer questions such as these. In the sites, testing was increased and decreased according to the offenders' behavior. Similarly, sanctions were not always applied in a consistent manner; thus it is not possible with our data to disentangle cause-and-effect relationships of this nature.

27. The recently completed Focused Offender Disposition program was designed to test both a newly developed assessment instrument for drug offenders and level of treatment (urine testing only versus testing plus treatment). Unfortunately, due in part to implementation difficulties, no differences were found among the study conditions in terms of treatment completion, failure, or rearrest (McBride & Inciardi, 1993). Thus the results do not appear definitive for answering questions such as those outlined above.

References

Anglin, M. D. (1988). The efficacy of civil commitment in treating narcotic addiction. In C. G. Leukefeld & F. M. Tims (Eds.), *Compulsory treatment of drug abuse: Research and clinical practice* (NIDA Research Monograph No. 86). Rockville, MD: National Institute on Drug Abuse.

Anglin, M. D., & Hser, Y.-I. (1990). Treatment of drug abuse. In M. Tonry & J. Q. Wilson (Eds.), *Drugs and crime* (Vol. 13). Chicago: University of Chicago Press.

Bureau of Justice Assistance (BJA). (1991). *American probation and parole association's drug testing guidelines and practices for adult probation and parole agencies.* Washington, DC: Author.

Carver, J. A. (1986). Drugs and crime: Controlling use and reducing risk through testing. *NIJ Reports.* Washington, DC: U.S. Department of Justice, National Institute of Justice.

Chaiken, J., & Chaiken, M. (1982). *Varieties of criminal behavior.* Santa Monica, CA: RAND.

Cook, L. F., Weinman, B., et al. (1988). Treatment alternatives to street crime. In C. G. Leukefeld & F. M. Tims (Eds.), *Compulsory treatment of drug abuse: Research and clinical practice* (NIDA Research Monograph No. 86). Rockville, MD: National Institute on Drug Abuse.

Erwin, B. S., & Bennett, L. A. (1987, January). New dimensions in probation: Georgia's experience with intensive supervision probation (IPS). *Research in Brief.* Washington, DC: U.S. Department of Justice, National Institute of Justice.

Gerstein, D. R., & Harwood, H. J. (Eds.). (1990). *Treating drug problems: Vol. 1. Institute of medicine.* Washington, DC: National Academy Press.

Goldkamp, J. S., Gottfredson, M. R., & Weiland, D. (1990). Pretrial drug testing and defendant risk. *The Journal of Criminal Law and Criminology, 81,* 585-652.

Hubbard, R. L., Marsden, M. E., Rachal, J. V., Harwood, H., Cavanaugh, E., & Ginzburg, H. M. (1989). *Drug abuse treatment: A national study of effectiveness.* Chapel Hill: University of North Carolina Press.

McBride, D. C., & Inciardi, J. A. (1993). The focused offender disposition program: Philosophy, procedures, and preliminary findings. *The Journal of Drug Issues, 23,* 143-161.

National Institute of Justice (NIJ). (1991). Drug use forecasting: Drugs and crime annual report. *Research in Action.* Washington, DC: U.S. Department of Justice, National Institute of Justice.

Nurco, D. N., Hanlan, T. E., & Kinlock, T. W. (1990). *Offenders, drugs, crime and treatment* (Draft). Washington, DC: U.S. Department of Justice, Bureau of Justice Assistance.

Petersilia, J. (1987). *Expanding options for criminal sentencing* (R-3544-EMC). Santa Monica, CA: RAND.

Petersilia, J., & Turner, S. (1990). *Intensive supervision for high-risk probationers: Findings from three California experiments* (R-3936-NIJ/BJA). Santa Monica, CA: RAND.

Petersilia, J., & Turner, S. (1993a). Intensive probation and parole. In M. Tonry & N. Morris (Eds.), *Crime and justice: A review of research.* Chicago: University of Chicago Press.

Petersilia, J., & Turner, S. (1993b). Evaluating intensive supervision probation/parole: Results of a nationwide experiment. *NIJ Research in Brief.* Washington, DC: U.S. Department of Justice, National Institute of Justice.

Petersilia, J., Turner, S., & Deschenes, E. P. (1992). Intensive supervision for drug offenders. In J. M. Byrne, A. Lurigio, & J. Petersilia (Eds.), *Smart sentencing: The emergence of intermediate sanctions.* Newbury Park, CA: Sage.

Petersilia, J., Turner, S., Kahan, J., & Peterson, J. (1985). *Granting felons probation: Public risks and alternatives* (R-3186-NIJ). Santa Monica, CA: RAND.

Toborg, M., Bellassai, J. P., Yezer, A.M.J., & Trost, R. P. (1989). *Assessment of pretrial urine testing in the District of Columbia: Summary report.* Washington, DC: U.S. Department of Justice, National Institute of Justice.

Turner, S., & Petersilia, J. (1992). Focusing on high-risk parolees: An experiment to reduce commitments to the Texas department of corrections. *Journal of Research in Crime and Delinquency, 29,* 34-61.

Turner, S., Petersilia, J., & Deschenes, E. (1992). Evaluating intensive probation/parole (ISP) for drug offenders. *Crime and Delinquency, 38,* 539-556.

Visher, C. A. (1990a). Incorporating drug treatment in criminal sanctions. *NIJ Reports.* Washington, DC: U.S. Department of Justice, National Institute of Justice.

Visher, C. A. (1990b). Linking criminal sanctions, drug testing, and drug abuse treatment: A crime control strategy for the 1990s. *Criminal Justice Policy Review, 3,* 329-343.

Visher, C. A., & McFadden, K. (1991). A comparison of urinalysis technologies for drug testing in criminal justice. *Research in Action.* Washington, DC: U.S. Department of Justice, National Institute of Justice.

Wilson, J. Q. (1990). Drugs and crime. In M. Tonry & J. Q. Wilson (Eds.), *Drugs and crime* (Vol. 13). Chicago: University of Chicago Press.

Wish, E. D. (1988). Identifying drug-abusing criminals. In C. Leukefeld & F. M. Tims (Eds.), *Compulsory treatment of drug abuse: Research and clinical practice* (NIDA Research Monograph No. 86). Rockville, MD: National Institute on Drug Abuse.

Wish, E. D., Cuadrado, M., & Martorana. J. (1986). Estimates of drug use in intensive supervision probationers: Results from a pilot study. *Federal Probation, 50,* 4-16.

Wish, E. D., & Gropper, B. A. (1990). Drug testing by the criminal justice system. In M. Tonry & J. Q. Wilson (Eds.), *Drugs and crime* (Vol. 13, pp. 321-391). Chicago: University of Chicago Press.

Wish, E. D., Toborg, M., & Bellassai, J. (1988). *Identifying drug users and monitoring them during conditional release* (National Institute of Justice briefing paper). Washington, DC: U.S. Department of Justice, National Institute of Justice.

15. Treating the Juvenile Drug Offender

ELIZABETH PIPER DESCHENES
PETER W. GREENWOOD

This chapter focuses on the problems of substance use and abuse among juvenile delinquents and their associated involvement in drug selling. It first examines the current literature on the characteristics of youths who use drugs, and the correlation among drug use, delinquency, and drug dealing. Second, we evaluate the existing literature concerning the treatment of substance abuse and the overall effectiveness of rehabilitation and treatment within the juvenile justice system. Finally, we combine the findings from previous research to present policy recommendations for the treatment of three types of juvenile delinquents: substance users who commit crimes, serious substance abusers addicted to drug use, and drug dealers.

Introduction

In the 1990s the juvenile drug offender represents a unique set of challenges and opportunities for public policy initiatives dealing with the problems of both drug use and delinquency. The cocaine epidemic and the introduction of crack have substantially changed the portrait of the drug world for teens. No longer is the problem one of just substance and alcohol use. Now it represents an attractive economic opportunity for young males: A chance to earn a reputation, and a high risk of being involved in a subculture of violence. The crack scene in the major urban areas in the United States is one in which young males 12 and 13 years of age are selling drugs, and young females become prostitutes to support their crack habit (Dembo, Williams, Schmeidler, Berry, Wothke, Getreu,

AUTHORS' NOTE: Support for the research described in this chapter was provided by the RAND Drug Policy Research Center, which is funded by the Ford and Weingart Foundations.

Wish, & Christensen, 1989; Inciardi & Pottieger, 1991; Johnson, Williams, Dei, & Sanabria, 1990b; Reuter, MacCoun, & Murphy, 1990). The youth who are being drawn into the crack trade, either as street dealers or users, are those from the poorest inner-city neighborhoods, with the least capacity for "success" through legitimate means (Greenwood, 1992; Johnson et al., 1990b).

The cocaine epidemic, however, is not widespread. In the general population of youths ages 12-17, drug and alcohol use are decreasing (NIDA, 1991). Among delinquents, the most frequently used drugs are marijuana and alcohol; only a small fraction of youths are users of hard drugs.[1] And in most urban areas, juvenile drug dealers report they do not use crack cocaine (Greenwood & Deschenes, 1993). Nonetheless, the continuation and escalation of drug use appear to be one of the major risk factors for delinquents who are released from residential programs (Greenwood & Turner, 1993). Even though many residential programs for delinquents have a substance abuse component, few programs are designed specifically for drug users or dealers, and thus lack appropriate treatment and aftercare.

Because youthful drug offenders vary considerably in their risk to the public, culpability, and treatment needs, there is need for a broad spectrum of sanctions and treatment options. The criminal justice system is the most powerful tool for holding juvenile offenders accountable for their actions (U.S. Government, 1989). In contrast to the adult criminal justice system, juvenile justice practitioners have access to a wider variety of treatment programs and resources that can be more easily tailored to each youth's individual problems and needs.[2] The issues now facing practitioners are the allocation of these resources among different categories of delinquent and drug-using youths, and the determination of what combinations of punitive and treatment-oriented responses are most effective in suppressing continued involvement in drugs and crime.

In this chapter we review what is known about the nature and extent of substance use among delinquents, and the effectiveness of various treatment approaches in reducing offending and drug use within the juvenile population. We conclude by suggesting various types of interventions and describing how they might be tested.

Drug Use and Delinquency: How Big an Overlap?

For many years there has been disagreement among researchers in this field as to the generality of deviance and the possibility of a causal relationship between drug use and crime. Many people believe that drug use leads to crime, while others suggest that delinquency precedes and causes drug use (Elliott & Ageton, 1976; Inciardi, 1979). However, most of the evidence supporting this belief is correlational (Clayton & Tuchfield, 1982). Another point of view contends that there are certain shared influences that lead to several different deviant behaviors. Jessor and Jessor (1977) suggest that unconventionality is the common underlying construct. Elliott, Huizinga, and Menard (1989) contend that delinquent peer group bonding has a principal influence on both delinquent behavior and drug use.

Although it generally has been shown that drug use is related to delinquency and crime (Chaiken & Johnson, 1988; Elliott et al., 1989; Fagan, Weiss, Cheng, & Watters, 1987; Gandossy, Williams, Cohen, & Harwood, 1980; Gropper, 1985; Watters, Reinarman, & Fagan, 1983), there is contradictory evidence concerning the magnitude and temporal ordering of that relationship because there is variation in the samples and the measures from one study or survey to the next. Some studies use official record data and others use self-reported information. In addition, the definitions of delinquency and drug use may vary. These methodological problems can sometimes blur the picture of the nature and extent of drug use and delinquency.

ESTIMATES OF DRUG USE PREVALENCE

Data from the National Household Survey indicate that in the general population the use of drugs other than alcohol is relatively low and has been declining in recent years (See Figures 15.1a and 15.1b). For most drugs lifetime prevalence among youths ages 12-17 and young adults ages 18-25 increased between 1976 and 1982 and decreased in 1985 and again in 1988. The prevalence of cocaine use, however, among youth ages 12-17 increased from 2% in 1976 to 4% in 1979 and remained relatively stable until 1988, when it declined to 3%. In comparison, marijuana use increased from 18% in 1976 to 24% in 1979 and decreased to 13% in 1988.

The patterns for current drug use within the past year are similar to those for lifetime prevalence (See Figures 15.2a and 15.2b), indicating a recent decrease in drug and alcohol use. For 1991, estimates of drug use during the past year among the general population of youths ages 12-17 range from 2% for cocaine use to 12% for marijuana use, and 46% for alcohol (NIDA, 1992).

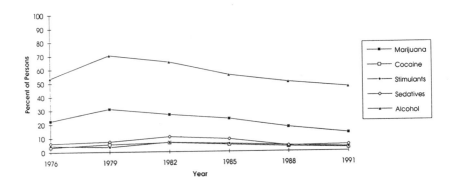

Figure 15.1a. Trends in Lifetime Prevalence of Drug Use: Youth Ages 12-17

SOURCE: National Institute on Drug Abuse, *National Household Survey, Population Estimates,* various years.

EVIDENCE OF THE RELATIONSHIP
BETWEEN DRUG USE AND DELINQUENCY

Estimates of the prevalence rates among juvenile offenders are at least five times higher than rates for the general population and have not shown any evidence of decreasing in the past few years. In 1980, among those youth ages 15-21 who self-reported committing index offenses in the National Youth Survey (Elliott et al., 1989), 32% reported using drugs other than marijuana and alcohol, and another 20% used marijuana.

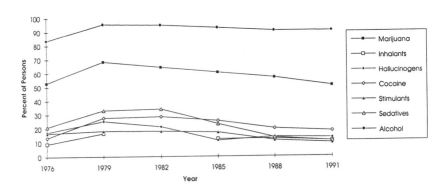

Figure 15.1b. Trends in Lifetime Prevalence of Drug Use: Young Adults Ages 18-25

SOURCE: National Institute on Drug Abuse, *National Household Survey, Population Estimates,* various years.

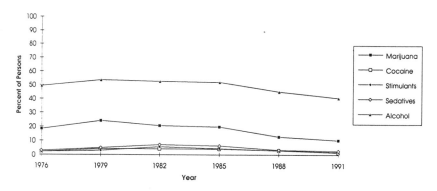

Figure 15.2a. Trends in Drug Use in Past Year: Youth Ages 12-17

SOURCE: National Institute on Drug Abuse, *National Household Survey, Population Estimates,* various years.

Data from the Drug Use Forecasting Study (DUF) for 1988 (U.S. Department of Justice, 1990) show that the frequency of recent marijuana use among male arrestees ages 15-20 ranged from less than 20% in St. Louis and Kansas City, to more than 50% in Chicago, New Orleans, and Portland (See Figure 15.3). Recent cocaine use among male arrestees in this age bracket ranged from 15% in Indianapolis, to more than 50% in New Orleans, New York, and Philadelphia.[3]

There is some evidence to indicate that delinquency and drug use may have similar underlying causes, but have an asymmetric relationship

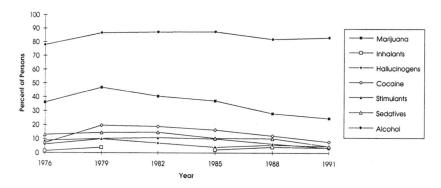

Figure 15.2b. Trends in Drug Use in Past Year: Young Adults Ages 18-25

SOURCE: National Institute on Drug Abuse, *National Household Survey, Population Estimates,* various years.

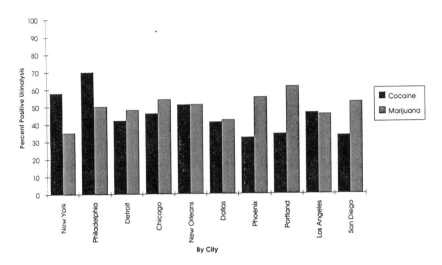

Figure 15.3. Cocaine and Marijuana Use by Male Juvenile Arrestees
SOURCE: National Institute of Justice, 1988 Drug Use Forecasting Study.

(Elliott et al., 1989; Rosenbaum, Deschenes, & Fagan, 1990). Findings from a small, geographically limited survey of students and dropouts in inner-city areas in 1984 and 1985 [4] indicate that although a majority of those who did not use drugs were petty offenders (72% of the male and 86% of the female non-users),[5] most of those who used hard drugs (64% of the males and 40% of the females) were multiple index offenders. Almost 60% of the males and 65% of the females were found not to be substance users (includes alcohol, marijuana, and hard drugs). This group reported committing very few offenses within the past year (an average of 7 for males and 2 for females). Users of hard liquor or marijuana (25% of the males and 23% of the females) reported between 50 (females) and 73 (males) offenses per year. The 17% of the males who used hard drugs reported committing almost one offense per day (323 offenses per year, 54 property offenses and 35 violent offenses), and the 12% of females who used hard drugs reported 243 offenses per year (37 property offenses and 28 violent offenses).

The initial results from the National Youth Survey panel data (Elliott et al., 1989) suggested that serious delinquency was related to poly-drug use. In looking at the age-specific prevalence rates, Menard and Elliott (1990) found that, in general, delinquency precedes drug use and peaks at about age 15. Drug use begins at a later age and the prevalence of poly-drug use (defined as use of amphetamines, barbiturates, hallucinogens, cocaine, and/or heroin four or more times in the past year) increases with age. Early onset of poly-drug use appears to be related to serious and persistent delinquency. Poly-drug users are a small proportion of the total sample (3% in later years). At younger ages the poly-drug users accounted for only 20% of all index offenses, but in the older cohorts the poly-drug users accounted for more than 70% of all index offenses. Thus as the cohorts age, there is an increasing prevalence of poly-drug use among serious offenders.

However, a reanalysis of the National Youth Survey data by Johnson, Wish, Schmeidler, and Huizinga (1991) indicates that relatively few youths are serious drug users and delinquents, and that the vast majority of youths commit minor delinquency or use some drugs. "Intensives," those who had three or more index offenses and three or more occasions of cocaine use in the past year, represented only 1.3% of the population surveyed but committed most of the robberies, felony thefts, and drug sales (Johnson et al., 1991, p. 223). In addition, they found a linear relationship between annual offense rates and type of drug use. Those who did not use drugs, or used only alcohol or marijuana, had significantly lower rates of delinquency than cocaine users.

In summary, although recent studies provide a wide range of estimates of the fraction of youth involved in delinquency or drugs, they all support the contention that the seriousness (hard drugs versus marijuana or alcohol) and frequency of drug use by offenders is one of the best predictors of their seriousness and frequency of offending. The more drug use, the higher the expected rate of offending.

DRUG USE AND DEALING

Although the relationship between serious delinquency and drug use is fairly consistent, there is more uncertainty as to the relationship between drug use and dealing. Research on heroin addicts (both adult and juvenile) has shown a strong correlation among heroin use, property crime, and dealing (Anglin & Speckart, 1988; Ball, Rosen, Flueck, & Nurco, 1981; Chein, 1964; Johnson, Goldstein, Preble, Schmeidler, Lipton, Spunt, & Miller, 1990a; Nurco, Schaeffer, Ball, & Kinlock, 1984). Other studies have shown that adolescent marijuana users are also involved in selling marijuana (Fields, 1986). With the change in drug use patterns from marijuana and heroin to cocaine and crack, the nature of the relationship between drug use and dealing may have also changed.

There is some evidence to suggest that the large profits available in the crack trade are attracting some young dealers who do not use that particular form of the drug (Greenwood, 1992). Self-reports of males leaving juvenile residential treatment facilities in Detroit and Pittsburgh between 1989 and 1990 suggest that the majority of crack dealers among this population do not use crack (Greenwood & Deschenes, 1993). Like other delinquents, they are more likely to use alcohol or marijuana. Eighty-two percent of the males from Detroit reported selling drugs. Of these, only 13% reported use of cocaine, although 80% reported use of some other drugs (including marijuana or alcohol). In comparison, in Pittsburgh, 59% of the males reported selling drugs, of which 40% reported use of cocaine, but only 10% of this was crack cocaine, and 58% of the dealers used some other kind of drug. Although they may have tried cocaine or crack at an earlier age, they claimed they did not use drugs while selling crack. In in-depth interviews, dealers in Detroit suggested that most cocaine or crack dealers do not use that substance because it impairs their ability to sell the drug; their motivation to sell drugs was primarily economic.[6] Similarly, in an ethnographic study of cocaine dealers in Harlem, Williams (1989) found that many of the dealers used cocaine but did not use crack.

Reuter, MacCoun, and Murphy (1990) report on an Urban Institute survey of 9th- and 10th-grade males (Altschuler & Brounstein, 1991) in high-risk areas of the District of Columbia, in which there was very little overlap between users and dealers. One out of six reported selling drugs (mostly marijuana) during the past year, and 55% of those who sold reported doing so more than five times. However, only 30% of those who sold drugs reported any use, which, while higher than the overall prevalence rate for the sample (11%), is considerably less than one might expect. By way of contrast, interviews with a sample of adult probationers who had been charged with selling drugs in the District found that 71% had used some drug other than marijuana during the 6 months prior to their current arrest. Fifty percent of the crack dealers had used crack, and another 11% had used cocaine[7] (Reuter et al., 1990).

Most other studies have also found high rates of usage among those who sell drugs, including crack. An early study of 100 youths in a city in New York State showed similar findings in the proportion of drug use and delinquency to the National Youth Survey. The authors (Carpenter, Glassner, Johnson, & Loughlin, 1988) conducted intensive interviews with a random sample of youths in school, a purposive sample of youths identified as drug users, and a sample of youths in local group homes or detention centers. Youths engaged in dealing drugs were the heaviest drug users. They were primarily involved in selling marijuana/hashish or amphetamine, and less often in selling cocaine, prescription drugs (such as Valium and codeine), and LSD. The primary motivation for selling drugs was to obtain a free supply. The youths did not appear to commit property crime in order to gain money with which to buy drugs.

A study of 254 seriously delinquent youths in Miami (Inciardi & Pottieger, 1991) showed that all of the youths had histories of multiple drug use. Eighty-four percent reported regular use of crack, beginning as early as age 13. Eighty percent of the youths were involved in the crack business. The greater the youths' involvement in the crack business, the more likely the daily or regular use of marijuana, depressants, and crack (p. 261). Of those who were heavily involved dealers (manufacturing, smuggling, wholesale, or retail), 87% reported using crack daily. Inciardi and Pottieger suggest that "the crack business is criminogenic in that it leads serious delinquents to become even more seriously involved in crime" (p. 268). Furthermore, they conclude that "the one major problem with the crack trade is that it facilitates crack addiction" (p. 268).

Research by Dembo et al. (1989) and Dembo, Williams, Getreu, Genung, Schmeidler, Berry, Wish, and LaVoie (1991) regarding the relationship among cocaine use, drug sales, and delinquency indicated a persistent relationship between drug sales and cocaine use. "Participating in drug sales in the year prior to initial interview was significantly and positively associated with testing urine-positive for cocaine at the time of the follow-up interview" (1989, p. 21). Dembo et al. (1989) hypothesize that although youths initially may have been dealers who did not use cocaine, the more they became involved in the drug culture by selling cocaine, the more likely they were to try the drug and become addicted to it. This reversal was found to be particularly true for the white males in the study.

What all of these studies suggest is that although some youths may enter the crack trade with the intention of not using the drug themselves, many are either not successful in maintaining their abstinence, or leave the business. Among older dealers, volume of sales and frequency of use are clearly related.

GANGS, VIOLENCE, AND DRUGS

In a study of 151 gang members in three inner-city neighborhoods in 1984 and 1985,[8] Fagan (1989) reported 63% of the gangs were involved in selling drugs, and 51% of the individual members were involved in drug sales. Although alcohol and marijuana were the most prevalent drugs used, heroin was used in 42% of the gangs and cocaine in 54%, with individual members reporting 35% regular use of cocaine and 13% frequent use. He found a strong relationship among violence, serious crime, frequent intoxication, and drug dealing. Drug use was more frequent among gangs involved in drug sales and serious crime.

Despite this evidence that suggests gangs are associated with the distribution of crack cocaine, particularly in New York and Los Angeles,[9] in other cities crack distribution appears to be non-gang related and more related to peer networks. Johnson et al. (1990a) describe the crack distribution in New York as a vertically organized model, with most of the dealing done by freelancers. This distribution system differs somewhat from that of heroin and marijuana (Mieczkowski, 1986), where markets are organized in a pattern known as the runner system. The crew boss acts as a supervisor and distributes the product to the runners, who build up a clientele on the street. The boss protects the runners and disciplines them. Recent interviews with a juvenile crack dealer in Detroit, who previously worked for a syndicate selling heroin, suggests that this form of distribution is also being used in that city for crack.[10]

Regardless of whether cocaine dealing is a gang or non-gang activity, it has come to be associated with violence. Numerous reports of shootings in Washington, D.C., Los Angeles, and New York indicate the increase in violent activity since the introduction of crack cocaine. Interviews with juvenile crack dealers in Detroit and Pittsburgh[11] and self-report data indicate that these individuals usually are armed with handguns, sawed-off shotguns, or even automatic rifles.

The Effectiveness of Correctional and Treatment Programs

A variety of placement alternatives are available for intervening with adjudicated juvenile offenders, ranging from diversion to voluntary community programs; community supervision at various levels of intensity; after-school and day-treatment programs; foster care; group homes and other types of community-based residential programs that allow youths some access to the community; to isolated wilderness programs and secure institutions. Within any one of these contextual settings youths can be exposed to a variety of treatment approaches, ranging from remedial education and vocational training, through life skills training, behavior modification, milieu therapy, Outward Bound/challenge approaches to social learning and cognitive-behavioral methods. During the

1960s and early 1970s, a great deal of optimism and experimentation was associated with many of these techniques.

However, following a number of critical reviews of previous evaluations, the best known of which were those by Lipton, Martinson, and Wilks (1975) and the National Academy of Sciences Panel on Research on Rehabilitative Techniques (Sechrest, White, & Brown, 1979), the accepted wisdom in this field became one of "nothing works." The evaluations could not be said to show that any one particular form of treatment was more effective than any other, or no treatment at all (Sechrest et al., 1979).

Although this view was challenged by a number of authors who pointed out the substantial number of experimental programs that had produced positive results, and various flaws in the experimental evidence, particularly evidence suggesting a considerable variation in the integrity with which particular treatment concepts were actually implemented (Gendreau & Ross, 1979; Greenwood & Zimring, 1985; Palmer, 1975, 1983), the "nothing works" position could still be said to reflect the conventional wisdom a decade later, when the National Academy organized a new research panel on the topic of "Criminal Careers and Career Criminals" (Blumstein, Cohen, Roth, & Visher, 1986).

The major development of the past decade that has begun to produce new evidence to refute the claim that "nothing works" is meta-analysis, a technique whereby the raw data from separate evaluations are used to construct standardized measures of treatment outcomes across individual studies, controlling on treatment and sample characteristics (Gendreau & Ross, 1987; Glass, McGraw, & Smith, 1981). A series of recent meta-analyses have begun to identify particular treatment approaches for juvenile offenders that do appear more likely to produce positive effects on recidivism.

Garrett's (1985) meta-analysis of 111 residential programs for adjudicated delinquents found that programs using behavioral and life skills approaches produced the largest positive results, averaging around 25% of the standard deviation of the recidivism rate for the control groups. Another meta-analysis of 90 community and residential programs for juvenile delinquents by Davidson, Redner, Blakely, Mitchell, and Emshoff (1987) also found that behavioral approaches produced the largest effect on recidivism, although the effects were so small that "they could not reject the null hypothesis." Programs based on group therapy and transactional analysis were more likely to produce negative effects.

More recently, Whitehead and Lab (1989) performed a meta-analysis on 50 evaluations of juvenile correctional programs appearing in professional journals from 1975 to 1984. The studies were divided into five categories of treatment: non-system diversion, system diversion, probation/parole/community corrections, institutional/residential, and specialty programs (Scared Straight, Outward Bound, and the like). Other groupings included behavioral or non-behavioral (because some previous meta-analyses had found behavioral interventions to be more effective); rigor of group assignment; and date. The two common statistics computed for all studies were χ^2 and *phi*.

The authors found their results "far from encouraging" and concluded that they clearly support the contentions of earlier researchers "that correctional treatment has little effect on recidivism." "System diversion" appeared to be the most promising form of intervention, with 7 out of 15 comparisons producing *phi* coefficients greater than .20. The comparison between behavioral and non-behavioral interventions found that although the former displayed a greater percentage of *phi* coefficients exceeding .20, they also showed a much greater number of negative *phi* values. The chronological analysis showed a trend toward less effective treatment in recent years.

In response to Whitehead and Lab, Andrews and his colleagues (1990), who had been promoting the notion that treatment did work if it was designed and implemented correctly, and applied to the appropriate types of offenders, performed their own meta-analysis on the same studies (and another group that they had been collecting in their files) and came up with dramatically different conclusions (Andrews, Zinger, Hoge, Bonta, Gendreau, & Cullen, 1990). Where Whitehead and Lab had been "discouraged," Andrews and his colleagues found that "appropriate" interventions reduced recidivism by more than 50%. The key to their analysis was in how they defined "appropriate" treatment in terms of risk, need, and responsivity.

In terms of risk, they hypothesized that higher levels of service are best reserved for higher risk cases, where there is more room for improvement. In terms of need, they hypothesized that it is better to focus on dynamic risk factors directly associated with criminal behavior, such as antisocial attitudes and feelings, antisocial peer associations, improved parenting, and anticriminal role modeling. In terms of responsivity, they hypothesized that appropriate services typically, but not exclusively, would involve the use of behavioral and social learning practices, such as modeling, graduated practice, rehearsal, role playing, reinforcement, extinction, prompting, resource provision, and detailed verbal guidance. Any form of service that involved forming antisocial individuals into groups was seen as counterproductive, except under the most exceptional circumstances.

The most comprehensive meta-analysis of juvenile delinquency interventions undertaken to date (Lipsey, 1991) includes 400 evaluations and a number of refinements designed to correct methodological problems identified in previous meta-analyses. This study supports the finding of previous studies that behavioral, skill-oriented, and multimodal approaches produce the largest effects, while deterrence approaches (shock incarceration) were more likely to produce negative effects. The Lipsey study also supports the finding of Andrews et al. (1990) that effective treatment approaches produce larger average treatment effects in a community, as opposed to institutional settings, and suggests that the more effective treatment approaches can reduce recidivism by 10% to 20%. Lipsey also found a moderate correlation between the duration or intensity of dosage and the magnitude of the effect.

At a more specific level of program detail, there are two basic methods of intervention that have produced positive effects across a number of replications. One is the family systems approach as developed by Alexander and Parsons (1973) in Utah, and Patterson, Chamberlain, and Reid (1982) in Oregon, and more recently applied by Gordon, Arbuthnot, Gustafsen, and McGreen (1988) in Ohio. This approach involves analyzing and improving communication skills and teaching parents contingency contracting. The technique requires a skilled and well-trained family counselor in order to secure the families' participation.

The other approach involves the use of very intensive supervision by college student volunteers who work with youth in the community. The specific techniques employed are advocacy, training in behavioral skills, and family therapy. Comparing this approach against several other community supervision models, Davidson et al. (1987) found that intensive supervision by college students resulted in significantly lower recidivism rates over a 2-year follow-up period, although there was no difference in self-reported delinquency.

Recent evaluations attempted to test the hypothesis that intensively supervised community reentry, when combined with a small secure residential program, can produce lower recidivism rates if the programs are implemented correctly. The Violent Juvenile Offender (VJO) Project, funded by the Office of Juvenile Justice and Delinquency Prevention (OJJDP), supported the design, implementation, and evaluation of a model intervention program, which was based on an integrated social learning, strain, and control theory perspective (Fagan, Rudman, & Hartstone, 1984). The model included three continuous phases: secure residential, community residential, and community reintegration. In four test sites, youth were randomly assigned between the experimental programs and standard correctional programs.

Direct observation and analysis of a number of process measures in the four test sites showed wide variation in the degree to which the experimental programs successfully implemented the design model (Fagan, 1990). In the two sites that implemented the model most successfully, one-year recidivism rates for experimental youth were found to be lower than those of the controls, but the sample sizes were too small to test for significance. The two sites with ineffective implementation were found to have recidivism rates equal to or greater than their controls.

A similar pattern prevailed in OJJDP's next experimental corrections initiative, which was designed to measure the effectiveness of several popular private correctional programs in dealing with chronic juvenile offenders (Greenwood & Turner, 1993). In each of three experimental sites, eligible youth were randomly assigned between the experimental private programs and traditional correctional placements. In two of the three sites, process and intermediate outcome data revealed that the private programs had not been successful in implementing the kind of programs they had initially proposed, and follow-up data collection was terminated. Only the Paint Creek Youth Center, near Cincinnati, Ohio, succeeded in implementing its plan for a small, staff-secure residential program, combined with intensively supervised reentry to the community. An evaluation focusing on the first 150 youths released for at least one year found that fewer of the experimental youths had been rearrested or returned to state custody, and fewer of them reported using drugs, but none of the differences were statistically significant (Greenwood & Turner, 1993).

In summary, the results of several recent meta-analyses suggest that the cognitive behavioral approach, combined with close supervision and advocacy, can reduce recidivism rates by 10% to 20%, especially when such programs are implemented in community settings. However, only a small fraction of juvenile offenders are currently exposed to such treatment. The remainder either are confined within an institutional setting or on probation with minimal supervision.

TREATMENT PROGRAMS FOR JUVENILE DRUG USERS

In the best of all worlds, judges, probation officers, and corrections officials should be able to turn to the research community for guidance concerning which types of drug treatment work most effectively for particular types of delinquents—and, in fact, they appear increasingly willing to do so. Unfortunately, the research community has little concrete advice to give in the way of programming for the prevention or treatment of substance abuse.

There are five commonly recognized major modalities of drug treatment: detoxification, outpatient drug-free, chemical dependency, therapeutic communities, and methadone maintenance (Institute of Medicine, 1990). Detoxification usually involves a short-term stay in a hospital, during which the patient's withdrawal is supervised. By itself, detoxification is not likely to promote continued abstinence. There are numerous types of outpatient programs based on psychotherapy and counseling or crisis intervention. Although retention rates in these programs are low, those who stay longer have better outcomes than do the dropouts and those not in programs.

A short-term residential or inpatient program combined with a long-term (1-2 years) outpatient therapy group is typical of chemical dependency programs. Many of these programs are based on the Minnesota model (28-day, 12-Step, or Hazelden type) in which the primary goal is abstinence. There has been very little research on the effectiveness of this approach. Therapeutic communities are a form of long-term (9-15 months) residential treatment that focus on changing behavior through encounter groups and peer pressure, also with the goal of abstinence. Rates of attrition are high for therapeutic communities. However, for those in residence, drug use and criminal activity are decreased, and those who graduate have better outcomes than do the dropouts. Methadone maintenance programs are only applicable to users of opiates, mostly heroin; however, they are perhaps one of the most widely studied programs. The programs involve substitution of a legal drug, methadone; and evaluations have shown inconsistent, yet mostly positive, results that may depend on the dosage levels.

Overall, existing evaluations of treatment programs, for both juveniles and adults, are extremely limited in the guidance they provide practitioners, because most focus on groups that are not representative of the clients with which most practitioners must currently deal, and many programs suffer from a variety of design defects.

To date, the majority of drug treatment evaluations deal with adults, most often heroin addicts, who appear to be quite different in their behavior and needs from the juvenile experimenters and users of marijuana, alcohol, cocaine, and/or amphetamine with whom the juvenile justice system must deal. And if the treatment literature tells us anything, it is that different types of substance abuse problems respond to different types of treatment (Office of National Drug Control Policy, 1990).

Most of the existing evaluations of drug treatment programs are not methodologically sound. The majority lack appropriate control groups, and very few involve random assignment among alternative treatment conditions. There is a great deal of inconsistency in how outcomes are measured and very little effort devoted to measuring the nature or quality of the services provided. Several of the major studies that suffer from these defects further muddy the waters by coming to different conclusions concerning which types of treatment appear most effective for particular client groups.

NATIONAL EVALUATIONS

Because few juveniles are heavily addicted to any drug, and opiates in particular, neither detox nor methadone maintenance programs have much to offer them. This leaves therapeutic communities and outpatient drug-free programs as the two basic modalities to which juveniles might be referred.

In the first major national study of treatment effectiveness, Sells and Simpson (1979) used data from the Drug Abuse Reporting Program (DARP) to compare outcomes across treatment modalities. Overall, they found significantly reduced drug use during treatment, and 4 to 6 years after treatment, across all treatment modalities. Reductions in opiate use were generally greater among treatment groups than among those who received no treatment, although significance levels were not reported. However, the percentage of adolescent subjects using marijuana daily, the adolescent drug of choice, remained constant (at 18%) for drug-free outpatient programs and increased for all the others (from 22% to 24% for therapeutic communities; 10% to 21% for methadone maintenance; and 14% to 22% for detox). Heavy alcohol use also remained unchanged or increased for all but drug-free outpatient subjects. The authors speculate that during the 1960s, when this treatment took place, marijuana and alcohol abuse may not have received as much attention as now.

In the second major national study, Hubbard, Cavanaugh, Craddock, and Rachal (1985) compared pre- and post-treatment behaviors for 240 clients, ages 18-19, or 17 and under, who were assigned to publicly funded residential or outpatient drug-free programs as part of the Treatment Outcomes Prospective Study (TOPS). They concluded that all residential treatment groups fared slightly better than outpatient groups. For example, daily marijuana use for residential clients under 17 years of age, who stayed in treatment at least 3 months, dropped from 79% (pre-treatment) to 12% (in the 12 months after treatment). Daily marijuana use among the same age group in outpatient programs actually increased from 48% to 54%.

Weekly use of drugs other than marijuana or alcohol, for patients 17 and under assigned to residential treatment, declined from 82% to 55% for those in treatment less than 3 months, and from 78% to 33% for those in treatment more than 3 months. Weekly use of other drugs by outpatient clients in the same age group decreased from 45% to 36% for those in treatment less than 3 months, but increased from 27% to 30% for those in treatment more than 3 months.

Although these national studies have provided some information on the types of treatment available for adolescent drug abusers, and indicate some degree of effectiveness, the DARP and TOPS studies are extremely limited in their application. First, the TOPS study did not have a control group, and in neither study were the clients randomly assigned to different modalities. Second, the majority of the research in the DARP and TOPS studies have been studies of adult opiate users.

In a recent review of these (DARP and TOPS) and other treatment evaluations, Anglin and Hser (1990) reached several conclusions regarding treatment for drug users. They suggested that although substantial improvement is possible in all modalities and programs, mixed modality programs (which are rarely implemented) have the greatest promise for bettering outcomes. Programs with flexible policies (in terms of individualized assessment of clients in major behavioral domains) and a case management approach were also found to be more effective. Other factors found to be predictive of such positive outcomes as increased client retention and decreased drug use, were employment, a stable marriage, a shorter drug use history, minimal criminality, and little psychiatric dysfunction. The length of time in treatment was found to be related to post-treatment outcomes for residential programs, but not necessarily for outpatient programs. Positive outcomes were related to staff experience, use of volunteers, use of practical problem-solving approach, and provision of special services (school, recreational, vocational, contraceptive, and relaxation training). And family involvement in treatment was found to improve the likelihood of treatment completion and reduce within-program problems.

The factors that Anglin and Hser (1990) believe to be associated with relapse include thoughts and feelings (cravings) about drugs, low involvement in productive activities such as work or school, and less satisfactory leisure activities.

The major problem with both the DARP and TOPS studies, and many of the other studies reviewed by Anglin and Hser (1990), is that they focus on programs that were not specifically designed for adolescents, and their pre/post designs and lack of comparable comparison groups make their results extremely difficult to interpret. The findings from a few small-scale, experimental programs, summarized in the next section, add considerable insight to our understanding of the available treatment for juvenile drug offenders.

EVALUATIONS OF INDIVIDUAL PROGRAMS

There are relatively few evaluations of drug abuse treatment programs designed specifically for adolescents, particularly delinquents, and few involve an experimental design. Many studies have used pre/post comparisons of adolescents in drug treatment (Friedman, Glickman, & Morrisay, 1986). Although different types of drug treatment have been shown to reduce the frequency of drug use, it is difficult to assess the impact of these programs because these studies lack control groups. In describing various programs, Kusnetz (1986) noted that the range of services provided varies from community outreach services to twice daily group counseling sessions and individual counseling every other day. The costs for treatment ranged from $62 per day for counseling to $418 per day for secure inpatient treatment (Kusnetz). In general, those adolescents who did the best were those motivated to change, regardless of the type of program (Kusnetz). However, in some instances, clients with family support who were less immersed in the drug culture tended to do better.

In a recent review of drug treatment programs targeted at juveniles, Catalano, Hawkins, Wells, Miller, and Brewer (1990-1991) concluded that some treatment is better than no treatment, but few comparisons of treatment method have consistently demonstrated the superiority of one method over another. Factors that appear to be associated with program completion or post-treatment outcomes include:

- age at onset of drug use
- primary drug of choice and abuse of multiple drugs
- number of prior arrests
- psychiatric symptomology
- degree of involvement in school
- time in treatment
- legal coercion into treatment
- drug cravings following treatment
- involvement in productive activities and active leisure

Hawkins, Lishner, Jenson, and Catalano (1987) and Hawkins, Jenson, and Catalano (1988) suggested that the most promising treatment approaches appear to be cognitive behavioral interventions combined with aftercare.

THE UNIQUE PROBLEM OF JUVENILE DEALERS

The treatment of both traditional juvenile delinquency and drug abuse focuses on family problems, antisocial attitudes, and improving prosocial skills, because these are areas in which most delinquent youth appear to have deficits. However, the rise of the crack trade has introduced a new form of juvenile deviance that may be more difficult to combat. Police departments around the country are consistent in their reports of adult drug dealers recruiting juveniles to work the streets for them. The primary motivations for this recruitment of juvenile labor appear to be that:

1. There is a decline of legitimate opportunities for young men in inner cities (Inciardi & Pottieger, 1991);
2. Juveniles face much less severe sanctions if they are apprehended rather than their adult counterparts; and
3. Juveniles may be more willing to engage in or risk the constant violence that appears to be associated with the crack trade in many cities.

With promises of front money, protection, status in the community, membership in an elite gang or posse, and incomes from $300 to $1,000 a week, it is not surprising that many enterprising young men from inner-city neighborhoods find drug dealing more attractive than the hopes of landing a minimum wage job (Johnson et al., 1990b; Reuter et al., 1990).

How is the juvenile justice system supposed to deal with this type of delinquent? Should victim awareness training be used to promote more empathy for their victims? This seems to have little promise if one believes that the clients (victims) are going to buy drugs anyway. Should juveniles be given a better appreciation of their own mortality? This approach also seems unlikely to work because dealers constantly face danger in their communities, even if they are not selling drugs. Can we provide these youths with alternative opportunities? What other jobs in the ghetto pay school dropouts $300 to a $1,000 per week, with flexible hours?

Some enterprising correctional administrators have taken to having the coroner bring fresh corpses into their juvenile facilities so the young dealers can get a better idea of what death really looks like. Others are attempting to educate young dealers concerning the harm they cause their community and to build on their sense of ethnic pride. Probation and parole officers can assist the youths in getting jobs, and keep pointing out the hazards of their former profession when the drug-related killings are reported in the paper. At this point we do not know if any of these ideas are effective in reducing drug dealing among juveniles.

EXPERIMENTAL EVALUATIONS

Six experimental evaluations that provide some information on inpatient and outpatient programs, family group homes, and aftercare services are not as encouraging. The first study, by Amini, Zilberg, Burke, and Salasnek (1983), examined an intensive psychodynamically oriented inpatient drug treatment program. A sample of 74 drug abusing delinquents was randomly assigned to either the inpatient program or conventional probation services for delinquents. No significant differences between the experimental inpatient group and the control group were found. However, significant and positive pre/post differences on various behavioral measures, such as type and level of drug use, were found among both groups but not between groups.

The second study was an evaluation of an experimental residential program for delinquents, based on the principles of Alcoholics Anonymous, that included counseling, family therapy, recreational, and educational components. The program had a reentry and aftercare phase and involved both the family and community in the treatment. In comparing the randomly selected treatment group ($N = 117$) to a waiting list group ($N = 27$) Grenier (1985) found that the treatment group showed significantly greater abstinence than the control group (66% versus 14%). The findings, however, may be biased. There was no pre-treatment test of the equivalence of the treatment and control groups, and any differences could be attributed to pre-treatment inequalities. Some of the difference might also be accounted for by the fact that varying methods were used in collecting the follow-up data.[12]

A third study, by Braukmann, Bedlington, Belden, Braukmann, Husted, Ramp, and Wolf (1985), evaluated Teaching Family group homes, which have several unique components that distinguish them from traditional group homes, including self-government, youth advocacy procedures, relationship development, and life skills training. The Teaching Family group home also has a live-in married couple who have been certified by the National Teaching-Family Association. The evaluation by Braukmann et al. showed that youths in the Teaching Family group homes have lower self-reported alcohol use and better prosocial skills during the time in the group home, compared both to delinquents in other group homes and to a no-treatment comparison group composed of friends of youths in the group homes. At one-year follow-up the experimental group remained higher in prosocial skills, but there were no differences between the three groups in drug and alcohol use.

Project ADAPT, a specially designed, intensive aftercare program that emphasizes skills training, is being evaluated by Hawkins and his colleagues in Washington State. In this study a group of 141 incarcerated juvenile offenders was randomly assigned to either Project ADAPT or the institution's standard program. Preliminary results have indicated that youths in Project ADAPT have significantly higher scores at the post-test in the three skill areas—drug and alcohol avoidance, social and problem-solving, and self-control—after the 10-week program. However, these differences did not remain in the 12-month follow-up (Hawkins, Jenson, Catalano, & Wells, 1991).

Similar results were found in an experimental evaluation of intensive aftercare programs for chronic delinquents in Detroit and Pittsburgh (Greenwood & Deschenes, 1993). Although youths in the Pittsburgh HomeQuest program reported that the program helped them stay off drugs, and the data indicate that a smaller proportion of the experimental group reported use of alcohol and marijuana at follow-up than at intake, there were no significant differences at 12-month follow-up between the experimental and control groups. There were also no significant differences in the rearrest rates or self-reported delinquency rates for youths in either Detroit or Pittsburgh, even though youths in the experimental programs had higher scores on measures of self-efficacy and coping skills than youths in the control groups.

The Paint Creek Youth Center (PCYC) is a small, privately run, staff-secure, residential program that utilizes a variety of intervention methods, including positive peer culture, individual case management, cognitive-behavioral training, family therapy, drug and alcohol counseling, and intensive supervision and advocacy during community reintegration. A recent evaluation of that program showed no significant differences in post-release arrests or self-reported delinquency or drug use between the treatment group and a randomly assigned comparison group placed in regular state training schools (Greenwood & Turner, 1993).

Conclusions and Implications

NEED FOR TREATMENT AND EFFECTIVE INTERVENTIONS

Although juvenile delinquents use drugs at rates that are 5 to 10 times higher than for nondelinquent youths, only a small fraction become seriously addicted to drugs while they are still within the jurisdiction of the juvenile justice system. However, because the prevalence of drug use continues to increase in the general population up to about age 20, involvement in the use or sale of drugs must be considered one of the primary risk factors for any delinquent. Longitudinal studies suggest that the use of drugs prolongs the delinquent career (Menard & Elliott, 1990). Elliott et al. (1989) suggest that drug prevention and treatment are central to controlling delinquency and drug use among multiple problem youths, and they point to the role of the peer group as a crucial element in the onset and maintenance of delinquency and drug use.

Our review of the literature suggests that several types of programs might be effective in controlling drug use and delinquency, but there is a need for more rigorous evaluations of such programs. Behavioral and cognitive learning techniques show promise for controlling both drug use and delinquency, yet preliminary results from Project ADAPT suggest that life skills training does not have a significant effect on preventing relapse to drug use. Family therapy has also been shown to be an important factor in treating adolescents, yet few programs have tested this component.

CLASSIFICATION FOR TREATMENT

Many jurisdictions currently evaluate offenders, according to a risk classification system, prior to placement. We contend that a similar approach needs to be taken in the case of drug-using or drug-involved offenders. Three types of treatment would appear to be indicated: diversion, intensive supervision, and residential programs based on behavioral-cognitive therapy, which include intensive aftercare. In addition, we contend that the drug dealer, regardless of whether he or she uses drugs, is uniquely different from other types of delinquents, and different options must be considered for dealers.

The drug user who is a minor offender or non-offender could be diverted from the criminal justice system, perhaps to be referred through the TASC program (Treatment Alternatives to Street Crime), if it exists within that state system. Depending on the severity of the drug-using behavior, the individual could be referred to any of a myriad of programs, from inpatient to outpatient drug-free, or community-based programs or group homes, to standard diversion programs (e.g., Davidson et al., 1987; Gordon et al., 1988), which use paraprofessionals as counselors, or wilderness programs.

Intensive supervision programs with urine testing may be a possible option for offenders who have failed in previous programs, but whose delinquency is not so serious that they have to be removed from the community. However, supervision is not likely to be effective without treatment. In addition, appropriate sanctions for program violations (e.g., dirty urine) should be provided.

The serious drug offender, addicted to drugs and also involved in delinquency (usually more serious offenses), should be placed in a residential program that uses a cognitive-behavioral approach. Depending on the severity of the delinquent behavior and the severity of the drug use, a range of alternatives may be appropriate, from wilderness programs, to positive peer culture or guided group interaction programs. In order to prevent relapse, these delinquents should be placed in an intensive aftercare program to facilitate community reintegration.

Regardless of the type of intervention applied, the most important concern should be the systematic evaluation of the effectiveness of various interventions for different types of juvenile delinquents and drug users. By evaluation, we are referring to a statistically controlled experimental design. More research of the quality of Project ADAPT needs to be conducted in different cities throughout the United States.

Regarding the problem of juvenile drug dealers, our review of the literature has shown that there is a good deal of variation across cities in how the drug trade is organized, the role that juveniles play in it, and their alternative opportunities (Ebener & Greenwood, forthcoming; Inciardi & Pottieger, 1991; Mieczkowski, 1986). These patterns are constantly changing with the competition, in response to law enforcement, and to meet the customers' tastes. Different types of responses by the juvenile justice system might be necessary, depending on the drug trade within each city.

One valuable area of research would be to start tracking and collecting data from several cohorts of young drug dealers (those recently convicted). By studying cohorts in several cities every few years, we would have a much better idea of trends in recruitment and career patterns. An even better design would be to track a complete cohort of delinquents because research shows that some juvenile drug dealers may be involved in a wide variety of crime (Inciardi & Pottieger, 1991).

A second avenue for research is to develop specific programs for drug dealers that can be empirically evaluated using an experimental design. Given that the crimes committed by drug dealers are economically motivated, it may be that we need to develop treatment programs that focus on this aspect. The use of day fines, one option that has been considered for adults, may be particularly appropriate for this group of delinquents. Boot camps or shock incarceration that provide short-term residential treatment with long-term reintegration or aftercare also hold promise.

The bottom line is that there are a number of promising leads but no consistent body of evidence to demonstrate how to reduce substance abuse among delinquents. Improvement in this area can only come about through more systematic experimentation and evaluation of alternative strategies. To ignore the substance abuse problems of this group of juveniles is to accept as inevitable their higher risk of continued criminal behavior and risk to public safety.

Notes

1. Hard drugs refers to cocaine, crack, LSD, amphetamines, heroin, Valium, Quaaludes, and other illegal substances.

2. Most states now spend about 50% more per day for juvenile residential placements ($25,000-$40,000 per year) than they do for incarcerating adults ($15,000-$22,000 per year).

3. Marijuana can be detected in the system up to 30 days after use, whereas cocaine use cannot be detected more than 48 hours after use.

4. Bronx, New York; New Orleans, Louisiana; Dallas, Texas; Chicago, Illinois; Los Angeles, California; San Diego, California.

5. Three or fewer incidents in the past year of minor theft, minor assault, vandalism, or illegal activities (buying or selling stolen goods, selling drugs).

6. These interviews were part of a research project at RAND by P. Greenwood and E. Deschenes (1993).

7. The low drug prevalence among young dealers in the Urban Institute survey is consistent with urinalysis data from the D.C. Pretrial Services Agency (with only 30% of juvenile arrestees testing positive in 1988 for any drug) and with a relatively high self-reported median age for first drug use among the adult dealers.

8. A survey was conducted in neighborhoods in South Central Los Angeles, University Heights in San Diego, and the west side of Chicago before the current crack cocaine epidemic.

9. Although the police assert there is gang involvement in dealing, Klein, Maxson, and Cunningham (1991) challenge this assertion. In their investigation of the involvement of gang members in crack dealing in Los Angeles, they found that gang members may deal drugs, but the gang does not run the crack business.

10. See previous note (6) regarding interviews.

11. See previous note (6) regarding interviews.

12. Semistructured telephone interviews were used for the controls, whereas questionnaires were administered 2 years after treatment for the experimentals.

References

Alexander, J. F., & Parsons, B. V. (1973). Short-term behavioral intervention with delinquent families: Impact on family process and recidivism. *Journal of Abnormal Psychology, 81,* 219-225.

Altschuler, D. M., & Brounstein, P. J. (1991). Patterns of drug use, drug trafficking, and other delinquency among inner city adolescent males in Washington, D.C. *Criminology, 29*(4), 589-622.

Amini, F. N., Zilberg, J., Burke, E. L., & Salasnek, S. (1983). A controlled study of inpatient vs. outpatient treatment of delinquent drug abuse adolescents: One year results. *Comprehensive Psychiatry, 23,* 436-444.

Andrews, D. A., Zinger, I., Hoge, R. D., Bonta, J., Gendreau, P., & Cullen, F. T. (1990). Does correctional treatment work? A clinically-relevant and psychologically-informed meta-analysis. *Criminology, 28*(3), 369-404.

Anglin, M. D., & Hser, Y.-I. (1990). Drug abuse treatment. In J. Q. Wilson & M. Tonry (Eds.), *Drugs and crime* (Vol. 13). Chicago: University of Chicago Press.

Anglin, M. D., & Speckart. G. (1988). Narcotics use and crime: A multisample, multimethod analysis. *Criminology, 26,* 197-233.

Ball, J. C., Rosen, L., Flueck, J. A., & Nurco, D. N. (1981). The criminality of heroin addicts: When addicted and when off opiates. In J. A. Inciardi (Ed.), *The drugs-crime connection.* Beverly Hills, CA: Sage.

Blumstein, A., Cohen, J., Roth, J. A., & Visher, C. A. (Eds.). (1986). *Criminal careers and career criminals* (Vol. 1). Washington, DC: National Academy of Sciences, National Research Council.

Braukmann, C. J., Bedlington, M., Belden, B., Braukmann, P., Husted, J., Ramp, K. K., & Wolf, M. M. (1985). Effects of community-based group-home treatment programs on male juvenile offenders—Use and abuse of drugs and alcohol. *American Journal of Drug and Alcohol Abuse, 11,* 249-278.

Carpenter, C., Glassner, B., Johnson, B. D., & Loughlin, J. (1988). *Kids, drugs, and crime.* Lexington, MA: Lexington Books.

Catalano, R. F., Hawkins, J. D., Wells, E. A., Miller, J., & Brewer, D. (1990-1991). Evaluation of the effectiveness of adolescent drug abuse treatment, assessment of risks for relapse, and promising approaches for relapse prevention. *The International Journal of the Addictions, 25*(9A & 10A), 1085-1140.

Chaiken, M. R., & Johnson, B. D. (1988). *Characteristics of different types of drug-involved offenders.* Washington, DC: U.S. Department of Justice, National Institute of Justice.

Chein, I. (1964). Narcotics use among juveniles. In R. Cavan (Ed.), *Readings in juvenile delinquency.* New York: Lippincott.

Clayton, R. R., & Tuchfield, B. S. (1982). The drug-crime debate: Obstacles to understanding the relationship. *Journal of Drug Issues, 12,* 153-166.

Davidson, W. S., II., Redner, R., Blakely, C., Mitchell, C., & Emshoff, J. (1987). Diversion of juvenile offenders: An experimental comparison. *Journal of Consulting and Clinical Psychology, 55*(1), 68-75.

Dembo, R., Williams, L., Getreu, A., Genung, L., Schmeidler, J., Berry, E., Wish, E., & LaVoie, L. (1991). A longitudinal study of the relationships among marijuana/hashish use, cocaine use and delinquency in a cohort of high risk youths. *Journal of Drug Issues, 21*(2), 271-312.

Dembo, R., Williams, L., Schmeidler, J., Berry, E., Wothke, W., Getreu, A., Wish, E., & Christensen, C. (1989). *The relationship between cocaine use, drug sales and other delinquency among a cohort of high risk youths over time.* Unpublished paper.

Ebener, P., & Greenwood, P. W. (forthcoming) *Substance abuse problems and programs in Newark: A needs assessment for Newark's fighting back initiative.* Santa Monica, CA: RAND.

Elliott, D. S., & Ageton, S. (1976). Subcultural delinquency and drug use. Appendix to *Drug use and crime: Report of the panel on drug use and criminal behavior* (NTIS No. PB 259/167). Springfield, VA: Research Triangle Institute.

Elliott, D. S., Huizinga, D., & Menard, S. (1989). *Multiple problem youth: Delinquency, substance use, and mental health problems.* New York: Springer-Verlag.

Fagan, J. (1989). The social organization of drug use and drug dealing among urban gangs. *Criminology, 27*(4), 633-667.

Fagan, J. (1990). Treatment and re-integration of violent delinquents: Experimental results. *Justice Quarterly, 7*(2), 233-263.

Fagan, J., Rudman, C. J., & Hartstone, E. (1984). Intervening with violent juvenile offenders: A community reintegration model. In R. A. Mathias (Ed.), *Violent juvenile offenders: An anthology* (pp. 207-230). San Francisco: National Council on Crime and Delinquency.

Fagan, J., Weis, J. G., Cheng, Y.-T., & Watters, J. K. (1987). *Drug and alcohol use, violent delinquency and social bonding: Implications for intervention theory and policy.* Final report submitted to the National Institute of Justice, URSA Institute, San Francisco.

Fields, A. B. (1986). Weedslingers: Young black marijuana dealers. In G. Beschner & A. Friedman (Eds.), *Teen drug use* (pp. 85-104). Lexington, MA: Lexington Books.

Friedman, C. J., Glickman, N. W., & Morrisay, M. R. (1986). Prediction to successful treatment outcome by client characteristics and retention in treatment in adolescent drug treatment programs: A large-scale cross validation study. *Journal of Drug Education, 16*(2), 149-165.

Gandossy, R. P., Williams, J. R., Cohen, J., & Harwood, H. J. (1980). *Drugs and crime: A survey and analysis of the literature.* Washington, DC: U.S. Department of Justice, National Institute of Justice.

Garrett, C. J., (1985). Effects of residential treatment of adjudicated delinquents. *Journal of Research in Crime and Delinquency, 22,* 287-308.

Gendreau, P., & Ross, R. R. (1979, October). Effective correctional treatment, bibliotherapy for cynics. *Crime and Delinquency, 25*(4), 463-489.

Gendreau, P., & Ross, R. R. (1987, September). Revivification of rehabilitation: Evidence from the 1980's. *Justice Quarterly, 4*(3).

Glass, G. V., McGraw, B., & Smith, M. L. (1981). *Meta-analysis in social research.* Beverly Hills, CA: Sage.

Gordon, D. A., Arbuthnot, J., Gustafsen, K. E., & McGreen, P. (1988). Home-based behavior-systems family therapy with disadvantaged juvenile delinquents. *The American Journal of Family Therapy, 16*(3), 243-255.

Greenwood, P. W. (1992). Substance abuse problems among high-risk youth and potential interventions. *Crime and Delinquency, 38*(4), 444-458.

Greenwood, P. W., & Deschenes, E. P. (1993). *The effects of intensive aftercare on the post-release behavior of chronic juvenile offenders.* Santa Monica, CA: RAND.

Greenwood, P. W., & Turner, S. (1993). Evaluation of the Paint Creek youth center: A residential program for serious delinquents. *Criminology.*

Greenwood, P. W., & Zimring, F. (1985). *One more chance: The pursuit of promising intervention strategies for chronic juvenile offenders.* Santa Monica, CA: RAND.

Grenier, C. (1985). Treatment effectiveness in an adolescent chemical dependency treatment program: A quasi-experimental design. *The International Journal of the Addictions, 20,* 281-291.

Gropper, B. A. (1985). Probing the links between drugs and crime. *NIJ Reports 188,* 4-8. Washington, DC: U.S. Department of Justice, National Institute of Justice.

Hawkins, J. D., Jenson, J. M., & Catalano, R. F. (1988). Delinquency and drug abuse: Implications for social services. *Social Service Review, 62*(2), 258-284.

Hawkins, J. D., Jenson, J. M., Catalano, R. F., & Wells, E. A. (1991). Effects of a skills training intervention with juvenile delinquents. *Research on Social Work Practice, 1*(2), 107-121.

Hawkins, J. D., Lishner, D. M., Jenson, J. M., & Catalano, R. (1987). Delinquents & drugs: What the evidence suggests about prevention and treatment programming. In B. S. Brown & A. R. Mills (Eds.), *Youth at high risk for substance abuse* (DHHS Pub. No. ADM 87-1537 ADAMHA). Rockville, MD: National Institute on Drug Abuse.

Hubbard, R. L., Cavanaugh, E. R., Craddock, S. G., & Rachal, J. V. (1985). Characteristics, behaviors, and outcomes for youth in the TOPS. In A. S. Friedman & G. M. Beschner (Eds.), *Treatment services for adolescent substance abusers.* Rockville, MD: National Institute on Drug Abuse.

Inciardi, J. A. (1979). Heroin use and street crime. *Crime and Delinquency, 25,* 335-346.

Inciardi, J. A., & Pottieger, A. (1991). Kids, crack, and crime. *Journal of Drug Issues, 21*(2), 257-270.

Institute of Medicine Committee for the Substance Abuse Coverage Study Division of Health Care Services. (1990). In D. R. Gerstein & H. Harwood (Eds.), *Treating drug problems: Vol. 1. A study of the evolution, effectiveness, and financing of public and private drug treatment systems.* Washington, DC: National Academy Press.

Jessor, R., & Jessor, S. L. (1977). *Problem behavior and psychosocial development: A longitudinal study of youth.* New York: Academic Press.

Johnson, B., Wish, E., Schmeidler, J., & Huizinga, D. (1991). Concentration of delinquent offending: Serious drug involvement and high delinquency rates. *Journal of Drug Issues, 21*(2), 205-229.

Johnson, B. D., Goldstein, P. J., Preble, E., Schmeidler, J., Lipton, D., Spunt, B., & Miller, T. (1990a). *Taking care of business: The economics of crime by heroin abusers.* Lexington, MA: D. C. Heath.

Johnson, B. D., Williams, T., Dei, K. A., & Sanabria, H. (1990b). Drug abuse in the inner city: Impact on hard-drug users and the community. In M. Tonry & J. Q. Wilson (Eds.), *Crime and justice: Vol. 13. Drugs and crime.* Chicago: University of Chicago Press.

Klein, M. W., Maxson, C. L., & Cunningham, L. C. (1991). *"Crack," street gangs and violence.* Los Angeles: University of Southern California, Center for Research on Crime and Social Control, Social Science Research Institute.

Kusnetz, S. (1986). Services for adolescent substance abusers. In G. Beschner & A. S. Friedman (Eds.), *Teen drug use* (pp. 123-153). Lexington, MA: Lexington Books.

Lipsey, M. W. (1991). Juvenile delinquency treatment: A meta-analytic inquiry into the variability of effects. In *Meta-analysis for explanation: A casebook.* New York: Russell Sage.

Lipton, D., Martinson, R., & Wilks, J. (1975). *The effectiveness of correctional treatment: A survey of treatment evaluation studies.* New York: Praeger.

Menard, S., & Elliott, D. S. (1990). Longitudinal and cross-sectional data collection and analysis in the study of crime and delinquency. *Justice Quarterly, 7*(1), 13-55.

Mieczkowski, T. (1986). Geeking up and throwing down: Heroin street life in Detroit. *Criminology, 24*(4), 645-666.

National Institute on Drug Abuse (NIDA). (1989). *National household survey on drug abuse: 1988 population estimates* (DHHS Pub. No. ADM 89-1636). Rockville, MD: National Institute on Drug Abuse.

National Institute on Drug Abuse (NIDA). (1991). *National household survey on drug abuse: 1990 main findings* (DHHS Pub. No. ADM 91-1788). Rockville, MD: National Institute on Drug Abuse.

National Institute on Drug Abuse (NIDA). (1992). *National household survey on drug abuse: 1991 population estimates* (DHHS Pub. No. ADM 92-1887). Rockville, MD: National Institute on Drug Abuse.

Nurco, D. C., Schaeffer, J. W., Ball, J. C., & Kinlock, T. W. (1984). Trends in the commission of crime among narcotic addicts over successive periods of addiction. *Journal of Drug and Alcohol Abuse, 10*, 481-489.

Office of National Drug Control Policy. (1990, June). *Understanding drug treatment.* Washington, DC: U.S. Department of Justice, Office of National Drug Control Policy.

Palmer, T. (1975). Martinson revisited. *Journal of Research in Crime and Delinquency, 12*, 133-152.

Palmer, T. (1983). The effectiveness issue today: An overview. *Federal Probation, 46*, 3-10.

Patterson, G. R., Chamberlain, P., & Reid, J. B. (1982). A comparative evaluation of a parent-training program. *Behavior Therapy, 13*, 638-650.

Reuter, P., MacCoun, R., & Murphy, P. (1990). *Money from crime: A study of the economics of drug dealing in Washington, D.C.* (R-3894-RF). Santa Monica, CA: RAND.

Rosenbaum, J. L., Deschenes, E. P., & Fagan, J. (1990, February). *Gender differences in delinquency and drug use.* Paper presented at the Western Society of Criminology meetings.

Sechrest, L., White, S. O., & Brown, E. D. (Eds.). (1979). *The rehabilitation of criminal offenders: Problems and prospects.* Washington, DC: National Academy of Sciences.

Sells, S. B., & Simpson, D. D. (1979). Evaluation of treatment outcomes for youths in the drug abuse reporting program (DARP): A follow-up study. In G. M. Beschner (Ed.), *Youth drug abuse: Problems, issues and treatments* (pp. 571-628). Lexington, MA: Lexington Books.

U.S. Department of Justice, National Institute of Justice, DUF (Drug Use Forecasting). (1990, March). *(1988) Drug use forecasting annual report: Drugs and crime in America.* Washington, DC: U.S. Department of Justice, National Institute of Justice.

United States Government. (1989). President George Bush: *National drug control strategy* (Presidential address). Washington, DC: Government Printing Office.

Watters, J. K., Reinarman, C., & Fagan, J. (1983). Causality, context, and contingency: Relationships between drug abuse and delinquency. *Contemporary Drug Problems: A Law Quarterly, 12*, 351-373.

Whitehead, J. T., & Lab, S. P. (1989, August). A meta-analysis of juvenile correctional treatment. *Journal of Research in Crime and Delinquency, 26*(3), 276-295.

Williams, T. (1989). *The cocaine kids.* New York: Addison-Wesley.

Epilogue

16. Drug Policy Initiatives: The Next 25 Years

DORIS LAYTON MacKENZIE

Twenty-five years ago, the President's Commission on Law Enforcement and the Administration of Justice conducted an exhaustive investigation of crime in the United States. The results of this investigation were reported in a series of nine task force reports summarizing the state of criminal justice at that time (Conley, 1993). The report on "Narcotics and Drug Abuse" represented the knowledge of experts at the time on drug use and abuse (Dupont & MacKenzie, 1993; President's Crime Commission, 1967). It is surprising to examine this report in light of what we know today. At the time there was little indication that a tidal wave of drug use was about to hit this country and that it would have a major impact on the criminal justice system. Nor was there any indication that the authors were aware of the earlier drug epidemic that hit the United States at the turn of the century.

The task force recommendations in the area of drug abuse focused on two areas: (a) enforcement and (b) research and evaluation. Most of their recommendations were realized: Staffs of the Bureaus of Customs and Narcotics were tremendously increased; states adopted drug abuse control legislation; federal drug abuse control laws were amended to strengthen record-keeping provisions; research was undertaken on the regulation of drugs and the effect of marijuana; educational materials were developed; and, at least for some period of time, sentencing laws were revised to give correctional professionals and courts more flexibility in sentencing drug offenders.

Despite these changes, illegal drug use continued to increase in the United States among the general population. In 1972, 28% of the young adults surveyed in the *National Household Survey* reported using marijuana in the past 30 days (NIDA, 1991a). By 1979 this percentage had increased to 35% for the same age group. Cocaine use showed a similar pattern of increase during the 1970s. Three percent of the 18-to-25-year-olds reported using cocaine in the past month in 1974, and this increased to more than 9% by 1979.

The good news is that during the 1980s the extent of illegal drug use appears to have declined. In the 1991 survey of young adults, 13% reported using marijuana in the past month and only 2% using cocaine, substantial drops from the peak use in 1979. In agreement with the household survey are statistics from the Drug Abuse Warning Network (DAWN), showing dramatic decreases in drug reported emergencies from 1988 to 1991 and, in addition, increasingly large proportions of the students in the high school seniors survey say they disapprove of illegal drug use (Johnston, O'Malley, & Bachman, 1991; NIDA, 1991b).

Although the above are positive signs that the drug epidemic is beginning to wane, the bad news is that the decline in illegal drug use does not appear to be occurring in all segments of the population. There is evidence that use remains high for those who come in contact with the criminal justice system. Particularly valuable in documenting this continuing drug use is an innovative system of Drug Use Forecasting (DUF), sponsored by the National Institute of Justice (NIJ), which takes advantage of the development of valid and reliable urine tests to measure recent drug use. Begun in 1987 DUF was designed to measure the extent of recent drug use among booked arrestees, as well as trends in drug use among this segment of the population (Herbert & O'Neil, 1991). In 1991 DUF urine tests of arrestees in 24 cities showed continued high levels of use, and there was no indication that use was declining. For example, 50% to 60% of the arrestees in the majority of cities tested positive for some illegal drug use. The lowest levels of use were in Omaha and Indianapolis, where 39% to 40% tested positive, still a substantial percentage of the arrestees. Cocaine was the most prevalent drug used in the majority of the sites.

What factors may have influenced this epidemic, and what have we learned in the past 25 years? As we begin the next 25 years the research reported in this volume points in four directions: (1) changes in policing strategies, (2) an emphasis on treatment, (3) system-level planning, and (4) the importance of evaluation.

Clearly indicated in the task force report of 25 years ago were the permissive attitudes that became popular during the 1970s among large segments of the population. The task force recommended more discretion and flexibility in sentencing, and a distinction be made between dangerous drugs and other drugs such as marijuana. Cocaine at the time was considered neither addictive nor a drug that might become a major social problem.

The love and peace expressed by the flower children of the age eventually led to acceptance and respect for some of their views; we got out of the war, sexual attitudes and behavior became more permissive, long hair and jeans were in style. The problem was that some of their ideas had destructive consequences. Acceptance of drugs and drug use was one such idea. Permissive attitudes toward drugs became widespread, as exemplified by a professor from a major university who encouraged people to "turn on, tune in, drop out." These permissive attitudes and the lack of knowledge regarding the dangerousness of certain drugs (e.g., cocaine) may have been in part responsible for an increasing number of middle-class drug users in the general population.

Despite the large increases in the number of law enforcement personnel, there was no corresponding decrease in drug dealing. It became evident that numbers alone would not reduce the problem; where resources were focused would be of utmost importance. Initially efforts to reduce the drug trade focused on disrupting the high-level drug operators who were involved in large-scale distribution (Kleiman & Smith, 1990). This getting "Mr. Big" strategy proved unsuccessful; other potential kingpins and existing organizations arose to replace those that were removed, and new drug wholesalers quickly appeared to replace the old.

Neither theory nor research evidence exist to support the attack "Mr. Big" strategy (Kleiman & Smith, 1990; Sviridoff & Hillsman, this volume). As Sviridoff and Hillsman point out, the earlier law enforcement efforts of interdiction at the borders, and targeting "Mr. Big" did not affect the problems associated with drug use.

Strategies changed, and as demonstrated by the chapters in this volume on police crackdowns (Worden, Bynum, & Frank), tactical narcotics teams (Sviridoff & Hillsman), and drug market analysis (Weisburd & Green), law enforcement efforts have begun to focus on street-level dealing. Practitioners search for ways to implement strategies for reducing street-level dealing, and researchers examine what specific strategies are effective in reducing the drug dealing and improving the quality of life in the targeted areas.

Throughout these chapters on law enforcement it is evident that one important factor in effective policing is community acceptance of and interaction with the police. It is no longer considered appropriate to judge police effectiveness only by the numbers of arrests or convictions. Community attitudes toward police, community fear of crime, police-citizen interaction, and the quality of life of the citizens are considered crucial variables and of utmost importance in evaluating law enforcement efforts. The difficulty of integrating this community perspective into police organizations, without losing the advantages of police professionalism, is clearly shown in the field experiments in Oakland and Birmingham (Uchida & Forst, this volume).

Furthermore, there is a realization that law enforcement is part of an overall criminal justice system that must be planned and coordinated. The public does not always discriminate among law enforcement, prosecution, and sanctioning. Police may arrest an individual, only to find that the courts and the correctional system are so overloaded that the response to the arrest is a quick plea bargain to time served. The offender is almost immediately back on the street. Those who might be deterred from involvement in the drug trade will hardly see this as a threat, and those who might cooperate with the police may reasonably question whether such limited returns are worth the time, effort, and danger such cooperation means to them personally.

Court and correction officials attempt to process the overwhelming numbers of drug offenders and drug-related crimes. For some time it was hoped that getting tough on crime, and particularly on drug offenders, would reduce the problem. More prisons were built to hold an increasing proportion of the population, and laws were passed to increase the number of mandatory sentences for drug offenders. Yet, as offenders continued to overflow the available space in the institutions, two things became obvious. First, treatment programs would be needed to decrease the rate of drug use among offender populations; and second, without careful system planning, it would not be possible to develop appropriate and effective methods of sanctioning drug-involved offenders.

The increase in drug use during the 1970s coincided with an occurrence in corrections that had a major impact on the field. This was the acceptance of the "nothing works" philosophy, arising from the review of correctional research by Martinson and his colleagues (Martinson, 1974). Although the legitimacy of the "nothing works" statement has been in debate since it was first uttered (Cullen & Gendreau, 1989), there was a wide acceptance of the conclusion. One wonders what impact this had on the development of treatment programs for offenders. It is clear, however, that many offenders did not receive treatment while in custody (Chaiken, 1989; U.S. Government Accounting Office, 1991). Today this is the very population that continues to use and abuse drugs. Research indicates that such programs can be successful in reducing drug use. The importance of developing appropriate treatment programs has become a top priority. Yet, there are still offenders, sanctioned by the system, who are released without receiving appropriate treatment.

We knew, 25 years ago, that there were treatment programs that worked, and we had evidence at that time that there might be benefits to coercing people into treatment (Dupont & MacKenzie, 1993). Had we put more effort into independent and objective evaluation of treatment programs, would we be further ahead in matching offenders to the treatment and sanctions that would be most effective in reducing drug use?

Another impact of the "nothing works" philosophy was the removal of some of the discretion in decision making from criminal justice professionals (Blumstein, 1989). The attitude seemed to be that if the corrections professionals could not develop effective programs, then why trust them to decide who to lock up and who to release. Decision making increasingly became the jurisdiction of policymakers, who responded to the public calls for harsh responses to crime. Fearful that they would be called upon to explain a Willie Horton decision, policymakers supported longer sentences and mandatory minimums.

As a result, a new penology developed that changed the focus from the individual offender to managing aggregate numbers of dangerous groups and system planning (Feeley & Simon, 1992). Prisons were built to incapacitate increasing numbers of offenders, interest centered on surveillance and custody as opposed to treatment and rehabilitation, and release decisions were made on the basis of classification for risk.

Today system planning continues to be a high priority in corrections. However, the pendulum has swung from a focus on the aggregate, the assessment of risk and incapacitation, to planning for the individual, intermediate sanctions, correctional options, and matching offenders to appropriate treatment and sanctions. There is a recognition that corrections is multidimensional. A rational sentencing policy is not limited to providing a range of punishments alone, but must include various purposes such as treatment, reparation, retribution, and costs (Harland, 1992).

Corrections can effectively change offenders, but how this change can and should be evaluated is undetermined. Upon release from prison, offenders, particularly those from the inner city, are faced with overwhelming problems. There is a debate about whether we should hold corrections accountable for recidivism rates, considering the social problems of the inner cities that may be the root cause of drug use and associated criminal activities (Johnson, Williams, Dei, & Sanabria, 1990).

Many questions remain about how to measure the effectiveness of public policy initiatives. Frequently we depend upon official arrest data for information about the type, extent, and severity of criminal activity. Yet research has demonstrated that official arrest data are severely flawed measures of criminal activity (Ball, Shaffer, & Nurco, 1983; Collins, Rachal, Hubbard, Cavanaugh, Craddock, & Kristiansen, 1982; Inciardi & Pottieger, 1991); it may be more accurate to consider arrest data as indicators of criminal justice involvement. Although self-report data may be more valid indicators of criminal activity, problems arise if respondents perceive that the information they give will or could be used against them.

Studies of the criminal activities of drug offenders present some particularly difficult problems. Self-report studies, in which confidentiality of data and immunity from prosecution have been secured, have consistently indicated that less than 1% of the offenses reported by drug abusers result in arrests (Ball, Rosen, Flueck, & Nurco, 1982; Inciardi, 1986; Inciardi & Pottieger, 1991). Furthermore, generic classification of crimes as burglary, larceny, and robbery tell us little about whether the crime was drug-related, and, if so, whether it was the result of a psychopharmacological state, motivation to obtain money in order to obtain or purchase drugs, or representing a conflict between those involved in drug distribution and those in drug trade.

Although there was an emphasis on research in the task force report of 25 years ago, this was in the limited areas of examination of the effect of marijuana, and on procedures to regulate drugs. Little was said about social science research examining different policing strategies, or the effectiveness of different types of treatment or correctional sanctions in reducing drug use and associated criminal activities.

The coordination between the evaluation work of the National Institute of Justice and the demonstration and block grant projects of the Bureau of Justice Assistance is a hopeful sign that more demonstration projects will receive independent evaluations. The advantage of such evaluations is the generalizations that can be made, and these, in turn, can be used to develop programs in other jurisdictions. Spending money to help one jurisdiction develop a demonstration project helps that specific jurisdiction. Spending money to understand what components are effective in the demonstration project means the results can be generalized to other jurisdictions. When such objective evaluations are conducted, many more jurisdictions can benefit from the knowledge obtained. As emphasized by Albert Reiss (this volume) there must be close cooperation between those who test and those who judge.

If we are to combat the problems of drugs and associated crime, we must have an understanding of the relationships between drugs and crime. Evaluations of public policy initiatives are important at one level to tell us what works. Equally as important is why it works. Future research must address both these aspects of evaluation if we are to develop effective programs.

References

Ball, J. C., Rosen, L., Flueck, J. A., & Nurco, D. N. (1982). Lifetime criminality of heroin addicts in the United States. *Journal of Drug Issues, 12*, 225-239.

Ball, J. C., Shaffer, J. W., & Nurco, D. N. (1983). The day-to-day criminality of heroin addicts in Baltimore: A study in the continuity of offense rates. *Drug and Alcohol Dependence, 12*, 119-142.

Blumstein, A. (1989). American prisons in a time of crisis. In L. I. Goodstein & D. L. MacKenzie (Eds.), *The American prison: Issues in research and policy*. New York: Plenum.

Chaiken, M. R. (1989). In prison programs for drug involved offenders. *National Institute of Justice Reports*. Washington, DC: U.S. Department of Justice, National Institute of Justice.

Collins, J. J., Rachal, J. V., Hubbard, R. L., Cavanaugh, E. R., Craddock, S. G., & Kristiansen, P. L. (1982). *Criminality in a drug treatment sample: Measurement issues and initial findings*. Research Triangle Park, NC: Research Triangle Institute.

Conley, J. A. (Ed.). (1993). *The president's crime commission: 25 years later* (ACJS/Anderson Monograph Series). Cincinnati, OH: Anderson.

Cullen, F. T., & Gendreau, P. (1989). The effectiveness of correctional rehabilitation: Reconsidering the "nothing works" debate. In L. I. Goodstein & D. L. MacKenzie (Eds.), *The American prison: Issues in research and policy*. New York: Plenum.

Dupont, R. L., & MacKenzie, D. L. (1993). Narcotics and drug abuse: An unforeseen tidal wave. In J. A. Conley (Ed.), *The president's crime commission: 25 years later* (ACJS/Anderson Monograph Series). Cincinnati, OH: Anderson.

Feeley, M. M., & Simon, J. (1992). The new penology: Notes on the emerging strategy of corrections and its implications. *Criminology, 30*, 449-474.

Harland, A. T. (1992). *Defining a continuum of sanctions: Some research and policy development implications*. Paper presented to the American Society of Criminology Annual Meeting, New Orleans, LA.

Herbert, E. E., & O'Neil, J. A. (1991). Drug use forecasting: An insight into arrestee drug use. *NIJ Reports*, 11-13. Washington, DC: U.S. Department of Justice, National Institute of Justice.

Inciardi, J. A. (1986). *The war on drugs*. Palo Alto, CA: Mayfield.

Inciardi, J. A., & Pottieger, A. E. (1991). Kids, crack, and crime. *Journal of Drug Issues, 21*, 257-270.

Johnson, B. D., Williams, T., Dei, K. A., & Sanabria, H. (1990). Drug abuse in the inner city: Impact on hard-drug users and the community. In M. Tonry & J. Q. Wilson (Eds.), *Drugs and crime: Vol. 13. Crime and justice* (pp. 9-67). Chicago: University of Chicago Press.

Johnston, L. D., O'Malley, P. M., & Bachman, J. G. (1991). *Drug use among American high school seniors, college students and young adults, 1975-1990* (DHHS Pub. No. ADM 91-1813). Rockville, MD: National Institute on Drug Abuse.

Kleiman, M.A.R., & Smith, K. D. (1990). State and local drug enforcement: In search of a strategy. In M. Tonry & J. Q. Wilson (Eds.), *Drugs and crime*. Chicago: University of Chicago Press.

Martinson, R. (1974). What works?—Questions and answers about prison reform. *Public Interest, 35*, 22-54.

National Institute on Drug Abuse (NIDA). (1991a). *National household survey on drug abuse: Population estimates 1991* (DHHS Pub. No. ADM 92-1887). Rockville, MD: National Institute on Drug Abuse.

National Institute on Drug Abuse (NIDA). (1991b). *Drug abuse and drug abuse research: The third triennial report to congress from the secretary, department of health and human services* (DHHS Pub. No. ADM 91-1704). Rockville, MD: National Institute on Drug Abuse.

President's Crime Commission. (1967). *The challenge of crime in a free society*. Washington, DC: Government Printing Office.

Author Index

Adler, P., 206
Adler, P. A., 161
Agar, M., 189
Ageton, S., 255
Akers, R. A., 193
Alderson, W., 66
Alexander, J. F., 265
Allison, M., 176
Altschuler, D. M., 209, 260
American Prosecutors Research Institute
    (APRI), 161
Amini, F. N., 272
Anderson, A. B., 192, 209, 210
Andrews, D., 184
Andrews, D. A., 264, 265
Andrews, M.P.A., 33
Anglin, D., 173
Anglin, M., 173, 175, 176
Anglin, M. D., 19, 21, 22, 30, 32, 33, 38,
    97, 226, 227, 232, 248, 259, 269
Annan, S., 81, 85, 92, 131
Arbiter, N., 29
Arbuthnot, J., 265, 275
Arling, G., 180
Ashford, J., 178
Atkinson, R., 176

Bachman, J. G., 154, 284
Baird, S., 180
Ball, J., 176
Ball, J. C., 19, 259, 288
Barnett, A., 111
Barnett, M., 51
Batani-Khalfani, A., 47, 49, 50
Battjes, R., 174
Bayley, D. H., 79, 80, 81, 99

Bea, K., 164
Bedlington, M., 272
Belden, B., 272
Belenko, S., 190, 191, 195, 196, 197, 199,
    205, 209
Bellassai, J. B., 34, 36
Bellassai, J. P., 241
Bellucci, P. A., 49
Bennett, L. A., 234
Berk, R. A., 193, 210
Berry, E., 253, 261
Bertucelli, S., 159, 162, 163
Beschner, G., 189
Biderman, A. D., 101
Biernacki, P., 206
Blakely, C., 263, 265, 275
Bluestone, D., 194
Blumstein, A., 21, 35, 192, 263, 287
Bocklet, R., 102, 161
Boland, B., 98
Bonta, J., 184, 264, 265
Bookstaber, R., 68
Bourgois, P., 51, 209
Boydstun, J. E., 98
Brakke, H., 155
Bratt, R., 129
Braukmann, C. J., 272
Braukmann, P., 272
Brecht, M., 21, 22, 176
Brennan, T., 174
Brewer, D., 270
Brounstein, P. J., 260
Brounstein, P. M., 209
Brown, B., 173, 174, 175
Brown, C. E., 81
Brown, E. D., 263
Brownstein, H. H., 49

Subject Index

About the Contributors

M. Douglas Anglin is adjunct associate professor in the Department of Psychiatry and Biobehavioral Sciences at UCLA. He is also director of the UCLA Drug Abuse Research Center. He earned his Ph.D. in social psychology from UCLA in 1979. Since then, he has been involved in more than 20 federally funded research projects, most of which deal with the evaluation of community treatment and other interventions for heroin and cocaine users. He serves as an adviser for a number of organizations, including the Los Angeles County Drug Abuse Program Office, the California Department of Corrections, the Federal Bureau of Prisons, the Office of National Drug Control Policy, and the National Academy of Sciences Institute of Medicine. He is author or co-author of nearly 70 articles for scientific books and journals.

Sampson O. Annan is the deputy director of research for the Police Foundation. He has more than 18 years' experience in survey research and program evaluation. He has managed numerous survey and evaluation research projects, including surveys for fear of crime experiments, anti-crime programs in public housing projects, police effectiveness study, modern policing and the control of illegal drugs, and spouse assault experiments. He directed the evaluation of *Narcotics Enforcement in Public Housing Developments,* conducted by the Police Foundation in Denver and New Orleans. He holds a B.S. in psychology and has pursued graduate studies in industrial psychology.

Timothy S. Bynum is a professor in the School of Criminal Justice and associate director of the Institute for Public Policy and Social Research at Michigan State University. For the past several years, he has worked with Robert Worden and James Frank on a comprehensive study, funded by the National Institute of Justice, of the impact of narcotics crackdowns. He currently is the principal investigator of a study on the impact of race and gender on police and juvenile court dispositions.

309

Elizabeth Piper Deschenes is a consultant to the Criminal Justice Program at RAND in Santa Monica, California. She has a B.A. (1975) in sociology from Colby College in Waterville, Maine. She received an M.A. (1979) and a Ph.D. (1983) in criminology from the University of Pennsylvania, where she worked with Drs. Wolfgang and Tracy on the 1958 Philadelphia Birth Cohort Study. Previously, she worked for URSA Institute on the Violent Juvenile Offender Project and for the UCLA Drug Abuse Research Center on studies of narcotic addicts. At RAND she is currently evaluating experimental correctional programs for adults and juveniles, including intensive supervision programs for different types of drug offenders, and residential and intensive aftercare programs for juvenile delinquents.

Jeffrey A. Fagan is an associate professor at the School of Criminal Justice of Rutgers University. His most recent publications include "Intoxication and Aggression," for *Drugs and Crime* (edited by Michael Tonry and James Q. Wilson) and *Drug Use and Delinquency Among Inner City Youths* (with Joseph Weis). He has published widely on the crack phenomenon in New York City, and edited a special issue of *Contemporary Drug Problems* on new research on crack. He is chair of the Working Group on the Social Ecology of Crime and Drugs for the Social Science Research Council's Committee on Research on the Urban Underclass. His current research includes the economic lives of women drug sellers and users in New York City, drug involvement among youth gangs, and organized crime activities by Chinese and other Asian youth gangs in New York. He also is editor of the *Journal of Research in Crime and Delinquency.*

Brian Forst is Associate Professor of Justice in the School of Public Affairs, The American University. He was director of research at the Institute for Law and Social Research from 1977 to 1985 and of the Police Foundation from 1985 to 1989. He has written widely on prosecution and sentencing, law enforcement, the deterrent effect of the death penalty, quantitative methods, and information technology.

James Frank is assistant professor of criminal justice at the University of Cincinnati. His present research interests are in the areas of citizen attitudes toward the police, citizens as co-producers of police outputs, and the relationship between police officer attitudes and behavior. He has published articles in *Justice Quarterly, American Journal of Sociology, Crime and Social Justice,* and *American Journal of Police.*

Heike P. Gramckow is Deputy Director of the Jefferson Institute for Justice Studies, Washington, D.C. She received her law degree from the University of Hamburg, Germany, and is currently working on her Ph.D. in law and criminal justice at the University of Hamburg. Specializing in international comparative justice studies, criminal justice systems and procedures, she has published several articles, including *The Drug Policy of the Bush Administration* (in German) and *An Ecology-Oriented European Market?* She has also co-authored several reports, including *Expedited Drug Case Management Programs: Issues for Program Development*; *Asset Forfeiture Programs: Impact and Implications*; and *Survey of Asset Forfeiture Programs in 1990*. She is a consultant to the Friedrich-Naumann Foundation, Washington, D.C.; serves as secretary to the International Criminal Justice/Law Enforcement Expert Systems Association; and is on the membership committee of the German American Law Association.

Lorraine Green is an Assistant Professor at the College of Criminal Justice at Northeastern University and is also a Senior Research Fellow at the Center for Crime Prevention Studies at Rutgers University. Dr. Green received her Ph.D. from Rutgers University and has worked as a Research Officer for several Australian government departments, including the Office of Crime Statistics, the South Australian Police Department, and the National Police Research Unit. Dr. Green was the Field Research Director for the National Institute of Justice-funded Drug Market Analysis Experiment and served as the Associate Director of the Center for Crime Prevention Studies (1991-1993), where she was responsible for coordinating several Center projects, including an evaluation of the Beat Health Program in Oakland, California, and a study that examined crime on the Rutgers-Newark University campus.

Peter W. Greenwood is a graduate of the U.S. Naval Academy with a Ph.D. from Stanford University. He is a senior researcher at RAND, where he has directed studies of detectives, prosecutors, criminal careers, selective incapacitation, the juvenile justice systems, juvenile corrections programs, and drugs. He is currently evaluating several innovative correctional programs for serious juvenile offenders, and is working with several cities in their efforts to combat drug abuse.

John R. Hepburn, Ph.D., earned his doctorate in sociology. He is a professor in the School of Justice Studies at Arizona State University. His research includes an evaluation of the Maricopa County Demand Reduction Program, which has adopted a policy of zero tolerance toward casual drug users, and the Focused Offender Disposition Program, which strives to assess the need for and success of treatment among probationers with a recent history of drug use.

Sally T. Hillsman is vice president for research at the National Center of State Courts, a nonprofit corporation serving the needs of the state courts. She was previously the associate director of the Vera Institute of Justice in New York City and its director of research. She has conducted research in a wide range of criminal justice areas, including intermediate sanctions, case processing, prosecution and court delay, and pretrial diversion, as well as policing and narcotics law enforcement. She currently administers the Center's national research agenda, court technology programs, and information services. She holds a Ph.D. in sociology from Columbia University.

Yih-Ing Hser is adjunct associate professor in the Department of Psychiatry and Biobehavioral Sciences at UCLA. She received her Ph.D. in cognitive psychology from UCLA. She has been awarded a Research Scientist Development Award from the National Institute on Drug Abuse since 1989. She is also currently associate director of the UCLA Drug Abuse Research Center. Her major research interests include human learning and memory, drug use epidemiology and treatment evaluation, and development and application of statistical methodologies.

Joan E. Jacoby is executive director of the Jefferson Institute for Justice Studies, Washington, D.C. She is the author of *The American Prosecutor: A Search for Identity;* co-author (with Edward Ratledge) of *Handbook on Artificial Intelligence and Expert Systems in Law Enforcement;* and has contributed chapters to other books, including *Theory and Research in Criminal Justice: Current Perspectives; Preventing Crime; The Prosecutor;* and *The Coming of Age of Information Technology.* Specializing in criminal justice systems and procedures for the past 20 years, she has also authored or co-authored numerous reports, including *Expedited Drug Case Management Programs: Issues for Program Development; Asset Forfeiture Programs: Impact Issues and Implications; Caseweighting Systems for Prosecutors; Basic Issues in Prosecution and Public Defender Performance.* She has also been published in the *Journal of Criminal Law and Criminology.*

Malcolm W. Klein is a professor of sociology, senior research associate at the Social Science Research Institute, and director of the Social Science

Research Institute, all at the University of Southern California. He earned his B.A. in psychology at Reed College (1952) and his Ph.D. in social psychology at Boston University (1961). He served as chair of the USC Sociology Department for 13 years, founded USC's Social Science Research Institute, and has received the university's Raubenheimer Award. He has served on the board of the American Society of Criminology, as chair of the criminology section of the ASA and SSSP, as president of the Association for Criminal Justice Research (California), as chair of NIMH crime and delinquency review committee, and has served on numerous national advisory panels and committees. In 1990 he received the E. H. Sutherland Award, the highest honor of the American Society of Criminology. He is author or editor of eight books and more than 60 articles and chapters in a broad range of areas, such as street gangs, diversion, deinstitutionalization, criminal justice planning, police handling of juvenile offenders, and comparative justice systems. His most recent research, with grants from the Centers for Disease Control, the Guggenheim Foundation, and the National Institute of Justice, involves the nature and control of street gang violence, and gang involvement in illegal drug distribution systems. He has been visiting professor of sociology at the University of Stockholm, and has published extensively about the juvenile justice systems in Western Europe, Russia, and China.

Douglas Longshore, Ph.D., earned his doctorate in sociology from UCLA in 1981. He is currently principal investigator at the Drug Abuse Research Center, Neuropsychiatric Institute, UCLA. Before joining UCLA, he was a social science analyst at the Program Evaluation and Methodology Division of the U.S. General Accounting Office in Washington, D.C., and a project director at the Studies and Evaluation Department, System Development Corporation, Santa Monica, California. His research interests include HIV risk among drug users, treatment evaluation, treatment utilization patterns, and equity issues in criminal justice.

Doris Layton MacKenzie is an associate professor in the Institute of Criminal Justice and Criminology, University of Maryland, and is currently working as a visiting scientist at the National Institute of Justice, U.S. Department of Justice. She graduated from The Pennsylvania State University with a Ph.D. in psychology. Before joining the Maryland faculty, she was an associate professor at Louisiana State University. Her research has focused on corrections and offenders. She has completed research and published papers on inmate adjustment, recidivism, prison crowding, and classification. She is co-editor of two recently published books, *The American Prison: Issues in Research and Policy* and *Measuring Crime: Large-Scale, Long-Range Efforts.*

Cheryl Lee Maxson is research assistant professor of sociology and research associate at the Social Science Research Institute, director of the Center for Research on Crime and Social Control, University of Southern California. Her recent research and publication activity is concerned with community responses to status offenders, street gang violence, and police identification and response to gang-related crime.

Joan Petersilia is director of the Criminal Justice Program at RAND in Santa Monica, California, and Associate Professor of Social Ecology at the University of California, Irvine. She has a B.S. (1972) in sociology from Loyola University of Los Angeles, an M.A. (1974) in sociology from The Ohio State University, and a Ph.D. (1990) in social ecology from the University of California, Irvine. She is a past president of the Association for Criminal Justice Research in California and the American Society of Criminology. She is a fellow of both the American Society of Criminology and the Western Society of Criminology, and the recipient of awards for her research from the American Probation and Parole Association and the California Probation, Parole, and Corrections Association. Her current work involves evaluating intensive probation and parole programs in 14 jurisdictions.

Albert J. Reiss, Jr., is the William Graham Sumner Professor of Sociology at Yale University and a lecturer in law, Yale Law School. He is the author of numerous scholarly works on law violations and their enforcement. He has contributed to methodology in the development of systematic social observation and the National Crime Victim Survey. Most recently he chaired the National Research Council's Panel on Understanding and Preventing Violence. He is an elected member of the American Academy of Arts and Sciences and a recipient of the Beccaria Gold Medal for distinguished work in criminology.

Wesley G. Skogan is professor of political science and urban affairs at Northwestern University. His research focuses on crime victims, crime prevention, fear of crime, and the interface between the police and the public.

Michele Sviridoff is currently director of research for the Midtown Community Court Project, which is coordinated by the Fund for the City of New York. Previously, as a senior research associate at the Vera Institute of Justice, she conducted research on New York City's Tactical Narcotics Teams; innovative neighborhood-oriented police programs, targeted at drug demand reduction, in eight cities; New York City's Civilian Complaint Review Board; and relationships between employment and crime in high-risk populations.

Susan Turner is a senior researcher in the criminal justice program at RAND in Santa Monica, California. She has a B.A. (1976) in psychology from the University of California, San Diego, and an M.A. (1978) and Ph.D. (1983) in social psychology from the University of North Carolina at Chapel Hill. She is a member of the American Society of Criminology, the American Probation and Parole Association, and the American Correctional Association. She is past president of the Association for Criminal Justice Research in California. Her current work involves correctional evaluations of intensive supervision probation and parole, work release, and Treatment Alternatives to Street Crime (TASC).

Craig D. Uchida is acting director of the Office of Criminal Justice Research at the National Institute of Justice. He received his Ph.D. in 1982 from the School of Criminal Justice, State University of New York at Albany. He has conducted research in law enforcement in a number of settings and on a variety of topics. He has published articles in the *American Sociological Review, The Journal of Criminal Law and Criminology, American Journal of Police,* and other criminal justice-related journals. In addition he has edited two books and written chapters for books on law enforcement issues.

David Weisburd is an associate professor of Criminology at the Hebrew University Law School in Jerusalem and the Director of the Center for Crime Prevention Studies at Rutgers University. Dr. Weisburd received his Ph.D. from Yale University and has served as a Research Associate at Yale Law School and the Vera Institute of Justice. He has been a Principal Investigator for a series of federally funded research programs in policing, including the Drug Market Analysis in Jersey City and the Minneapolis Hot Spots Patrol Experiment. Professor Weisburd is author or editor of *White Collar Crime Reconsidered,* with Kip Schlegal (1992); *Police Control and Control of the Police,* with Craig Uchida (1993); *Jewish Settler Violence: Deviance as Social Reaction* (1989); and *Crimes of the Middle Class* (1991). He has also published numerous scholarly articles and reports.

Robert E. Worden is assistant professor of criminal justice and of public policy at the State University of New York at Albany. His research focuses primarily on developing theories of police decision making and behavior, and on evaluating the outcomes of police policies and strategies. He is co-principal investigator for a study of police drug crackdowns, which is funded by a grant from the National Institute of Justice.